Frontiers of Environmental Economics

Edited by
Henk Folmer

Professor of General Economics, Wageningen University and Professor of Environmental Economics, Tilburg University, The Netherlands

H. Landis Gabel

Professor of Economics and Management and Associate Dean, INSEAD, France

Shelby Gerking

Professor of Economics, University of Wyoming, USA

Adam Rose

Professor and Head of Department of Energy, Environmental and Mineral Economics, Pennsylvania State University, USA

Edward Elgar
Cheltenham, UK • Northampton, MA, USA

Published by
Edward Elgar Publishing Limited
Glensanda House
Montpellier Parade
Cheltenham
Glos GL50 1UA
UK

Edward Elgar Publishing, Inc.
136 West Street
Suite 202
Northampton
Massachusetts 01060
USA

A catalogue record for this book
is available from the British Library

Library of Congress Cataloguing in Publication Data

Frontiers of environmental economics / edited by Henk Folmer ... [et al.].
    Includes index.
    1. Environmental economics.   2. Natural resources.   I. Folmer, Henk, 1945–

    HD75.6.F76   2000
    333.7—dc21   00–026459

ISBN 1 84064 226 2

Typeset by Manton Typesetters, Louth, Lincolnshire, UK.
Printed in Great Britain by MPG Books Ltd, Bodmin, Cornwall.

Contents

v

Figures

Tables

Contributors

Thomas Aronsson is Professor of Economics at Umeå University in Sweden. He is currently doing research on welfare economics, public economics and environmental economics. He is one of the authors of *Welfare Measurement, Sustainability and Green National Accounting* (1997, Cheltenham, Edward Elgar).

Robert U. Ayres is Sandoz Professor of Environment and Management, Professor of Economics and Director of the Centre for the Management of Environmental Resources at INSEAD, in Fontainebleau, France. He has published more than 190 journal articles and book chapters and has authored or co-authored 16 books on topics ranging from technological change, manufacturing and productivity to environmental and resource economics. His most recent books are *Accounting for Resources 1 and 2* (1998, 1999, Cheltenham UK and Northampton, USA, Edward Elgar), *Turning Point: The End of the Growth Paradigm* (1998, London, Earthscan).

Marcel Boyer is President and CEO of CIRANO, a multi-university liaison and transfer centre. He is also Jarislowsky Professor of Technology and International Competition at Polytechnique-Montréal and Professor of Economics at the University of Montréal. An elected member of the Royal Society of Canada and a member of the board of the NBER, he is Chairman of NCM2, a network of seven Canadian research centres regrouping some 250 scientists in Mathematics, Operational Research, Computer Science and Economics. He is the co-editor, with R.E. Kilhlstrom, of *Bayesian Models in Economic Theory* (1984, Amsterdam, North Holland).

Carlo Carraro is Professor of Econometrics and Environmental Economics at the University of Venice, Italy. He is also the research director of FEEM, Milan and research fellow of CEPR, London. He is the author/editor of more than 20 books, among which are *Environmental Policy and Market Structure* (1996, Boston, Kluwer Academic Publishers), *International Environmental Negotiations* (1997, Cheltenham, Edward Elgar), *New Directions in the Economic Theory of the Environment* (1997, New York, Cambridge University Press), *International Environmental Agreements on Climate Change* (1999, Dordrecht, Kluwer Academic Publishers).

Thomas D. Crocker is J.E. Warren Distinguished Professor of Energy and Environment in the Department of Economics and Finance at the University of Wyoming. Author or co-author of nearly 150 papers and two books in resource and environmental economics, his was the original (1966, New York, W.W. Norton and Co.) proposal and analysis of tradable environmental permit systems

Ronald G. Cummings holds the Noah Langdale, Jr. Chair in Environmental Policy at Georgia State University. Previous positions include Professor and Chairman at the Department of Economics, University of New Mexico, and at the Department of Resource Economics, University of Rhode Island, and Program Director (Mexico City) for Resources for the Future, Inc. He served as policy sciences editor for the journal *Water Resources Research* between 1984 and 1987, and as managing editor for the *Journal of Environmental Economics and Management* between 1987 and 1997. He is the author of a number of books and journal articles dealing with the management of natural resources and environmental systems.

Henk Folmer is Professor of General Economics at Wageningen University and Professor of Environmental Economics at Tilburg University, The Netherlands. He served as first President of the European Association of Environmental and Research Economics from 1987 to 1993. He served on the EC Task Force on the Single Market and the Environment. He has written a large number of publications in a wide variety of international outlets in the fields of environmental and resource economics, econometrics, labour economics and regional economics. He is co-editor of the annual publication *The International Yearbook of Environmental and Resource Economics: A Survey of Current Issues* (Edward Elgar).

H. Landis Gabel is Professor of Economics and Management and Associate Dean at INSEAD in Fontainebleau, France. He founded the Centre for the Management of Environmental Resources there in 1989. Recent books, edited with others, include *Principles of Environmental and Resource Economics Second Edition* (2000, Cheltenham, Edward Elgar) and the *European Casebook on Industrial and Trade Policy* (1996, Prentice Hall).

Shelby Gerking is Professor of Economics at the University of Wyoming, Laramie, Wyoming. He is the author of a number of articles on valuing environmental resources, regional growth, development and policy that have appeared in journals including the *Review of Economics and Statistics, Journal of Environmental Economics and Management, Journal of Risk and Uncertainty, Southern Economic Journal* and *Journal of Regional Science.*

Michael Hoel is Professor of Economics at the University of Oslo, Norway. He has published articles in a number of economic journals on environmental economics, resource economics, labour economics and other applications of microeconomic theory.

Robert Kaufmann is an Associate Professor at the Center for Energy and Environmental Studies at Boston University. He has written two books and more than 40 peer review papers in journals such as *Nature, Science* and *The American Journal of Agricultural Economics*. These papers have won awards from the International Association of Energy Economists and the National Wildlife Federation.

Howard Kunreuther is the Cecilia Yen Koo Professor of Decision Sciences and Public Policy at the Wharton School, University of Pennsylvania as well as Co-Director of the Wharton Risk Management and Decision Processes Center. He has a long-standing interest in ways that society can better manage low probability–high consequence events as they relate to environmental, technological and natural hazards. He is the author with Paul Freeman of *Managing Environmental Risk through Insurance* (1997, Boston, Kluwer Academic Publishers) and co-editor (with Richard Roth, Sr) of *Paying the Price: The Status and Role of Insurance Against Natural Disasters in the United States* (1998, Washington, D.C., Joseph Henry Press).

John List is Associate Professor of Agricultural and Natural Resource Economics at the University of Arizona, Tucson. He has authored several papers in journals, including *American Economic Review, Journal of Environmental Economics and Management, Land Economics* and *American Journal of Agricultural Economics*.

Karl-Gustaf Löfgren is Professor of Economics at Umeå University in Sweden. He is co-author of *Disequilibrium Macroeconomics in Open Economies* (1984, Oxford, Basil Blackwell), *The Economics of Forestry and Natural Resources* (1985, Oxford, Basil Blackwell) and *Welfare Measurement, Sustainability and Green National Accounting* (1997, Cheltenham, Edward Elgar). He has published journal articles in many fields of economics, among others macroeconomics, labour economics and environmental economics and natural resources.

Anil Markandya is Professor of Economics at the University of Bath. He obtained his doctorate from the London School of Economics in 1974 and has taught at University College London, at universities in Australia, France, Italy and the United States. From 1992 to 1996 he was Research Associate at

the Harvard Institute of International Development and is now a Faculty
Associate there. He is author of around two hundred books, monographs,
articles and reports on environmental economics, including the landmark
Blueprint for a Green Economy (1989, Earthscan) and *Reconciling Trade and
the Environment* (1999, Cheltenham, Edward Elgar).

Michael McKee is a Professor in the Economics Department and a member of
the Executive Committee of the Public Finance Consortium at the University
of New Mexico. He earned his PhD from Carleton University in Ottawa,
Canada and has taught at several universities in Canada, the United States
and in Auckland, New Zealand. His research interests are in taxation and
environmental economics. He uses laboratory experimental markets in his
research. He has published in several of the leading journals including the
American Economic Review, *Economic Inquiry*, the *Journal of Environmental
Economics and Management* and *Land Economics*.

Charles Perrings is Professor of Environmental Economics and Head of the
Environment Department, University of York. Previously he was Professor of
Economics at the University of California, Riverside and Director of the
Biodiversity Programme at the Beijer Institute, Stockholm. He is editor of the
journal *Environment and Development Economics*; author of *Economics of
Ecological Resources: Selected Essays* (1997, Cheltenham UK and North-
ampton, MA, Edward Elgar), and co-editor of *Biological Diversity: Economic
and Ecological Issues* (1995, Cambridge, Cambridge University Press), and
Biodiversity Conservation: Problems and Policies (1994, Dordrecht, Kluwer
Academic Press).

Rüdiger Pethig is Professor of Economics at the University of Siegen, Ger-
many. He is the co-author of *Trade and Environment* (1980, Amsterdam,
Elsevier) and the editor of *Conflicts and Cooperation in Managing Environ-
mental Resources* (1992, Berlin, Springer-Verlag) and of *Valuing the
Environment: Methodological and Measurement Issues* (1994, Boston, Kluwer
Academic Publishers).

Adam Rose is Professor and Head of the Department of Energy, Environmental and Mineral Economics at The Pennsylvania State University. He is
currently involved in research on global climate change, economics of natural
hazards, natural-resource-dependent economies, new energy technologies and
applied general equilibrium modelling. He has authored several books and
numerous articles published in such journals as *Energy Economics*, *Energy
Journal*, *Resource and Energy Economics*, *Journal of Environmental Economics and Management*, *Environment and Development Economics*, *Journal*

of Regional Science, Energy Policy and *Resources Policy*. He served as the American Economic Association representative to the American Association for the Advancement of Science from 1986 to 1992. His research has been funded by the United Nations, US Environmental Protection Agency, US Department of Energy, Center for Clean Air Policy, Multidisciplinary Center for Earthquake Engineering Research, California Air Resources Board and several private firms. He is a member of the editorial boards of the *Journal of Regional Science*, *Resource and Energy Economics*, *Resources Policy* and *Pacific and Asian Journal of Energy*.

Jason F. Shogren is the Stroock Distinguished Professor of Natural Resource Conservation and Management, and Professor of Economics at the University of Wyoming. Before returning to his alma mater, he taught at Appalachian State, Iowa State and Yale universities. In 1997, Shogren served as the senior economist for environmental and natural resource policy on the Council of Economic Advisors in the White House. He was an associate editor of the *Journal of Environmental Economics and Management*, and is currently an associate editor of the *American Journal of Agricultural Economics*. Recent publications include *Environmental Economics* (1997, Oxford, Oxford University Press) and *Private Property and the Endangered Species Act* (1998, Austin, University of Texas Press); and essays on risk, conflict, valuation, environmental policy and experimental economics.

Bernard Sinclair-Desgagné is Professor of Technology Economics and Policy at the Ecole Polytechnique de Montréal and Senior Researcher at CIRANO, the Interuniversity Research Center for the Analysis of Organizations. His most recent research can be found in journals such as *Econometrica* (1994), the *Journal of Law, Economics and Organizations* (1999), the *European Economic Review* (1996) and *Journal of Environmental Economics and Management* (1995, 1997).

Laura Taylor is Assistant Professor of Economics in the Andrew Young School of Policy Studies, Georgia State University, USA. Her publications have appeared in such journals as the *American Economic Review*, the *Journal of Environmental Economics and Management*, *Land Economics* and *Environmental and Resource Economics*.

Tom Tietenberg, the Mitchell Family Professor of Economics at Colby College in Waterville, Maine, is the author or editor of ten books (including *Environmental and Natural Resource Economics* (1992, New York, HarperCollins), one of the best-selling textbooks in the field) as well as over 60 articles and essays on environmental and natural resource economics.

Elected President of the Association of Environmental and Natural Resource Economists by his colleagues in 1987–88, he has consulted on environmental policy with the United Nations, World Bank, the InterAmerican Development Bank, the Agency for International Development and the US Environmental Protection Agency.

David Wheeler is Lead Economist in the Environment Unit of the World Bank's Development Research Group. He received his undergraduate degree from Princeton University (1968) and his PhD in Economics from the Massachusetts Institute of Technology (1974). Before joining the World Bank in 1990, Wheeler was a tenured Associate Professor of Economics at Boston University (1976–90). He has also been a visiting professor at MIT's Department of Urban Studies and Planning (1978–79) and the National University of Zaire (1973–75); Director of the Development Studies Project in Jakarta, Indonesia (1987–89); and co-founder of the Boston Institute for Developing Economies. After joining the World Bank, Wheeler was asked to establish the Environment Unit in the Development Research Group. As Lead Economist, he directs a team that works on environmental policy and research issues in collaboration with policy makers and academics in Brazil, Colombia, Mexico, China, India, Indonesia, the Philippines and other developing countries. He has published numerous books and articles on issues related to development and environment.

Acknowledgements

This book would not have been possible without the financial support of several generous organizations and the professional support of capable staff. Foremost, we wish to thank the Association of European Universities (CRE) for initiating the project. It represents an extension to the graduate student/ professional level and a broadening to include American representation of their prior initiative to promote education in environmental economics. We are also grateful to the Dean's Office of the College of Earth and Mineral Sciences of The Pennsylvania State University and to the John S. Bugas Endowment of the University of Wyoming for financial support of the Conference at Airlie Center, Virginia, at which the papers in this volume were first presented and extensively discussed by the authors and editors.

The brunt of the organization of the conference was ably undertaken by Jan Moyer of The Pennsylvania State University. Jill Bernaski assisted in that effort and also produced the conference brochure. Additional funding support was provided to Shelby Gerking for his travel and editorial duties by the Center for Economic Research of Tilburg University, and by the Netherlands Organization for Scientific Research (NWO).

Introduction

Henk Folmer, H. Landis Gabel, Shelby Gerking and Adam Rose

Environmental and natural resource economics is a young sub-area of economics compared to others, such as international trade, industrial organization and public finance. Young though it may be, however, one could argue that the diagnosis of the problems at its heart has been made and most of the public policy prescriptions have been written. It may be, as has also been argued, that the patient too often chose to ignore the doctor's advice, but that does not contradict the claim that this area of economics has come a long way in a short time to establish a secure theoretical paradigm and a set of policy-relevant research results.

To elaborate, we have long understood the principles of market externalities and market failure that underlie the misallocation of environmental resources at a point in time. Recently, scholars have shown increasing interest in intertemporal resource misallocation, prompted by the appearance of the term 'sustainability' in the mid 1980s. Although the term itself continues to defy clear definition, if it is given some clear definition as a starting point, analysis can typically be pushed through to yield interesting insights. To the extent that the growing environmental 'problem' traces its root cause less in market failure and more in the twin pressures of population growth and economic development, again the diagnosis is clear even if implementation of policy prescriptions might prove difficult or impossible.

All this is to argue that environmental economics is a 'normal science' with the advantages and liabilities that this entails for researchers. Its accepted paradigm is the product of the research of preceding generations of academics, which guides the research of the next. Yet research in a normal science is surely less original, less exciting and perhaps less enervating, than pre-paradigmatic research. One imagines that for a normal science, all the really important academic work has been done, the Nobel Prize winners named (even if history still keeps their names secret) and that the field is on the declining side of the marginal product curve.

This may indeed be true, but we the editors believe that environmental and natural resource economics has yet to tackle some very important research

1

topics and that it will be a growth market for years in the future. Our belief motivates this book.

The objective of this book is to focus attention on areas of environmental and natural resource economics and management that we believe have received insufficient research attention and thus should constitute fertile areas for future exploration. We have tried to bring together in this volume a mix of eminent European and American scholars to provide a research agenda and to stimulate cross-fertilization within and across various disciplines like economics, geography, biology and ecology. The language and the methodology common to each chapter are economics, yet all chapters are accessible to a wider audience than academic economists. The papers are original research contributions, but they are less developed in a mathematical or empirical sense than would be expected for major journal publication. We hope they may reach researchers and policy makers in the public sector, professional staff in research institutes and think tanks and consultants doing environmental work with either public or private sector clients.

Although we feel that environmental and resource economics is mature, our belief that it will be a future growth market provokes some questions. Why might some areas have been under-researched? What were the barriers to progress? Where are the specific growth areas of the future? In the collection of chapters that follows, we can see some answers to these questions.

First, one might attack the proposition that the field is mature; that it has an established and adequate paradigm. Most economists, however, would probably accept that this is so, but, as the reader will see in several of the following chapters, this view is not unanimous. Obviously, an attack on the basic paradigm would open up a vast research agenda. Some of the chapter authors are sceptical of the existence of a paradigm (see Ayres's chapter on industrial ecology); others of its adequacy in light of unsolved problems (see Kaufmann's chapter on ecological economics). The main attack on the paradigm comes from ecology, but Kaufmann reminds the reader that in science, as in poker, something always beats nothing. That is, if ecology or ecological economics are to take the research agenda forward, it must be by demonstrating empirically that they perform better than their neoclassical economic rival.

Many of the following chapters see future research opportunities in interdisciplinary work; for example, joint work between environmental economists and ecologists (see Kaufmann, Ayres, Perrings), organizational theorists (see Gabel and Sinclair-Desgagné), engineers (see Ayres), behaviouralists (see Kunreuther), biologists and geographers (see Crocker and Shogren).

Just as interdisciplinary opportunities for new research lie unexploited, so too do opportunities for more intra-disciplinary research. These opportunities can take at least two different forms. One is between different sub-areas of economics. Examples include research that links regional and urban economics, the 'new economic geography', and environmental economics (see Gerking and List); the integration of organizational economics and environmental economics (see Gabel and Sinclair-Desgagné); and technological change, R&D and endogenous growth (see Carraro).

The second form of intra-disciplinary research brings to environmental economics methodologies previously used only elsewhere in economics. Experimental economics is an example. Cummings, McKee and Taylor see exceptional opportunities to use that methodology to contribute to areas of environmental economics where old problems still lie unsolved.

Experimental economics is a logical step following the growing application of game theory in environmental economics. However, within the area of game theory there also exist ample opportunities for new research. Evolutionary game theory is a rapidly developing area. However, applications of this field in environmental economics are still scarce. Similar observations apply to interconnected game theory. This field has proven to be instrumental in the explanation of seemingly irrational behaviour in the practice of environmental policy and the development of instruments to promote cooperation with respect to international environmental problems.

Of course, new observations (real or imagined) that contradict the predictions of conventional models confront the researcher with new challenges. We see one in the claim that strict environmental policy might help the competitiveness of firms subject to it (Gabel and Sinclair-Desgagné). Tietenberg and Wheeler's chapter on information strategies shows another instance in which research has been stimulated by observation, in this case of an induced response to environmental concerns.

Like new observations of practice, new policy issues often appear on the horizon and attract academic attention. Concern for pollution havens that trade liberalization has provoked is an example that comes up in a number of chapters (for example, Gerking and List, Ayres, Carraro). Another is the concern for carbon leakage in light of the Kyoto agreement (see Hoel). We see in the chapter by Gerking a curious case in which a topic – spatial issues – may shift meaning as new problems replace old ones in the literature. When Horst Siebert wrote about 'Spatial aspects of environmental economics' for the *Handbook of Natural Resource and Energy Economics* in 1985, he wrote mostly about the geographical dispersion of pollutants. Fifteen years later, most research attention focuses on industrial and labour location decisions.

Another emerging area of research interest – interest generated by events – is that of catastrophic risk. The chapter by Boyer and Sinclair-Desgagné is interesting in terms of this 'Introduction' because it takes up an emerging area – major technological risk – via an interdisciplinary approach (see the Gabel and Sinclair-Desgagné chapter). Corporate governance and the firm's

internal organizational structures and systems have not traditionally interested economists. This chapter shows another novelty that may prompt research
in the future. That is its shift of audience from the public policy maker to the
corporate policy maker. The former has been virtually the exclusive target of
advocacy writing in the past, but the latter may be the growth market as we
look forward.

Catastrophic risk is the topic of the Kunreuther chapter, too, but here the
focus is more on natural hazards: acts of God rather than acts of corporate
principals and agents. As do others, the author sees the need to consider
alternatives to the conventional expected utility-maximizing model of choice,
which is a cornerstone of the neoclassical economics paradigm.

Finally, as stimuli for new research, there are simply problems that have
long been around but have not been solved. Several appear in the following
chapters. An example is the valuation problem that global externalities create
for green accounting (see Aronsson and Löfgren). More generally, a number
of authors (Kaufmann, Markandya, Carraro) point to the need for more
applied empirical work to inform theory and to guide policy.

SUMMARY OF CONTRIBUTIONS

The first chapter, by Thomas Aronsson and Karl-Gustaf Löfgren, addresses
the question of how to measure green net national product welfare indices
that explicitly account for changes in environmental capital. The authors
examine situations involving global external effects, which can cause fundamental valuation problems, yet have been frequently ignored in related studies.
Aronsson and Löfgren explore the relationship between appropriate national
and global welfare measures, on the one hand, and national and global tax
policies used to improve resource allocation on the other. If countries act
cooperatively, it turns out that the global welfare level is appropriately measured by a static index related to the sum of the countries' green net national
products. When countries do not act cooperatively, however, this simple
result no longer holds.

Chapter 2, by Robert Kaufmann, turns attention to issues in ecological
economics. It begins by describing the field, outlining inherent conflicts
between economic development and ecological preservation and reasons
why ecologists have not been satisfied with the way in which economic
models frequently characterize man's relationship with the environment.
The chapter also speculates on the future development of ecological economics, concluding that ecological economists must begin to (1) represent
key components of the ecological economic system better than more traditional economic models and (2) improve public policy regarding resource

and environmental management. This perspective is then more fully developed by arguing that the field of ecological economics might usefully become more interdisciplinary and emphasize empirical studies to a greater extent in the future.

The chapter by Shelby Gerking and John List begins by noting the growing importance of the spatial dimension and focuses on the interaction between environmental and natural resource economics and regional and urban economics. This intersection is characterized by the fact that the environment both affects and is affected by geographic movements of labour, capital and other mobile factors of production. The chapter treats traditional topics in this area, such as amenity valuation, human migration, the construction of quality of life indices, and industrial location as well as the more recently emerging issue of the possible impact of the spatial concentration of pollution on economically disadvantaged groups. Future research directions suggested highlight the role of 'new economic geography' models, endogeneity of environmental policy and regional growth.

Tom Tietenberg and David Wheeler look at public and private attempts to increase the availability of information about pollution. These disclosure strategies form the basis for what some have called the 'third wave' in pollution control policy, coming after legal regulation and market-based instruments. While these strategies have become commonplace in natural resource settings, they are less familiar in a pollution control context. However, research on and experience with this approach are now growing both in the OECD and developing countries. Following a review of the conceptual foundations of disclosure strategies, the chapter considers how the policy setting influences the type of information strategy employed. Examples of innovative disclosure strategies in the US, Latin America and Asia, and the channels through which they operate are followed by a review of empirical research on their effectiveness and suggestions for where future research might be helpful.

In the next chapter, Ronald Cummings, Michael McKee and Laura Taylor outline the applicability of experimental methods to issues in environmental economics and policy and then offer a view of future research opportunities in this area. Experimental methods are particularly relevant to further development of environmental economics because of their capacity to frame hypotheses, generate data (particularly when field observations are unavailable) and demonstrate the consequences of policy alternatives to policy makers. These themes are drawn out in detail by considering applications of experimental methods to valuation of environmental amenities or damages, policy design issues related to compliance with environmental rules and regulations and issues involving market-based policies and privatization. Examples chosen from these areas support the view that the interface of experimental economics with environmental economics represents a challenging yet highly promising area for further research.

H. Landis Gabel and Bernard Sinclair-Desgagné examine the effects of environmental regulations from the perspective of a firm. Their starting point is to recognize that neoclassical economists assume that perfectly rational and efficient firms represent a crucial link between environmental regulatory policy and the allocation of environmental resources. Yet, in reality, firms are quite complex; they may have titular principals, but they are actually run by agents to whom a great deal of autonomy is delegated. Thus firms' activities are imperfectly controlled and coordinated by a set of interrelated management systems and procedures for operationalizing the principals' objectives. This chapter applies this view to show how it is possible for strict environmental regulations to be win–win (the 'Porter hypothesis') by simultaneously reducing the firms' private costs as well as external costs imposed on the environment.

In Chapter 7, Michael Hoel studies the links between international trade and transboundary pollution problems when capital is mobile. The general point is that actions taken by a country (or group of countries) will affect equilibrium prices of internationally traded goods, which in turn will affect production and consumption decisions as well as emissions. An important example in this regard is 'carbon leakage', which is a potential problem under the Kyoto agreement because developing countries have no quantitative commitment to scale back their greenhouse emissions. This chapter explores the carbon leakage problem from a theoretical viewpoint, concluding that industrialized countries should have the same carbon tax in all sectors and then supplement this instrument with appropriate import and export tariffs. The possibility of inducing developing countries to cut back on emissions by offering transfer payments is also explored.

The next chapter, by Anil Markandya, considers links between poverty, the environment and development. The chapter is developed around six research questions: (1) Does an increase in poverty within a community lead to increased environmental degradation? (2) Will an environment inhabited by the poor become more degraded than one inhabited by the rich? (3) How have important social changes resulted in concurrent increases in poverty and environmental degradation? (4) Does a deterioration of the ambient environment hurt the poor more than the rich? (5) Do policies to change the environment hurt the poor more than the rich? (6) Do increases in economic development over the long run ameliorate poverty and improve the environment? A survey of current literature suggests that existing research in these areas is strong on theory but that greater emphasis should be placed on high-quality empirical work in the future.

Robert Ayres contributed Chapter 9 on the topic of industrial ecology, which is the study of materials, energy flows and transformations in an economic system and across its boundaries. Cross-boundary impacts on the biosphere have economic implications because they affect environmental services to humans. The services in question range from climatic stabilization and nutrient cycling to food supply and waste assimilation. Thus, industrial ecology overlaps resource and environmental economics. From this perspective, Ayres discusses trade and tax policy, economic growth, welfare and dematerialization, which benefits the environment by conserving value and by reducing dissipative uses of materials. He concludes that environmental assets are a crucial part of national wealth and, among other things, should play a more important role in economic growth analyses in the future. A specific research area to be targeted would be to determine whether technologies are selected by a 'survival of the fittest' mechanism or whether accidents, non-economic factors or path dependence appear to be equally or more important. Unless a survival of the fittest mechanism dominates, there may be a significant potential for double dividends and support for the Porter hypothesis.

The analysis of natural or environmental capital continues in the next chapter, written by Thomas Crocker and Jason Shogren. They model the nexus of private land uses, collective environmental protocols (constraints) and ecosystem services by depicting ecosystems as lotteries. They argue that for an ecosystem to provide protection against natural or man-made hazards, landowners must often exercise self-restraint over land use. A fundamental non-convexity exists in an owner's preferences if he chooses a discrete self-restraint alternative. Moreover, policy makers who disregard non-convex owner preferences for ecosystem configurations are likely to invest excessively in ecosystem care. Overprotection creates an environmental threshold that truncates both public and private opportunities to fill the void with lotteries to smooth preferences across states of nature.

In Chapter 11, Marcel Boyer and Bernard Sinclair-Desgagné focus on the issue of environmental risks associated with technology development. Large corporations are major developers of new technologies that are both an engine of growth in an economy as well as a source of new hazards, as illustrated by recent and highly publicized industrial accidents. Their chapter begins by reviewing these hazards and then models the way in which corporate boards assess prospective liability, including new environmental liability rules that apply to financial creditors. It then analyses internal mechanisms for implementing policies toward risk, such as stakeholders' involvement and selective audits, in a multi-task principal–agent framework. Further research is suggested to refine the definition of major technological risks and to study the evolution of regulation concerning corporate liability, the development of new insurance markets and institutions for sharing major risks.

In Chapter 12, Howard Kunreuther also focuses on aspects of environmental risk by asking what alternative strategies are appropriate for reducing losses and providing protection against natural and environmental hazards that create potentially catastrophic losses to individuals, firms and society. The chapter emphasizes the importance of combining market mechanisms, such as incentives and insurance, with regulations and standards, and then illustrates this view based on a study of Hurricane Andrew in Florida in 1992. This discussion leads to a proposed programme for hazard management that is developed around improving estimates of risk, property inspections, building codes, mitigation incentives and the use of benefit–cost analysis. Specific suggestions show how each element in this programme can be strengthened by further research.

Charles Perrings's chapter advances understanding of the concept of sustainability of economic growth and development. It focuses on advances that stem from the application of the ecological concept of system resilience to environmental economics. The chapter begins with a critical review of empirical evidence provided by estimates of the environmental Kuznets curve and then turns to approaches for modelling sustainability using the concept of resilience applied in a Markov framework. However, much future research is needed to identify the transition probabilities associated with specific institutional conditions, and to weight those probabilities in terms of social objectives. This effort is quite important because real economy–environment systems generally involve states that are only partially observable and controllable and decision processes that are adaptive, that involve learning and that include conflicting objectives of agents who often behave strategically.

Carlo Carraro, in Chapter 14, analyses the role of technological innovation and diffusion to control and reduce polluting emissions. First, the main effects of environmental innovation on growth and emissions are highlighted. Then the incentives for firms to undertake R&D and carry out innovation are reviewed. Market imperfections and externalities imply that public innovation policies are necessary to supplement firms' investments in environmental innovation. Hence, the chapter discusses how R&D and innovation are linked to environmental policies, analyses how optimal policy mixes can be designed and focuses on the impact of related externalities on technological diffusion, crowding-out and endogenous growth. Given the international dimension of many environmental problems, the chapter also discusses the impact of environmental innovation on the geographic distribution of polluting industries and of environmental policies on the international dissemination of innovation. The first part of the chapter is devoted to theoretical models, whereas the second part provides a survey of empirical attempts to model environmental technological innovation and diffusion.

In the final chapter, Rüdiger Pethig looks to the future of environmental economics. He organizes his contribution around methods of analysis rather than specific environmental problems, beginning with theoretical concepts and their ramifications and then turning to the role of interdisciplinary research, empirical work and the potential impact that environmental economics can have on policy formulation. In consequence, this chapter has a broader focus than the others. Yet, Pethig resists any temptation to advance a specific research agenda of his own, preferring to conclude that substantive research opportunities can arise from honestly addressing a few basic questions. For example, how much empirically sound theoretical knowledge has really been accumulated and how does empirical research and hypothesis-testing compare with other areas of economics? How much economy–environment interaction is accounted for in current environmental economics research and what is the still unused potential to draw on other disciplines' ecology-related knowledge? Answering these types of questions on the basis of reliable information certainly would promote successful corrective policies.

CONCLUDING THOUGHTS

Although the coverage of this volume is broad, we do not claim to have encompassed all of the areas of important future research nor all of the main topics within the areas covered. The following omissions are especially noteworthy. Extensive empirical work on environmental justice has been done over the past several years, primarily empirical studies of the negative environmental effects on ethnic or racial minorities and low-income groups. However, much of this work is *ad hoc* and thus disconnected from welfare economics or any formal conceptual base. The issue is whether this empirical research can stand on its own or whether it will require a theoretical foundation, including revisions or extensions of traditional welfare economics.

Another important area only partially addressed in this volume is the economics of natural hazards. This topic may fit into environmental economics if one were to think of positive attributes of the environment as resources and negative ones as hazards. The chapter by Kunreuther offers many other links. One basic consideration to emphasize is that a natural hazard is not solely a natural phenomenon; it is an interaction between the human use system and the environment. Thus the acceleration of natural disasters in recent years has not been caused so much by any increase in the frequency or severity of the natural stimulus as by our increased vulnerability to human actions such as the build-up of structures in flood plains. More empirical work is needed on the extent of this vulnerability now and in the future and on accurately measuring losses from natural disasters so that appropriate cost–benefit studies of mitigation can be undertaken. This will require more collaboration with geologists, meteorologists and engineers and could benefit from some cross-fertilization from benefits valuation in other areas of environmental economics.

Still another area is environmental valuation, which has been a dominant force in environmental economics for the past twenty years. In this volume this work has been extended to analysing ecosystems as lotteries and to formal rules for applying experimental techniques. Still further extensions are necessary, however.

Future research opportunities in interdisciplinary work are not restricted to further interaction between environmental economists and physical scientists but also include other social sciences, notably sociology and psychology. For instance, environmental economists have largely ignored the role of social networks in the development and diffusion of innovation. Such aspects have been left to sociologists who in their turn have shown little or no interest in typical economic concepts, such as profit and utility maximization and their determinants. As standard econometrics shows, omission of systematic explanatory variables, such as social networks, leads to biased estimators of the coefficients of variables included in the analysis as well as of their variances. Similar observations apply to the interaction between economics and psychology, in particular with respect to valuation of environmental quality. What have often appeared as anomalies to economists, such as the discrepancy between the willingness to pay and the willingness to accept, have long been well-understood phenomena to psychologists.

'Observation' is another area where environmental economics is still in its infancy. Most research has been theoretical. In spite of the elegance of the results and the many important insights that have been obtained in theoretical environmental economics, there undoubtedly exists a growing need for empirical research. Without empirical support the impact of environmental economics in policy making will remain limited. Because environmental issues hardly played a role in public policy until the late 1970s, there exist only short-run (multivariate) time series of such variables as emissions, environmental policy, employment, firm birth, exports, etc. Moreover, there exist substantial differences among countries. For instance, compared to the United States, most European countries are lagging behind. Lack of data seriously hampers analysis of such important issues as the impact of environmental policy on foreign trade and location behaviour of firms. In particular, cross-national comparisons are seriously hampered. For the further development of environmental economics, systematic collection of data is a prerequisite. Only then will it become possible for environmental economics to reach the stage of elegance and practical importance it should.

Despite notable advances in environmental economics and clear progress in reducing environmental pollution, extensive pollution problems persist. Several reasons can be offered, including the fact that environmental economics is still a relatively new field and the fact that economic advice goes only as far as policy makers take it. Still another explanation is that our current paradigm does not require us to eliminate all pollution; we only reduce it to the point where the marginal benefits equal the marginal costs. One of the most valuable insights offered by environmental economists in the current paradigm, although it can sometimes be embarrassing when taken out of context, is that the optimal level of pollution is not zero. At the same time, most of us would prefer a world where pollution is reduced substantially below the current level. Marginal benefits increase with population and affluence, but the major mechanism for reducing pollution in the future will reduce the costs of attaining it. Some would suggest that competitive pressures and good foresight should cause this to happen. Others would point to the public goods nature of R&D, myopia in decision making and uncertainty about the future, implying that either market strengthening or market intervention is needed. Therefore, a very pressing area of future research would be developing incentives and institutions for reducing transaction and mitigation costs over time. The second major area of research would be to close the gap between good economics and good policy making by improving risk communication, institutional design and the decision-making process with respect to the environment.

1. Green accounting and green taxes in the global economy

Thomas Aronsson and Karl-Gustaf Löfgren

1 INTRODUCTION

The question of the proper design of the national accounts has been subject to extensive research during the last decade. One of the major issues here has been to design so-called green net national product (NNP) welfare measures by explicitly accounting for environmental damage and accumulation (decumulation) of environmental capital.[1] The first-best valuation (or accounting) principles are well known from Weitzman (1976). It is also clear, from the studies by Aronsson and Löfgren (1993, 1995) and Aronsson, Johansson and Löfgren (1997), how the impact of externalities should be handled so as to measure welfare in the uncontrolled market economy. The valuation problems implicit in green accounting are, to a large extent, related to environmental externalities. However, since the main purpose of the previous studies has been to measure the national welfare level, the global nature of these externalities has frequently been neglected. This chapter extends the analysis of green accounting to a global economy, where pollution caused by production in one country affects the well-being of consumers in other countries. We shall, in particular, explore the relationship between, on the one hand, the appropriate national and global welfare measures and, on the other, the national and/or global policies used to improve the allocation of the resources.

The analytical framework for studying global external effects is well known from previous work on, for example, international pollution control. Global external effects are routinely analysed in terms of Nash non-cooperative differential games in open loop or feedback loop form.[2] From research on oligopoly equilibria, such as Loury (1986), Polansky (1992) and in a recent paper by Tahvonen and Salo (1996), it is clear how the implementation problem is solved. However, in most instances the games are played between nations, and it is not always spelt out how the solution is implemented in a market economy.[3] The idea must be that the nations impose 'Pigouvian-related taxes' in the domestic product markets. These taxes are suboptimal, since the externalities are not fully internalized in the Nash solution. The latter creates complications for welfare measurement reminiscent of those discussed in Aronsson and Löfgren (1993, 1995).

We shall treat the valuation and implementation problems in three cases. The first is where the nations play a non-cooperative Nash game in open loop form. Here, we derive the welfare measures for each country as well as a global welfare measure. The second is the cooperative solution. This solution constitutes an important reference case for green accounting at the global level. The reason is that, to be able to measure welfare at the global level by observables related to the sum of the countries' green NNPs, it is necessary for the countries to coordinate their environmental policies so as to implement the cooperative solution. The latter can be accomplished by a global, Pigouvian-related, tax and transfer system. These taxes are directly useful for accounting purposes at the global level by solving a missing information problem in market data. Interestingly, however, it is not straightforward to split the sum of green NNPs into national welfare measures: even if the economies follow the cooperative solution, welfare measurement at the national level usually requires more information than can be found in each country's market data.

The third case refers to valuation problems arising in the imperfectly controlled market economy. We begin with the observation that 'cooperation' need not mean full implementation of a cooperative solution; it can also refer to smaller projects. We analyse the welfare effects of one such project: namely if, in a non-cooperative equilibrium, the countries agree to slightly raise the emission taxes. Our final concern is to study what we have called 'the close to cooperative solution'. This is interesting in the sense that a (first-best) cooperative solution concept is extremely difficult to implement in practice due to enormous information requirements. To make the implementation problem a bit more practical, we use the willingness-to-pay approach to construct a set of emission taxes, which are closely related to those supporting the cooperative solution. The fundamental questions to ask are whether the approximation of the Pigouvian tax structure contributes to increasing the welfare level, in comparison with the uncontrolled market economy, and whether these taxes are useful for green accounting in a similar way to Pigouvian taxes along a cooperative solution. The latter is also relevant from a methodological perspective, since it focuses on the willingness-to-pay technique as a means of collecting policy-relevant information.

2   A TWO-COUNTRY ECONOMY

This section analyses a two-country model and its implications for welfare measurement. The purpose is here to derive the appropriate national and global welfare measures under both the Nash non-cooperative open loop solution and the cooperative solution. The problem of implementing these solutions in the decentralized economy and, hence, the informational content of market data are dealt with in section 3. To focus on how to handle the (global) external effects arising from pollution, we shall neglect international trade. Terms of trade effects and their complications for welfare measurement are discussed by Asheim (1996).

2.1   The Model

As has been conventional in the literature on green accounting, let us neglect population growth and normalize the population in each economy to equal one. The instantaneous utility function facing the consumer in country i, $i = 1, 2$, takes the form

$$u_i(t) = u_i(c_i(t), z_i(t))$$

where $c_i(t)$ is consumption at time t and $z_i(t)$ is an indicator of environmental quality at time t. The instantaneous utility function is increasing, twice continuously differentiable and strictly concave in its arguments. If we denote the part of the stock of pollution generated by production in country i by x_i, the indicator of environmental quality in country i is defined by the concave function

$$z_i(t) = z_i(x_1(t), x_2(t))$$

where $\partial z_i / \partial x_1 < 0$ and $\partial z_i / \partial x_2 < 0$ for all x_1, x_2.

Output is produced by labour (normalized to one), physical capital and emissions (through the use of energy input). Net output is determined by the production function

$$y_i(t) = f_i(k_i(t), g_i(t))$$

where k_i is the capital stock per unit of labour and g_i is energy per unit of labour. Note that y_i measures net output, which means that the depreciation of physical capital has been accounted for. We assume that the function $f_i(\cdot)$ is twice continuously differentiable and strictly concave as well as non-decreasing in g_i. The stock of physical capital accumulates according to

$$\dot{k}_i(t) = f_i(k_i(t), g_i(t)) - c_i(t) \tag{1.1}$$

The stock of pollution accumulates through the release of emissions. In the model, these originate from the production of energy. To simplify the analysis, we will disregard the process of producing energy and assume that emissions in country i at t are equal to $g_i(t)$, which means that the differential equation for $x_i(t)$ is written

$$\dot{x}_i(t) = g_i(t) - \gamma x_i(t) \tag{1.2}$$

where γ is the rate of depreciation.

2.2   The Nash Non-cooperative Open Loop Solution

It is well known that differential games are very difficult to solve analytically, and that an equilibrium solution may not exist.[4] However, given that a solution does exist, it turns out that envelope properties of the value function enable us to derive a set of results relevant for both welfare comparisons and cost–benefit analysis. To see this, suppose to begin with that the resource allocation in each country is decided upon by a planner, who takes the path for the part of the stock of pollution created by the other country as exogenous. For country i, the planner chooses $c_i(t)$ and $g_i(t)$ to maximize

$$U_i(0) = \int_0^\infty u_i(c_i(t), z_i(t)) e^{-\theta t} dt$$

subject to the equations of motion for k_i and x_i, initial conditions $k_i(0) = k_{i0}$ and $x_i(0) = x_{i0}$ and terminal conditions $\lim_{t \to \infty} k_i(t) \geq 0$ and $\lim_{t \to \infty} x_i(t) \geq 0$. The parameter θ represents the rate of time preference, which is assumed to be identical across the countries.

The present-value Hamiltonian is written

$$H_i(t) = u_i(c_i(t), z_i(t)) e^{-\theta t} + \lambda_i(t) \dot{k}_i(t) + \mu_i(t) \dot{x}_i(t) \tag{1.3}$$

where λ_i and μ_i are present-value shadow prices in terms of utility. The additional necessary conditions are (neglecting the time indicator)[5]

$$\frac{\partial u_i(c_i, z_i) e^{-\theta t}}{\partial c_i} - \lambda_i = 0 \tag{1.4}$$

$$\lambda_i \frac{\partial f_i(k_i, g_i)}{\partial g_i} + \mu_i = 0 \tag{1.5}$$

$$\dot{\lambda}_i = -\lambda_i \frac{\partial f_i(k_i, g_i)}{\partial k_i} \tag{1.6}$$

$$\dot{\mu}_i = -\frac{\partial u_i(c_i, z_i)e^{-\theta t}}{\partial z_i} \frac{\partial z_i}{\partial x_i} + \mu_i \gamma \tag{1.7}$$

$$\lim_{t \to \infty} \lambda_i \geq 0 (= 0 \text{ if } \lim_{t \to \infty} k_i > 0) \tag{1.8}$$

$$\lim_{t \to \infty} \mu_i \geq 0 (= 0 \text{ if } \lim_{t \to \infty} x_i > 0) \tag{1.9}$$

Now, let

$$\Lambda_i^n(t) = (c_i^n(t), g_i^n(t)), \forall t$$

solve planner i's optimization problem. We define $(\Lambda_1^n, \Lambda_2^n)$ to be a Nash equilibrium, if

$$U_1(\Lambda_1^n, \Lambda_2^n) \geq U_1(\Lambda_1, \Lambda_2^n), \text{ all } \Lambda_1$$

$$U_2(\Lambda_1^n, \Lambda_2^n) \geq U_2(\Lambda_1^n, \Lambda_2), \text{ all } \Lambda_2$$

and refer to the solution vectors, Λ_1^n and Λ_2^n, as the equilibrium strategies of the two players.

We shall measure the national welfare level of each country by its value function (which in this case coincides with the present value of future utility facing the consumer), and the global welfare level by the sum of the value functions. The following general theorem simplifies the analysis:

Theorem 1 *If the Hamiltonian is continuously differentiable with respect to t, it follows that $dH_i(t)/dt = \partial H_i(t)/\partial t$ along an optimal solution.*

The proof of theorem 1 is straightforward and follows because the indirect effects of time via control, state and costate variables will vanish along an optimal solution (see, for example, Seierstad and Sydsaeter, 1987, p. 277). For the particular model discussed here, theorem 1 implies

$$\frac{dH_i^n(t)}{dt} = -\theta u_i(c_i^n(t), z_i^n(t))e^{-\theta t} + \frac{\partial u_i^n(\cdot)e^{-\theta t}}{\partial z_i(t)} \frac{\partial z_i^n(t)}{\partial x_j(t)} \dot{x}_j^n(t) \tag{1.10}$$

where $j \neq i$, $u_i^n(\cdot) = u_i(c_i^n, z_i^n)$, $z_i^n = z_i(x_1^n, x_2^n)$, and the superindex '$n$' is used to denote the Nash non-cooperative open loop solution. The second term on the right-hand side comes from the direct effect of time on planner i's present-value Hamiltonian via $x_j(t)$, which is 'exogenous' as long as the planners do not coordinate their decisions. Solving equation (1.10) and transforming the solution to current value terms gives the national welfare measure for country i[6]

$$\theta V_i^n(t) = H_i^{n^c}(t) + \int_t^\infty \Omega_i^n(s) e^{\theta t} ds \qquad (1.11)$$

where $V_i^n(t) = \int_t^\infty u_i(c_i^n(s), z_i^n(s)) \exp(-\theta(s-t)) ds$ is the value function of country i along the non-cooperative open loop solution and $H_i^{n^c}(t) = H_i^n(t) e^{\theta t}$ the current-value Hamiltonian. The term $\Omega_i^n(t)$ is a short notation for the last term on the right-hand side of equation (1.10), that is, the influence of pollution accumulation in country j on the instantaneous utility of the consumer in country i. Note that the non-cooperative open loop solution only internalizes the external effects caused by domestic pollution accumulation. The external effect from the pollution created by the other country remains uninternalized, and the last term in equation (1.11) measures the present value of the (uninternalized part of the) marginal external effect.

The current-value Hamiltonian is interpretable as a measure of the green NNP in utility terms, that is, it measures the current 'utility consumption' plus the discounted utility value of the present net investments (in physical capital and pollution). To transform $H_i^{n^c}(t)$ into what looks like a real NNP concept, let us follow Hartwick (1990) and Mäler (1991) and approximate the instantaneous utility by a linear function, that is

$$u_i(c_i^n, z_i^n) \approx \lambda_i^{n^c} c_i^n + \frac{\partial u_i(c_i^n, z_i^n)}{\partial z_i} z_i^n$$

where $\lambda_i^{n^c}(t) = \lambda_i^n(t) e^{\theta t}$. From this approximation, we obtain the following linearized version of the welfare measure in real terms[7]

$$\frac{\theta V_i^n(t)}{\lambda_i^{n^c}(t)} \approx c_i^n(t) + \dot{k}_i^n(t) + \rho_i^n(t) z_i^n(t) - \tau_i^n(t) \dot{x}_i^n(t) \qquad (1.12)$$

$$+ \frac{1}{\lambda_i^{n^c}(t)} \int_t^\infty \Omega_i^n(s) e^{\theta t} ds$$

where $\rho_i^n = (\partial u_i^n(\cdot)/\partial z_i) \lambda_i^{n^c}$ and $\tau_i^n = -\mu_i^n / \lambda_i^n$. The first row in equation (1.12) is the green NNP, in real terms, at time t. For the economy discussed here, the green NNP is the sum of the conventional NNP (the first two terms), the willingness to pay for environmental quality at time t (the third term)[8] and the value of additions to the stock of pollution at time t (the fourth term). In a decentralized setting, the interpretation of $(\tau_1^n(t), \tau_2^n(t))$ would be in terms of emission taxes, which are designed to support the non-cooperative open loop solution.

According to equations (1.11) and (1.12), it is obvious that market data alone do not contain all the relevant information for measuring the national welfare level. This is so because, as long as part of the external effects arising from pollution remains uninternalized, welfare becomes a function of time itself via the marginal external effect. The implication is that, to measure the national welfare level, we would require knowledge of the future paths taken by both economies (so as to obtain an estimate of the last term on the right-hand side of equation (1.12)).

Measurement of the global welfare level gives a similar conclusion. Adding the two national welfare indicators gives

$$\theta \sum_{i=1}^{2} V_i^n(t) = \sum_{i=1}^{2} \left[H_i^{nc}(s) + \int_t^{\infty} \Omega_i^n(t) e^{\theta t} ds \right] \qquad (1.13)$$

Equations (1.11) and (1.13) can be summarized as follows:

Proposition 1   *If the economies follow the Nash non-cooperative open loop solution, each national welfare measure is affected by external effects caused by pollution accumulation in other countries. These external effects also remain uninternalized at the global level. The implication is that observable market data do not contain all relevant information for measuring national and global welfare.*

A somewhat unattractive feature of the open loop solution is that the players choose all the values of their controls at the outset of the game. Note, however, that if we were to relax the open loop assumption and, instead, redo all analyses under a feedback loop (by conditioning the control variables on the state of the economies), the qualitative conclusions about welfare measurement, from proposition 1, would remain.[9] Essentially, when the countries do not cooperate so as to fully internalize the global external effects, the static green NNP will fail to work as a welfare measure at both the national and global levels. This leads us to turn to the cooperative solution.

2.3   The Cooperative Solution

To derive the cooperative solution, where the external effects are fully internalized at the global level, suppose to begin with that a global planner maximizes the sum[10] of the countries' utility functions, $U_1(0)$ and $U_2(0)$, subject to equations of motion for the state variables (k_1, k_2, x_1 and x_2) as well as to the initial and terminal conditions defined above. Among the necessary conditions, we find[11]

$$\frac{\partial u_i(c_i, z_i)e^{-\theta t}}{\partial c_i} - \lambda_i = 0 \tag{1.14}$$

$$\lambda_i \frac{\partial f_i(k_i, g_i)}{\partial g_i} + \mu_i = 0 \tag{1.15}$$

$$\dot{\lambda}_i = -\lambda_i \frac{\partial f_i(k_i, g_i)}{\partial k_i} \tag{1.16}$$

$$\dot{\mu}_i = -\frac{\partial u_i(c_i, z_i)e^{-\theta t}}{\partial z_i}\frac{\partial z_i}{\partial x_i} - \frac{\partial u_j(c_j, z_j)e^{-\theta t}}{\partial z_j}\frac{\partial z_j}{\partial x_i} + \mu_i\gamma \tag{1.17}$$

$$\lim_{t \to \infty} \lambda_i \geq 0 (= 0 \text{ if } \lim_{t \to \infty} k_i > 0) \tag{1.18}$$

$$\lim_{t \to \infty} \mu_i \geq 0 (= 0 \text{ if } \lim_{t \to \infty} x_i > 0) \tag{1.19}$$

for $i = 1, 2$ and $i \neq j$. Let

$$\Lambda_i^*(t) = (c_i^*(t), g_i^*(t)), \forall t$$

for $i = 1, 2$ solve the planner's optimization problem where the superindex '*' is used to denote the cooperative solution.

Turning to the welfare analysis, let $H^*(t) = \Sigma_i H_i^*(t)$ denote the present-value Hamiltonian along the cooperative solution, where

$$H_i^*(t) = u_i(c_i^*(t), z_i^*(t))e^{-\theta t} + \lambda_i^*(t)\dot{k}_i^*(t) + \mu_i^*(t)\dot{x}_i^*(t))$$

From theorem 1, we obtain

$$\frac{dH^*(t)}{dt} = -\theta \sum_{i=1}^{2} u_i(c_i^*(t), z_i^*(t))e^{-\theta t} \tag{1.20}$$

since the only non-autonomous time dependence of the global economic system originates from the utility discount factor, when the external effect has become fully internalized at the global level. Solving equation (1.20) and transforming the solution to current value terms gives

$$\theta \sum_{i=1}^{2} V_i^*(t) = H^{*c}(t) = \sum_{i=1}^{2} H_i^{*c}(t) \tag{1.21}$$

where $H_i^{*c}(t) = H_i^*(t)e^{\theta t}$. We have just proved the following result:

Proposition 2 *If the economies follow the cooperative solution, then the current value Hamiltonian for the global economy, which can be interpreted as the sum of the green NNPs in utility terms, is the appropriate global welfare measure.*

The interpretation of the global welfare measure in terms of the sum of the green NNPs is further emphasized by linearizing the welfare measure. Applying the same procedure as in subsection 2.2 we find

$$\theta \sum_{i=1}^{2} V_i^*(t) \approx \sum_{i=1}^{2} \lambda_i^{*c}(t) \left[c_i^*(t) + \dot{k}_i^*(t) + \rho_i^*(t)z_i^*(t) - \tau_i^*(t)\dot{x}_i^*(t) \right] \tag{1.22}$$

where $\rho_i^* = (\partial u_i^*(\cdot)/\partial z_i)\lambda_i^{*c}$ and $\tau_i^* = -\mu_i^*/\lambda_i^*$. Clearly, if the economies follow the cooperative equilibrium, all terms in equation (1.22) would be observable (or recoverable) at time t. In the context of decentralized economies, $(\tau_1^*(t), \tau_2^*(t))$ are also interpretable as emission taxes, which are set so as to make these economies reproduce the cooperative solution. The usefulness of Pigouvian emission taxes for green accounting in a cooperative economy is obvious from equation (1.22). These taxes, together, measure the social value of additions to the stock of pollution and provide, therefore, the same information as market prices in a competitive economy.

Since the countries act as 'one decision maker' in the cooperative solution, it is not straightforward to split the global welfare measure into two static national welfare measures. Consider the following proposition:

Proposition 3 *If the economies follow the cooperative solution, each national welfare measure contains more information than is provided by its contribution to the (global) current-value Hamiltonian.*

To see this, let us apply theorem 1 to the equation for $H_i^*(t)$

$$\frac{dH_i^*(t)}{dt} = -\theta u_i(c_i^*(t), z_i^*(t))e^{-\theta t} + \Gamma_i^*(t)$$

where

$$\Gamma_i^*(t) = \frac{\partial u_i^*(\cdot)e^{-\theta t}}{\partial z_i}\frac{\partial z_i^*(\cdot)}{\partial x_j}\dot{x}_j^*(t) - \frac{\partial u_j^*(\cdot)e^{-\theta t}}{\partial z_j}\frac{\partial z_j^*(\cdot)}{\partial x_i}\dot{x}_i^*(t)$$

for $i \neq j$, is a short notation for the non-autonomous time dependence following, since $H_i^*(t)$ neither contains $u_j^*(\cdot)$ nor μ_j^*. The national welfare measure will take the form

$$\theta V_i^*(t) = H_i^{*c}(t) + \int_t^\infty \Gamma_i^*(s)e^{\theta t}ds \tag{1.23}$$

This means that the national welfare measure contains forward-looking components, unless the following (rather restrictive) conditions are fulfilled simultaneously: (1) the effect of x_i on $u_j(\cdot)$ is identical to the effect of x_j on $u_i(\cdot)$, and (2) $\dot{x}_i$ and $\dot{x}_j$ are identical along the optimal path. Note also that, even if these forward-looking components remain in the national welfare measures, they will disappear at the global level, that is, $\Sigma_i\Gamma_i^*(t) = 0$ for all t. This is so because the marginal benefits and costs of pollution control only balance at the global level in the cooperative equilibrium. From the point of view of an individual country, there is still a discrepancy between what the country pays, in pollution charges, and the benefits the country receives from pollution control. This makes the individual economies non-autonomous time dependent (in addition to the non-autonomous time dependence caused by the utility discount factor).

3   THE MARKET ECONOMY

This section concerns three interrelated issues. The first is to show, very briefly, that the solution concepts in section 2 are (at least in theory) implementable in a market economy. The second refers to a small cooperative project; in this case, an agreement to (slightly) raise the emission taxes, when the preexisting equilibrium is the Nash non-cooperative open loop solution. We wish to determine, by cost–benefit analysis, whether such an agreement is welfare improving in comparison with non-cooperative behaviour. The final concern is to examine the possibility of approximating the cooperative solution via (non-Pigouvian) emission taxes, which are based on currently observable (or collectable) willingness-to-pay information. The latter is also relevant for accounting, to the extent that these taxes reduce (or eliminate) the 'missing information problem' in market data caused by external effects.

    It is convenient to begin with a brief description of the outcome in the controlled market economy. Suppose an emission tax, $\tau_i^0(t)$, is imposed on the firm in each country, and that the tax revenues, $\tau_i^0(t)g_i(t)$, are given to the consumer in the form of a lump-sum transfer. To take a short cut to the decentralized solution, note that the fundamental difference between a planner solution and the market economy is that the stock of pollution is not a state variable in the latter case; it is, instead, a side effect of the firm's decision to pollute, and its path is exogenous to the consumer.

In addition to the initial condition for the physical capital stock and the transversality condition, the necessary conditions obeyed by the decentralized solution are

$$\frac{\partial u_i(c_i^0, z_i^0)e^{-\theta t}}{\partial c_i} - \lambda_i^0 = 0 \tag{1.24}$$

$$\frac{\partial f_i(k_i^0, g_i^0)}{\partial g_i} - \tau_i^0 = 0 \tag{1.25}$$

$$\dot{\lambda}_i^0 = -\lambda_i^0 \frac{\partial f_i(k_i^0, g_i^0)}{\partial k_i} \tag{1.26}$$

$$\dot{k}_i^0 = f(k_i^0, g_i^0) - c_i^0 \tag{1.27}$$

for $i = 1, 2$ and $t \in [0, \infty)$. The time indicator has been suppressed, and the superindex '0' is used to denote the solution in the controlled market economy conditional on $\tau_i^0(t)$. Note also that these equations are general equilibrium conditions, that is they are obtained by combining the necessary conditions for the consumer and the firm in each country.

3.1   A Pigouvian View

We mentioned in section 2 that the shadow prices of pollution in real terms are interpretable as Pigouvian-related taxes. With the decentralized solution at our disposal, we will justify these statements:[12]

Proposition 4   *(i) If $\tau_i^0(t) = \tau_i^n(t) = -\mu_i^n(t)/\lambda_i^n(t), \forall t$ and $i = 1, 2$, the decentralized economies replicate the Nash non-cooperative open loop solution.*
   (ii) If $\tau_i^0(t) = \tau_i^*(t) = -\mu_i^*(t)/\lambda_i^*(t), \forall t$ and $i = 1, 2$, the decentralized economies replicate the cooperative solution.

Proof: To prove the first part, replace $\tau_i^0(t)$ in equation (1.25) by $\tau_i^n(t) = -\mu_i^n(t)/\lambda_i^n(t)$. It follows that $(c_i^n(t), g_i^n(t), k_i^n(t), \lambda_i^n(t)), t \in [0, \theta)$, obey the necessary conditions in equations (1.24)–(1.27). Finally, solving equation (1.2) gives $x_i^n(t)$. The proof of the second part is analogous. ∎

We shall refer to $\tau_i^n(t)$ as the 'non-cooperative' Pigouvian tax and $\tau_i^*(t)$ as the 'full' Pigouvian tax[13] for country i. To emphasize the difference between the two Pigouvian-related emission tax paths even further, let us solve equations (1.7) and (1.17), respectively, subject to the transversality condition[14]

$$\mu_i^n(t) = \int_t^\infty \frac{\partial u_i^n(s)e^{-\theta s}}{\partial z_i} \frac{\partial z_i^n(s)}{\partial x_i} e^{-\gamma(s-t)} ds$$

$$\mu_i^*(t) = \int_t^\infty \left[\frac{\partial u_i^*(s)e^{-\theta s}}{\partial z_i} \frac{\partial z_i^*(s)}{\partial x_i} + \frac{\partial u_j^*(s)e^{-\theta s}}{\partial z_j} \frac{\partial z_j^*(s)}{\partial x_i} \right] e^{-\gamma(s-t)} ds$$

Clearly, $\mu_i^n(t)$ and, hence, $\tau_i^n(t)$, only take into account that pollution in country i affects the utility of the consumer in country i (a consequence of the non-cooperative solution concept). The implication is that non-cooperative Pigouvian taxes only capture part of the social value of additonal pollution, which explains the 'missing information problem' in market data. The latter problem is absent at the global level in the cooperative solution, because $\mu_i^*(t)$ and, therefore, $\tau_i^*(t)$, reflect all direct utility effects of pollution caused by country i.

3.2 Tax Reforms in the Non-cooperative Equilibrium

If the countries behave non-cooperatively, they can clearly do better by coordinating their tax policies. However, 'coordinating tax policies' need not necessarily imply attempts to implement the cooperative equilibrium. It is perhaps more realistic to assume that countries agree upon smaller projects, the purpose of which is to improve the resource allocation in comparison with a non-cooperative regime. The concern of this subsection is the welfare effects of the implementation of such projects. More specifically, what happens if, in a Nash non-cooperative open loop equilibrium, the countries agree to raise their emission taxes?

The initial tax structure is the non-cooperative Pigouvian tax paths. We want to measure the welfare effects of increasing these emission taxes to $\tau_1^n(t) + \alpha$ and $\tau_2^n(t) + \beta$, respectively, for all t, where α and β are small positive constants. In each country, the additional tax revenues are given to the consumer in the form of a lump-sum subsidy.

The value function is written

$$W^n(0;\xi) = \sum_{i=1}^2 V_i^n(0;\xi) = \int_0^\infty \left[\sum_{i=1}^2 u_i(c_i^n(t;\xi), z_i^n(t;\xi)) \right] e^{-\theta t} dt \qquad (1.28)$$

where ξ is a parameter vector with α and β as two of its elements. The cost–benefit rules we are looking for can be obtained by differentiating the value function with respect to α and β, respectively, and evaluating the resulting derivatives at the points where $\alpha = 0$ and $\beta = 0$. It is straightforward to derive these measures by using the dynamic envelope theorem.[15] We show in the appendix that the cost–benefit rule for α takes the form

$$
\frac{\partial W^n(0;\xi)}{\partial \alpha} = \int_0^\infty \left[\frac{\partial u_1(c_1^n(t), z_1^n(t))}{\partial z_1} \frac{\partial z_1^n(t)}{\partial x_2} \frac{\partial x_2^n(t)}{\partial \alpha} \right.
$$

$$
\left. + \frac{\partial u_2(c_2^n(t), z_2^n(t))}{\partial z_2} \frac{\partial z_2^n(t)}{\partial x_1} \frac{\partial x_1^n(t)}{\partial \alpha} \right] e^{-\theta t} dt
$$

(1.29)

where the parameter vector ξ has been suppressed for notational convenience.

In general, what causes a small change in taxation to have an impact on the welfare level is that this tax was not set optimally prior to the reform. In the non-cooperative open loop framework discussed here, part of the external effects of pollution remains uninternalized. This means that we can expect α to affect the welfare level via the uninternalized part of the external effect. According to equation (1.29), this is precisely what happens, since α affects $u_1(\cdot)$ via x_2 and $u_2(\cdot)$ via x_1. Any effect of α via control, state and costate variables will vanish from the welfare change measure as a consequence of optimization.[16] To interpret equation (1.29), note that the second term within the bracket is positive, since $\partial x_1^n(\cdot)/\partial \alpha < 0$. On the other hand, the sign of $\partial x_2^n(\cdot)/\partial \alpha$ cannot be determined a priori, which means that the first term within the bracket can be either positive or negative. It depends on how the increase in α (via the decrease in x_1^n) affects the marginal utility of consumption and, hence, production (and pollution accumulation) in country 2.

The cost–benefit rule for β is analogous to equation (1.29): the welfare effect cannot be determined a priori, since $\partial x_1^n(\cdot)/\partial \beta$ can be either positive or negative. Hence, the welfare effect we are looking for, $\partial W^n(0;\xi)/\partial \alpha + \partial W^n(0;\xi)/\partial \beta$, is in general ambiguous.[17] To be able to sign the welfare effect of the tax project, we would need additional information about the preferences. Consider the special case of additive utility functions:

Proposition 5   *If $u_i(c_i, z_i) = \phi_i(c_i) + \kappa_i z_i$ and $z_i = \rho_i^i x_i + \rho_i^j x_j$ for $i = 1, 2$, and $j \neq i$, where κ_i, ρ_i^i and ρ_i^j are constants, then $\partial W^n(0;\xi)/\partial \alpha > 0$ and $\partial W^n(0;\xi)/\partial \beta > 0$.*

The proof rests on the fact that, in the case of additive separability and linearity, a change in $\alpha(\beta)$ will neither affect the marginal utility of consumption nor the emission tax in country 2 (1) and, therefore, not its decision to produce goods and accumulate pollution. It follows that $\partial x_2^n(\cdot)/\partial\alpha$ and $\partial x_1^n(\cdot)/\partial\beta = 0$, implying that the 'ambiguous parts' of the welfare change measures (for example, the first term of equation (1.29)) will vanish. Although special, the utility function underlying proposition 5 is interesting from the point of view that the national welfare effect of each reform is equal to zero; $\partial V_1^n(0;\xi)/\partial\alpha = 0$ and $\partial V_2^n(0;\xi)/\partial\beta = 0$. The (positive) global welfare effect originates from the influence of α on country 2 (via the decrease in x_1) and of β on country 1 (via the decrease in x_2). *In other words, if the policy maker in one country does not believe that the other country will stick to the agreement, he/she will have no incentive to raise the emission tax.*

3.3 'Close to' the Cooperative Solution

The emission tax paths implicit in the cooperative solution, that is, the 'full' Pigouvian tax paths, play two distinct roles in the context of a market economy: these taxes bring the economy to the socially optimal path, and they are directly useful for accounting purposes (see equation (1.22)). However, the implementation problems are enormous; we would require the policy makers to solve a command optimum problem in a dynamic economy. To make the implementation problem a bit more practical, suppose we were to construct static approximations of the full Pigouvian taxes using currently available (or collectable) willingness-to-pay information.[18] Two questions immediately arise. First, will the approximation of the Pigouvian taxes improve the welfare level compared with the uncontrolled market economy? Second, is the information provided by such taxes useful from the point of view of social accounting?

By static approximations of the full Pigouvian taxes we mean a set of emission taxes resembling those that would support the cooperative solution when the marginal utilities of pollution are constant. However, since the full Pigouvian taxes are, in general, forward looking, we shall also assume that the taxes are revised repeatedly as new willingness-to-pay information becomes available. In a recent paper, Aronsson and Löfgren (1999), we explore these approximations of the Pigouvian taxes in the context of a 'one-country' economy. In that case, it was possible to recover the relevant information through willingness-to-pay questions to the consumer. Here, as we shall see, things become more complicated when two countries are involved.

To construct a static analogue to the full Pigouvian tax for country i at time t, we use how a change in x_i affects the utilities of the consumers in countries i and j at time t. Specifically, and as we shall explain below, we would like to measure the sum of the following two terms

$$R_{ii}^0(t)/\lambda_i^{0c}(t) = \frac{\partial u_i(c_i^0(t), z_i^0(t))}{\partial z_i} \frac{\partial z_i(x_i^0(t), x_j^0(t))}{\partial x_i}/\lambda_i^{0c}(t)$$

$$R_{ji}^0(t)/\lambda_i^{0c}(t) = \frac{\partial u_j(c_j^0(t), z_j^0(t))}{\partial z_j} \frac{\partial z_j(x_i^0(t), x_j^0(t))}{\partial x_i}/\lambda_i^{0c}(t)$$

where $\lambda_i^{0c}(t) = \partial u_i^0(t)/\partial c_i$. If we were to ask the consumer in country i how much he/she is willing to pay (in terms of reduced consumption) to reduce domestic pollution marginally at time t, and if the consumer reveals the correct willingness to pay, the answer would be the marginal rate of substitution between $x_i(t)$ and $c_i(t)$, that is $-R_{ii}^0(t)/\lambda_i^{0c}(t)$. It is more difficult to obtain information about the second term by means of the willingness-to-pay technique, since the consumer in country j would be willing to pay $-R_{ji}^0(t)/\lambda_j^{0c}(t)$, rather than $-R_{ji}^0(t)/\lambda_i^{0c}(t)$, for a marginal reduction of x_i at time t. Therefore, to identify the number $-R_{ji}^0(t)/\lambda_i^{0c}(t)$, we would also need information about the relative marginal utility of consumption at the equilibrium, $\lambda_i^{0c}(t)/\lambda_j^{0c}(t)$. The latter is (in principle) recoverable by econometric methods, since estimates of consumer demand parameters provide information about the utility functions.

Suppose, for the argument, we are actually able to collect all this information via the willingness-to-pay technique and econometric analysis of consumer demand. We could then use this information to construct static approximations of the full Pigouvian taxes. Clearly, collecting all this information takes time, which itself gives rise to complications. Suppose that it takes dt units of time until new information becomes available, and consider

$$\overline{\tau}_i^0(t) = -\left[\overline{R}_{ii}^0 + \overline{R}_{ji}^0\right]/\left[(\theta+\gamma)\lambda_i^{0c}(t)\right] \qquad (1.30)$$

as a possible approximation of the full Pigouvian tax for country i on the time interval $(t, t + dt)$, where $\overline{R}_{ii}^0$ and $\overline{R}_{ji}^0$ are constants and equal to $R_{ii}^0(t)$ and $R_{ji}^0(t)$, respectively. To design these emission tax rates, we have only used information that is available (or recoverable) at time t. The reader may think of $\overline{\tau}_i^0(t)$ as a static approximation of a full Pigouvian tax. To see this interpretation more clearly, note that the firm in country i contributes to the utility at the margin by $\lambda_i^{0c}(t)(\partial f_i(t)/\partial g_i)$, since using energy enables the firm to produce goods. However, producing goods also means adding to the stock of pollution. The latter decreases utility at the margin by $-\lambda_i^{0c}(t)\overline{\tau}_i^0(t)$, which is a constant approximation of the marginal value of pollution. In other words, the marginal product of energy at time t will, in this way, be equal to a static approximation of the future marginal cost of pollution.

We shall begin by examining whether the approximation of the full Pigouvian tax structure solves the 'missing information problem' usually invalidating static welfare measures at the global level. In other words, given the approximation of the full Pigouvian taxes, is it possible to measure the global welfare using a static index (interpretable as the sum of green NNPs) in a way similar to what we did in equation (1.21)? Substitute the expression for $\bar{\tau}_i^0(t)$ into equation (1.25). It follows that the necessary conditions in equations (1.24)–(1.27) look as if they were derived from the following pseudo Hamiltonian (where the superindex '0', as before, denotes the controlled market economy)

$$
\begin{aligned}
H_p^0(t) = &\sum_{i=1}^{2} u_i(c_i^0(t), z_i^0(t))e^{-\theta t} + \sum_{i=1}^{2} \lambda_i^0(t)\dot{k}_i^0(t) \\
&+ \sum_{i=1}^{2} \left[\overline{R}_{ii}^0 + \overline{R}_{ji}^0\right] \frac{1}{\theta + \gamma} e^{-\theta t} \dot{x}_i^0(t)
\end{aligned}
\tag{1.31}
$$

for $i \neq j$, which is also the sum of green NNPs in utility terms, discounted to present value, given the approximation of the emission tax discussed above. In the appendix, we show that the time derivative of equation (1.31) takes the form

$$
\frac{dH_p^0(t)}{dt} = -\theta \sum_{i=1}^{2} u_i(c_i^0(t), z_i^0(t))e^{-\theta t} \text{ on } (t, t+dt)
\tag{1.32}
$$

At first glance, equation (1.32) may seem to be the differential equation we are looking for. Integrating over each short time interval and summing these integrals up to time T gives

$$
H_p^0(T) = H_p^0(t) - \theta \sum_{s=t}^{T-ds} \int_{s}^{s+ds} \sum_{i=1}^{2} u_i(c_i^0(\zeta), z_i^0(\zeta))e^{-\theta \zeta} d\zeta
\tag{1.33}
$$

To prove the welfare equivalence of the pseudo Hamiltonian, we would need to assume that $H_p^0(T)$ approaches zero when T goes to infinity; a mathematical property of the present-value Hamiltonian in 'well-behaved' infinite horizon control problems derived by Michel (1982). However, this result does not apply here, because equation (1.32) only holds on $(t, t+dt)$. Discrete information collection introduces discontinuities into the problem. This implies, for example, that the upper limit of integration on $(s, s+ds)$ will, in general, differ from the lower limit of integration on $(s + ds, s + 2ds)$. Every such point of discontinuity may contribute to make the limit of $H_p^0(T)$ different from zero. An interpretation is that the loss of information, which arises when the data collection involves a discrete element, may invalidate the interpretation of the sum of static green NNPs as a global welfare measure.

Only if the prediction errors caused by the discontinuities sum to zero, which would imply that the pseudo Hamiltonian approaches zero when time goes to infinity, are we able to derive the welfare measure

$$\theta W^0(t) = H_p^{0^c}(t) \qquad (1.34)$$

where $H_p^{0^c}(t) = H_p^0(t)e^{\theta t}$ and $W^0(t)$ is the value function. We summarize the results by the following claim:

Claim 1 *If we approximate the full Pigouvian tax rate by $\bar{\tau}_i^0(t)$, and if the contribution to future utility from the discontinuities becomes small on average in the sense that $\lim_{T \to \infty} H_p^0(T) \approx 0$, then the global welfare level at time t is closely approximated by the sum of the countries' green NNP measures. Moreover, the approximations of the full Pigouvian tax rates play the same role in social accounting in the decentralized economy as the full Pigouvian tax rates would do in the decentralized version of the cooperative solution.*

Given the conditions in claim 1, we have reconciled the growth-theoretical approach to social accounting with the (static) willingness-to-pay approach to environmental services. Note also that the consumers, endowed with perfect foresight, know the policy rule and are assumed to reveal their true willingness to pay when asked by the policy maker. However, if lying would improve the resource allocation, the perfect foresight consumers have an incentive not to reveal their true willingness to pay.[19] This suggests an interesting complication: for claim 1 to apply, the policy rule (based on correct willingness-to-pay information) must take the economy reasonably close to the cooperative solution.

Under the appropriate linearity and separability assumptions, $\bar{\tau}_i^0(t)$ measures the full Pigouvian tax of country i:

Proposition 6 *If willingness-to-pay information can be collected continuously, and if the following two conditions hold; (1) $u_i(c_i, x_i) = \phi_i(c_i) + \kappa_i z_i$, where κ_i is a constant, and (2) $z_i = \rho_i^i x_i + \rho_i^j x_j$, where ρ_i^i and ρ_i^j are constants, then $\bar{\tau}_i^0(t) = \tau_i^*(t)$.*

To see this result, note that $\bar{\tau}_i^0(t) = (\kappa_i \rho_i^i + \kappa_j \rho_j^i)/[(\theta + \gamma)\lambda_i^{0^c}]$ for all t is the full Pigouvian tax path for country i given conditions (1) and (2). Proposition 6 gives a sufficient condition for the tax to be Pigouvian and for the economy to follow the socially optimal path.[20] It is not a necessary condition, since $\bar{\tau}_i^0$ and τ_i^* are always equal in a steady state. The latter means that the 'close to cooperative economy' has the same steady state, if it exists, loosely speaking as the cooperative equilibrium.

It is not possible to prove that the approximations of the full Pigouvian taxes are welfare improving, compared with the uncontrolled market economy, in the general case. On the other hand, the cooperative equilibrium and the controlled market economy have the same steady state solution, when the market equilibrium is defined conditional on the approximation of the Pigouvian tax paths. Therefore, provided the tax policy takes the economy to a (unique) steady state, we will eventually approach the cooperative solution, in the neighbourhood of which the tax policy always improves the welfare of future generations.

4   CONCLUSIONS

Global external effects cause fundamental valuation problems relevant for green accounting, which have not been addressed in previous studies. In this chapter, we explore the relationships between, on the one hand, the appropriate national and global welfare measures and, on the other, the national and/or global tax policies used in an attempt to improve the allocation of resources. We would like to emphasize the following results:

- If the economies follow a non-cooperative Nash solution, neither the national welfare level nor global welfare can be exactly measured by a static index related to the green NNP. The reason is that only part of the external effect becomes internalized in a non-cooperative solution. The uninternalized part of the external effects, at both the national and global levels, will cause the economic system to be non-autonomous time dependent, which creates valuation problems reminiscent of those caused by disembodied technological change.
- If the economies follow the cooperative solution, the global welfare level is appropriately measured by the sum of the individual countries' green NNPs. However, since the cooperative solution means that the countries act as 'one decision maker', it is not, in general, straight-forward to split the sum of the green NNPs into national welfare measures. The reason is that, even if the external effects have become internalized at the global level, there is still an imbalance between costs and benefits of pollution control at the national level in the cooperative equilibrium. Therefore, an interesting implication of the welfare analyses in the non-cooperative and cooperative equilibria is that observable static indices do not suffice for measuring national

welfare, regardless of whether or not the countries cooperate in order to control for external effects.

- Despite the fact that the emission taxes are not optimally chosen in the non-cooperative open loop equilibrium, an agreement to (slightly) increase these taxes will, in general, give rise to an ambiguous welfare effect.
- To implement the cooperative (and even a non-cooperative) solution in the market economy, we would require an enormous amount of information. We show that it is, in principle, possible to use currently available willingness-to-pay information to derive 'a close to cooperative solution', which has the same steady state (if it exists) as the cooperative solution. It remains an open question whether 'the prediction errors' caused by the approximation of the Pigouvian tax structure will invalidate the welfare interpretation of the sum of national green NNP measures. In real-world situations, distortionary taxation creates additional complications for welfare measurement,[21] and it is unclear to what extent it pays to look for approximations of first-best Pigouvian taxes. Analysing a second-best version of the cooperative solution might be a natural next step. However, approximations of second-best taxes in economies with transboundary pollution is clearly worth a paper of its own, and is left for future research.

5   APPENDIX

Tax Reforms in the Non-cooperative Open Loop Equilibrium

The value function is written

$$W^n(0;\xi) = \sum_{i=1}^{2} V_i^n(0;\xi) = \int_0^{\infty} \left[\sum_{i=1}^{2} u_i(c_i^n(t;\xi), z_i^n(t;\xi)) \right] e^{-\theta t} dt \qquad (1.A1)$$

where ξ is a parameter vector with α as one of its elements. Let us follow the approach to the dynamic envelope theorem suggested by Leonard (1987) and define the present-value Hamiltonians

$$\hat{H}_i(t;\xi) = u_i(c_i^n(t;\xi), z_i^n(t;\xi)) e^{-\theta t} + \lambda_i(t) \dot{k}_i^n(t;\xi) + \mu_i(t) \dot{x}_i^n(t;\xi)$$

for the arbitrary and differentiable functions $\lambda_i(t)$ and $\mu_i(t)$. Replacing $u_i(t;\xi)e^{-\theta t}$ by $\hat{H}_i(t;\xi) - \lambda_i(t)\dot{k}_i^n(t;\xi) - \mu_i(t)\dot{x}_i^n(t;\xi)$ in equation (1.A1), and applying the rules of partial integration, gives

$$W^0(0;\xi) = \int_0^\infty \sum_{i=1}^2 [\hat{H}_i(t;\xi) + \dot{\lambda}_i(t)k_i^n(t;\xi) + \dot{\mu}_i(t)x_i^n(t;\xi)]dt$$
$$- \sum_{i=1}^2 \lambda_i(t)k_i^n(t;\xi) \,|_0^\infty - \sum_{i=1}^2 \mu_i(t)x_i^n(t;\xi) \,|_0^\infty \qquad (1.A2)$$

Note that the functions λ_i and μ_i are arbitrary and do not depend on ξ. The cost–benefit rule we are looking for is obtained by differentiating equation (1.A2) with respect to α and evaluating the derivative at the point where $\alpha = 0, \lambda_i(t) = \lambda_i^n(t;\xi)$ and $\mu_i(t) = \mu_i^n(t;\xi)$.[22] We shall also require that the terminal conditions do not bind, in which case the transversality conditions in equations (1.8) and (1.9) hold as strict equalities. Formally,

$$\frac{\partial W^n(0;\xi)}{\partial \alpha} = \int_0^\infty \sum_{i=1}^2 \left[\frac{d\hat{H}_i(t;\xi)}{d\alpha} + \dot{\lambda}_i^n(t;\xi)\frac{\partial k_i^n(t;\xi)}{\partial \alpha} \right.$$
$$\left. + \dot{\mu}_i^n(t;\xi)\frac{\partial k_i^n(t;\xi)}{\partial \alpha} \right] dt \qquad (1.A3)$$

since $k_i(0)$ and $x_i(0)$ are exogenous and $\lim_{t\to\infty} \lambda_i^n(t;\xi) = \lim_{t\to\infty} \mu_i^n(t;\xi) = 0$. Note that

$$\frac{d\hat{H}_i}{d\alpha} = \frac{\partial \hat{H}_i}{\partial c_i}\frac{\partial c_i^n}{\partial \alpha} + \frac{\partial \hat{H}_i}{\partial g_i}\frac{\partial g_i^n}{\partial \alpha} + \frac{\partial \hat{H}_i}{\partial x_i}\frac{\partial x_i^n}{\partial \alpha} + \frac{\partial \hat{H}_i}{\partial x_j}\frac{\partial x_j^n}{\partial \alpha} + \frac{\partial \hat{H}_i}{\partial k_i}\frac{\partial k_i^n}{\partial \alpha} \qquad (1.A4)$$

for $i \neq j$ evaluated along the non-cooperative open loop solution. Substituting equation (1.A4) into equation (1.A3), and using the necessary conditions in equations (1.4)–(1.7), we obtain equation (1.29).

The Properties of the Pseudo Hamiltonian

Differentiating equation (1.31) with respect to time we obtain (neglecting the time indicator)

$$\frac{dH_p^0}{dt} = \sum_{i=1}^2 \left[\frac{\partial H_p^0}{\partial c_i}\frac{dc_i^0}{dt} + \frac{\partial H_p^0}{\partial g_i}\frac{dg_i^0}{dt} + \frac{\partial H_p^0}{\partial k_i}\frac{dk_i^0}{dt} + \frac{\partial H_p^0}{\partial \lambda_i}\frac{d\lambda_i^0}{dt} \right.$$
$$\left. + \frac{\partial H_p^0}{\partial x_i}\frac{dx_i^0}{dt} \right] + \frac{\partial H_p^0}{\partial t}$$

Now, $\partial H_p^0 / \partial c_i = \partial H_p^0 / \partial g_i = 0$ and $(\partial H_p^0 / \partial \lambda_i)(d\lambda_i^0 / dt) = -(\partial H_p^0 / \partial k_i)(dk_i^0 / dt)$.

What then remains is

$$\frac{dH_p^0}{dt} = \sum_{i=1}^{2} \frac{\partial H_p^0}{\partial x_i} \frac{dx_i^0}{dt} + \frac{\partial H_p^0}{\partial t}$$

Using $\bar{R}_i^0 = \bar{R}_{ii}^0 + \bar{R}_{ji}^0$, we have (for $i \neq j$)

$$\frac{dH_p^0}{dt} = \sum_{i=1}^{2} \left[\left(\frac{\partial u_1^0}{\partial z_1} \frac{\partial z_1^0}{\partial x_i} + \frac{\partial u_2^0}{\partial z_2} \frac{\partial z_2^0}{\partial x_i} \right) - \frac{\bar{R}_i}{\theta + \gamma} \gamma \right] e^{-\theta t} \frac{dx_i^0}{dt}$$
$$- \theta \sum_{i=1}^{2} u_i(c_i^0, x_i^0) e^{-\theta t} - \sum_{i} \frac{\bar{R}_i}{\theta + \gamma} e^{-\theta t} \theta \frac{dx_i^0}{dt}$$
$$= -\theta \sum_{i=1}^{2} u(c_i^0, x_i^0) e^{-\theta t}$$

Note here the property of the pseudo Hamiltonian; it is constructed such that the non-autonomous time dependence from the external effect, via the stock of pollution, is offset by the time dependence of the approximation of the present value shadow price of pollution, which gives the desired differential equation for $H_p^0(t)$.

ACKNOWLEDGEMENTS

The authors would like to thank Martin Weitzman as well as participants in seminars at the University of Umeå, Stockholm School of Economics and Ulvön for helpful comments and suggestions. The chapter has also been improved by comments from Tom Crocker, Michael Hoel and H. Landis Gabel. A research grant from HSFR is also gratefully acknowledged.

NOTES

1. Empirical attempts have also been made to improve the accounting practices along these lines; see Repetto *et al.* (1989), US Environmental Protection Agency (1991) and Hultkrantz (1992).
2. The reader is referred to Mäler (1989), Barrett (1990, 1994), Carraro and Siniscalco (1993), Cesar (1994), Tahvonen (1994) and Mäler and de Zeeuw (1995) to mention a few. More details are available in a recent survey by Missfeldt (1996).
3. An exception is van der Ploeg and de Zeeuw (1992).
4. Explicit solutions usually require a set of simplifying assumptions; see, for example, Hoel (1978), Clark (1980), Levhari and Mirman (1980), Dockner, Feightinger and Jörgensen (1985) and Tahvonen (1994). In a more general setting, however, very few insights emerge (even in terms of qualitative statements). One of the most comprehensive statements of the theory has been provided by Basar and Olsder (1982).
5. The transversality conditions are necessary provided that certain growth conditions are fulfilled. These growth conditions serve as upper bounds on the influence of the state

variables on the functions involved. For further details, the reader is referred to Seierstad and Sydsaeter (1987, theorem 16, chapter 3).

6. We have used $\lim_{t\to\infty} H_i^n(t) = 0$, which follows provided that certain regularity conditions are fulfilled; see Michel (1982) and Seierstad and Sydsaeter (1987, p. 245).

7. Note that this 'market-related' approximation of the present value of future utility can also be obtained by using the prices in a competitive economy directly in a way similar to Dixit, Hammond and Hoel (1980). See also Asheim (1997).

8. Note that $\rho_i^n = (\partial u_i^n(\cdot)/\partial z_i)/\lambda_i^n$ measures the marginal rate of substitution between environmental quality and consumption at time t, which is recoverable by means of a static willingness-to-pay question to the consumer.

9. See also Löfgren (1999).

10. This assumption is made to preserve simplicity. The results to be derived below are also valid under a more general welfare function.

11. See note 5.

12. For a similar interpretation of non-cooperative and cooperative equilibria in terms of market solutions, see also van der Ploeg and de Zeeuw (1992).

13. It is sometimes argued that a cooperative solution is difficult to implement, since one country may gain by free riding, provided the other countries follow the agreement. However, this argument misses the fact that implementation means taxing firms in a decentralized economy. When the Pigouvian taxes have been introduced, and if we disregard the possibility of tax avoidance, individual firms have no incentives to deviate from the socially optimal behaviour. We would, instead, argue that the difficult problem is to find these Pigouvian taxes.

14. We assume that the terminal conditions on the stocks of pollution are not binding, in which case we can use $\lim_{t\to\infty} \mu_i^n(t) = 0$ and $\lim_{t\to\infty} \mu_i^*(t) = 0$.

15. See Seierstad (1981) and Seierstad and Sydsaeter (1987). A theorem on the differentiability of the value function in infinite horizon optimal control problems, which has been derived by Atle Seierstad, is presented by Aronsson, Johnsson and Löfgren (1997, appendix to chapter 4). As indicated by Jensen and Lockwood (1998), it may be rather restrictive to assume differentiability of the value functions in a feedback loop Nash equilibrium. They show, within a class of linear-quadratic differential games, that the value function may be discontinuous, even if the game itself has a very simple structure. They also give sufficient conditions for differentiability, which turn out to be related to the conditions for a unique equilibrium.

16. Note the absence of the so-called tax-base effects via the preexisting emission taxes. These tax-base effects, which normally would influence the welfare effect following a tax change, are offset by terms that have to do with the effect of the reform on the domestically created pollution. The reason is that the non-cooperative open loop solution internalizes the domestic part of the external effects arising from pollution.

17. Note that this conclusion does not depend on the tax increases being permanent. An agreement to temporarily increase the emission taxes would also give rise to an ambiguous welfare effect, since a temporary increase in α (β) can affect $x_2^n(x_1^n)$ in either direction.

18. The potential usefulness of willingness-to-pay information to improve the national accounts was recognized in some of the older literature on social accounting; see, for example, Peskin and Peskin (1978).

19. Note that, if the consumers do not reveal their true willingness to pay, the calculations behind claim 1 are no longer valid.

20. Note that, if the utility function is non-linear in the pollution arguments, continuous information collection does not imply that the tax path is Pigouvian, since the instantaneous shadow price of pollution is not correctly estimated in this case.

21. See Aronsson (1998).

22. Note that, even if the stock of pollution is not a state variable in the decentralized economy, $\mu_i^n(t;\xi)$ is implicitly defined by the non-cooperative Pigouvian tax.

REFERENCES

Aronsson, T. (1998), 'Welfare measurement, green accounting and distortionary taxes', *The Journal of Public Economics*, **70**, 273–95.

Aronsson, T. and K.-G. Löfgren (1993), 'Welfare consequences of technological and environmental externalities in the Ramsey growth model', *Natural Resource Modeling*, **7**, 1–14.

Aronsson, T. and K.-G. Löfgren (1995), 'National product related welfare measurement in the presence of technological change, externalities and uncertainty', *Environmental and Resource Economics*, **5**, 321–32.

Aronsson, T. and K.-G. Löfgren (1999), 'Pollution tax design and green national accounting', *European Economic Review*, **43**, 1458–74.

Aronsson, T., P.-O. Johansson and K.-G. Löfgren (1997), *Welfare Measurement, Sustainability and 'Green' National Accounting – A Growth Theoretical Approach*, Cheltenham, UK and Northampton, MA: Edward Elgar.

Asheim, G.B. (1996), 'Capital gains and "Net National Product" in open economies', *Journal of Public Economics*, **59**, 419–34.

Asheim, G.B. (1997), 'Adjusting green NNP to measure sustainability', *The Scandinavian Journal of Economics*, **99**, 355–70.

Barrett, S. (1990), 'The problem of global environmental protection', *Oxford Review of Economic Policy*, **6**, 68–79.

Barrett, S. (1994), 'Self-enforcing international environmental agreements', *Oxford Economic Papers*, **46**, 878–94.

Basar, T. and G.J. Olsder (1982), *Dynamic Noncooperative Game Theory*, London: Academic Press.

Brock, W. (1977), 'A polluted golden age', in V.L. Smith (ed.), *Economics of Natural and Environmental Resources*, New York: Gordon and Breach.

Carraro, C. and D. Siniscalco (1993), 'Strategies for the international protection of the environment', *Journal of Public Economics*, **52**, 309–28.

Cesar, H.S.J. (1994), *Control and Game Models of Greenhouse Effects*, Lecture Notes in Economics and Mathematical Systems 146, Springer-Verlag.

Clark, C.M. (1980), 'Restricted access to common property fishing resources: a game theoretic analysis', in P.T. Liu (ed.), *Dynamic Optimization and Mathematical Economics*, New York: Plenum Press.

Dixit, A., P. Hammond and M. Hoel (1980), 'On Hartwick's rule for regular maximin paths for capital accumulation', *Review of Economic Studies*, **47**, 551–6.

Dockner, E., G. Feightinger and S. Jörgensen (1985), 'Tractable classes of nonzero-sum open loop Nash differential games: theory and examples', *Journal of Optimization Theory and Applications*, **14**, 179–97.

Hartwick, J. (1990), 'Natural resources, national accounting and economic depreciation', *Journal of Public Economics*, **43**, 291–304.

Hoel, M. (1978), 'Distribution and growth as a differential game between workers and capitalists', *International Economic Review*, **19**, 335–50.

Hultkrantz, L. (1992), 'National accounts of timber and forest environmental resources in Sweden', *Environmental and Resource Economics*, **2**, 283–305.

Jensen, H. and B. Lockwood (1998), 'A note on discontinuous value functions and strategies in affine quadratic differential games', *Economics Letters*, **61**, 301–6.

Leonard, D. (1987), 'Costate variables correctly value stocks at each instant', *Journal of Economic Dynamics and Control*, **11**, 117–22.

Levhari, D.R. and L.J. Mirman (1980), 'The great fish war: an example using a dynamic Nash–Cournot solution', *Bell Journal of Economics*, **11**, 322–44.

Löfgren, K.-G. (1999), 'Welfare measurement and cost–benefit analysis in Nash and Stackelberg differential fish games', *Natural Resource Modeling*, **12**, 291–305.

Loury, G. (1986), 'A theory of oligopoly: Cournot–Nash equilibrium in exhaustible resource markets with fixed supplies', *International Economic Review*, **27**, 285–301.

Mäler, K.-G. (1989), 'The acid rain game', in H. Folmer and E. van Jerland (eds), *Valuation Methods and Policy Making in Environmental Economics*, Amsterdam: Elsevier.

Mäler, K.-G. (1991), 'National accounts and environmental resources', *Environmental and Resource Economics*, **1**, 1–15.

Mäler, K.-G. and A. de Zeeuw (1995), 'Critical loads in games of transboundary pollution control', Working Paper 7.95, Fondazione Eni Enrico Mattei.

Michel, P. (1982), 'On the transversality conditions in infinite horizon optimal control problems', *Econometrica*, **50**, 975–85.

Missfeldt, F. (1996), 'Game-theoretic modelling of transboundary pollution: a review of the literature', mimeo, Economics Department, University of Stirling.

Peskin, H.M. and J. Peskin (1978), 'The valuation of nonmarket goods in income accounting', *Review of Income and Wealth*, **24**, 71–91.

Polansky, S. (1992), 'Do oil producers act as oligopolists?', *Journal of Environmental Economics and Management*, **23**, 216–47.

Repetto, R., W. Magrath, M. Wells, C. Beer and F. Rossini (1989), *Wasting Assets: Natural Resources in the National Income Accounts*, Washington, DC: World Resources Institute.

Seierstad, A. (1981), 'Derivatives and subderivatives of the optimal value function in control theory', Memorandum from Institute of Economics University of Oslo, 26 February.

Seierstad, A. and K. Sydsaeter (1987), *Optimal Control Theory with Economic Applications*, Amsterdam: North-Holland.

Tahvonen, O. (1994), 'Carbon dioxide abatement as a differential game', *European Journal of Political Economy*, **10**, 686–705.

Tahvonen, O. and S. Salo (1996), 'Oligopoly equilibria in nonrenewable resource markets', mimeo, The Finnish Forest Research Institute.

US Environmental Protection Agency (1991), *Environmental Investments: The Cost of a Clean Environment*, Washington, DC: Island Press.

van der Ploeg, F. and A.J. de Zeeuw (1992), 'International aspects of pollution control', *Environmental and Resource Economics*, **2**, 117–39.

Weitzman, M.L. (1976), 'On the welfare significance of national product in a dynamic economy', *Quarterly Journal of Economics*, **90**, 156–62.

2. The environment and economic well-being

Robert Kaufmann

1 INTRODUCTION

The nascent discipline of ecological economics is at a critical point. It was developed by ecologists and economists to remedy flaws that they perceived in the economic approach to resource and environmental management. To do so, these scientists developed a logically consistent model of human interactions with the environment. This ecological economic model is irreconcilable with many aspects of the mainstream economic model. This led to a considerable body of empirical research that tested the explanatory power of the ecological economic model relative to the mainstream economic model. In general, the ecological model performed well.

Despite these successes, I believe that ecological economics is on the verge of being absorbed by mainstream economics. Many of the articles published in the journal *Ecological Economics* could be published in mainstream economic journals. While this is not bad, it causes me to wonder whether the ecological economic model is useful, or whether ecological economics is another name for resource and environmental economics. Put simply, is there a future for ecological economics?

I believe ecological economics has a future beyond mainstream economics. This optimism is based on my belief that the ecological economic model can be used to generate insights that are not available to those who start with the economic model. In this chapter, I describe the evolution and general nature of the ecological economic model, how ecological economics has lost its way, and how it can right itself. To regain its viability, ecological economics must compete directly with the mainstream economics in the policy arena. It can compete successfully by using the interdisciplinary model that underlies ecological economics rather than the single-discipline model that is economics and by embracing the complications of the real world through statistically rigorous empirical analyses rather than eliminating these complications in the pursuit of elegant theory. Should ecological economics do so, the quality of resource and environmental management will improve significantly, which would benefit all.

2 WHAT IS ECOLOGICAL ECONOMICS?

The intellectual evolution of ecological economics can be traced back several centuries to the French physiocrats (Cleveland, 1987). In spite of this history, much of the recent research agenda has evolved from the conflict between economic development and ecological preservation. This conflict caused economists and ecologists to interact. In these interactions, ecologists and economists were nearly always on opposite sides.

The confrontational nature of these interactions shaped the intellectual development of ecological economics. As the contact between ecologists and economists continued, ecologists began to understand the world view of economists. Rather than mitigate the division between ecologists and economists, this understanding exacerbated the conflict. Several aspects of the economic model contradicted the ecologists' world view. Convinced that the economic paradigm was fundamentally flawed, a group of ecologists and some economists developed an alternative model of human interactions with the environment. The following description of this model is not meant to be a literature review. Rather, it my idiosyncratic view of ecological economics.

Material and Energy Flows

Ecologists analyse natural ecosystems by tracing the flow of matter and energy among organisms and between organisms and their environment. These flows allow ecologists to identify the factors that determine the rate of biological productivity (the total amount of energy available to the biological organisms in a system). By following the flow of energy and matter through food webs, ecologists can understand how the natural systems function and how they react to disturbance.

Ecological economists reasoned that a similar approach could be applied to economic systems. But discussion of material and energy and material flows plays a minor role in the economic literature. Instead, economists focus on money flows. To economists, money flows contain the information that ecologists obtain from energy and material flows. In a proper functioning market, the price of a material or energy flow conveys information about the availability of that material or energy flow (marginal cost) and its usefulness to the system (marginal utility).

This interpretation of money flows does not satisfy ecological economists. Aside from the missing information that is acknowledged by economists (for example, environmental externalities), ecological economists argue that money flows are an incomplete substitute for measuring material and energy flows. Money flows do not obey the laws of thermodynamics, in the same way that material and energy flows must (Georgescu-Roegen, 1971; Odum, 1971). As

a result, analyses based on money flows may lead to theory or policy that
violates the laws of thermodynamics, which is a physical impossibility.

Ecological economists point out that the basic model of the economic
system is a perpetual motion machine. This model shows firms and households exchanging factors of production and goods and services in a circular
flow. This circular flow violates the second law of thermodynamics. Ecological economists argue that the understanding of the economic system can be
improved by studying the material and energy flows that make the diagram
consistent with the laws of thermodynamics.

From a thermodynamics perspective, economic production is a work process that increases the organization state of matter. Such changes oppose the
tendency towards a greater state of disorder dictated by the second law of
thermodynamics. As such, economic production does not occur spontaneously. Rather, energy must be used to oppose the tendency towards disorder.
Energy powers the circular flow of goods, services and factors of production
between firms and households.

The source of this energy is dictated by the laws of thermodynamics. The
first law of thermodynamics states that matter and energy cannot be created
or destroyed; therefore humans must obtain them from the environment. The
second law of thermodynamics implies that the ability of energy to do work
declines as energy is used to do work. Consequently, new sources of energy
must be obtained continuously from the environment. Ecological economists
use this dependence on environmental sources of matter and energy to redefine the boundaries of the economic system. The economic system is a
subsystem of the environmental system. As such, energy and matter are the
only primary inputs. Capital and labour are derived from environmental
sources of energy and matter.

The redefinition of primary inputs is *prima facie* evidence for studying
material and energy flows. The availability of energy is measured using the
concept of energy return on investment (EROI). EROI measures the amount
of energy obtained from the environment relative to the amount of energy
used to obtain it. A feasible energy source must have an EROI greater than
1.0. An EROI of 1 or less implies that no energy remains to power the non-
energy sectors of the economy. EROI provides a useful supplement to economic
analyses because market imperfections can distort energy prices. In one case,
analyses of EROI indicated that firms were making a profit extracting oil with
an EROI less than 1.0 (Gilliland, 1975).

Ecological economists also use material and energy flows to measure the
impact of economic activities on the environment. As indicated by the first
law of thermodynamics, all of the energy and matter used by the economic
system must come from the environment. Extracting these resources entails a
suite of environmental impacts. Similarly, humans cannot destroy matter or

energy; therefore all the matter and energy extracted from the environment eventually returns to the environment as wastes. These wastes also entail a suite of environmental impacts. By tracing material and energy flows from the environment to the economic system and back to the environment, ecological economists assess the environmental impacts specific to economic activities.

Limits

There is a basic disagreement between ecological economics and mainstream economics about the notion of limits. Ecological economists believe that the size and material well-being of human populations is ultimately limited by environmental factors. On the other hand, mainstream economists believe that economic well-being, especially in the short term, is limited by allocative efficiency.

The notion that environmental factors constrain the ultimate size and economic well-being of the human population was put forward by Thomas Malthus. This line of inquiry was dropped from the mainstream economic research agenda because the predictions of Malthus, Jevons and more recent analyses, such as the Club of Rome, proved to be too pessimistic. At the same time, unprecedented rates of technical change convinced many mainstream economists that human ingenuity could overcome any environmental constraint.

The failure of previous predictions and rapid rates of technical innovation have not dissuaded ecological economists of the notion that environmental factors limit economic activity. They start their analysis using the notion of overshoot. Non-human populations overshoot their carrying capacity, which is the maximum number of individuals that a given area of the environment can support indefinitely. Ecological economists argue that technical innovations may allow human populations to exceed their carrying capacity, but this overshoot is temporary. Much of the technical change during the industrial revolution is based on the use of non-renewable resources. These technologies will lose their effectiveness as the availability of energy and material resources declines.

Herman Daly (1991) uses the notion of the plimsoll line to illustrate the difference between ecological economists and mainstream economists regarding the role of limits. The plimsoll line indicates how low in the water a boat may sit safely. By focusing on allocative efficiency, mainstream economists concentrate on how to load the boat in the most efficient way. That is, spacing the cargo evenly is more efficient than loading all of the cargo at the bow – such an unbalanced load may cause the ship to capsize. On the other hand, ecological economists are concerned about how much cargo can be placed on the boat. That is, there is a limit on the amount of cargo that the ship can carry, regardless of how efficiently it is loaded.

Consistent with this analogy, ecological economists try to identify environmental factors that may limit the size and material well-being of the human population. They focus on the supply of natural resources and the ability of the environment to process wastes. Many ecological economists argue that the quantity of energy that can be extracted from the environment with a large EROI will ultimately limit the size and material well-being of human society (Hall, Cleveland and Kaufmann, 1986; Gever *et al.*, 1986). They are particularly concerned about the energy resources that will ultimately replace conventional supplies of oil and natural gas, which many believe will be depleted within a century. Ecological economists also focus on the ability of the environment to dilute and detoxify wastes. Currently, humans emit carbon dioxide into the atmosphere faster than the ocean and terrestrial biota can take up that carbon. As a result, the atmospheric concentration of CO_2 is increasing and the resultant increase in the radiative forcing of the atmosphere may change the climate in a way that reduces human well-being.

Value

Ecological economists also have a fundamental disagreement with mainstream economists regarding the source of value. Mainstream economists believe that value is a subjective human assessment. According to this perspective, natural ecosystems have value to the extent that humans assign value to them. On the other hand, ecological economists believe that natural ecosystems have value, whether or not humans recognize their contribution.

Ecological economists use the laws of thermodynamics and the economic notion of opportunity costs to quantify the value of natural ecosystems. Natural ecosystems support economic activity by producing natural resources and processing wastes. These contributions to economic activity are termed environmental life support. In the first step of economic production, environmental life support produces natural resources by concentrating and rearranging matter and energy in a way that opposes the tendency towards a greater state of entropy. For example, copper is scattered randomly throughout the earth's crust. In a few places, environmental life support produces ores by concentrating copper ten- to 100-fold relative to crustal rock (Lovering, 1969). In the final step of economic production, environmental life support provides waste treatment services by diluting and detoxifying the by-products of economic activity. For example, environmental life support decomposes organic wastes and purifies water.

The contribution of environmental life support is critical to economic activity because it affects the quantity of human capital and labour that is used by the economic system to produce a good or render a service. In general, the quantity of capital or labour that is required to produce a good or service is related inversely to the quantity of work done by environmental life support to produce a natural resource or process wastes (Chapman and Roberts, 1983). For example, environmental life support does more work to support large concentrations of fish in areas of high productivity, such as coastal upwelling, than the amount of work done to support low concentrations of fish in areas of low productivity, such as open oceans. The extra work done by natural capital has value to the economic system because less capital and labour generally is required to harvest fish from areas with high population densities. At the other end of economic production, environmental life support reduces the amount of capital and labour used to dilute and detoxify wastes. For example, environmental life support does more work to oxygenate freshwater ecosystems that can process ten units of organic wastes than ecosystems that can process one unit of organic wastes. The increased effort by environmental life support has value to the economic system because less human capital and labour is needed to detoxify organic wastes in freshwater ecosystems that can process ten units per day than one unit per day.

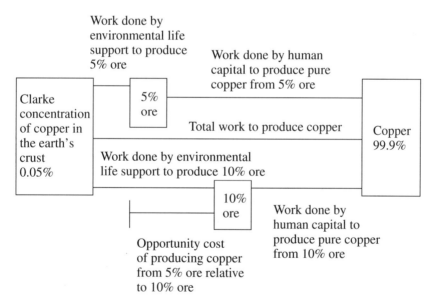

Figure 2.1   *The opportunity costs of depleting ores that contain 10 per cent copper and replacing them with ores that contain 5 per cent copper*

The inverse relation between the amount of work done by environmental life support and the quantity of human capital and labour that is required to produce a unit of economic output or dispose of a unit of waste is used to assess the value of ecosystems. This value is measured using the economic notion of opportunity cost. The opportunity cost of environmental life support is the amount of human capital and/or labour that must be used to maintain a given level of economic activity in the face of a reduction in environmental life support. As society exhausts ores in which environmental life support has increased the concentration of copper to 10 per cent, society must increase the use of capital and labour to maintain a constant level of copper production from ores in which environmental life support has increased the concentration of copper to 1 per cent (Figure 2.1). Similarly, as society overwhelms the ability of natural capital to processes organic wastes, society must build and maintain sewage treatment plants to stabilize the concentration of waste in the environment.

3   HOW WILL ECOLOGICAL ECONOMICS EVOLVE?

The literature generated by ecological economists contains two important short-comings. First, a significant fraction of the ecological economics literature can be characterized as 'economics bashing'. Criticism of the economic model served as a jumping-off point for ecological economics, but the literature is now replete with these criticisms, many of which are repeated *ad nauseum*. Criticizing the economic model by itself is not a fruitful research agenda. Ecological economics must move beyond criticism and offer something positive.

Unfortunately, ecological economics is short of such alternatives, and this lack constitutes the second shortcoming. While some ecological economists may be saving their best efforts for 'their' journal *Ecological Economics*, I would assume that many ecological economists would like to demonstrate the 'superiority' of their theoretical model by reporting empirical results that contain insights not available to results generated from the economic model. Many of the economics journals that focus on resource and environmental issues have a strong empirical component and so editors are often looking for papers that 'build a better mousetrap', regardless of the theoretical framework used to generate it. The absence of statistically rigorous analyses in *Ecological Economics* or mainstream economics journals implies to me that many of the models generated by ecological economists have not surpassed the ability of economic models to represent resource and environmental issues or their ability to formulate policy.

If ecological economics is to survive, and I believe it will, ecological economics must stop bashing economics and compete directly with economics. In short, it is time for ecological economists to 'put up or shut up'. To demonstrate its viability, ecological economics research should be evaluated against two criteria: (1) Do the models developed by ecological economists represent the relevant components of behaviour of the ecological economic system 'better' than economic models? (2) Can the models developed by ecological economists be used to formulate policy that improves resource and/or environmental management relative to the current policy regime? If the models developed by ecological economists cannot do better, ecological economics will be nothing more than an interesting, but short-lived, criticism of mainstream economics.

The criteria for the success of ecological economics are stringent. Given the current state of resource and environmental management, there is good reason to believe that ecological economics can develop better models and better policy. To do so, I suggest that researchers use an interdisciplinary approach and emphasize empirical analysis over theory.

Interdisciplinary Approach

Much of the progress in both the natural and social sciences has been generated by researchers following a reductionist, single-discipline approach. To solve a set of problems, researchers identify the set of relevant variables. These variables constitute a system and are said to be endogenous to that system. Variables that have a small or indirect effect on the problem are ignored and/or held constant and are said to be exogenous. Differentiating endogenous and exogenous variables is necessary to reduce the number of variables to a manageable size. By reducing the number of variables, analysts can analyse the interactions among variables in a controlled manner.

The boundaries that identify the variables endogenous to the economic system were drawn by analysts interested in an array of issues that are known today as economics. This set of boundaries enables economists to make significant progress in areas that are of concern to economics. But many of the variables that are important to resource and environmental management are exogenous to the economic system. As such, the system boundaries of the mainstream economic model impede the analysis of interactions between humans and their environment.

To avoid these impediments, ecological economists should use an interdisciplinary approach. The variables that affect the availability of natural resources and/or the environmental impacts of human activity lie within the boundaries of biology, geology and chemistry. Based on these linkages, ecological economists must redraw the system boundaries to endogenize the relevant variables, regardless of discipline.

Much of the effort to expand system boundaries has simply linked existing models from different disciplines. Linking existing models from disparate

disciplines seems a logical way of expanding the system boundaries to include the relevant variables, but this approach cannot overcome the
shortcomings that are built into the single-discipline models. In the process of
building single-discipline models, many variables are eliminated because
their effects are hard to represent in a manner that is consistent with the
effects of the other endogenous variables. These variables remain 'missing'
even after the single-discipline models are linked. I illustrate the limits associated with linking existing models with efforts to assess the effect of climate
change on agriculture. To quantify these effects, analysts use the temperature
and precipitation forecast from a climate model to drive a physiological
model of crop yield. The economic effects of the change in yield are assessed
with an economic model.

Yield models based on crop physiology (for example, Andresen and Dale,
1989; Jones and Kiniry, 1986; Stapper and Arkin, 1980) cannot simulate the
effect of the economic environment on the behaviour of farmers. As a result,
yield models based on crop physiology are designed to be 'free from region-
specific or management-specific effects' on the assumption that farmers follow
optimum management techniques (Liverman *et al.*, 1986). Without these
effects, yield models based on crop physiology cannot assess many important
strategies for mitigating or adapting to climate change.

Conversely, it is not possible to use economic models of yield because
many of these models do not include weather effects. Temperature and precipitation clearly affect crop yields. Yet many economic models of crop yield
exogenize these variables because the effects of temperature or precipitation
on yield cannot be simulated in a way that is consistent with the effects of
other economic variables. Economic models often simulate yield with a
production function that represents the effect of capital, labour and purchased
inputs (for example, Cooke and Sundquist, 1989). Consistent with economic
theory, the production function is specified in a way that increasing the use of
a purchased input increases output. But this is not consistent with the effect
of temperature or precipitation on yield. Physiological analyses indicate that
there is an inverted U-shaped relation between weather variables and yield.
This implies that the marginal product of a weather variable is positive as the
weather variable increases towards the physiological optimum from below.
But the marginal product is negative as the weather variable increases beyond
the optimum. As a result, it is not possible to simulate the effect of weather
variables on yield using a production function.

To represent the effects of weather and economic variables on crop yield,
analysts need to build a new model, one that is consistent with determinants
from a variety of disciplines. An interdisciplinary model that satisfies this
criterion was published in *The American Journal of Agricultural Economics*
by Kaufmann and Snell (1997). The model represents the effect of weather,

economic and technical variables on corn yield in a way that is consistent with biological and economic theory. Weather variables are specified for periods that correspond to the phenological stage of development (for example, tassel initiation, silking) rather than the human calendar. The effect of temperature and rainfall during phenological stages is specified in a way that is consistent with the notion of a physiological optimum. Recently, Kaufmann *et al.* (1998) showed that the model's predictive accuracy could be increased by using a simple bucket model to track soil moisture instead of direct measurements of precipitation.

Similarly, the model represents the effect of economic and policy variables in a way that is consistent with economic theory and farmer behaviour. The change in the use of purchased inputs is represented with a proxy that is derived from marginal productivity theory. The effect of the policy environment on farmer behaviour is simulated by the difference between the lagged price of corn and the loan rate announced by the Commodity Credit Corporation (CCC). A large positive difference between the loan rate and the previous year's price indicates a relatively high price floor. This increases the farmer's willingness to buy and apply factor inputs, which increases yield.

Finally, the model represents the technical and demographic determinants of corn yield. Plant breeding has changed the rate at which cultivars move between stages of development. By tracking the phenological development of corn, the model can simulate changes in the type of cultivar planted. The model also simulates the effects of farm, farmland and farmer characteristics on yield, and the economies of scale associated with the knowledge and technology used to grow corn. In addition it simulates the effect of land quality on yield with a proxy that is based on the Ricardian notion of land-use patterns. A recent modification to the model (Snell *et al.*, 2000) represents the effect of a farmer's age on production.

The development of the hybrid yield model required considerable effort relative to simply linking existing models. This extra effort appears worthwhile because the hybrid model adds to our understanding of yield and extends our ability to assess the effect of climate change on agriculture. The model results indicate that corn yield is determined by both the physical and social variables that are not statistically independent. When the model is estimated with only climatic or social variables, the regression coefficients change in ways that are consistent with crop physiology and economic behaviour. The physiological optima calculated from the regression coefficients that are estimated by the model with only weather variables (restricted model) are similar to the optima calculated from the results estimated from the complete set of determinants (Figure 2.2). Physiological optima are determined largely by plant genetics and therefore are relatively unaffected by the social environment.

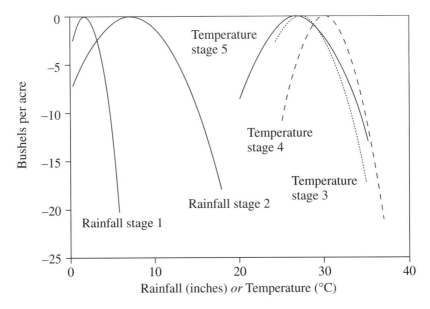

*Figure 2.2   The change in yield associated with climate variables that have
a physiological optimum*

On the other hand, the parabolic effects of weather variables on yield that
are estimated by the restricted model are steeper than the parabolic effects
estimated by the unrestricted model. This change in shape is consistent with a
link between weather conditions and economic behaviour. Unfavourable climatic conditions (far from the physiological optimum) reduce the marginal
productivity of purchased inputs. The reduction in marginal product lowers
the optimal use of purchased inputs. Conversely, good weather increases the
marginal product of purchased inputs, which increases the optimal use of
purchased inputs.

The positive relation between weather and the marginal product of purchased inputs implies that the negative effect of poor weather on yield is
exacerbated by a reduction in the use of factor inputs. Omitted variable bias
forces models that exogenize economic variables to fold the effect of reduced
use of purchased inputs into the regression coefficients for climate. Consistent with this bias, the reductions in yield caused by climatic conditions away
from the physiological optimum that are estimated by the restricted model
are more severe than the reductions estimated by the unrestricted model. This
change in the effect of weather variables on yield implies that physiological
models overstate the effect of weather variables on yield because they ignore
the response by farmers.

Because it includes variables that represent the social and natural environment, the hybrid model improves the ability to assess the effect of climate change on agriculture. Existing models cannot assess the cost-effectiveness of strategies for adaptation because farmer behaviour is not included in the crop physiology models, except with regard to the type of cultivar or row spacing. The hybrid model can be used to evaluate strategies for adaptation to climate change because the hybrid model correlates corn yield directly to farm programmes that influence the decision-making process of farmers. The ability to tie farm programmes to yield is especially important to decision makers because preliminary analyses indicate that these programmes may play a significant role in promoting adaptation to climate change (Lewandrowski and Brazee, 1992). It may be possible for the government to promote responses that offset the effect of climate change on agriculture, but the ability to do so does not ensure cost-effectiveness. Decisions to implement policies that offset the effect of climate change must weigh the economic loss of the physical reduction in yield and output caused by climate change against the costs incurred by policies that encourage adaptation. The ability to simulate the effect of policy variables on corn yield allows the hybrid model to generate much of the information needed to assess the cost-effectiveness of government policies that promote adaptation to climate change.

Similarly, the government may attempt to offset negative effects of climate change on total output via programmes that encourage farmers to increase the number of acres planted. Increasing acres planted increases total output, but less rapidly than the increase in acres because increasing the number of acres planted pushes farmers on to marginal land and reduces average yield. The effect of land quality on yield simulated by the hybrid model can be coupled with estimates for the cost of government programmes that increase acres planted to assess the economic effectiveness of this strategy for adaptation to climate change.

Empirical Analysis versus Theory

For many topics associated with natural resource and environmental management, the theory that underlies ecological economics differs from the theory that underlies mainstream economics. These differences provide an opportunity for ecological economics to demonstrate its mettle. To do so, ecological economics must describe the mechanisms of a process better than economic theory. More importantly, the policies that are implied by that description must be more effective than those implied by the economic model. If these criteria are satisfied, ecological economics will flourish as a discipline.

How should ecological economists demonstrate their capabilities? I believe that ecological economists should: (1) focus on topics designated as important by current policy debate; (2) generate empirical models using appropriate quantitative techniques; and (3) use these results to generate feasible policies that will succeed where existing policies are ineffective. Put simply, ecological economists must solve important problems better than mainstream economics.

I suggest that ecological economists let the environmental policy debate shape much of their research agenda. Graduate students should be directed to research topics based on their relevance to the current policy environment. Some may argue that 'current events' should not drive an academic research agenda, but allowing the policy debate to drive the research agenda has allowed mainstream economics to reach its current position of dominance. A flood of young economists examined the relation among energy prices, energy consumption and economic activity following the oil price shocks of the 1970s and 1980s.

This effort allowed mainstream economics to displace the body of knowledge that was developed by ecological economists prior to the oil shocks, because ecological economists failed to make their research results relevant to policy makers. The importance of policy relevance is illustrated by the role of EROI in US energy policy. In 1974, US law (PL-93-577) mandated that EROI be used to evaluate the feasibility of alternative sources of energy. The inclusion of this criterion may have been the high-water mark of ecological economics. Based on this success, ecological economists set about calculating the EROI for a host of energy sources. Nevertheless, policy makers rarely used EROI to evaluate alternative technologies (GAO, 1982). They failed to do so because ecological economists did not develop EROI to meet the needs of policy makers. For example, EROI did not account for qualitative differences among the fuels recovered from the environment and the fuels used to extract them. Because of such shortcomings, the use of EROI and the role of ecological economists in US energy policy has been marginalized.

To avoid a repeat of this fiasco, ecological economists must ensure that the policy implications of their research are feasible. If the policy community decides that the relation between energy use and economic activity is of critical importance, ecological economists must translate the implications of their research into usable policy suggestions. Ecological economists cannot simply argue that the current policy is not feasible – they must propose alternatives. The policy community needs alternatives, and poor policy suggestions will fill the vacuum of no policy suggestions.

In addition to offering feasible alternatives, ecological economists will regain access to the policy debate only if the empirical component of their analyses satisfies the standards set by recent advances in quantitative techniques. To do so, ecological economists must analyse real-world data using proper techniques. I emphasize analysis of real-world data because policy makers have rightfully become suspicious of parametrized models. Both mainstream economists and ecological economists can parametrize models that are generally consistent with observed behaviour. But the feasibility of policy based on these models can be differentiated only if the theoretical relations that underlie the model are tested against real-world data in a statistically meaningful fashion.

To do so, ecological economists must make use of recent advances in time series econometrics. The most important of these advances is the development of techniques that can detect relations among non-stationary variables (Stock and Watson, 1993; Johansen and Juselius, 1990; Johansen, 1988; Engle and Granger, 1987). The simplest non-stationary variable (other than a deterministic time trend) is a random walk (Y), which is given by the following equation

$$Y_t = Y_{t-1} + \varepsilon_t \tag{2.1}$$

in which ε_t is a normally distributed random error term with a mean value of zero. Although the mean value of ε is zero, as is the long-run value of Y, the value of Y will 'walk' randomly away from zero for extended periods. These movements away from zero make it appear as though the variable is 'trending' up or down; therefore, the variable is said to have a stochastic trend.

The presence of a stochastic trend is critical to the technique used to estimate the relations between variables. Granger and Newbold (1974) find that the diagnostic statistics generated by ordinary least squares indicate meaningful relations between unrelated non-stationary variables more often than implied by random chance. These relations are termed 'spurious regressions'. Spurious regression results make it appear as though variables are related when in fact they are not. Spurious regressions erode the confidence in policy suggestions based on empirical analyses because the time series for many resource and environmental variables (and economic variables) contain a stochastic trend.

To differentiate between spurious and meaningful regressions, a large part of the recent econometric time series literature deals with estimation and inference in the presence of non-stationary variables. Engle and Granger (1987) define the notion of cointegration: a property displayed by variables that share a common stochastic trend. Cointegration analysis is also related to 'Granger causality'. If two variables share a common trend, there may be Granger causality in one or more directions between them (Cuthbertson, Hall and Taylor, 1992). This allows the analyst to describe the statistical ordering of the variables.

Because these methodologies have been developed by time series econometricians, they have been used by many mainstream economists to analyse resource and environmental issues. Ecological economists have been less willing to adapt them, and so much of their empirical analysis cannot be interpreted in a statistically meaningful fashion. As such, these results are rightfully dismissed. If ecological economists are to establish their ability to develop policy relative to mainstream economists, they must abandon ordinary least squares in favour of more sophisticated techniques that can generate statistically meaningful results.

The importance of using the proper econometric techniques to test hypotheses about issues that are important to policy makers can be illustrated by the debate about the strength of the relation between energy use and GDP. The strength of this relation is critical to the debate about climate change. If the link between energy use and economic activity is strong, it will be difficult (expensive) to reduce carbon emissions. Conversely, if the relation between energy use and economic activity is weak, and/or the causal order runs from economic activity to energy use, policies to reduce carbon emissions will have relatively little effect on economic activity.

Debate about the strength of the relation between energy use and economic activity is a major fault line that splits ecological economists from mainstream economists. Based on the thermodynamic importance of energy described in section 2, most ecological economists argue that there is a strong link between energy use and economic activity. On the other hand, most mainstream economists argue that energy use and economic activity are linked loosely and the degree of coupling at any point in time depends on relative prices and the level of technical know-how.

Theoretical disagreements about the strength of the relation between energy use and economic activity are tested empirically by quantifying the factors that determine the amount of energy required to produce a real currency unit of GDP (the *E/GDP* ratio) and the causal order in the relation between energy use and GDP. Mainstream economists have produced a variety of models for the *E/GDP* ratio and the causal order in the relation between energy use and GDP. In general, economic models simulate the *E/GDP* ratio using a deterministic time trend (sometimes known as an autonomous increase in energy efficiency – AIEE) and/or energy prices. The authors claim that these models simulate historical changes in the *E/GDP* ratio fairly well (Nordhaus, 1994; Manne and Richels, 1992). Similarly, economic analyses indicate that there is no causal order in the relation between energy use and economic activity (Kraft and Kraft, 1978; Akarca and Long, 1980; Hamilton, 1983; Burbridge and Harrison, 1984; Yu and Hwang, 1984; Yu and Choi, 1985; Erol and Yu, 1987; Ammah-Tagoe, 1990; Abosedra and Baghestani, 1991).

Ecological economists argue that these empirical results are flawed because mainstream economic models ignore qualitative differences among the types of energy consumed and differences in the energy intensity of the goods and services produced. The effect of these changes on the *E/GDP* ratio can be quantified by estimating a model that has the general form given by equation (2.2):

$$\frac{E}{GDP} = \alpha + \beta_1 \ln\left(\frac{Coal}{E}\right) + \beta_2 \ln\left(\frac{Gas}{E}\right) + \beta_3 \ln\left(\frac{Oil}{E}\right)$$
$$+ \beta_4 \ln\left(\frac{Primary\ electricity}{E}\right) + \beta_5 \ln\left(\frac{PCE}{GDP}\right) \qquad (2.2)$$
$$+ \beta_6 (Product\ mix) + \beta_7 (Energy\ price)$$

where *E* = *Coal* + *Gas* + *Oil* + *Primary electricity* (measured in heat units such as kcals), *GDP* is real GDP (measured in real currency units), *Primary electricity* is electricity generated from hydro, nuclear, solar or geothermal sources, *PCE* is personal consumption expenditures spent directly on energy by households (real currency units), *Product mix* measures the fraction of GDP that originates in energy-intensive sectors (for example, chemicals) or non-energy-intensive sectors (for example, services) and *Energy price* is a measure of real energy prices (real currency units).

The effect of changes in the types of fuels consumed on the *E/GDP* ratio is measured by the fraction of total energy consumption from individual fuels. The signs on the regression coefficients β_2, β_3 and β_4 are expected to be negative because natural gas, oil, and primary electricity can do more useful work (and therefore generate more economic output) per heat unit than coal. The types of goods and services produced and consumed also have a significant effect on the *E/GDP* ratio. The *E/GDP* ratio can be viewed as a weighted average of the energy intensity of the goods and services produced or consumed. A change in the fraction of real GDP that is associated with production or consumption from a specific sector will affect the *E/GDP* ratio if the energy intensity of that sector differs significantly from the weighted average.

Equation (2.2) can be used to account for much of the variation in the energy/GDP ratio in the US between 1929 and the 1980s (Gever *et al.*, 1986; Cleveland *et al.*, 1984). Kaufmann (1992) obtains similar results for France, the UK, Germany and Japan during the post-war period. Despite this consistency, the results were estimated before time series econometricians had developed techniques to assess the relation among non-stationary variables. The variables in equation (2.1) are generally non-stationary; therefore the results described above could be spurious.

To test whether the results are spurious, I estimate a vector error correction model (VECM) using the techniques developed by Johansen (1988) and

Johansen and Juselius (1990) to determine whether there is a cointegrating relation among the variables in equation (2.2) for historical data for the US between 1929 and 1997. To ease the difficulties associated with the identification of cointegrating vectors, I specify a partial system in which the variables on the right-hand side of equation (2.2) are exogenous.

The results of the Schwartz information criteria and the Hannon Quinn information criteria indicate that the VECM should contain one lag. The values for λ_{max} and λ_{trace} (40.75) indicate that the system contains one cointegrating vector. The regression coefficients in this cointegrating vector are statistically significant and have signs that are consistent with the effects described above (Table 2.1). The alpha for this cointegrating relation is statistically significant and has the correct sign – negative. Together, these results imply that the relation between the *E/GDP* ratio and the variables in equation (2.2) is not spurious, at least not for the US between 1929 and 1997. Conversely, this result implies that the relation between the *E/GDP* ratio and a time trend and/or prices is spurious.

The cointegrating relation between the *E/GDP* ratio and the variables on the right-hand side of equation (2.2) implies that the relation between energy use and GDP should be stronger than a mere correlation. Stern (1993) inves-

Table 2.1   *Cointegration model for the US energy/GDP ratio 1929–97*
               based on equation (2.2)

Variable	β	Standard error	t-statistics
E/GDP	1.00		
ln (*Coal/E*)	0.00		
ln (*Oil/E*)	0.174	0.027	6.4
ln (*Gas/E*)	0.048	0.011	4.4
ln (*Primary electricity/E*)	0.081	0.011	7.4
PCE/GDP	−7.236	0.279	25.9
P_{cut}	0.000		
P_{max}	0.057	0.015	3.8
P_{rec}	0.000		
Trend	0.000		
α	−0.816	0.116	7.3
R^2	0.83		
Identifying restrictions	$\chi^2(4) = 1.64$		
Serial correlation	$\chi^2(1) = 0.756$		

Note: P_{cut}, P_{max}, P_{rec}, values for fuels, related products and power disaggregated for asymmetric effects as described by Gately (1992).

tigates this possibility by estimating a vector autoregression (VAR) which includes capital, labour and energy in which total energy use is measured in a way that accounts for qualitative differences among fuels. Tests indicate that energy cannot be excluded from the VAR. This result indicates that energy use 'Granger causes' GDP. To evaluate whether this result in spurious, Stern (1998) includes the same variables in a VECM and estimates the VECM with the techniques described above. The results confirm the conclusion that energy use has a causal effect on economic activity.

Conclusions about the relation between energy use and economic activity derived from analyses of the *E/GDP* ratio and causal order contradict some of the policy implications generated by economic models. Most importantly, the results indicate that there is no autonomous increase in energy efficiency (AIEE). That is, energy use and carbon emissions will not shrink on their own.

In addition to identifying shortcomings in current policy, the results of the ecological economic model point to ways in which policy can be improved. The results generated from equation (2.2) identify interfuel substitution and household energy conservation as two of the more cost-effective means for reducing carbon emissions. Kaufmann (1994) demonstrates the effectiveness of interfuel substitution by estimating the value of the marginal product of coal, oil, natural gas and primary electricity from a modified version of equation (2.2). He finds that the value of the marginal product of coal is less than the value of the marginal product of oil and natural gas. This implies that interfuel substitution can reduce carbon emissions more effectively than indicated by their relative carbon contents. In 1992, the value of the marginal product of oil relative to coal was 3.33. This implies that only 0.33 units of oil are needed to replace one unit of coal at the margin. As a result, substituting 0.333 units of oil for one unit of coal reduces the quantity of carbon emitted by more than 75 per cent, which is significantly greater than the 30 per cent reduction implied by the carbon content of oil relative to coal.

The results from equation (2.2) also imply that efforts to conserve energy are most effective when directed at the household sector. The fraction of GDP spent directly on energy by households has a large effect on the *E/GDP* ratio. The sharp reduction in personal consumption expenditures on energy during the Second World War is largely responsible for the sharp, albeit temporary, reduction in the *E/GDP* ratio. This sensitivity is consistent with the results of input–output analyses, which indicate that the energy intensity of household fuel purchases are an order of magnitude greater than the energy intensity of non-energy goods and services (Hannon, 1982). The large effect of household purchases of energy on the *E/GDP* ratio, along with the relatively small fraction of GDP spent on energy by households, imply that the cost-effectiveness of efforts to reduce carbon emissions could be increased by directing conservation programmes at the household sector.

4   CONCLUSION

I have tried to argue that ecological economics stands to be absorbed by mainstream economics. To avoid this fate, ecological economics must do what economics has done so well – provide policy suggestions to decision makers. To regain this foothold, I have described the criteria for a productive research agenda. I hope that analysts find these suggestions useful. The success will affect the survival of millions of species, including our own.

REFERENCES

Abosedra, S. and H. Baghestani (1991), 'New evidence on the causal relationship between United States energy consumption and gross national product', *Journal of Energy and Development*, **14**, 285–92.

Adams, F.G. and P. Miovic (1968), 'On relative fuel efficiency and the output elasticity of energy consumption in western Europe', *Journal of Industrial Economics*, **17**, 41–56.

Akarca, A. and T. Long (1980), 'On the relationship between energy and GNP: a reexamination', *Journal of Energy and Development*, **5**, 326–31.

Ammah-Tagoe, F.A. (1990), 'On woodfuel, total energy consumption and GDP in Ghana: a study of trends and causal relations', mimeo, Center for Energy and Environmental Studies, Boston University, Boston, MA.

Andresen, J.A. and R.F. Dale (1989), 'Prediction of county-level corn yield using an energy-crop growth index', *Journal of Climate*, **2**, 48–56.

Burbridge, J. and A. Harrison (1984), 'Testing for the effects of oil price rises using vector autoregressions', *International Economic Review*, **25**, 459–84.

Chapman, P.F. and F. Roberts (1983), *Metal Resources and Energy*, London: Butterworth.

Cleveland, Cutler J. (1987), 'Biophysical economics: historical perspective and current research trends', *Ecological Modelling*, **38**, 47–73.

Cleveland, C.J., R. Costanza, C.A.S. Hall and R. Kaufmann (1984), 'Energy and the United States economy: a biophysical perspective', *Science*, **225**, 890–97.

Cooke, S.C. and W.B. Sundquist (1989), 'Cost efficiency in US corn production', *American Journal of Agriculatural Economics*, **71** (November), 1003–10.

Cuthbertson, K., S.G. Hall and M.P. Taylor (1992), *Applied Econometric Techniques*, Ann Arbor, MI: University of Michigan Press.

Daly, H.E. (1991), 'Elements of an environmental macroeconomics', in R. Costanza (ed.), *Ecological Economics*, New York: Oxford University Press, pp. 32–46.

Engle, R.E. and C.W.J. Granger (1987), 'Cointegration and error-correction: representation, estimation, and testing', *Econometrica*, **55**, 251–76.

Erol, U. and E.S.H. Yu (1987), 'On the causal relationship between energy and income for industrialized countries', *Journal of Energy and Development*, **13**, 113–22.

Gately, D. (1992), 'Imperfect price-reversibility of US gasoline demand: asymmetric responses to price increases and declines', *Energy Journal*, **13** (4), 179–207.

General Accounting Office (1982), 'DOE funds new energy technologies without estimating potential net energy yields', GAO/IPE-82-1, Washington, DC.

Georgescu-Roegen, N. (1971), *The Entropy Law and the Economic Process*, Cambridge, MA: Harvard University Press.

Gever, J., R. Kaufmann, D. Skole and C. Vorosmarty (1986), *Beyond Oil: The Threat to Food and Fuel in the Coming Decades*, Cambridge, MA: Ballinger.

Gilliland, M. (1975), 'Energy analysis and public policy', *Science*, **189**, 1051–6.

Granger, C.W.J. (1969), 'Investigating causal relations by econometric models and cross-spectral methods', *Econometrica*, **37**, 424–38.

Granger, C.W.J. and P. Newbold (1974), 'Spurious regressions in econometrics', *Journal of Econometrics*, **2**, 111–20.

Hall, C.A.S., C.J. Cleveland and R.K. Kaufmann (1986), *Energy and Resource Quality: The Ecology of the Economic Process*, New York: Wiley Interscience.

Hamilton, J.D. (1983), 'Oil and the macroeconomy since World War II', *Journal of Political Economy*, **91**, 228–48.

Hannon, C. (1982), 'Analysis of the energy cost of economic activities: 1963–2000', *Energy Systems and Policy Journal*, **6**(3), 249–78.

Johansen, S. (1988), 'Statistical analysis of cointegration vectors', *Journal of Economic Dynamics and Control*, **12**, 231–54.

Johansen, S. and K. Juselius (1990), 'Maximum likelihood estimation and inference on cointegration with application to the demand for money', *Oxford Bulletin of Economics and Statistics*, **52**, 169–209.

Jones, C.A. and J.R. Kiniry (1986), *CERES-Maize: A Simulation Model of Maize Growth and Development*, College Station, Texas: A&M Press.

Kaufmann, R.K. (1992), 'A biophysical analysis of the energy/real GDP ratio: implications for substitution and technical change', *Ecological Economics*, **6**, 35–56.

Kaufmann, R.K. (1994), 'The relation between marginal product and price in US energy markets', *Energy Economics*, **16**, 145–58.

Kaufmann, R.K. and S. Snell (1997), 'A biophysical model of corn yield: integrating physical and economic determinants', *American Journal of Agricultural Economics*, **79**(1), 178–80.

Kraft, J. and A. Kraft (1978), 'On the relationship between energy and GNP', *Journal of Energy and Development*, **3**, 401–3.

Lewandrowski, J. and R. Brazee (1992), 'Government farm programs and climate change: a first look', in J.M. Reilly and M. Anderson (eds), *Economic Issues in Global Climate Change*, Boulder, CO: Westview Press.

Liverman, D.M., W.H. Terjung, J.T. Hayes and L.O. Mearns (1986), 'Climatic change and corn yields in the North American Great Plains', *Climatic Change*, **9**, 327–47.

Lovering, T.S. (1969), 'Mineral resources from the land', *Resources and Man*, Committee on Resources and Man, National Academy of Sciences, San Francisco: W.H. Freeman and Company.

Manne, A.S. and R. Richels (1992), *Buying Greenhouse Insurance: The Economic Costs of CO_2 Limits*, Cambridge, MA: MIT Press.

Masih, A.M.M. and R. Masih (1996), 'Energy consumption, real income and temporal causality: results from a multi-country study based on cointegration and error-correction modelling techniques', *Energy Economics*, **18**, 165–83.

Nordhaus, W. (1994), *Managing the Global Commons: The Economics of Climate Change*, Cambridge, MA: MIT Press.

Odum, H.T. (1971), *Environment, Power, and Society*, New York: Wiley Interscience.

Snell, S.E., R.K. Kaufmann and L. Scuderi (2000), 'An interdisciplinary model of corn yield: precipitation versus soil moisture', paper presented at the American Meteorological Society meeting, Davis, CA, August.

Snell, S.E., L. Scudieri, R.K. Kaufmann and S. Gopal (2000), 'Model calculated soil moisture or precipitation for yield modelling?', paper presented at the 24th Conference on Agricultural and Forest Meteorology, University of California at Davis, 15 August.

Stapper, M. and G.F. Arkin (1980), *CORNF: A Dynamic Growth and Development Model for Maize*. Ag. Exp. State Programs and Model Documentation 80-2, Texas A&M University.

Stern, D.I. (1993), 'Energy use and economic growth in the USA: a multivariate approach', *Energy Economics*, **15**, 137–50.

Stern, D.I. (1998), 'A multivariate cointegration analysis of the role of energy in the US macroeconomy', Working Papers in Ecological Economics 9803, Centre for Resource and Environmental Studies, Australian National University, Canberra, ACT 0200, Australia.

Stock, J.H. and M.W. Watson (1993), 'A simple estimator of cointegrating vectors in higher order integrated systems', *Econometrica*, **61**(4), 783–820.

Yu, E.S.H and J.-Y. Choi (1985), 'The causal relationship between energy and GNP: an international comparison', *Journal of Energy and Development*, **10**, 249–72.

Yu, E.S.H. and B. Hwang (1984), 'The relationship between energy and GNP: further results', *Energy Economics*, **6**, 186–90.

Yu, E.S.H. and J.C. Jin (1992), 'Cointegration tests of energy consumption, income, and employment', *Resources and Energy*, **14**, 259–66.

3. Spatial economic aspects of the environment and environmental policy

Shelby Gerking and John List

1 INTRODUCTION

The spatial dimension in economic analysis has been a subject of resurgent interest in the 1990s beginning with Krugman's (1991a, 1991b) application of models by Dixit and Stiglitz (1977) to 'economic geography'. By 1998, *The Economist* magazine's listing of top economists under the age of 35 included three (Edward Glaeser, Glenn Ellison and Andrei Schleifer) who have contributed key papers on the location of industry and economic growth in cities. Spatial issues have also recently attracted increasing attention among natural resource and environmental economists. As indicated by Deacon *et al.* (1998, p. 393), spatial aspects of resource use may turn out to be as important as the more frequently studied temporal dimension. They suggest that links between land use, land-use policy, ecosystem function and open space and other directly valued environmental amenities represent key areas where additional research may have a high payoff. Sanchirico and Wilen (1999) treat these links in greater depth and Bockstael and Irwin (2000) provide a comprehensive survey of land-use issues from an environmental perspective.

This chapter examines additional spatial aspects by focusing on the intersection between environmental and natural resource economics and regional and urban economics. The main theme developed is that the environment and government policy to protect it both affect and are affected by geographic factor mobility, both within and between countries. This interaction has not been extensively treated; yet, it contains a broad range of interesting research questions such as: to what extent do environmental attributes offset human migration patterns?; and how is the environment affected when people move? Industry location patterns in response to environmental policy changes have been the subject of much empirical work, but how does the location of industry and, more generally, economic growth affect the spatial distribution of environmental problems? Do environmental problems become more or less spatially concentrated in the face of economic growth? Does the spatial distribution of environmental hazards adversely affect the members of economically disadvantaged groups including the poor and members of certain minority groups?

The remainder of this chapter is divided into three sections. Section 2 examines connections between factor rewards, labour mobility and amenity values. Section 3 develops issues related to the environment, capital mobility and industrial location. Each of these sections works toward the above questions by first critically reviewing results of prior studies and then suggesting a few directions for additional research. Implications and conclusions are briefly summarized in section 4.

2   FACTOR REWARDS, LABOUR MOBILITY AND AMENITY VALUES

2.1   Theory

Beginning in the 1970s, economists developed theoretical models to investigate the link between the environment and environmental policy and the interregional pattern of factor rewards and industrial outputs. For example, Forster (1977), Comolli (1977) and Yohe (1979) adapted general equilibrium models from international trade theory (for example, Jones, 1965, 1971 and Batra and Casas, 1976) for this purpose. A common feature of these models is that they focus on only one country or region and do not explicitly consider geographic factor mobility. Instead, the main distinctions between the models developed in these three papers rest on how the environment is incorporated (see Forster, 1981, pp. 106–7). Comolli and Forster treat the current flow of pollution as a joint output of the production process, whereas Yohe treats the current flow of pollution as a factor of production. Also, Comolli assumes that pollution is not an argument in the utility function; however, consumers are still negatively affected by environmental deterioration because emissions from one sector accumulate in the environment and interfere with production in the other sector. Forster, on the other hand, assumes that the stock of pollution directly affects the utility of consumers, but has no effect on output levels. Yohe's model focuses only on the production side; in consequence, consumer preferences are ignored.

Forster (1981) carefully outlines the rather dramatic differences in results produced by these models, so there is no need to review them here. Nevertheless, it is worth noting that they initiated the application of analytical techniques from international trade theory in environmental economics. These techniques, when coupled with ideas from Rosen's (1974, 1979) seminal work on hedonic prices and implicit markets, continue to be a dominant form of theoretical analysis as models were extended to incorporate spatial aspects of the environment and environmental policy.

Roback (1982) developed a general equilibrium approach to modelling effects of the environment on the spatial distribution of economic activity and factor rewards that continues to be influential today.[1] The perspective taken in this model continues to inspire controversy in migration research and serves as the basis for many recent empirical attempts to compute dollar values of amenities and urban quality of life indices. The model allows environmental amenities to affect both utility of consumers and productivity of firms and its main contribution rests on showing how amenity values are determined through interaction of labour and land markets. Prior empirical literature had attempted to estimate values of environmental amenities using data on either wages (Nordhaus and Tobin, 1972; Getz and Huang, 1978; Rosen, 1979; Henderson, 1982) or land rents (Ridker and Henning, 1967; Polinsky and Rubinfeld, 1977), but not data from both markets together.

Roback's model posits a system of small regions in which each region employs an identical constant returns to scale production function to produce a single composite good (X) using labour (H), land (L) and the amenity (A). Workers, identical everywhere and spatially mobile at zero cost, consume X, use land for residential purposes and enjoy the amenity. Land is the same in each region; in consequence, the only way to tell regions apart is by their differing endowments of A. The price of the composite good ($P = 1$) is determined on a competitive world market and labour and land are paid their marginal value products (W for labour and R for land). Also, equilibrium has three characteristics that arise from the assumptions of competition, constant returns to scale in production, and perfect interregional labour mobility. First, worker utility levels are as high as possible and are the same in each region. Second, entrepreneurs earn zero profits and cannot achieve lower production costs by relocating. Third, labour and land are fully employed in each region.

This model can be used to demonstrate how variation in A between regions affects equilibrium factor rewards, output of the composite good, and population size (that is, number of workers). Wages and land rents are uniquely determined via interaction of worker preferences and costs faced by entrepreneurs: changes in the endowments of labour and land have no effect on these factor rewards. To illustrate more fully how factor rewards are determined, consider two regions (R_1 and R_2) that are endowed with differing amounts of the amenity (A_1 and A_2). Denote the indirect utility function of workers in R_i as

$$V_i = V(W_i, R_i, A_i) \tag{3.1}$$

and the cost function of X producers in R_i as

$$C_i = C(W_i, R_i, A_i). \tag{3.2}$$

Let $A_1 > A_2$ and assume that the amenity reduces costs of producing X. Then, as illustrated in Figure 3.1 (adapted from Roback, 1982, p. 1261), workers in the high amenity region (R_1) may be paid either higher or lower wages than in R_2, while R_1 land earns unambiguously higher rents than land in R_2. However, in spite of the ambiguous effect of amenity levels on wages, the wage/rental ratio always ends up lower in the high amenity region (R_1). Thus, the percentage increase in land rents is greater than any possible corresponding increase in wages.

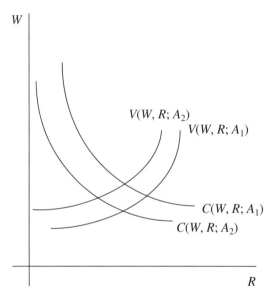

Figure 3.1   Determination of wages and land rents

Additionally, the spatial distribution of amenities affects the interregional distribution of X production and population of workers through the full employment conditions of the model. Roback (1982) does not discuss these conditions, although they necessarily arise from the assumptions of constant returns to scale in production and competition in all markets. Full employment conditions do receive attention in her later work (Roback, 1988). In any case, in the model at hand, they require that all land is used either for X production or for worker residences

$$L = C_r X + kH \tag{3.3}$$

and that all workers are employed in X production

$$H = C_w X \qquad (3.4)$$

In equations (3.3) and (3.4), k denotes per worker utilization of land (and is a function of the W/R ratio), and C_r and C_w denote derivatives of the cost function which are interpreted as the per unit use of land and labour, respectively, in the production of X.

As previously discussed, supplies of L and H have no effect on equilibrium values of W and R; however, regions with differing amounts of A would be expected to produce different amounts of X and have different worker populations. For example, a region like R_1 above with relatively more A will have lower unit costs of producing X. Also, the lower wage/rental ratio in R_1 means that: (1) X producers will economize on their use of land by utilizing more labour-intensive production methods and (2) workers will have lower real incomes and consume less housing relative to the composite good. Thus, amenity levels affect X and H; however, the direction of effect is, in general, ambiguous.

A limitation of Roback's analysis is that it treats only natural or non-produced amenities. Gyourko and Tracy (1989) extend her model to include public services produced by local governments and taxes levied to finance them.[2] This extension allows for the possibility that local governments can choose public service levels, including those that may affect environmental quality. Workers and firms are assumed to be freely mobile between regions. Firms produce a single composite good under conditions of constant returns to scale that is sold on a world market at a fixed price (unity). Equilibrium wages and land rents are again determined through interaction of worker preferences and firm costs in a manner similar to that illustrated in Figure 3.1. The Gyourko and Tracy model, however, produces a broader set of comparative static results for changes in factor rewards in response not only to changes in natural amenities, but also to changes in government services and taxes.

As indicated in the preceding discussion, the Roback and Gyourko and Tracy models have the property that, in equilibrium, unit costs and worker preferences uniquely determine factor rewards. This property is also exhibited in related models in which a non-traded good is added (Roback, 1982) or two or more types of interregionally mobile workers are present (Roback, 1988; Beeson, 1991). The intuition here is that under the assumptions of competition in all markets, constant returns to scale in production, and zero mobility costs, $n + 1$ interregional markets (one for goods and one for each type of labour) exactly determine $n + 1$ factor rewards (see Ethier and Svensson, 1986, for further discussion). This correspondence between the number of markets and the number of factors is in certain respects similar to standard textbook treatments of the 2×2 Heckscher–Ohlin (H–O) model in international trade theory in which factor rewards are determined by relative commodity output prices alone and factor endowments do not matter.

The Roback, Gyourko and Tracy, and related models, however, differ from the H–O model in an important respect. In the H–O model, commodity trade equalizes factor prices between countries (or regions). Thus, the issue of whether factors are mobile does not arise because there is no incentive to move. In the models reviewed here, workers *must* be freely mobile; otherwise, utility levels would never be equalized across regions. In fact, the assumption of free worker mobility is a key simplification that assists in breaking the link between factor endowments and equilibrium factor rewards.

To better appreciate the potential role of factor endowments and migration on the spatial distribution of factor rewards, consider five variants of the basic model. First, Blomquist, Berger and Hoehn (1988) present a model in which a representative urban area in an interregional system is assumed to have two counties, each with a different level of amenities. (These authors also present a related model in which urban areas are composed of a central business district and surrounding residential zone [Hoehn, Berger and Blomquist, 1987].) Their model allows for amenity variation both within and between urban areas. Additionally, production costs are subject to congestion or agglomeration effects and the model endogenously determines a city size variable incorporated directly into the production cost function. Other features of the model are similar to Roback's (1982), except that production uses capital, but does not use land. Capital is spatially mobile and receives a return that is fixed by international markets.

In the Blomquist, Berger and Hoehn model, equilibrium again occurs when neither workers nor firms can gain by relocating, so unit production costs always equal output price and utility levels are the same everywhere. The analysis focuses on how wages and land rents are affected by differences in amenity levels within an urban area. Cross-county effects emerge because a change in amenities in one county results in a change in urban population, which in turn affects production costs of all firms located there. A curious feature of the Blomquist, Berger and Hoehn model, however, is that city size is determined along with factor rewards through interaction of indirect utility and unit production cost equations. The fact that all factors must be fully employed (given the assumptions of competition in all markets and constant returns to scale production technology) is not utilized. Thus, although factor rewards depend on city size, city size is independent of the aggregate endowment of available labour.

As a second extension of the basic framework, assume that in the Blomquist, Berger and Hoehn model the composite good had been produced using labour and interregionally immobile capital. Because capital is no longer mobile between regions, factor rewards to be determined (3.3) would outnumber interregional markets (3.2) (see Batra and Casas, 1976; Ethier and Svensson, 1986; and Jones, 1971 for further details and interpretation). Factor endowments then would come into play (through full employment equations like (3.3) and (3.4)) in the determination of factor rewards. In this situation, wages and rents would still vary from one region to another, but this variation would no longer be entirely attributable to interregional differences in amenity levels. A possible implication of this outcome is that amenity values should be calculated net of factor endowment effects. Notice that factor endowments may also affect the interregional pattern of factor rewards if a fixed supply of land is zoned for different purposes (that is, industrial or residential). Zoning may be 'natural' if there are actually two (or more) types of land with each type better suited for one purpose than others.

A third extension of the model, considered by Mueser and Graves (1995), arises when interregional labour mobility costs are introduced. These authors develop a dynamic model to explain the migration process. Central features of their analysis are that individuals face relocation costs as they consider migration to regions offering higher utility levels and that firms face adjustment costs in changing their levels of employment. These frictions prevent the spatial distribution of output and population from adjusting instantaneously. Nevertheless, Roback's (1982) definition of regional equilibrium illustrated in Figure 3.1 explains how a steady state position is attained when the system experiences no exogenous shocks for an extended period of time.

The introduction of adjustment costs into the analysis, however, may require modifications in Roback's concept of long-run equilibrium. As discussed previously, migration only will occur as long as monetized utility differentials between regions exceed migration costs. Thus, interregional utility levels may not necessarily be equalized, factor endowments become a determinant of factor rewards, and long-run equilibrium can no longer be characterized using Figure 3.1. Indifference curves in W,R space cannot be drawn on the assumption of a fixed utility level. Moreover, within limits determined by migration costs, regional utility levels and solutions for W and R may no longer be unique. Instead, there may be a range of possible values for utility levels, wages and land rents within which workers would have no incentive to relocate. Dickie and Gerking (1998) develop a model that is suggestive of these outcomes, but consider only the case in which monetized utility differentials are exactly equal to migration costs. Additional work may be warranted to consider the broader situation where migration costs define a range in which regional utility levels can vary.

A fourth extension of the basic model could be developed using ideas drawn from the 'new economic geography' literature. For example, Krugman

(1991a, 1991b) analyses a two-region model, adapted from the work of Dixit and Stiglitz (1977), that envisions increasing returns to scale in production, monopolistic competition in output markets, and positive costs of transporting commodities between regions. In this model, real wages are the same in each region only when the work force happens to be split equally between them. Otherwise, real wages end up unequal and the magnitude of the difference depends on three parameters: (1) the share of consumer expenditure devoted to all manufactured goods, (2) the elasticity of substitution on the demand side between individual manufactured products and (3) the size of commodity transportation charges.

Environmental amenities could be introduced into the model either on the consumption side or the production side (or both). Amenity differences between regions, then, would represent a fourth reason why real wages might diverge. An advantage of this extension would be to see how amenities interact with other parameters of the model to determine the interregional pattern of factor rewards. Unlike Roback's analysis, there would be no expectation of a simple link between amenities and factor rewards. In fact, results obtained would, in all likelihood, come from computer simulations or applications of evolutionary game theory. Krugman (1998) discusses these possibilities in more detail and Kilkenny (1998) uses the 'new economic geography' framework to examine the connection between rural development and transportation costs.

Finally, a fifth extension might involve making a region's amenity level endogenous. In the Roback framework as well as in several later analyses, amenity levels are treated as fixed regional characteristics. However, pollution may result as a by-product of production, and congestion may arise as the number of workers in the region increases. From here, a number of modelling possibilities might be pursued. Pollution or congestion might enter utility functions of regional residents or interfere with production or both. Similar to other extensions suggested above, endogenous amenity levels would represent another reason why interregional differences in factor prices may reflect more than simply compensation for differences in particular regional characteristics. This point turns out to be an important criticism of many of the amenity valuation and quality of life studies treated in the next subsection.

2.2   Interregional Amenity Valuation and Quality of Life Indices

The basic model, developed from equations (3.1)–(3.4), has frequently been used to support empirical estimates of the value of amenities and to compute indices of quality of life. In these studies, the implicit price (P_A) of an amenity is usually calculated from a simple manipulation of the indirect utility function (equation (1.1))

$$P_A = k(dR/dA) - (dW/dA) \tag{3.5}$$

In equation (3.5), k again denotes land used for consumption (residential) purposes per worker. The magnitudes of dR/dA and dW/dA, of course, depend on whether A is an amenity in consumption or production or both. P_A is interpreted as the payment a worker must make for a small increase in amenity levels available only through costless migration. This section discusses selected quality of life studies and is divided into two parts, treating hedonic and revealed preference approaches. Additional research is suggested in light of possible theoretical extensions developed in the previous section.

Hedonic studies
Roback (1982) empirically illustrates the use of equation (3.5) to compute values of amenities. Her results, which are based on wage data from the '1973 Current Population Survey' and residential site price data from FHA qualifying families, are only suggestive because data on land prices were admittedly weak. Blomquist, Berger and Hoehn (1988) then conducted a broader empirical investigation based on housing expenditure and wage data available from the 1 in 1000 A Public-Use Sample of the 1980 United States Census. Because their analysis used data on housing expenditure, rather than land prices, equation (3.5) was reformulated so that the P_A is equal to the derivative of the price of housing with respect to A weighted by the quantity of housing purchased less the wage effect, dW/dA.

Blomquist, Berger and Hoehn present estimates of values for 16 different amenities, such as precipitation, heating and cooling degree days, air quality, and extent of violent crime. A monetized quality of life index is computed for 253 counties by summing the amounts of available amenities in each, weighted by their full, implicit prices. Estimates of these prices were based on hedonic wage and housing expenditure equations, which included measures of the amenities as explanatory variables. Coefficients of the amenity variables were generally significantly different from zero and plausibly signed. Because these coefficients were constrained to be the same for each county, variation in the quality of life index between counties reflects only differences in amounts of amenities present. Pueblo, Colorado turned out to have the highest quality of life ranking at $3289, followed by Norfolk, Virginia at $2106. St Louis, Missouri had the lowest ranking at –$1857.

Gyourko and Tracy (1991) also estimate amenity values and constructed quality of life indices using the 1980 United States Census of Population and Housing 1 in 1000 A Public-Use Sample. Estimates in this study pertain to 130 cities rather than counties. In keeping with their model (outlined above), a central focus of the analysis rests on the contribution of local fiscal variables, as contrasted with pure amenities, as well as the possibility that location rents may be at least partially capitalized into public sector wages. Coefficient estimates reported generally have expected signs. Estimated full implicit prices indicate that public services (that is, health, education and safety) are 'goods', while higher taxes generally are 'bads'. Also, both individual- and city-specific disturbance variances included in equations estimated are significantly different from zero. The interpretation of this result, however, is uncertain; yet it holds considerable importance for calculation of quality of life indices. On the one hand, as Gyourko and Tracy indicate, the city-specific disturbance may reflect unmeasured housing quality or human worker capital, in which case it should not be included in the index. On the other hand, if it reflects omitted amenity or fiscal variables that would have been included in the regressions had appropriate data been available, then it should be included. Another possibility, not considered by these authors, is that the city-specific disturbance term may reflect utility differences between cities that arise because of imperfect worker mobility.

In any case, Gyourko and Tracy present quality of life rankings, with and without city-specific effects. For some cities, whether city-specific effects are included makes little difference; San Diego, CA ranked fourth under both approaches. However, without accounting for city effects, Boise, ID ranked 108th; whereas in the rankings with group effects it was second. Overall, the rank correlation between the two sets of estimates was 0.63. Also, Pueblo, CO, which was ranked first by Blomquist, Berger and Hoehn, ranked 66th when city effects are excluded and 96th when city effects are included. This example illustrates a point more fully discussed by Gyourko (1991) that the quality of life rankings are imprecise and can change substantially with changes in the underlying amenity and public service variables as well as with changes in data sets and econometric methods employed.

Revealed preference studies
Herzog and Schlottmann (1993) implemented one of the first studies that used the revealed preference approach to estimating values of amenities. Citing the work of Greenwood *et al.* (1991), these authors contend that the assumption of equilibrium in the labour and land markets substantially weakens the applicability of the hedonic method to valuing amenities. They propose to illustrate how this problem can be corrected by estimating the value of urban scale from a migration (M) function in which the total differential, dM, is set equal to zero. This approach, however, may be deficient if there are relocation costs associated with moving. In this situation, as the authors observe in a footnote, setting $dM = 0$ would not imply constant utility between regions.

Kahn (1995, p. 224) discusses four specific problems associated with the hedonic approach to calculating quality of life indices. First, all amenities and local public services must be exhaustively enumerated and observed.[3] Second, unmeasured city-specific attributes may be correlated with included attributes, resulting in biased and inconsistent estimates. Third, included attributes may have a high degree of intercorrelation (recall that Blomquist, Berger and Hoehn, 1988 used 16 area-specific attributes in their wage and housing expenditure regressions). Fourth, returns to human capital characteristics may differ across regions. Kahn attempts to avoid these problems by developing an alternative method for calculating quality of life indices that is based on revealed preference. This method is based on three assumptions: (1) migration costs are zero, (2) all agents in the economy have identical preferences defined over consumption and a set of city-specific attributes, and (3) all agents have equal skills. Then, if people in city A are observed to have lower consumption than people in city B, then city A must be the 'nicer' of the two.

Kahn's revealed preference method was implemented by ranking quality of life in five US cities (New York, Houston, Chicago, San Francisco and Los Angeles) using Census data for 1980 and 1990. Equations for wages and rental expenditures were estimated for each city. This approach allowed for intercity variation in characteristic prices and the constant term in each equation is interpreted as the net effect of all city-specific amenity and local fiscal variables. Estimates obtained were used to predict wage and rental expenditures for each sample member in each of the five cities. Surpluses were then calculated by subtracting predicted rental payments from predicted wages. Cities with the highest surpluses (Chicago and Houston) were judged to have a relatively low quality of life: the extra amount available for consumption is treated as compensation for lower levels of natural amenities and poorer local fiscal conditions.

Cragg and Kahn (1997) also use migration data to estimate the value of climate and quality of life. Their study is base on data from the 1 per cent samples from the '1990 Census of Population and Housing'. The idea here is to determine the extent to which migrants pay for amenities through changes in wages and rents when they move from one state to another. The sample consists entirely of migrants; thus, the decision to move is not considered. Rather, a conditional multinomial logit model is estimated to explain which of the lower 48 US states was chosen when migrants relocated. In this model, migrants are assumed to maximize utility by maximizing consumption of market goods and natural amenities. The value of market goods consumption was measured by the difference between after-tax income and the rental price of a four-room home.

Migrants were assumed to know what their consumption bundle would be in each of their possible 47 destination states. Thus, equations were estimated for wages, weeks worked and home rental prices, and consumption values were imputed for each migrant in each state. Wage equation estimates were significantly affected by whether returns to worker characteristics were constrained to be equal across states. In any case, the implied consumption values were then used to estimate parameters of the conditional multinomial logit model. These parameters, in turn, were used to make calculations of willingness to pay for environmental amenities. In particular, the authors ask (p. 277), 'if an environmental good's quantity increased by one standard deviation, how much private consumption could we take away from that person such that his probability of moving to a given state would remain unchanged?'

The resulting estimates showed that: (1) the most highly valued environmental attribute was a higher average February temperature and (2) older people and non-college graduates valued environmental attributes more highly than did younger people and college graduates. Also, willingness-to-pay estimates for individual amenities exceeded corresponding estimates of actual payments computed from the hedonic wage and rental equations. State-by-state quality of life rankings using the migration approach placed warm winter states (Florida, Arizona and California) at the top. The hedonic approach, which placed greater weight on cooler summers than warmer winters, ranked California 25th and moved Arkansas and Oklahoma to 3rd and 4th, respectively.

Although the revealed preference approach has certain advantages over that used by Blomquist, Berger and Hoehn (1988) and Gyourko and Tracy (1991), it has at least three limitations. First, as discussed by Rauch (1993) and noted by Kahn (1995), cities with larger amounts of human capital per worker may be more productive and have higher wages than other cities. Thus, a relatively large surplus for a city may reflect higher productivity rather than a lower quality of life. Second, the method assumes that all worker attributes are observed which, of course, may not be true. As Kahn (1995) points out, if workers with greater unobserved ability self-select into the nicest cities, relatively high surplus values may no longer correspond to lower quality of life. Third, workers are assumed to be perfectly mobile, so that utility is the same in all cities. However, if workers face relocation costs, utility levels will not be identical everywhere. In a given city, some workers may be earning positive quasi-rents, while the quasi-rents for others are negative. Kahn attempts to limit this potential problem by restricting his sample to renters, who are more mobile than homeowners, and by reporting the median of individual surpluses for a city. Nevertheless, utility differences may not 'average out' and large surplus values still may reflect higher levels of utility, rather than a lower quality of life.

2.3   Environmental Amenities and Migration

An important test of the usefulness of equation (3.5) to value amenities and to compute quality of life indices rests on whether workers are freely mobile between geographic areas. On the one hand, several papers by Graves and others (for example, Graves, 1976, 1980; Graves and Linneman, 1979; and Graves and Mueser, 1993) argue that interregional labour markets are highly efficient and that any utility differences that arise are quickly arbitraged away through migration. As a result, observed migration occurs mainly, if not exclusively, in response to amenity demand changes that accompany increasing household incomes or life-cycle events such as retirement. On the other hand, the more traditional human capital view (Sjaastad, 1962) is that utility differences between regions can be persistent because labour market adjustment through migration can be a slow process. This view accommodates the possibility that migration can be related to increased demand for amenities; however, economic opportunities (that is, not yet arbitraged utility differences) are generally thought to be the primary motivating factor.[4]

Evans (1990) and Hunt (1993) have extensively reviewed the literature on the relative roles of amenities and economic opportunities in the migration decision. Based on available empirical evidence, both authors conclude that greater support can be found for the more traditional view that emphasizes utility differences and differences in economic opportunities between regions. However, the matter appears to be far from settled. Results from three recent papers attempting to contrast the two views of migration show why.

Greenwood and Hunt (1989) examine the role of amenities in migration using two different data sets. They model migration as a function of both natural amenities and variables measuring economic opportunity. Coefficients of both types of variables turned out to be statistically significant; however, the economic opportunity variables, such as employment growth in a region, appeared to be more important in explaining migration. Greenwood and Hunt offer several reasons to explain why these findings differ so greatly from those of Graves. Aside from differences in data and model specification, they argue that if migrants are attracted to jobs, and if employment growth has been greatest in amenity-rich areas, then Graves's estimated linkage between amenities and migration may be at least partly spurious.

Mueser and Graves (1995), in a paper discussed previously, argue that measures of economic opportunity, such as employment growth, both affect and are affected by migration. Greenwood and Hunt recognized this important source of simultaneity and based their conclusions on instrumental variable estimates. Mueser and Graves, on the other hand, attempt to avoid the problem entirely by estimating a reduced-form equation. In particular, they examine net migration (constructed by cohort-survival methods) between US county aggregates in three decades; 1950–60, 1960–70 and 1970–80. Explanatory variables included measures of industrial composition, amenities, settlement patterns and demographic characteristics. Key findings are that migrants move to more desirable climates, avoid areas in which manufacturing and agriculture dominate the industrial structure, and avoid areas with a high percentage of blacks. Also, standardized coefficients for each group of variables indicated that the climate-related amenities dominated the industrial composition variables in explaining net migration rates. This procedure for comparing the importance of groups of variables, however, invokes the questionable assumption that all relevant factors in a group can be enumerated and measured.

Greenwood *et al.* (1991) consider more directly whether variations in real income between regions (actually, states) reflect only compensation for amenity differences. Their approach was to model net migration as a function of real after-tax earnings (RY) using panel data in an instrumental variable, fixed effects framework and interpret the constant term shifters as a measure of the relative effects of amenities. They then solve for values of real after-tax earnings (RY^*) that would make net migration in each state equal to zero. Differences between RY and RY^* were interpreted as measuring the extent to which interregional utility differences are important. These differences, however, were statistically significant at the 10 per cent level only for seven states.

Although the Greenwood *et al.* paper is often cited as an important defence of the traditional view of migration, the fact that interregional utility differences are statistically significant in so few cases leaves open the possibility that Graves's view of amenities and migration is largely correct. However, as argued above, both the model and the empirical work presented by Mueser and Graves to defend their position appear to be deficient. As a result, Greenwood's (1985, p. 532) call 'for a simultaneous analysis of spatial utility and profit maximization with migration of both households and firms providing the dynamic adjustment' remains appropriate today. Theoretical difficulties in constructing such a model have already been discussed and Hunt (1993) points out several empirical challenges to be overcome, including convincingly identifying the equations in the system. In any case, additional theoretical and empirical work on migration and interregional earnings differences is clearly warranted to split utility effects from amenity effects.

A serious complication in this regard, however, is the likely endogeneity of both utility and amenity levels. As indicated in section 2.1, for example, levels of amenities and utility may erode in the face of natural population growth as well as from immigration. In its most general form, this idea dates back to Malthus and was a centrepiece in the limits to growth literature in the 1970s (see Cropper and Griffiths, 1994 for an elaboration of this point).

However, as Cropper and Griffiths argue, there is little compelling empirical evidence on the extent to which population pressure results in environmental degradation, holding per capita income constant. Using a fixed effects model for panel data from 64 countries, they show that deforestation increased with increases in rural population density. More recently, Amacher *et al.* (1998) also found an interactive relationship between environmental quality and migration using data from the Philippines. In particular, they note that migration flows are larger to destinations where the public share of forest land is larger, but these are the regions experiencing most rapid deforestation.

Although these results were obtained in the context of tropical deforestation, the general point made surely applies to broader circumstances. Migrants may well be attracted by environmental amenities, but the environment they hoped to enjoy can be substantially altered if large numbers of people arrive. Air and water quality issues in rapidly expanding urban areas of both developed and developing countries represent additional examples in this regard (that is, consider the air pollution problems of Mexico City and Los Angeles). In any case, it would be useful to think of environmental quality and migration as jointly dependent variables in a broader model of economic and ecological relationships. Perhaps then the migrant attractive power of environmental attributes could be jointly estimated with the extent to which additional migrants affect the environment or the resources devoted to environmental cleanup. Greenwood and Hunt (1984) make somewhat similar estimates in a migration and job-growth context in the 'chicken and egg' literature initiated by Muth (1971).

3 ENVIRONMENTAL REGULATION AND FIRM LOCATION

This section analyses evidence concerning interrelationships between the environment and industrial location. The starting point is to consider the well-established strand of literature that examines how industrial location responds to the environment and environmental policy. Tannenwald (1997), Levinson (1996a), Olewiler (1994) and Gunther (1991) have recently provided thorough literature reviews in this area; consequently, the discussion here focuses mainly on possible future research directions. A limitation of this literature, however, is that the environment is frequently treated as an exogenous determinant of firm location. Firm location, of course, can lead to changes in the natural environment and in environmental policy. Potentially interesting research questions in this regard are raised at the end of this section.

3.1 Models of Firm Location

Prior empirical analyses of environmental policy and firm location have often been based on the very simple idea that firms choose locations where expected profits are highest. The perspective taken is that either geographic movements by one firm or plant have no perceptible effect on economic or environmental conditions at the location selected or that all such effects can be treated as external to the firm. Viewed in this light, the firm's location problem involves comparison of numerous exogenous spatial cost and demand factors including labour market conditions, market size and accessibility, business taxes, public services, external economies, energy costs and environmental compliance expenditures. With regard to costs of compliance with environmental policies, Gray (1997a, 1997b) cites officials in the pulp and paper industry who conjecture that 'the main influence of environmental regulations ... come(s) through difficulties in getting construction permits, due either to delays in permit issuance or to uncertainty about whether the permit would be issued at all'. This phenomenon is not confined to this sector, as many environmental regulations often go beyond specifying numerical discharge standards and require that a firm install specific abatement technologies prior to opening a new plant (Jaffe *et al.*, 1995).

3.2 Empirical Evidence

The simple theoretical framework described above has led researchers to pursue empirical specifications that attempt to explain changes in employment, plant expansions, relocations or births by using variables that are presumably arguments in a firm's cost function. Domestic evidence of the effects of environmental regulation can be split according to type of data set utilized. Duffy-Deno (1992) and Crandall (1993) use aggregate data for Standard Metropolitan Statistical Areas (SMSAs) and states, respectively, and find that environmental regulation does not significantly affect employment growth or total earnings. Other studies examine Dun and Bradstreet data. These include McConnell and Schwab's (1990) county study of the automobile assembly industry, Bartik's (1988) state-level study of *Fortune 500* companies, and Crandall's (1993) state-level study of plant start-ups. Although various measures of regulatory stringency are used in these studies, findings generally indicate that environmental regulation does not significantly alter firm location patterns. Still other (and more recent) studies use 'Census of Manufacturers' data to analyse firm-level location decisions. This group includes state-level studies (Levinson, 1996b and Gray, 1996, 1997b), and county-level studies (Kahn, 1997 and Henderson, 1996, 1997). These studies tend to be somewhat more sophisticated and often find that stringency of environmental regulations affects the spatial allocation of pollution-intensive firms; however, effects tend to be small.

3.3 Future Research Directions

Why do current studies find that environmental regulations have small effects on economic activity? One explanation, advanced by Cropper and Oates (1992), is that other types of firm outlays, such as expenditures for labour and energy, swamp any effect of environmental regulations. Levinson (1996b), however, notes that environmental compliance costs, while small relative to other types of costs, have been increasing in recent years. Additionally, he conjectures that allocation of mobile investment could still be affected if these costs exhibit enough interregional variation. In consequence, it is important to test for the extent of differences in environmental policies between geographic locations.

A potential scenario would be that as compliance expenditures have risen steadily since the early 1970s, environmental policies across space have become more similar, confounding any effects of increased compliance expenditures. This premise is entirely possible given recent findings of spatial income convergence (Gottschalk and Smeeding, 1997). Indeed, assuming that local income levels partially determine environmental outcomes, income convergence may be a precursor to conditional convergence (or convergence to a constant differential) of environmental policies.[5] Furthermore, if environmental policies have converged through time, results would shed light on why domestic firm location studies have consistently found environmental regulations as insignificant determinants in a firm's decision set, even though US firm-level compliance expenditures (for pollution abatement) have risen steadily since the early 1970s. Tests for spatial convergence of environmental policies might follow procedures developed in the interregional income convergence literature (see, for example, Carlino and Mills, 1993, 1996).

Complementary to the convergence explanation is the argument that environmental compliance expenditures are important in certain contexts. For example, it may be the case that current empirical studies fail to pick up the effects of environmental regulation because they misspecify the firm's final choice set. If a firm narrows its choice set down to geographical sites in relatively close proximity, such as between a city and one of its suburbs, state-level empirical studies may be reporting biased estimates. This argument has its roots in the tax competition literature. A basic finding is that the smaller the area of study, the larger the influence of tax rates. For example, intra-regional studies typically present tax elasticities that are at least four times greater than estimated interregional tax elasticities (Wasylenko, 1997). The intuition behind this phenomenon is that smaller areas tend to have less variation in other important location factors, such as labour markets, climate and energy costs, which in turn accentuate any differences in tax packages.

A natural experiment to test this premise in the environmental arena is to compare results from studies that vary the heterogeneity of the final choice set. This can be done by comparing results from US domestic studies of Standard Metropolitan Statistical Areas (SMSAs) (Duffy-Deno, 1992), counties (Kahn, 1997; Henderson, 1996, 1997), and states (Levinson, 1996b; Gray, 1996, 1997b) with comparable coefficient estimates from international studies (Leonard, 1984, 1988; Tobey, 1990; Grossman and Krueger, 1991; Low and Yeats, 1992a, 1992b). Evidence from the majority of studies in each category suggests stringency of environmental regulation deters manufacturing activity, but the magnitude of this result is generally small.

These results suggest that the influence of environmental regulation is relatively homogeneous across geographic decision sets. However, if firms narrow their final choice set to smaller geographical areas than states, counties or SMSAs across the US, existing studies run the risk of presenting erroneous estimates. This shortcoming can be addressed in at least two ways. First, with existing county-level data, contiguous sets of counties could be grouped so as to analyse the location decision within each set. For example, a model similar to a conditional logit model could be estimated here, except here the final choice set is not the entire population (or randomly selected counties), but is contiguous counties. Alternatively, one could estimate a nested logit model that pools contiguous cross-sections in each branch.

A second technique to further disaggregate the firm-level decision is to narrow the decision process even further, such as to a choice set of a city or one of its suburbs. The analysis could then test if city ordinances regarding pollution control spur the firm to locate in the suburb. One intriguing data set that could potentially meet this standard is the *Thomas Register*. City-level data on the entire inventory of firms that entered, survived and exited within the product markets can be compiled from the *Thomas Register of American Manufacturers*. The *Thomas Register*, first published in 1906, is a widely used source of information by purchasing agents of all companies and public agencies. Lavin (1992), in extensively describing various sources of business information, states that the *Thomas Register* is the best example of a directory which provides information on manufacturers by focusing on products. According to Lavin (1992), 'The *Thomas Register* is a comprehensive, detailed guide to the full range of products manufactured in the United States ... Covering only manufacturing companies, it strives for a complete representation within that scope.' Its completeness is a consequence of strong incentives on the part of the manufacturers to be included in the listing, since inclusion broadens the market for their products at no additional cost to them.

Measurement problems represent another source of explanations for the current empirical evidence. Three examples appear to be particularly important in this regard. For example, existing empirical work may lack adequate control for improved environmental quality due to more stringent environmental regulations.[6] As previously mentioned, wage rates will partially account for this problem. If increased environmental quality is not fully capitalized in wages, however, potential omitted variable bias could lead to an understatement of the effects of environmental regulation. This problem is akin to shortcomings in early studies of taxation and industrial location that failed to control for public services in the regression equation. Helms (1985) developed an innovative approach to mitigate this problem by using a balanced government budget equation to allow inclusion of all revenue and expenditure items in the regression equation (see also Evans and Karras, 1994 and Dalenberg and Partridge, 1995). Although an approach directly comparable to this technique is not readily apparent to solve the omitted variable problem in the regulatory competition literature, there should at least be some recognition of the services that environmental factors provide.

A second issue concerns the measurement of regulatory stringency. Enforcement has been measured by variables such as local spending on environmental quality control, industry-level compliance cost expenditures per dollar of value-added and counts of numbers of environmental statutes. Although this criticism has been previously noted (see Tannenwald, 1997, and Henderson, 1996), it cannot be entirely mitigated because the concept of regulatory stringency is simply difficult to measure. Additionally, most empirical models look at environmental regulation from a single dimension and find little evidence of negative affects of environmental factors. Nevertheless, simple intuition implies that environmental regulations can affect not only marginal costs of production but also start-up costs. Exclusion of either aspect may lead to serious biases in estimated parameter values.

A third measurement issue concerns the unit of analysis. Due to data constraints, many location studies use aggregate manufacturing data. In consequence, results may indicate that the effect of environmental regulation is minimal, even though certain individual industries (perhaps heavily polluting or geographically footloose) are significantly influenced by pollution control policies.[7] One extension in this direction is to examine individual industries that may have the mobility to arbitrage away any regulatory discrepancies that exist. For example, when Levinson (1996b) focuses on the response of individual industries to environmental policy, heavy polluters, such as producers of petroleum and coal products, turn out to be among the most strongly affected. Additionally, effects of environmental regulations in manufacturing may well not be representative of the outcome of environmental regulation in other sectors. Capital may be more or less geographically mobile in other economic sectors. An example in this regard might be exploration for certain minerals, such as copper. The location of this activity may respond not only to environmental regulations concerning drilling, but also to downstream regulations concerning production and smelting. Perhaps an international study would be useful in this context to ensure a larger range in stringency of environmental regulations considered.

Besides these measurement issues discussed above, many potential research topics remain in the interjurisdictional competition area. For example, Deily and Gray (1991), Crandall (1993) and Kahn (1996) have recently presented results that support an interesting premise relating local business cycles to local environmental regulations. For example, their findings suggest that regulators may advance special deals that stretch out compliance schedules of individual industries, particularly those industries which are large employers. Hence, enforcement may not be as random as first perceived, as regulators' policing of polluters appears to recognize the local trade-off between the environment and jobs. On the other hand, findings from these papers suggest that employment growth in polluting industries is inversely related to regulatory stringency. Together, these findings suggest that environmental regulation may tend to smooth out the local business cycle; that is, periods of growth are slowed by environmental regulations, while recessionary periods are made less severe because environmental regulations tend to protect the interest of large, existing firms (see also Pashigian, 1985). Nevertheless, this important phenomenon deserves more attention.

This research agenda could begin with examining firm hazard rates in US counties that are either have or have not attained federal air quality standards.[8] These results could then be compared to the intuition of Stigler (1971), who argued that a plant with an older capital stock is more likely to be closed than a plant with a newer capital stock, *ceteris paribus*, simply because major reinvestment decisions should arise in the older plant first. However, there is a caveat to Stigler's argument concerning environmental regulations – we are not in a world of *ceteris paribus*. For example, current US environmental regulations are written in a manner that regulates new sources of pollution much more stringently (new source bias) than older sources (older firms have been 'grandfathered' into less restrictive standards and have a relative advantage). Whether environmental regulations extend the life of plants is an open conjecture, but if they do, this would be important to the smoothing of local business cycles, particularly in areas of contraction.

Other important research problems also abound. For example, although numerous empirical studies have attempted to quantify the relationship between environmental regulation and the growth and location of economic activity, one neglected area of research is the effect that environmental regulation has on firm *relocation* decisions. A study of this nature is important for numerous reasons. First, productivity growth and expansion in *existing* plants account for a large amount of regional growth over time (see, for example, Gray and Shadbegian, 1998). Second, a study of firm relocations represents a test of the anecdotal evidence that prevailed during the North American Free Trade Agreement (NAFTA) negotiations. Third, examining relocation data provides a test of whether the location decisions of new start-up plants are more sensitive to environmental regulation than the relocation of existing plants.

As indicated at the beginning of this section, endogeneity of environmental attributes and environmental policy represents another important dimension to consider. In regard to the types of single-equation models just discussed, endogeneity issues arise because the location of industry and higher pollution levels are positively correlated cross-sectionally. Thus, firm entry and more stringent pollution standards potentially coincide, resulting in problematic regression estimates. Studies that fail to lag independent variables, or use panel data techniques inappropriately, may be presenting biased coefficient estimates. One approach to deal with this problem is due to Holtz-Eakin (1994) and Holtz-Eakin, Newey and Rosen (1988).

The issue of endogeneity, however, is much broader than is evident from a single-equation context. Relocation of industry or, more generally, economic growth may result in shifts in the spatial pattern of environmental problems. One possibility is that, over time, heavily polluting industries may become a less important part of a region's economic base. Kahn (1999) refers to the resulting decline in pollution levels as a 'silver lining' to be factored into calculations of regional welfare. Another possibility is that urban areas may grow more rapidly than rural areas and that new cities may end up located in close proximity to older ones. Economic growth may, therefore, come in the form of urban growth with greater spatial concentration of sources of pollution. Air pollution resulting from automobile transportation might represent an example in this regard, but surely there are others. Additionally, pollution problems brought about by industry location patterns may be unevenly distributed across urban areas. This prospect raises the question of who faces the worst pollution problems; that is, the issue of environmental justice recently studied by Brooks and Sethi (1997) and Arora and Cason (1999). As noted by Glickman (1999), environmental justice has recently attracted more attention than perhaps any other environmental issue. Also, it raises the issue of spatial discounting: how do perceptions of environmental hazards change as distance from the site increases? Does this spatial decay factor change when different types of hazards are considered? Do environmental hazards tend to result in greater dispersion of economic activity?

4 CONCLUSION

This chapter has focused on spatial economic aspects of the environment and environmental policy. It has treated this topic by looking at the intersection between environmental and natural resource economics and regional and urban economics. This perspective yields the obvious, but infrequently treated, observation that the environment both affects and is affected by geographic factor mobility. Much of the empirical literature on human migration and capital mobility takes the environment and environmental policy as an exogenous input into the decision-making process. This approach has yielded numerous important insights concerning the responsiveness of factors to environmental attributes and policy. However, a more complete understanding will be obtained from a broader framework that recognizes that factor mobility and aspects of the environment are interactively determined. Additionally, this broader framework will aid in developing emerging topics concerning the political role of economic growth in spatially concentrating environmental problems and the role of environmental hazards in spatially dispersing economic activity.

ACKNOWLEDGEMENTS

We thank Henk Folmer and other participants at the conference, 'Frontiers in Environmental Economics', for numerous constructive suggestions. Also, Gerking gratefully acknowledges the hospitality of CentER, Tilburg University, where portions of this chapter were completed, as well as visiting grant B46-386 from the Netherlands Organization for Scientific Research (NWO).

NOTES

1. Mathur and Stein (1993) develop an alternative interregional model of the economic effects of amenity differences. Roback's analysis, however, has been by far more prominent in stimulating further research.
2. Related extensions have considered relationships between factor rewards and public infrastructure (Dalenberg and Partridge, 1997; Haughwout, 1998). Also, Voith (1991) examines capitalization of locational attributes into wages and land rents and distinguishes between types of committees.
3. This point has also been addressed recently by Jensen and Leven (1997).
4. These two views have frequently been characterized in the migration literature as 'equilibrium vs disequilibrium'. However, referring to the traditional view as the disequilibrium perspective may be somewhat misleading. It merely emphasizes distortions, such as migration costs, that Graves and others assume are small enough to ignore.
5. Convergence up to a constant differential, or conditional convergence, is stressed since optimal environmental regulation should take into account other factors that affect potential

damages. These factors include assimilative capacities, demographic characteristics, geographic characteristics, etc.

6. This omitted variable bias may be attenuated in panel data contexts; for example, quality of the environment can be picked up by the fixed costs.

7. A few recent exceptions are McConnell and Schwab (1990, automobiles), Henderson (1996, chemicals) and Levinson (1996b, various industries).

8. Interestingly, Black and Henderson's (1999) recent contribution to the theory of urban growth did not touch on environmental issues.

REFERENCES

Amacher, Gregory S., Wilfredo Cruz, Donald Grebner and William F. Hyde (1998), 'Environmental motivation for migration: population pressure, poverty, and deforestation in the Philippines', *Land Economics*, **74**, 92–101.

Arora, Seneca and Timothy N. Cason (1999), 'Do community characteristics influence environmental outcomes? Evidence from the toxic release inventory', *Southern Economic Journal*, **65**, 691–716.

Bartik, Timothy (1988), 'The effects of environmental regulations on the location of business in the US', *Growth and Change*, **19**, 22–44.

Batra, Ravindra and Francisco R. Casas (1976), 'A synthesis of the Heckscher–Ohlin and neoclassical models of international trade', *Journal of International Economics*, **6**, 21–38.

Becker, Randy and Vernon Henderson (1997), 'Births, survival, and investment in polluting industries under air quality regulations', working paper, Brown University.

Beeson, Patricia (1991), 'Amenities and regional differences in returns to worker characteristics', *Journal of Urban Economics*, **30**, 224–41.

Black, Duncan and Vernon Henderson (1999), 'A theory of urban growth', *Journal of Political Economy*, **107**, 252–84.

Blomquist, Glenn C., Mark C. Berger and John P. Hoehn (1988), 'New estimates of the quality of life in urban areas', *American Economic Review*, **78**, 89–107.

Bockstael, Nancy E. and Elena G. Irwin (2000), 'Economics and the land use–environment link', in Thomas Tietenberg and Henk Folmer (eds), *International Yearbook of Environmental and Resource Economics: 2000–2001*, Cheltenham, UK and Northampton, MA: Edward Elgar.

Brooks, Nancy and Rajiv Sethi (1997), 'The distribution of pollution: community characteristics and exposure to air toxics', *Journal of Environmental Economics and Management*, **32**, 233–50.

Carlino, Gerald and Leonard Mills (1993), 'Are US regional economies converging? A time-series analysis', *Journal of Monetary Economics*, **32**, 335–46.

Carlino, Gerald and Leonard Mills (1996), 'Testing neoclassical convergence in regional incomes inequality', *Regional Science and Urban Economics*, **26**, 565–90.

Comolli, Paul M. (1977), 'Pollution control in a simplified general-equilibrium model with production externalities', *Journal of Environmental Economics and Management*, **4**, 289–304.

Cragg, Michael and Matthew E. Kahn (1997), 'New estimates of climate demand: evidence from location choice', *Journal of Urban Economics*, **42**, 261–84.

Crandall, Robert W. (1993), *Manufacturing on the Move*, Washington, DC: The Brookings Institution.

Cropper, Maureen and Charles Griffiths (1994), 'The interaction of population growth with environmental quality', *American Economic Review, Papers and Proceedings*, **84**, 250–54.

Cropper, Maureen and Wallace Oates (1992), 'Environmental economics: a survey', *Journal of Economic Literature*, **30**, 675–740.

Dalenberg, Douglas and Mark Partridge (1995), 'The effects of taxes, expenditures, and public infrastructure on metropolitan area employment', *Journal of Regional Science*, **35**, 617–40.

Dalenberg, Douglas R. and Mark D. Partridge (1997), 'Public infrastructure and wages: public capital's role as a productive input and household amenity', *Land Economics*, **73**, 268–84.

Deacon, Robert T. *et al.* (1998), 'Research trends and opportunities in environmental and natural resource economics', *Environmental and Resource Economics*, **11**, 383–97.

Deily, Mary and Wayne Gray (1991), 'Enforcement of pollution regulations in a declining industry', *Journal of Environmental Economics and Management*, **21**, 260–74.

Dickie, Mark and Shelby Gerking (1998), 'Interregional wage disparities, relocation costs, and labor mobility in Canada', *Journal of Regional Science*, **38**, 61–88.

Dixit, Avinash K. and Joseph E. Stiglitz (1977), 'Monopolistic competition and optimum product diversity', *American Economic Review*, **67**, 297–309.

Duffy-Deno, Kevin T. (1992), 'Pollution abatement expenditures and regional manufacturing activity', *Journal of Regional Science*, **32**, 419–36.

Ethier, Wilfred J. and Lars E.O. Svensson (1986), 'The theorems of international trade with factor mobility', *Journal of International Economics*, **20**, 21–42.

Evans, Alan W. (1990), 'The assumption of equilibrium in the analysis of migration and interregional differences', *Journal of Regional Science*, **30**, 515–31.

Evans, Paul and Gergios Karras (1994), 'Are government activities productive? Evidence from a panel of US states', *Review of Economics and Statistics*, **76**, 1–11.

Forster, Bruce A. (1977), 'Pollution control in a two-sector dynamic general equilibrium model', *Journal of Environmental Economics and Management*, **4**, 305–12.

Forster, Bruce A. (1981), 'Environmental regulation and the distribution of income in simple general equilibrium models', in Maurice B. Ballabon (ed.), *Economic Perspectives: An Annual Survey of Economics*, Volume 2, London: Harwood Academic Publishers.

Getz, Malcolm and Y.C. Huang (1978), 'Consumer revealed preference for environmental goods', *Review of Economics and Statistics*, **60**, 449–58.

Glickman, Theodore S. (1999), 'Measuring environmental equity with geographical information systems', in Wallace E. Oates (ed.), *The RFF Reader in Environmental and Resource Management*, Washington, DC: Resources for the Future.

Gottschalk, Peter and Timothy Smeeding (1997), 'Cross-national comparisons of earnings and income inequality', *Journal of Economic Literature*, **35**, 633–87.

Graves, Philip E. (1976), 'A reexamination of migration, economic opportunity, and the quality of life', *Journal of Regional Science*, **16**, 107–12.

Graves, Philip E. (1980), 'Migration and climate', *Journal of Regional Science*, **20**, 227–37.

Graves, Philip E. and Peter D. Linneman (1979), 'Household migration: theoretical and empirical results', *Journal of Urban Economics*, **6**, 383–404.

Graves, Philip E. and Peter R. Mueser (1993), 'The role of equilibrium and economic perspectives on regional labor migration', *Journal of Regional Science*, **33**, 69–84.

Gray, Wayne B. (1996), 'Manufacturing plant location: does state pollution regulation really matter?', mimeo, Clark University.

Gray, Wayne B. (1997a), 'Discussion of "State Regulatory Policy and Economic Development"', *New England Economic Review*, 99–103.

Gray, Wayne B. (1997b), 'Plant location: do different industries respond differently to environmental regulation?', mimeo, Clark University.

Gray, Wayne B. and Ronald Shadbegian (1998), 'Do firms avoid environmental regulation by shifting production?', mimeo, Clark University.

Greenwood, Michael J. (1985), 'Human migration: theory, models, and empirical studies', *Journal of Regional Science*, **25**, 521–44.

Greenwood, Michael J. and Gary L. Hunt (1984), 'Migration and interregional employment redistribution in the United States', *American Economic Review*, **74**, 957–69.

Greenwood, Michael J. and Gary L. Hunt (1989), 'Jobs versus amenities in the analysis of metropolitan migration', *Journal of Urban Economics*, **25**, 1–16.

Greenwood, Michael J., Gary L. Hunt, Dan S. Rickman and George I. Treyz (1991), 'Migration, regional equilibrium, and the estimation of compensating differentials', *American Economic Review*, **81**, 1382–90.

Grossman, Gene M. and Alan B. Krueger (1991), 'Environmental impacts of a North American Free Trade Agreement', Woodrow Wilson School Discussion Papers in Economics No. 158.

Gunther, W. (1991), 'Plant locations and environmental regulations', in David McKee (ed.), *Energy, the Environment, and Public Policy*, New York: Praeger, pp. 55–64.

Gyourko, Joseph (1991), 'How accurate are quality of life rankings across cities?', *Federal Reserve Bank of Philadelphia Business Review*, 3–12.

Gyourko, Joseph and Joseph Tracy (1989), 'The importance of local fiscal conditions in analyzing local labor markets', *Journal of Political Economy*, **97**, 1208–31.

Gyourko, Joseph and Joseph Tracy (1991), 'The structure of local public finance and the quality of life', *Journal of Political Economy*, **99**, 774–806.

Haughwout, Andrew F. (1998), 'Aggregate production functions, interregional equilibrium, and the measurement of infrastructure productivity', *Journal of Urban Economics*, **44**, 216–27.

Helms, L. Jay (1985), 'The effect of state and local taxes on economic growth: a time-series cross-section approach', *The Review of Economics and Statistics*, **67**, 574–82.

Henderson, J. Vernon (1982), 'Evaluating consumer amenities and interregional welfare differences', *Journal of Urban Economics*, **11**, 32–59.

Henderson, J. Vernon (1996), 'Effects of air quality regulation', *American Economic Review*, **86**, 789–813.

Henderson, J. Vernon (1997), 'The impact of air quality regulation on industrial location', *Annales d'Economie et de Statistique*, **45**, 123–37.

Herzog, Henry W. and Alan M. Schlottmann (1993), 'Valuing amenities and disamenities of urban scale: can bigger be better?', *Journal of Regional Science*, **33**, 145–65.

Hoehn, John P., Mark C. Berger and Glen C. Blomquist (1987), 'A hedonic model of interregional wages, rents, and amenity values', *Journal of Regional Science*, **27**, 605–20.

Holtz-Eakin, Douglas (1994), 'Public-sector capital and the productivity puzzle', *Review of Economics and Statistics*, **76**, 12–21.

Holtz-Eakin, Douglas, Whitney Newey and Harvey Rosen (1988), 'Estimating vector autoregressions with panel data', *Econometrica*, **56**, 1371–95.

Hunt, Gary L. (1993), 'Equilibrium and disequilibrium in migration modeling', *Regional Studies*, **27**, 341–9.

Jaffe, Adam, Steven Peterson, Paul Portney and Robert Stavins (1995), 'Environmental regulation and the competitiveness of US manufacturing: what does the evidence tell us?', *Journal of Economic Literature*, **33**, 132–63.

Jensen, Mark J. and Charles L. Leven (1997), 'Quality of life in central cities and suburbs', *Annals of Regional Science*, **31**, 431–49.

Jones, Ronald W. (1965), 'The structure of simple general equilibrium models', *Journal of Political Economy*, **73**, 557–72.

Jones, Ronald W. (1971), 'A three-factor model in trade, theory, and history', in J.N. Bhagwati *et al.* (eds), *Trade, Balance of Payments and Growth*, Amsterdam: North-Holland.

Kahn, Matthew E. (1995), 'A revealed preference approach to ranking city quality of life', *Journal of Urban Economics*, **38**, 221–35.

Kahn, Matthew E. (1997), 'Particulate pollution trends in the United States', *Regional Science and Urban Economics*, **27**, 87–108.

Kahn, Matthew E. (1999), 'The silver lining of rust belt manufacturing decline', *Journal of Urban Economics*, **46**, 360–76.

Kilkenny, Maureen (1998), 'Transport costs and rural development', *Journal of Regional Science*, **38**, 293–312.

Krugman, Paul (1998), 'Space: the final frontier', *Journal of Economic Perspectives*, **12**, 161–74.

Krugman, Paul (1991a), 'Increasing returns and economic geography', *Journal of Political Economy*, **99**, 483–99.

Krugman, Paul (1991b), *Geography and Trade*, Cambridge, MA: MIT Press.

Lavin, Michael R. (1992), *Business Information: How to Find It, How to Use It*, 2nd edition, Phoenix, AZ: Oryx Press.

Leonard, H. Jeffrey (1984), *Are Environmental Regulations Driving US Industry Overseas?*, Washington, DC: Conservation Foundation.

Leonard, H. Jeffrey (1988), *Pollution and the Struggle for the World Product*, Cambridge: Cambridge University Press.

Levinson, Arik (1996a), 'Environmental regulations and industry location: international and domestic evidence', in Jagdish Bhagwati and Robert E. Hudec (eds), *Fair Trade and Harmonization: Prerequisites for Free Trade?, Volume 1: Economic Analysis*, Cambridge, MA: MIT Press.

Levinson, Arik (1996b), 'Environmental regulations and manufacturer's location choices: evidence from the Census of Manufactures', *Journal of Public Economics*, **61**, 5–29.

Low, Patrick and Alexander Yeats (1992a), 'Do 'dirty' industries migrate?', in Patrick Low (ed.), *International Trade and the Environment*, Washington, DC: World Bank.

Low, Patrick and Alexander Yeats (1992b), 'Trade measures and environmental quality: the implications for Mexico's exports', in Patrick Low (ed.), *International Trade and the Environment*, Washington, DC: World Bank.

Mathur, Vijay K. and Sheldon H. Stein (1993), 'The role of amenities in a general equilibrium model of migration and growth', *Southern Economic Journal*, **59**, 394–409.

McConnell, Virginia and Robert Schwab (1990), 'The impact of environmental regulation on industry location decisions: the motor vehicle industry', *Land Economics*, **66**, 67–81.

Mueser, Peter R. and Philip E. Graves (1995), 'Examining the role of economic opportunity and amenities in explaining population redistribution', *Journal of Urban Economics*, **37**, 176–200.

Muth, Richard F. (1971), 'Migration: chicken or egg?', *Southern Economic Journal*, **37**, 295–306.

Nordhaus, William D. and James Tobin (1972), 'Is growth obsolete?' in *Economic Research: Retrospect and Prospect, Volume 5, Economic Growth*, New York: Columbia University Press.

Olewiler, Nancy (1994), 'The impact of environmental regulation on investment decisions', in Jamie Benidickson, Bruce Doern and Nancy Olewiler (eds), *Getting the Green Light: Environmental Regulation and Investment in Canada*, Ottawa, Ontario: C.D. Howe Institute, pp. 53–110.

Pashigian, Peter (1985), 'Environmental regulations: whose self-interests are being protected?', *Economic Inquiry*, **23**, 551–84.

Polinski, A. Mitchell and Daniel L. Rubinfeld (1977), 'Property values and the benefits of environmental improvements: theory and measurement', in Lowdon Wingo and Alan Evans (eds), *Public Economics and the Quality of Life*, Baltimore, MD: Johns Hopkins University Press.

Rauch, James E. (1993), 'Productivity gains from the geographic concentration of human capital: evidence from the cities', *Journal of Urban Economics*, **34**, 380–400.

Ridker, Ronald G. and John A. Henning (1967), 'The determinants of residential property values with special reference to air pollution', *Review of Economics and Statistics*, **49**, 246–57.

Roback, Jennifer (1982), 'Wages, rents and the quality of life', *Journal of Political Economy*, **90**, 1257–78.

Roback, Jennifer (1988), 'Wages, rents, and amenities: differences among workers and regions', *Economic Inquiry*, **26**, 23–41.

Rosen, Sherwin (1974), 'Hedonic prices and implicit markets: product differentiation in pure competition', *Journal of Political Economy*, **82**, 34–55.

Rosen, Sherwin (1979), 'Wage-based indexes of urban quality of life', in Peter Mieszkowski and Mahlon Straszheim (eds), *Current Issues in Urban Economics*, Baltimore, MD: Johns Hopkins University Press.

Sanchirico, James N. and James E. Wilen (1999), 'Bioeconomics of spatial exploitation in a patchy environment', *Journal of Environmental Economics and Management*, **37**, 129–50.

Sjaastad, Larry A. (1962), 'The costs and returns of human migration', *Journal of Political Economy*, **70**, Supplement, 80–93.

Stigler, George (1971), 'The theory of economic regulation', *Bell Journal of Economics and Management Science*, **2**, 3–21.

Tannenwald, Robert (1997), 'State regulatory policy and economic development', *New England Economic Review*, 83–97.

Tobey, James A. (1990), 'The effects of domestic environmental policies on patterns of world trade: an empirical test', *Kyklos*, **43**, 191–209.

Voith, Richard P. (1991), 'Capitalization of local and regional attributes into wages and rents: differences across residential, commercial, and mixed use communities', *Journal of Regional Science*, **31**, 127–45.

Wasylenko, Michael (1997), 'Taxation and economic development: the state of the economic literature', *New England Economic Review*, 37–53.

Yohe, Gary W. (1979), 'The backward incidence of pollution control – some comparative statics in general equilibrium', *Journal of Environmental Economics and Management*, **6**, 187–98.

4. Empowering the community: information strategies for pollution control

Tom Tietenberg and David Wheeler

INTRODUCTION

The Demand for Disclosure Strategies

The first phase of pollution control involved applying traditional legal remedies such as emissions standards. Over time, however, it became clear that these traditional regulatory approaches to pollution control were excessively costly in some circumstances (Tietenberg, 1985) and incapable of achieving the stipulated goals in others (Tietenberg, 1995). Failures have been especially common in developing countries, where legal and regulatory institutions are often weak (Afsah and Laplante, 1996a). In response to these deficiencies the second phase of pollution control focused on market-based approaches such as tradable permits, emission charges, deposit-refunds and performance bonds (Hahn, 1989; OECD, 1989; Tietenberg, 1990; OECD, 1994, 1995). In some instances they have substituted for traditional remedies, but in most cases they have complemented them. In the OECD and Eastern Europe, these approaches have added both flexibility and improved cost-effectiveness to pollution control policy. Pollution charges have also contributed to improved environmental performance in developing Asia and Latin America, with particularly noteworthy examples in China (Wang and Wheeler, 1996), Malaysia (Vincent, 1993) and Colombia (Arbeláez, 1998).

Even the addition of market-based approaches, however, has not fully solved the problem of pollution regulation. In the industrialized countries the system remains overburdened by the sheer number of substances to be controlled. Neither staffs nor budgets are adequate for the task of regulating all of the potentially harmful substances that are emitted by firms and households. In many developing countries, these difficulties are compounded by the problems associated with designing, implementing, monitoring and enforcing market-based regulations.

To counter these problems, phase three in the evolution of pollution control policy involves investment in the provision of information as a vehicle for making the community an active participant in the regulatory process. The timing of this increasing role for disclosure strategies seems to emanate from the increasing perceived need for more regulatory tools (as described above); the falling cost of information collection, aggregation and dissemination; and the rising demand for environmental information from communities and markets. Rising benefits and falling costs imply that public disclosure merits a close look, even if it has been perceived as inefficient in the past.

The disclosure strategies considered in this chapter involve public and/or private attempts to increase the availability of information on pollution to workers, consumers, shareholders and the public at large. Provision of greater information may either complement or replace traditional regulation strategies. Disclosure strategies seek to enlist market forces in the quest for efficient pollution control. And in so doing they interact in sometimes complex ways with traditional standard-setting and enforcement strategies. Whether they complement phase one and two strategies or substitute for them, they involve a rather different role for government – one which seems to offer the possibility of fulfilling the large and growing need for pollution control despite limited budgets and staffs. But how real is this promise?

The Conceptual Foundation for Disclosure Strategies

The starting point for thinking about information approaches to pollution control is the Coase theorem (Coase, 1960). In his landmark essay Coase pointed out that pollution control situations have a certain symmetry. Inefficient pollution imposes costs on victims which exceed the costs of controlling that pollution. In other words the marginal benefits of pollution control exceed the marginal costs. The existence of inefficient pollution damage therefore provides a motivation for the victims to take corrective action, even in the absence of any such incentives by the polluters.

What economists have learned rather recently is that the list of victims can be very large indeed, much larger than originally thought. The list of potential victims includes not only the traditional categories of those harmed directly by the pollution, but also those who may be disturbed by it even if they are not directly affected. The fact that this 'non-use' value of pollution control can be quite large has become a familiar result to those conducting contingent value surveys. The pressure to control pollution therefore can arise from victims experiencing both use and non-use damages.

One standard precondition for decentralized processes to work efficiently is for the decision makers to have full information. In the case of victims taking action to control pollution, this precondition is not likely to be met.

Information about environmental risks is asymmetrically distributed. In a typical case, the best knowledge of emission profiles is held by the polluters and/or regulators, not the victims. Furthermore, the polluters are unlikely to share the information with victims in the absence of outside pressure to do so. In addition, bureaucratic inertia and/or legal constraints have frequently prevented information sharing by regulators.

However, even if information on emissions is provided, this may not be sufficient for victims to understand the severity of the risk they face. Such understanding can only occur when knowledge of emission levels is combined with information on exposure and on the exposure/risk relationship.

In the past the Coasean insight has been dismissed as a foundation for policy[1] for several reasons.

- In multiple victim circumstances it ignores the public good nature of information. When coupled with the very real transactions costs associated with the collection and dissemination of information, this characteristic tends to undermine the incentive of any individual to derive and to share information on the nature and extent of pollution damage with other victims.
- The approach appears to force the victim to pay for controlling pollution damage which he/she did not cause, an outcome which violates the well-established 'polluter pays' principle of pollution control.

Since, as discussed below, both of these flaws turn out to be remediable, the traditional lack of interest in Coasean approaches may have been misplaced.

Overview

While disclosure (particularly labelling) strategies have become common in natural resource settings (organic agriculture and forest certification programmes, for example), they are less familiar in a pollution control context. Yet the number of applications in this new arena is increasing in both OECD and developing countries.

Generally these disclosure strategies are justified on ethical grounds. Victims are seen as having the right to know the environmental risks to which they have been exposed. In this chapter we explore quite a different justification – that providing greater information can be part of a larger strategy to promote efficient pollution control.

This chapter will review what we know and do not know about the use of disclosure strategies to control pollution. It is important to note that this review will not cover two related fields. First, we shall not examine the rather large literature on the relationship between regulator and polluter when the stakeholders have private information (Lewis, 1996). Second, we shall not examine the literature on the role of strategies (for example, auditing) for increasing the amount of information available to the firm itself (Sinclair-Desgagné and Gabel, 1997). Our focus is rather on information made available to consumers, workers, shareholders and the public at large.

Following a review of the conceptual foundations for disclosure strategies, the chapter will consider how the policy setting influences the type of information strategy employed. Examples of innovative disclosure strategies (in the US, Latin America and Asia), and the channels through which they operate, will be followed by a review of the empirical research on their effectiveness. The chapter will close with the authors' sense of what we have learned and where further research would be particularly helpful.

THE CONTEXT

Tailoring disclosure strategies to the specific context requires an understanding of the various types of situations that can arise and the policy-relevant characteristics that differentiate them. For the purposes of this study we shall consider two broad pollution types (product pollution and process pollution) and four specific settings (the household setting, the consumption setting, the employment setting and the community setting).

Pollution Types

Pollution can arise either from the consumption or use of products ('product' pollution) or the production of those products ('process' pollution). Examples of the former include the consumption of foods contaminated with pesticides, the use of aerosol sprays with ozone-depleting chemicals, driving automobiles, heating homes with polluting fuels, etc. Examples of the latter include water pollution from pulp and paper mills, air pollution from steel mills, hazardous waste pollution from chemical plants, radiation from nuclear power plants, etc.

The Setting

The point of departure for disclosure strategies is an understanding of the economic incentives that face the parties to an environmental pollution situation. Do they have incentives to take actions to control pollution? Are these incentives compatible with an efficient outcome, or do the incentives create a bias toward too little or too much control?

Analysing the answers to these questions begins with isolating the role of information in the process. In the absence of government intervention, will the efficient amount of information be generated? Or will the amount of information supplied normally be inefficiently large or small? Will it normally be made available to victims?

Given the answers to the above questions, what possible role for government is involved? Does this role complement or substitute for traditional regulation?

The household setting
Indoor pollutants, though increasingly recognized as significant contributors to human health problems, have not traditionally been addressed by conventional regulation. Two classic examples of dangerous indoor pollutants are radon gas[2] and lead paint.[3]

Do homeowners have an incentive to control these forms of pollution? Assuming they have full information, homeowners have three major possible responses when confronted with the risk of radon or lead contamination. They can decide not to control; they can undertake some control; or they can attempt to solve the problem by selling the house to someone else.

For the first two choices, homeowner incentives are compatible with efficiency. Because those who would bear the damage and those who would pay for the control are in the same household, theory would lead us to expect an efficient balancing of the benefits and the costs. Control would be undertaken until the marginal cost of additional control equalled the value of the marginal damage reduced by the expenditure.

The third choice, however, opens the possibility of an inefficiency. The cheapest solution may well be selling the home to an unsuspecting buyer, thereby passing any control costs on to them. This is a clear externality: what is cheapest for the homeowner is not cheapest for society as a whole.

Do households have efficient incentives to invest in information? Information on radon or lead has one of the characteristics of a public good – indivisibility. Information shared with one party does not diminish the stock of information available to be shared with many other parties. Information about radon or lead, however, does not automatically have the second characteristic of a public good – non-exclusivity. The establishment of exclusive rights could be possible, at least in principle.

What does this suggest about the role for government? For the externality case it seems necessary to ensure that only full information transfers of property take place. Once good information is available on safe levels and a test is developed, sellers with low/no radon have a clear incentive to disclose that fact, via a test certificate that is verifiable. They can sell their house for more. This is just like termite damage.

An informed buyer should reduce the offer price by an amount that reflects the cost of controlling the radon or lead. Linking the selling price to the pollution situation by full disclosure would restore efficient incentives and offer the seller a choice – controlling the pollution (and raising the price) or accepting a lower selling price.

In fact, current policy in the US corresponds closely to this recommendation. As of 6 December 1996, all home buyers and tenants have the right to know about potential lead-based paint hazards before they buy or rent older housing under a programme jointly sponsored by the US Environmental Protection Agency (USEPA) and the US Department of Housing and Urban Development. Prospective tenants or buyers of pre-1978 residential dwellings – including single-family homeowners – can ask for and receive information on known lead-based paint hazards before purchasing or renting.[4]

The US government has also played an important research and development (R&D) role in this context. It has conducted basic research to discover appropriate risk thresholds for lead and radon[5] and has widely disseminated this information. It has also made sure that low-cost test kits are available. However, it has been up to the market to supply the test kits at a reasonable price, and up to households to decide what they should do with the results.

This is a very different policy than would be implied by traditional regulation. The regulatory solution would involve the definition of a standard which would then have to be applied, with appropriate monitoring and enforcement, to every 'at risk' household. Even if physically possible, which is doubtful, this approach would not normally be expected to produce efficient outcomes. The homeowner would not generally be free to balance the benefits and costs of remediation.

The product consumption setting
Consider now a situation of product pollution in which damage is inflicted directly on consumers of that product. Examples might include fruits or vegetables with residues of pesticides, heating systems that leak harmful gases, carpets or dry cleaning which emit toxic fumes left over from the manufacturing or cleaning process, etc.

Here we have a case where the polluter and the pollutee are different. Yet the apparent conclusion that an externality is present is not necessarily valid.

Since consumers and producers are linked by the purchase decision, pollution inflicted on consumers is not necessarily an externality. Consumers who are aware that a product is exposing them to an environmental risk can either avoid purchasing it (if, for example, a riskless substitute is available) or purchase it only at a lower price that reflects the associated damage or the cost of preventing or mitigating it. In either case, the producer has an incentive to alter its products and/or pricing to balance the potential loss of sales against the costs of eliminating or mitigating the pollution problem.

Will the market supply the proper amount of information about the risk to ensure that consumers are fully informed? Not necessarily. Since producers have something to lose by providing this information (a loss of sales or lower prices), they will only provide it if prodded by some outside force.[6] Individual consumers do not normally have an incentive to acquire the information, since their *individual* gains are so small (even when *societal* gains are large) in comparison to the costs of an appropriate product-testing programme.[7] Hence, even in cases where the costs of ensuring informed consumers can be justified on efficiency grounds, private incentives will not necessarily produce that outcome.

What is the implied role for government? If the environmental risk is so large that rational consumers would not purchase the product, the government typically bans it. A common case, however, arises when the environmental risk exceeds the benefits of the product for some consumers, but not for others. In such a case, firms should offer products that pose varying environmental risks, leaving the market to sort out the market share going to each type of product. Under reasonably competitive conditions, product labelling should provide the requisite information. For example, vegetable producers who use no pesticides will label their produce as 'organic', thereby affording consumers the opportunity to make an informed choice. In general, produce labelled as organic has been able to command a price premium for the lower environmental risk it poses.

However, it is clear that consumers need reliable benchmarks for evaluating producers' claims. Without an enforceable standard by which the term 'organic' is defined, its credibility will be rapidly undermined under competitive conditions. Here the government may have a role in standardizing the information provided and sanctioning those who misrepresent their products.

A different sort of information is needed when the pollution arises from the use of the product. For example, pesticides are clearly toxic by design, not default. Banning pesticides simply because they are toxic to some species is not practical. Effective government policies in this case will recognize that risks to pesticide users will vary with their application practices. Typically, government-mandated labels provide detailed instructions on 'proper' (damage-minimizing) application procedures. Application of especially risky pesticides may be limited to licensed applicators who are required to undergo special training.[8]

Like their counterparts in the household setting, disclosure strategies in the product consumption setting provide an alternative to traditional regulation. In some cases disclosure strategies can substitute for traditional regulation (as when private labelling produces informed consumers), and in some cases can complement traditional regulation (as when pesticides posing an unacceptable risk are banned, but others are controlled by requiring precautionary labels or licensed applicators).

The occupational setting
The employment setting provides a very different set of interactions between polluters and pollutees. Employers typically control the overall production process, which includes decisions about the toxicity of the substances employees face. However, employees have at least some control over their actual exposure to risk.

What incentives do fully informed employers and employees have with respect to controlling those risks? Are those incentives likely to be compatible with efficiency? Consider first the incentives of the employees. If they bear both the cost of taking precautions and the expected damage from exposure, employees will maximize their welfare by taking all cost-justified precautions to reduce risk, and by seeking wage increases to compensate for the remaining risk.[9]

The employer must choose how much to invest in risk reduction. Since fully informed employees will demand compensation for any remaining risk, a cost-minimizing employer will invest to the point where the incremental cost of risk reduction is equal to the wage increment that will compensate employees for the residual risk.

All of this, however, depends on fully informed workers (and employers). Will normal market processes guarantee the efficient generation and sharing of occupational risk information?

The answer seems to depend on the nature of the employment situation. Individual employees are unlikely to be willing to bear the cost of acquiring information about the risk, since their expected individual benefits are likely to pale in the face of their individual costs. When employees band together, however, as in labour unions, providing that information may become desirable because the collective benefits will outweigh the cost of acquiring the information.[10]

How about employers? In general, employers do not have an incentive to inform their workers about environmental risks. Fully informed workers are likely to demand higher wages; workers who are ignorant of the risks they face are not.

What role does this suggest for the government? It may be minimal when labour organizations such as unions are large and well organized. However, the recent decline of unionization in the US has produced a growing need for other sources of information.

The original thrust of US government policy (the Occupational Safety and Health Act [OSHA] in 1970) was strictly regulatory. The government promulgated thousands of very detailed standards, which in many cases prescribed specific actions to be undertaken by employers. Empirical analysis performed up to the mid 1970s clearly indicated that this approach was ineffective (Viscusi, 1992, pp. 181–205). In response to this lack of success, the Carter and Reagan administrations proposed major reforms. The evidence on that period is more mixed. Analysts have found some statistically significant effects of OSHA on worker safety, but these effects were neither dramatic in magnitude nor robust across different measures of risk (Viscusi, 1992, pp. 206–22).

Risk communication became an important element of the policy in 1983, when the 'Hazard Communication Standard' introduced uniform hazard communication requirements for manufacturers. Under this standard, each employee who is, or may be, exposed to hazardous chemicals in the workplace must receive information and training tailored to the nature of the risk. The Emergency Planning and Community Right-to-Know Act prescribes three different types of risk communication instruments: container labels, Material Safety Data Sheets (MSDS)[11] and training sessions. In this case risk communication is designed to complement, rather than substitute for, other policies.

The community setting
From an economic point of view, the most difficult setting for pollution disclosure involves situations where the polluter and pollutee have no formal contractual relationship and large numbers of parties are involved.

The relationship between polluters and their neighbouring communities provides a good example of this problem. Whereas disclosure strategies can build upon the purchase relationship for consumption-related pollution, and the wage relationship for employment-related pollution, community–polluter relationships are not mediated by specific behavioural linkages.

The community case is the large numbers case where the basic Coase theorem is most problematic, not only because of the high bargaining costs due to the large number of parties and the public good nature of information supply, but also because of the free-rider motive in the large numbers case even in the presence of perfect information (Kennedy *et al.*, 1994). How important is the free-rider problem in practice in the disclosure context? Just how empowering is disclosure when the benefits from taking action are not exclusive? These are two of the questions we seek to answer.

DISCLOSURE STRATEGIES FOR THE COMMUNITY SETTING

The typical information strategy involves four separate functions: (1) establishing mechanisms for discovering environmental risks, (2) ensuring the reliability of the information, (3) publicizing or sharing the information and (4) acting on the information.

Detecting Environmental Risks

The necessary first step in an efficient information approach is discovering the extent and magnitude of environmental risks. Environmental risks will normally be detected only after some investment in information is made. Who should make that investment? What incentives do they face?

Assessment of environmental risk requires knowledge of a complex causation process. Relevant considerations include the emissions volumes of pollutants, the resulting degree of exposure, and the sensitivity of the population to this exposure.

Full information requires knowledge of all these links in the process, but notice that the types of information involved are quite different. Some information is general – for example, atmospheric pollutant concentrations apply to the population at large – while other information is specific to individual polluters.

The government may be in the best position to identify the general elements of environmental risk. These elements are of interest to the largest number of citizens, and one-time collection of risk-related information by a central body eliminates duplication of effort.

Polluters themselves are an obvious source of firm-specific risk information. They have the best information about their inputs, products and processes, and they may be well positioned to assess exposure of third parties to harmful emissions. However, they normally do not have the proper incentives to detect or to reveal the risks that they generate, in the absence of the threat of liability or some other outside force.

The polluters are not the only possible source of firm-specific information. In the US, for example, an alternative approach to monitoring places some responsibility on private enforcers. An example is provided by the 'riverkeepers' system. Typically hired by associations of citizens who live along the river, riverkeepers constantly oversee a network of monitoring stations, usually with help from many volunteers. These associations are funded by voluntary dues from the members.

Ensuring Reliable Information

Information has both a quantity and quality dimension. Effective risk communication requires that the requisite information be reliable, as well as available. Inaccurate or partial information can be worse than no information at all, if it promotes either a false sense of security or unjustified fears. And firms have incentives to mislead the public, either by overstating their environmental accomplishments or by selective omission (noting the positive outcomes and ignoring or burying the negative ones).

Accurate information can be promoted by standardizing the method of collection (specifying acceptable collection instruments and procedures, for example, as well as the nature of the information to be gathered) and by ensuring significant losses for those who falsify information.[12] The ISO 14000 process, a set of voluntary environmental management standards crafted by the International Standards Organization, represents one international attempt to standardize the requirements for certification of good environmental practice.

When allegations of a potentially actionable environmental risk are raised from the community, a process must be established to verify and validate the claims. Lodging a complaint does not ensure its validity. The organization that receives the complaint may be the regulatory authority, a court, or perhaps a special commission that is responsible for judging the claims. Its function is to determine whether the party bringing the claim has met the required burden of proof.

Disseminating the Information

For a disclosure strategy to work, the necessary information must reach the pollutees in a usable form. This step may be automatically satisfied by information provided by the community itself, but not for information produced by the government or the polluter.

Transparency is the key to ensuring the availability of useful information.[13] In practice this means that the information must be in a form that can be used by the community, and the community must have access to it.[14]

Information disclosure can either be voluntary or mandatory. In a well-known voluntary system, organic farmers identify themselves as 'green producers', subject to certification procedures. Since disclosure is voluntary, conventional farms have no obligation to list the types and amounts of the pesticides used. On the other hand, most community right-to-know approaches (such as the Toxic Release Inventory described below) require all firms to provide emission information.[15]

For complaints against public officials, private enforcers will have the necessary information only if the relevant decision processes are open to public scrutiny. For example, community leaders may wish to ensure that environmental impact assessments filed by developers comply with procedural requirements and are truthful. Timely access to the assessments is especially important, since nearly completed projects are difficult to enjoin.[16]

Monitoring of polluters is a prerequisite for initiating complaints against them. In most cases polluters themselves report their emissions to the authorities. Transparency is ensured when the mandated periodic reports are accessible to the public. When publicly available, they can be used by private enforcers as the basis for raising non-compliance claims.[17]

Acting on the Information

Once the information is generated about an environmental risk, the next step is to define what can be done with it. The options range from letting the information generate its own pressure through preexisting channels to establishing new channels for pressure to be applied.

Existing channels can be used in many different ways.

- In the *product market*, consumers may choose less environmentally harmful products when effective information makes the choices clear. In addition to the obvious case where consumers may be directly harmed by the product (such as pesticides), this channel can be used by consumers who choose green products such as chlorine-free paper, even if they are not directly harmed by the pollution. Product market effects are enhanced when large buyers (large chains or the government, for example) decide to include environmental considerations in their purchasing decisions.

- In the *capital market*, owners of shares of common stock in polluting firms may decide to invest in companies with a 'greener' record, either for moral reasons or because they believe that environmentally benign firms will ultimately face fewer clean-up costs and will therefore be more competitive. Some evidence suggests that green firms may have higher rates of return.[18] The ability of investors to make these choices has been facilitated by the rise of green mutual funds, which screen firms using well-defined environmental performance criteria. In the Netherlands, the government subsidizes green funds by exempting their income from taxation.

- In the *labour market*, environmentally responsible employers may find it easier to hire employees, and to retain employee loyalty. This could be because employees perceive that such employers are likely to be more financially stable over the long run, or because they have a moral preference for supporting green activities with their labour.

- In the *legislature*, when existing regulation seems inadequate, the information may build community support for additional legislation.[19]

- In the *judicial system*, parties directly harmed by the pollution may seek redress through a variety of channels.

  - Victims can recover compensatory damages by suing polluters (these are called 'tort law' actions).

– Judicial oversight actions can be brought against public enforcement authorities that are not fulfilling their statutory responsibilities.[20] The results of these judicial actions can also be made available to the public.

– Citizens can use the information to assert their legal right to a clean environment. Following the United Nations Conference on the Human Environment at Stockholm in 1972, many countries incorporated environmental considerations into their constitutions. These *constitutional principles* generally hold that the State and all its citizens are responsible for environmental protection; all humans have the right to a healthy environment; the State and all citizens must foster development that is environmentally appropriate. Some constitutions, like those of Colombia, Ecuador and Chile, establish the right of people to live in an unpolluted environment. As a result of these constitutional provisions, the right to a clean and safe environment has become a fundamental right for each individual, enforceable through judicial action.

– The public can be given certain enforcement powers to act on the disclosure directly. *Private enforcement actions* differ from more conventional liability actions because their initiators are not seeking compensation for pollution-related damages. Rather, the private enforcers are seeking to bring non-complying polluters into compliance, or to prevent pollution that is perceived as violating individual rights to a clean environment. Private enforcement actions can either be *direct* ('citizen suits', in which private enforcers bring claims before the judiciary on their own behalf) or *indirect* ('complaint actions', in which enforcers are only allowed to file complaints with a designated legal authority).[21]

SELECTED FUNCTIONING PROGRAMMES

Practical application of these principles can be illustrated by reference to some representative programmes.

The Toxic Release Inventory Program

The Toxic Release Inventory (TRI) was enacted by the US Congress in January 1986 as a part of the Emergency Planning and Community Right-to-Know Act (EPCRA). It is designed to provide information to the public on

Table 4.1   TRI releases, 1988–94

	1988	1992	1993	1994	1988–1994	Change %
Total facilities	21 046	22 593	21 938	21 336	+290	1.38
Total forms	66 571	70 238	68 567	66 777	+206	0.31
	Pounds	Pounds	Pounds	Pounds	Pounds	%
Total air emissions	2 252 904 433	1 560 000 713	1 385 442 978	1 340 980 491	–911 923 942	–40.48
Surface water	176 726 741	195 589 595	203 003 168	47 011 773	–129 714 968	–73.40
Underground injection	625 967 221	366 495 726	294 846 947	306 651 731	–319 315 490	–51.01
On-site land releases	480 451 877	327 557 956	274 062 285	282 267 922	–198 183 955	–41.25
Total releases	3 536 050 272	2 449 643 990	2 157 355 378	1 976 911 917	–1 559 138 355	–44.09

Source: EPA (1994).

releases of toxic substances into the environment. Most of the substances involved are not themselves subject to release standards.

TRI states that firms that *use* 10 000 pounds or more of a listed chemical in a given calendar year, or firms which *import, process or manufacture* 25 000 pounds or more of a listed chemical must file a report on each of the chemicals in existence within the plant if they also have ten or more full-time employees.

Reporting of emissions or use of listed chemicals is accomplished annually. The reports include such information as the name of the company, name of the parent company if it exists, toxic release and frequency of release, as well as the medium in which the chemical is released.[22] The information is available to the public. Firms must also separately report emissions to their state and local authorities as well as to fire and emergency officials. Whether the data supplied by these reports meet the reliability standard described above is not clear.

According to these reports, has TRI reduced toxic emissions into the environment? Apparently it has. According to official EPA data, total releases are down by a bit over 44 per cent since the programme's inception (Table 4.1). However, this does not necessarily imply that toxic risk has also declined by 44, since risk factors for different toxins can differ by orders of magnitude.

The 33/50 Program

To complement and reinforce the TRI Program, the EPA initiated the 33/50 Program in February 1991. This programme set national goals of 33 per cent reduction in 17 priority toxic chemicals by 1992, and 50 per cent reduction by 1995. The reductions were to be achieved voluntarily by programme participants,[23] and compliance with the guidelines was to be measured using the TRI reports. The programme emphasizes pollution prevention rather than end-of-pipe control.

The initial invitation list, which contained the names of 555 companies with substantial chemical releases, was subsequently expanded to 5000. Some 1300 corporations ultimately signed up to participate in the 33/50 Program. Participants collectively reduced their emissions by more than 50 per cent, a total of 757 million pounds of pollutants, by 1994 – a year ahead of schedule.

Proposition 65

Proposition 65 was established in the state of California by popular vote in November of 1986, after the inception of the Toxic Release Inventory by the

EPA. Prop. 65 requires companies producing, using or transporting one or more of 480 listed chemicals to notify those who are potentially affected. Chemicals are listed as carcinogenic or causing reproductive harm. When their use or potential exposure levels exceed unacceptable risk thresholds established by a group of approved scientists, the affected people must be notified. The risk threshold is uniquely determined for each chemical and depends upon its intrinsic potency or the potency of a released mixture.

Notification (by means of warning labels) must be placed on all products that will cause adverse health effects when used for a prolonged period of time. Notification must also be made by a company whose toxic emissions to air, ground or water exceed levels deemed safe for prolonged exposure.[24]

The third form of notification involves workers in the plant emitting the toxins. Workers must be warned of the potential danger if toxic chemicals defined by Prop. 65 are used in manufacturing a product or created as a by-product of manufacturing.

Only companies with ten or more full-time workers are required to notify endangered people of exposure. Non-profit organizations like hospitals, recycling plants and government organizations, which account for over 65 per cent of California's pollution, are not required to comply with Prop. 65.

Under the Proposition, private citizens, other industry members and environmental groups can sue companies that fail to notify people of exposure in an appropriate fashion. Plaintiffs who make a successful legal claim get to keep a substantial portion of the settlement; this encourages private enforcement of the law and reduces government monitoring. Industry members also have a strong incentive to monitor each other, so that one company does not cheat and look greener than its rivals.

EPA Audit Policy

What incentives can the government provide for encouraging the discovery of private environmental information? One possibility is to apply weaker sanctions to firms reporting environmental problems before they are detected by the regulators. On 22 December 1995, USEPA implemented an ambitious new policy which reduces, but *does not* waive, fines for non-compliant companies that audit themselves and promptly disclose and correct their own violations (60 Fed. Reg. 66706). USEPA believes that such audits should be made public. About 100 companies had taken advantage of the EPA programme by February of 1997 (*Greenwire*, 18 February 1997).

As of 1997, 24 states had passed similar measures and 16 states were actively considering them (*Greenwire*, 14 August 1997). Achieving the right balance between sticks and carrots has not been easy. For example, some states have carried positive incentives beyond EPA's 'comfort zone' by granting *immunity* from prosecution rather than reduced fines to firms which disclose and correct their own violations.[25]

Despite these problems, data provided by the EPA show that the Audit Policy is having some effect on corporate behaviour. One hundred and five companies have disclosed violations at more than 350 facilities under the policy. EPA has already settled matters with 40 companies and 48 facilities, waiving all penalties in most cases. In some cases even criminal penalties have been waived.[26]

Private Enforcement Actions

Increasingly, provisions for better environmental information also give citizens the right to submit environmental complaints to administrative or judicial boards.[27] In Latin America and the Caribbean, for example, complaints are frequently triggered by perceived violations of regulatory procedures or citizens' environmental rights, not by failure to comply with specific legal discharge standards. In the US and Europe, actions are more commonly related to the latter.[28]

Administrative actions may result in the imposition of civil penalties, the creation of compliance orders or both. Successful negotiations between control authorities and violators typically produce consent decrees, which create compliance schedules and/or provide for the collection of civil penalties. Civil penalties may be imposed to eliminate the economic benefit from noncompliance. Sometimes citizens who initiate actions even receive monetary rewards, although that is currently the exception rather than the rule.[29]

At the next level, private enforcers may be empowered to do more than raise complaints.[30] Citizens empowered as private attorneys-general are authorized to initiate civil proceedings against any polluter violating the terms of its pollution permit. In the US these proceedings may be initiated by any 'person', defined as an 'individual, corporation, partnership, association, state, municipality, political subdivision of a state and any agency department or instrumentality of the US or any officer, agent or employee thereof'.[31]

Under several US statutes, citizens may sue for appropriate civil penalties as well as an injunction against pollution. Civil penalties are calculated to remove any 'significant economic benefits' from non-compliance with federal environmental statutes.

With only a few exceptions, under the American Rule each party in a court case must bear its own litigation expenses. The 'private attorney-general' approach, created during the 1970s, extends the common benefit approach by allowing reimbursement for actions performed in the general public interest. Otherwise, the courts have ruled, few people would have an incentive to protect the public good. Congress has affirmed this approach by including attorney fee reimbursement procedures in the citizen suit provisions of the environmental statutes (Jordan, 1987).

Citizen groups are only reimbursed for successful or partially successful claims. When an action is proved to be harassing or frivolous, attorney fee awards can also be made to the defendants. That is apparently a rare occurrence.

Indonesia's Public Disclosure Program[32]

Indonesia's regulatory structure for controlling pollution is weak due to budget constraints, staffing deficiencies and corruption in the judicial system. Faced with a growing industrial sector in the mid 1990s, Indonesia's National Pollution Control Agency (BAPEDAL) decided to initiate a programme called PROPER (Program for Pollution Control, Evaluation and Rating), which would rate and publicly disclose the environmental performance of Indonesian factories.

Indonesia has chosen a single-index approach to the provision of information. Under this approach BAPEDAL compiles raw pollution information and aggregates it into a single, easy-to-interpret colour rating for environmental performance.

- A *black* rating is assigned to factories that have made no attempt to control pollution and are causing serious damage.
- A *red* rating is assigned to factories that have some pollution control, but fall short of compliance with national regulatory standards.
- A *blue* rating is assigned to factories that are in compliance with national regulatory standards.
- A *green* rating is assigned to factories whose emissions control and environmental management procedures significantly exceed those needed for compliance.
- A *gold* rating is reserved for world-class performers, those that rank among the cleanest plants of that type anywhere in the world.

In the pilot phase of PROPER, 187 plants were rated. When the programme was officially launched in June 1995, only the names of the five green plants were publicly announced. The 121 plants rated as red or black were privately notified and given until December 1995 to improve their performance. Full disclosure was implemented on 29 December; the pilot phase results are displayed in Table 4.2.

These data suggest that PROPER's short-term impact in the below average category has been substantial. Before full disclosure in December, half the black plants made successful efforts to upgrade their status, along with a

Table 4.2 *Indonesia disclosure programme (number of firms in each classification category, various dates)*

Colour	June 1995	December 1995	September 1996
Gold	0	0	0
Green	5	4	5
Blue	61	72	94
Red	115	108	87
Black	6	3	1

Source: Data provided by the World Bank.

substantial number of red plants. By September 1996, only one plant remained black, and red plants had fallen by 24 per cent. No short-term impact is observable in the overcompliance range, but this is not surprising. Attaining green or gold status will require longer-term investments, while rapid installation of basic abatement equipment can be sufficient to escape from a black rating.

Has PROPER been expensive? A *very* conservative estimate is provided by the programme's first 18 months of operation. This estimate is overly conservative for two reasons. First, most of the expenses were devoted to reorganization and upgrading of BAPEDAL's monitoring, data processing and technical analysis capabilities – all costs which would have been incurred for implementation of *any* effective pollution control programme, whether command and control or market based. Appropriately imputed costs for PROPER would actually be determined at the margin by applications of the ratings methodology to existing data and public dissemination of the results. Obviously, these would be far lower than the full costs of agency upgrading. Second, during the first 18 months, all parties were high on the learning curve and technical assistance was provided by expensive foreign consultants. Since then, the PROPER team has operated independently of foreign assistance.

The conservative cost estimate is indeed sobering – because it is so small. For the first 187 plants, fully accounted administrative costs of about $100 000 were sufficient to reduce biochemical oxygen demand (BOD) emissions by approximately 40 per cent. The implied cost is about $535/plant for 18 months: about $360/year, or $1/day. Other benefits have included a sharp improvement in BAPEDAL's general performance, as the new information-handling standards have taken hold, and a much higher level of credibility with industry, NGOs and the general public. Recalling that the previous regime was almost totally ineffective, it is difficult to avoid the conclusion that PROPER has been very successful in improving environmental performance at very low public cost.

As PROPER becomes better known, the concept is spreading. The Philippines' Department of Environment and Natural Resources (DENR) has begun a public disclosure programme called EcoWatch which is similar to Indonesia's PROPER. The programme started in 1997, when President Ramos publicly introduced EcoWatch accompanied by the leaders of around 20 Philippines business associations. The associations signed an agreement with DENR to support EcoWatch by providing information for programme development and encouraging participation by members (*Manila Bulletin*, April 1997 as cited in http://www.worldbank.org/NIPR/comrole.htm/ecowatch). In June 1998, President Ramos initiated public disclosure by publicly congratulating the recipients of the first blue awards. After a change in administration, the new government has reaffirmed its support for EcoWatch and announced its intention to expand the programme.

Mexico and Colombia are also beginning similar programmes. The Mexican programme, called PEPI (Public Environmental Performance Index) will use pollution reports generated by the new national environmental licensing programme. Colombia plans to use data generated by its new water pollution charge programme to rate and publicly disclose the environmental performance of polluters.

Green Electricity Pricing[33]

As of 1997, 13 electric utilities in the United States had adopted some form of green pricing. Under a green pricing scheme the customer is asked to pay a premium of up to 15 per cent of the normal bill.[34] In return the utility uses renewable energy sources according to a set formula.

Surveys consistently reveal that from 56 per cent to 80 per cent of respondents indicate a willingness to pay more for environmentally friendly energy sources. Green pricing attempts to tap this willingness to pay as a means of financing renewable energy sources that are not quite cost effective. (The cost-effective sources would presumably be added to the mix even without green pricing.)

Green pricing provides an example of a voluntary information disclosure strategy. Utilities prepared to offer green options to consumers can advertise that fact, but other utilities are under no obligation to follow suit.

EMPIRICAL ANALYSIS

The literature on economic analysis of disclosure strategies is rather young, but it does contain some useful, if partial, information.

Doyle *et al*. (1990)

In the early stages of this study, a review of the literature on risk communication and self-protective behaviour found that traditional information and awareness programmes (such as advertising campaigns and public service announcements) are likely to fail when they are targeted at the general population.

- To test this hypothesis for radon, the study sent a mail survey to 920 households that had purchased radon test kits as part of an intensive information and awareness campaign in the Washington, DC area. Over 100 000 test kits were purchased as a result of the campaign. Although about 33 000 homes in this area exceeded the EPA action level for radon by a factor of five or more (with a radon reading of 20 picocuries per litre or higher), the survey results indicated that *only 1.2 per cent of this group had taken convincing remedial action as a result of the campaign*. In addition, only about a third of the homes in this 1.2 per cent group conducted a post-mitigation retest to confirm that mitigation had been effective.
- In contrast, a separate telephone survey of 303 home buyers in Boulder County, Colorado found that over 40 per cent of recently purchased homes were tested for radon gas at the time of home sale, and that this testing was often motivated by information provided by the realtor. Even though no intensive information and awareness campaign has been conducted in Colorado, and no state laws currently apply to radon, *54 per cent of tested homes in the sample that had radon levels above the EPA action level underwent mitigation (with 87 per cent of those completing follow-up testing) as part of the home sale transaction*.

The authors attribute this difference to powerful economic incentives which apply at the point of home sale. Such targeted information appears to elicit much more action than information directed at the general population.[35]

Magat and Viscusi (1992)

This was among the first studies to examine the potential role of hazard warnings. Through a series of carefully defined experiments, the authors attempted to estimate not only the value of hazard warnings, but also how their structure might influence their effectiveness. Their results suggest several conclusions.

- Consumers did react to warning labels, and their reactions implied significant perceived benefits.
- Information overload is a potentially serious problem. Because of cognitive limitations, the marginal cost of complete information will generally exceed the marginal benefit of providing it. As information increases, marginal benefits may even become negative because confusion increases.
- Making information available to consumers is insufficient to guarantee that they will respond. The information must be organized for efficient processing. Label design matters.[36]

Arora and Cason (1996)

Using an econometric model, the authors assess the factors that influence a firm's decision to participate in EPA's 33/50 Program. Their study draws the following conclusions.

- The largest firms with the greatest toxic releases are the most likely to participate in this voluntary programme.
- There is no evidence that firms free ride on emission reductions prior to the programme's initiation, or that they participate to divert attention from poor compliance with mandatory regulations.
- Firms in industries that are closer to final consumers (proxied by normalized advertising expenditures) are more likely to participate in the programme.

Naysnerski and Tietenberg (1992)

The information used in this analysis included data on 1205 citizen actions: plaintiffs, defendants, filing dates for notices and/or complaints, penalties and statutes involved in the claim. The analysis examined the effects of various incentives on the types of claims filed. The following conclusions emerged from this study.

- Disclosure plays a key role in determining the effectiveness of private enforcement, since the disclosed information is the basis for bringing the actions. The effectiveness of citizen suits has been greatly affected by the magnitude of the burden of proof environmental groups are forced to bear. Proof of violation is relatively easy to establish under the Clean Water Act because regulated firms are required to file publicly available Discharge Monitoring Reports. Lacking the government's power to conduct on-site inspections, citizen groups are heavily dependent on these self-monitoring reports.

- The effectiveness of the citizen suit process is affected to a large degree by the incentives offered private enforcers in the programme. In particular, allowing private enforcers to extract penalties which are earmarked for environmental improvement, and to be reimbursed for legal expenses, increases the attractiveness of the process for private enforcers.
- For one class of polluters, public facilities, citizen suits seem a distinctly superior form of enforcement.
- Since citizen suits are typically based on proving non-compliance with specific effluent/emission standards, determining that citizen suits have led to greater compliance does not necessarily indicate that they have led to greater cost-effectiveness. Complete compliance is not necessarily cost effective if the effluent/emission standards are not themselves cost effective.
- Since the evidence suggests that private enforcers respond to specific incentives, a bias will be created if the incentives are not applied uniformly to the various pollutants. Those programmes that reward private enforcers will be preferred, whether or not they address the most serious problems.

This study suggests that coupling disclosure with private enforcement can be effective, but efficiency depends on programme design.

Muoghalu, Robison and Glascock (1990)

This study examined the capital market impacts of hazardous waste mismanagement lawsuit filings and settlements for the 1977–86 period. The sample contained 128 initial lawsuits against firms and 74 case settlements that were announced in the print media (generally the *Wall Street Journal*).

- Though significant results were obtained for the day of the announcement, no significant results were obtained for the two control periods: from two to five days *prior to* and one to five days *after* the announcement.
- The results indicate that stockholders suffered, on average, a statistically significant loss in market value of 1.2 per cent at the *filing* of the lawsuit, but no significant abnormal returns at the *disposition* of the suit.

Laplante and Lanoie (1994)

This study examines the capital market effects on Canadian firms of some 47 announcements of environmental events, including environmental regulation violations (12), initiation of legal action (9), settlement of suits (13) and investments in emissions control (13) during the period 1982–91. Their findings are:

- Announcements of incidents and the filing of lawsuits did not trigger any significant abnormal stock market returns.
- Announcements of suit settlements that resulted in fines resulted in a decline in value of about 2 per cent.
- Announcements of investments in emissions control equipment resulted in an abnormal loss on the day of the announcement of about 1.2 per cent.

These results contrasted with those for American firms in Muoghalu, Robison and Glascock (1990), who found that the American stock market reacted to the initiation of a lawsuit. The authors attribute the difference to less credible enforcement of environmental regulations in Canada; Canadian investors were apparently only influenced by the outcome.

Badrinath and Bolster (1996)

This article examines stock market reactions to 730 EPA judicial actions for a sample of publicly traded firms from 1972 to 1991.

- The market value of the average affected firm dropped 0.43 per cent during the week of settlement.
- While high relative fines appear to have affected stock market prices, the analysis uncovered no consistent relationship between the magnitude of relative fines and prices.
- The estimated market penalty was larger for more recent actions and for repeat offenders.

The authors note that, while these results reflect an environment that does not promote public information about enforcement actions, they do suggest substantial social benefits from providing more systematic information.

Hamilton (1995)

This event study uses data on 436 publicly traded companies to ascertain whether stock prices were affected by the announcement of emissions information by the Toxic Release Inventory. The results are complemented by a study of media coverage of TRI announcements in 1989.[37]

- Holding emissions constant, news stories about firms were negatively related to the dispersion of their pollution across facilities, and to the amount of public information about their pollution patterns prior to TRI disclosure.
- Most of the publicly traded firms in the sample did not receive any coverage of their TRI releases in the print sources traced by the study.
- For those companies which reported TRI data to the EPA, the average abnormal return on the day the information was made public was negative and statistically significant.
- These effects were smaller for firms where investors had previous information about pollution patterns (such as companies with exposure at Superfund sites).

This study suggests that disclosure does have stock market impacts, but the magnitude of the impacts depends on the treatment of the disclosure by the press and how much knowledge investors already have.

Konar and Cohen (1997)

Comparing the 40 firms with the largest abnormal reductions in stock prices to a control group of otherwise similar firms, this analysis finds:

- The top 40 firms were among the top one third of polluting firms (per dollar revenue) in their industries, but did not necessarily have the largest emissions.
- The top 40 firms subsequently reduced their emissions more than other firms in the industry (including those firms with the largest TRI reported emissions/revenue prior to the TRI disclosure).
- The top 40 firms made more significant attempts to improve their environmental performance by reducing the number and severity of oil and chemical spills.
- The top 40 firms had a lower likelihood of large fines from the government in subsequent years.

This study suggests that stock market effects are ultimately translated into real environmental improvements.

Khanna *et al.* (1997)

This study also examines stock market and waste management responses to TRI disclosure, but in this case the sample period is 1990–94 and the focus is on the chemical industry.

- Chemical firms incur statistically significant losses in market value during the one-day period following the disclosure of the Toxic Release Inventory.
- These losses have a significant negative impact on subsequent on-site releases and a significant positive impact on wastes transferred off-site for recycling and treatment, but their impact on total toxic wastes generated by the firms is negligible.

The key aspect of this study was its deeper analysis of the changes in environmental behaviour that followed the capital market effects of disclosure. TRI disclosure promoted a reduction in on-site releases and off-site recycling, but it did not encourage pollution prevention.

Khanna and Damon (1997)

This paper examines the motivations for participating in the voluntary 33/50 Program and its implications for toxic releases. It demonstrates that benefits due to potentially avoided costs of liabilities and compliance provide strong incentives for participation.

- After controlling for sample selection bias and the impact of other firm-specific characteristics, the paper shows that programme participation led to a statistically significant decline in toxic releases over the period 1991–93.
- Participation also had a statistically significant negative impact on the short-run profits of firms, but it had a positive and statistically significant affect on market value, indicating that investors expected costs of participating to be more than offset by lower future environmental liabilities.

Dasgupta and Wheeler (1996)

This study examines environmental complaints lodged in China by citizens over the 1987–93 period to discover the factors that seem to explain the number of complaints. The results indicate:

- The incidence of complaints mirrors abatement benefits and the intensity of exposure for visible pollutants, although this is not true for less visible pollutants with similar risk.
- Regions with higher education levels tend to initiate many more complaints, all other things being equal. This implies that a reliance on complaints alone would result in inappropriately low allocation of inspection resources to less educated, relatively 'silent' regions.

This study raises the possibility that complaint processes may be biased against poorer and less educated communities. It reflects the findings of several studies that suggest that richer, better-educated communities in developing countries control pollution more effectively, through formal regulation or informal pressure.[38]

Dasgupta, Laplante and Mamingi (1997)

This event study for developing countries parallels earlier studies for the US and Canada. It focuses on stock market reactions to environmental news in Argentina, Chile, Mexico and the Philippines. None of these countries has a strong record of enforcing environmental regulations. However, the study finds that:

- Stock values rise when good environmental performance is publicly recognized by the government.
- Stock values fall in response to publicized citizens' complaints about polluters.
- Environmental news seems to induce much greater valuation changes in these emerging markets than in North American stock markets.

Dasgupta, Hettige and Wheeler (1998)

This survey-based econometric analysis controls for many determinants of environmental performance in Mexican factories, including differences between firms that are publicly traded and privately held.

- Other things equal, the results indicate significantly better performance for plants owned by publicly traded firms.
- Furthermore, the results suggest that environmental performance is improved by exposure to public scrutiny in developing countries, as well as in industrial economies.

SUMMARY AND CONCLUSIONS

The information that we have in hand at this point is too sketchy to allow us to draw firm conclusions. It is possible, however, to generate some hypotheses which are consistent with the available evidence. If and when these hypotheses are upheld by other studies, they could form a basis for both understanding information approaches and for enhancing their effectiveness.

Overall Effectiveness

- Disclosure strategies can be effective in motivating environmental improvement. However, the form of disclosure seems to be critical.
Disclosure of overall performance seems to encourage pollution abatement, while focusing only on some pollutants may simply result in
substitution toward undisclosed forms of pollution.

- When information disclosure is coupled with voluntary compliance
programmes, the evidence suggests that the largest firms with the
greatest emissions are the most likely to participate. No evidence suggests that firms free ride on emission reductions prior to the programme's
initiation, or that they participate to divert attention from poor compliance with mandatory regulation. In other words voluntary compliance
programmes can result in real, not merely reported, environmental
improvement.

- For one class of polluters, public facilities, combining disclosure with
the empowerment of private enforcers has apparently been more effective than traditional public enforcement.

- Public announcements do seem to affect stock market valuations of
firms, but these effects seem lower for known polluters. The different
results for Canada and the US suggest that the enforcement culture
may determine whether it is the initiation of the action or the final
settlement that affects value. In the new stock markets of Latin America
and Asia, public announcements have strong effects on firms' valuation
despite the weakness of formal regulation.

- Large declines in stock market value seem to motivate firms to improve their environmental performance.

- The green pricing information suggests that at least some consumers
are willing to pay higher prices for products with lower environmental
impact, even when the consumers are not directly affected by the
pollution.

- Public disclosure has significantly reduced pollution in a variety of
settings (for example, TRI in the US; PROPER in Indonesia). In the
case of PROPER, at least, abatement has been induced at very low
public cost. However, the evidence on the *cost-effectiveness* of these
programmes remains sparse. Promotion of compliance with inappropriate regulatory standards is not generally cost effective, of course.
On the other hand, public disclosure can facilitate a diversity of local
solutions to pollution problems which no formal regulatory system
(market-based or otherwise) could encompass. New measurement strategies may be necessary for rigorous cost-effectiveness analysis in this
context.

The Determinants of Effective Strategies

- The quality and quantity of information conveyed can have a large impact on the effectiveness of the programme. However, too much information can produce cognitive overload and lower the effectiveness of disclosure. The form in which information is conveyed seems to matter a great deal.
- The US experience with provision of radon information to homeowners suggests that a targeting strategy can have a strong impact on programme effectiveness.
- Incentives created by complementary aspects of disclosure programmes can also be important. Private enforcers, for example, seem to respond to incentives such as earmarking penalties for environmental improvement and the reimbursement of legal costs. Also important is the burden of proof environmental groups are forced to bear in bringing claims against polluters. Properly designed disclosure strategies can lower this burden of proof significantly.

Biases in Disclosure Strategies

- Firms in industries that are closer to final consumers (proxied by normalized advertising expenditures) are more likely to participate in voluntary compliance programmes that are accompanied by disclosure.
- Complaint processes seem to reflect damages for visible pollutants, but not for less visible pollutants.
- Complaint processes seem to work quite well in areas with relatively high income and education levels, but they work less well in poorer areas with lower education levels.
- Although citizen suits have apparently led to greater compliance, greater compliance does not necessarily guarantee greater cost-effectiveness. Complete compliance is not necessarily cost effective if the effluent standards are not themselves cost effective.
- Since the evidence suggests that private enforcers respond to specific incentives, their actions against polluters will be biased toward high-incentive problems, whether or not these are the most serious for public welfare.

Remaining Questions

The current level of evidence provides no guidance on whether disclosure strategies are producing efficient outcomes or not. The fact that they are effective does not necessarily mean that they are efficient. Reaching that conclusion requires much better information than we currently have on both the marginal benefits and marginal costs of information provision strategies. We currently do not have enough information to begin to assess where the next investments in information provision should be made. Important questions for future research include:

- Do these investments in the provision of information yield rates of return that compare favourably with other pollution control policy investments or not? First-round results from PROPER suggest an excellent rate of return, but more work is necessary.
- Which types of information provision yield the highest rates of return?
- What form should the disclosure take? Under what circumstances might highly aggregated and structured information (as in the Indonesia programme) be preferred to the provision of more raw data (as with the Toxic Release Inventory)? When might the provision of raw data be preferred?
- How cost effective are various channels of information provision (for example, newspaper articles, internet)?
- Are there diminishing returns to the provision of information as the number of substances and circumstances covered by disclosure increases? Does the public become saturated?
- Does the effectiveness of disclosure diminish over time as it becomes a more common form of regulation?
- What are the distributional implications of information strategies?

ACKNOWLEDGEMENTS

The authors are indebted to H. Landis Gabel, Robert U. Ayres and Howard Kunreuther for helpful comments.

NOTES

1. I was one of those who was quick to dismiss it (see Tietenberg, 1992).
2. The Environmental Protection Agency has estimated that between 5000 and 20 000 lung cancer deaths per year in the United States can be attributed to exposure to radon gas. This colourless, odourless gas (a product of natural radioactive decay) tends to enter homes from the ground or through the water supply.
3. The USEPA has also estimated that more than 1.7 million American children under the age of six have unsafe blood-lead levels, making lead poisoning a significant environmental health hazard for young children. Most of those children are poisoned by deteriorated lead-based paint and the contaminated soil and dust it generates. Children with too much lead in their bodies can experience lowered IQ, reading and learning disabilities, impaired

hearing and other problems. More than 80 per cent of the US housing stock built before 1978 – some 64 million residences – is estimated to contain lead paint.

4. In the case of sales transactions, home buyers can also request up to ten days to conduct a lead-based paint risk assessment or inspection at their own expense prior to finalizing a sales contract. The new requirements apply to sales and rentals of residences built before 1978, the year the sale of residential lead-based paint was banned. Specific notification and right-to-know language must be included in the contract or lease, along with signed statements from all parties verifying that the requirements have been met.

5. For the analysis behind the radon standard see Marcinowski and Napolitano (1993).

6. In principle one such outside force could be liability law. If producers are held liable for the pollution damages caused by their products, they will have an incentive to balance the expected liability costs against the costs of controlling the pollution. In practice, however, this channel does not work very well. For a detailed assessment of why not see Dewees (1992).

7. Another interesting possibility would be for a competitor to supply the information, thereby diverting sales to his/her own product. One example of this involves milk. Distributors that have specifically prohibited their suppliers from milking cows injected with growth hormone advertise the absence of this hormone in their milk, thereby assigning significance to the silence of their competitors.

8. This strategy will not be sufficient if the risky chemicals are readily available to non-licensed applicators. In the US the state of Mississippi had to evacuate a record 281 households in response to the spraying of methyl parathion, a toxic farm pesticide, in hundreds of Gulf Coast homes and businesses. Five day-care centres, a motel and a restaurant were also closed. Two men face charges of spraying commercial pesticides without a licence (*Greenwire*, 18 November 1996).

9. Not all occupational risk situations, however, fit this description. In some cases the cost of taking precautions may be borne by the employer (as when special equipment is involved). In others the damage may be borne by other workers instead of, or in addition to, the worker who controls the risk. In either case no presumption of efficient behaviour can be made.

10. Unions would be expected to produce more efficient information flows since they represent many workers and can take advantage of economies of scale in the collection, interpretation and dissemination of information. Available evidence suggests that most wage premia for risk are found for unionized workers (see Viscusi, 1983).

11. MSDS are required of all chemical manufacturers and importers. Employers using such substances must obtain the relevant sheets from their suppliers and make them available to employees. These sheets contain information on the characteristics of the substance, proper handling procedures and emergency and first aid procedures.

12. This may be one area where criminal penalties are justified (see Segerson and Tietenberg, 1992).

13. In the United States the Center for Environmental Information and Statistics became operational and open to the public early in 1998. The Center provides easy access for the public to EPA's massive environmental information resources through computers and other means.

14. The Sector Facility Indexing Project (SFIP) initiated by the USEPA is a community-right-to-know and data integration pilot project that provides environmental performance data for facilities within five industrial sectors: automobile assembly, petroleum refining, pulp mills, iron and steel and primary non-ferrous metal production (aluminium, copper, lead and zinc). The ultimate goal of the SFIP is to publish information regarding each profiled facility, and provide a publicly accessible database of current information which will allow for customized data searches (62 Federal Register 19573).

15. The mandatory versus voluntary dimension is becoming an important issue in a US proposal to provide pollution information on electric utilities as part of the deregulation process. This proposal would provide consumers with information on the emissions profiles of each of the utilities from which they would be able to secure power, thereby enabling them to choose on environmental as well as economic grounds. An unresolved issue is

whether it would be sufficient to let the green utilities identify themselves, or to require all utilities to disclose their emissions profiles.

16. In practice, unfortunately, timely access may be the exception rather than the rule in many countries. In commenting on the Mexican system Alanis-Ortega (1995, p. 9) states: 'While government bodies may let you consult a document, obtaining a copy is generally more difficult. Not all offices have copy machines and most often it is prohibited to take a document out of the government office to make copies. Another limiting factor is that many government offices in Mexico do not have an organized document system, a place to store their documents that is readily available to the public or to the staff, to manage and organize such information. At times documents are not even available to the very government officials that are legally responsible for the information.'

17. For an analysis of the consequences of various rules for making regulatory information available to private enforcers see Che and Earnhart (1997).

18. A study conducted by Richard Clough of Duke University indicated that portfolios invested in 'environmentally responsible' companies generally return one to three percentage points more annually than the holdings of 'irresponsible' companies (*Investor's Business Daily*, 27 May 1997).

19. Hamilton (1997), for example, found that US legislators were more likely to vote for disclosure strategies when they had a large number of Superfund sites in their district.

20. In January 1997 France's largest water distribution company, Lyonnaise des Eaux, filed an 'unprecedented' lawsuit against the French government for failure to meet European Union directives regulating permissible nitrate levels in one of the country's rivers. Lyonnaise had been fined after Brittany residents sued the firm for supplying water that contained high nitrate concentrations. The company seeks $900 000 in compensation for damage to its reputation and for the cost of maintaining a special water-treatment plant to meet the standards (Andrew Jack, *Financial Times*, 24 January 1997).

21. Private enforcement mechanisms are currently used in both the United States and Europe to enforce environmental standards, as well as in Latin America (Tietenberg, 1996). In the US some fourteen statutes authorize citizen suits, and some thousands of claims have been initiated (Naysnerski and Tietenberg, 1992). According to Sand (1991), in Europe the number of public and private environmental complaints filed rose from about 10 in 1982 to 460 in 1989. More than half of these have been filed by private individuals or organizations.

22. Polluters must report the scientific as well as the common name for the chemical being addressed by that form, and provide a risk rating. The ratings are: immediate (acute) health hazard, delayed (chronic) health hazard, fire hazard, sudden release of pressure hazard, and reactive hazard (40 C.F.R. § 370.2).

23. Aside from good publicity, there seems to be little evidence of any other *quid pro quo* for participation. For example, participants apparently did not face diminished enforcement pressure as a result of their participation (see Arora and Cason, 1996).

24. In practice, notification on labels has sometimes been so small as to attract little attention from the consumer. Notification of community-type risks has frequently been via the classified advertisement sections of the newspapers, which few people read. An increasing body of research suggests that the form of the risk communication matters (see Magat and Viscusi, 1992).

25. In one, for example, the EPA ruled that Idaho must revise its 'controversial' environmental audit law to ensure it does not interfere with the state's authority to enforce air pollution regulations. The Idaho Audit Act grants immunity from civil and criminal penalties to companies that disclose and correct environmental problems during self audits (*Lewiston Morning Tribune*, 4 December as cited in *Greenwire*, 4 December 1997).

26. For example, in one such case, on 7 February 1996, the United States Department of Justice announced that Chiquita Brand International was not prosecuted due to its voluntary disclosure that its subsidiary, John Morrell and Company, had illegally dumped slaughterhouse waste into the Big Sioux River in Sioux Falls, South Dakota for years, and had deliberately submitted false discharge monitoring reports to conceal its crimes. John Morrell and Company and several of Morrell's corporate officials now stand convicted of

conspiracy and various Clean Water Act felonies. However, the government has declined to prosecute Chiquita, citing the parent company's voluntary disclosure and cooperation as the prime factors (http: //es. inel.gov/oeca/epapolguid.html (21 March 1997)).

27. This section draws upon Tietenberg (1996).
28. Complaint processes have also been established in both China and India. In India, for example, an environmental audit procedure has been developed for the 500 megawatt Dahanu Thermal Power project. The authorities in charge of the project distribute summaries of the results of environmental monitoring to the local community. Community groups can then check emissions against legal standards and seek redress through the courts as necessary (World Bank, 1992).
29. On 7 February 1997 EPA approved monetary awards to 20 citizens who helped the Agency take successful enforcement actions under the Clean Air Act (CAA). These were the first monetary awards given under the CAA, which authorizes EPA to make awards of up to $10 000 after an enforcement action is concluded for reporting violations or assisting the Agency in enforcement proceedings. The Agency awarded the $10 000 maximum to a citizen who helped EPA conclude a major asbestos enforcement case. The citizen learned that children were playing with bags of a powdery substance in an abandoned industrial building and, suspecting that the material was asbestos, warned the children, contacted the local air pollution control agency, and provided other information about the large quantity of asbestos improperly stored there.
30. This section is based on Naysnerski and Tietenberg (1992).
31. 42 USC 7602(e).
32. This section is based upon Afsah, Laplante and Wheeler (1996b). This paper is available on the web at http://www.worldbank.org/nipr/work_paper/1672/index.htm.
33. This section is based upon Moscovitz (1993) and Lamarre (1997).
34. Despite the fact that in Detroit Edison's Solar Currents plan customers pay an average of 14 per cent more, the programme has quickly became oversubscribed. Some 70 customers are currently on a waiting list.
35. This study was subsequently published in concise form as Fisher *et al.* (1991).
36. The USEPA is in the early stages of considering whether to require 'talking labels' on products like pesticides and herbicides. Under a proposal being circulated among interested parties, computer chips like those found in toys and greeting cards would play brief warnings when activated by a button (Mike Magner, Newhouse/*S.F. Examiner*, 31 December 1996 as cited in *Greenwire*, 31 December 1996).
37. This information was compiled from the Nexis database and the *Wall Street Journal* index for 1989.
38. See for example Pargal and Wheeler (1996), Hettige *et al.* (1996), and Hartman, Huq and Wheeler (1997).

REFERENCES

Afsah, S. and B. Laplante (1996a), 'Program-based pollution control management: the Indonesia Prokasih Program', World Bank, Policy Research Dept, Working Paper No. 1602, May.
Afsah, S., B. Laplante and D. Wheeler (1996b), 'Controlling industrial pollution: a new paradigm', World Bank, Policy Research Dept, Working Paper No. 1672.
Alanis-Ortega, Gustavo (1995), 'Private enforcement of environmental regulations: El Tamarindo in Jalisco, Mexico: A Case Study', a draft report to the Inter-American Development Bank, Washington, DC (September).
Arbeláez, T., S. Dasgupta, B. Laplante and D. Wheeler (1998), 'Colombia's pollution charge system: implementation, impact and implications: research proposal', World Bank, Development Research Group, April.

Arora, S. and T.N. Cason (1996), 'Why do firms volunteer to exceed environmental regulations? Understanding participation in EPA's 33/50 Program', *Land Economics*, **72**(4), 413–32.

Badrinath, S.G. and P.J. Bolster (1996), 'The role of market forces in EPA enforcement activity', *Journal of Regulatory Economics*, **10**(2), 165–81.

Che, Y.-K. and D. Earnhart (1997), 'Optimal use of litigation: should regulatory information be withheld to deter frivolous suits?', *Rand Journal of Economics*, **28**, 120–34.

Coase, R. (1960), 'The problem of social cost', *The Journal of Law and Economics*, **3**(October), 1–44.

Dasgupta, S. and D. Wheeler (1996), *Citizen Complaints as Environmental Indicators*, Washington, DC: World Bank.

Dasgupta, S., H. Hettige and D. Wheeler (1998), *What Improves Environmental Performance? Evidence from Mexican Industry*, Washington, DC: World Bank.

Dasgupta, S., B. Laplante and N. Mamingi (1997), *Pollution and Capital Markets in Developing Countries*, Washington, DC: World Bank.

Dewees, D. (1992), 'Tort law and the deterrence of environmental pollution', in T.H. Tietenberg (ed.), *Innovation in Environmental Policy*, Cheltenham, UK: Edward Elgar, pp. 139–64.

Doyle, J.K., Gary H. McClelland, William D. Schulze, Paul A. Locke, Steven R. Elliott, Glenn W. Russell and Andrew Moyad (1990), 'An evaluation of strategies for promoting effective radon mitigation', Washington, DC: Environmental Protection Agency.

EPA (1994), 'The 1994 TRI Data Release report', EPA pulication 745-R-96-002, available on-line at http://www.epa.gov/opptintr/tri/ttintro.htm.

Fisher, A. *et al.* (1991), 'Communicating the risk from radon', *Journal of the Air & Waste Management Association*, **41**(11), 1440–45.

Hahn, R.W. (1989), 'Economic prescriptions for environmental problems: how the patient followed the doctor's orders', *The Journal of Economic Perspectives*, **3**(2), 95–114.

Hamilton, J.T. (1995), 'Pollution as news: media and stock market reactions to the toxics release data', *Journal of Environmental Economics and Management*, **28**(1), 98–113.

Hamilton, J.T. (1997), 'Taxes, torts, and the toxics release inventory: Congressional voting on instruments to control pollution' *Economic Inquiry*, **35**(4), 745–62.

Hartman, R., M. Huq and D. Wheeler (1997), *Why Paper Mills Clean Up: Determinants of Pollution Abatement in Four Asian Countries*, Washington, DC: World Bank.

Hettige, H., M. Huq, S. Pargal and D. Wheeler (1996), 'Determinants of pollution abatement in developing countries: evidence from South and Southeast Asia', *World Development*, **24**(12), 1891–904.

Hettige, H., M. Singh, S. Pargal and D.Wheeler (1997), 'Formal and informal regulation of industrial pollution: comparative evidence from Indonesia and the United States', *World Bank Economic Review* (Fall).

Jordan, S.J. (1987), 'Awarding attorneys fees to environmental plaintiffs under a private attorney general theory', *Boston College Environmental Affairs Law Review*, **14**, 287 311.

Kennedy, P.W. *et al.* (1994), 'Pollution policy: the role for publicly provided information', *Journal of Environmental Economics and Managment*, **26**(1), 31–43.

Khanna, M. and L. Damon (1997), 'EPA's Voluntary 33/50 Program: impact on toxic releases and economic performance of firms', Environmental and Resource Economics Working Paper No. 8, Program in Environmental and Resource Economics, University of Illinois at Urbana-Champaign.

Khanna, M., W.R.H. Quimio et al. (1997), 'Toxics release information: a policy tool for environmental protection', Department of Agricultural and Consumer Economics, University of Illinois at Urbana-Champaign.

Konar, S. and M.A. Cohen (1997), 'Information as regulation: the effect of community right to know laws on toxic emissions', *Journal of Environmental Economics and Management*, **32**(1), 109–24.

Lamarre, L. (1997), 'Utility customers go for the green', *EPRI Journal*, **22**(2), 6–15.

Laplante, B. and P. Lanoie (1994), 'Market response to environmental incidents in Canada', *Southern Economic Journal*, **60**, 657–72.

Lewis, T. (1996), 'Protecting the environment when costs and benefits are privately known', *Rand Journal of Economics*, **27**(4), 819–47.

Magat, W.A. and W.K. Viscusi (1992), *Informational Approaches to Regulation*, Cambridge, MA: MIT Press.

Marcinowski, F. and S. Napolitano (1993), 'Reducing the risks from radon', *Air and Waste*, **43**, 955–62.

Moscovitz, D. (1993), 'Green pricing: why not customer choice?', *The Electricity Journal*, **6**(8), 42–9.

Muoghalu, M.I., H.D. Robison and J.L. Glascock (1990), 'Hazardous waste lawsuits, stockholder returns and deterrence', *Southern Economic Journal*, **57**, 357–70.

Naysnerski, W. and T. Tietenberg (1992), 'Private Enforcement', in T.H. Tietenberg (ed.), *Innovation in Environmental Policy*, Cheltenham: Edward Elgar, pp. 109–36.

Naysnerski, W. and T. Tietenberg (1992), 'Private enforcement of environmental law', *Land Economics*, **68**(1), 28–48.

OECD (1989), *Economic Instruments for Environmental Protection*, Paris: Organization for Economic Cooperation and Development.

OECD (1994), *Applying Economic Instruments to Environmental Policies in OECD and Dynamic Non-Member Countries*, Paris: Organization for Economic Cooperation and Development.

OECD (1995), *Environmental Taxes in OECD Countries*, Paris: Organization for Economic Cooperation and Development.

Pargal, S. and D. Wheeler (1996), 'Informal regulation of industrial pollution in developing countries: evidence from Indonesia', *Journal of Political Economy*, **104**(6), 1314.

Sand, P.H. (1991), 'International cooperation: the environmental experience', in J.T. Mathews (ed.), *Preserving the Global Environment: The Challenge of Shared Leadership*, New York: W.W. Norton, pp. 236–79.

Segerson, K. and T. Tietenberg (1992), 'The structure of penalties in environmental enforcement: an economic analysis', *Journal of Environmental Economics and Management*, **23**(2), 179–200.

Sinclair-Desgagné, B. and H.L. Gabel (1997), 'Environmental auditing in management systems in public policy', *Journal of Environmental Economics and Management*, **33**(3), 331–46.

Tietenberg, T. (1995), Design lessons from existing air pollution control systems: the United States', in S. Hanna and M. Munasinghe (eds), *Property Rights in a Social and Ecological Context: Case Studies and Design Applications*, Washington, DC: World Bank.

Tietenberg, T. (1996), *Private Enforcement of Environmental Regulations in Latin*

America and the Caribbean: An Effective Instrument for Environmental Management?, Washington, DC: Inter-American Development Bank.

Tietenberg, T.H. (1985), *Emissions Trading: An Exercise in Reforming Pollution Policy*, Washington, DC: Resources for the Future.

Tietenberg, T.H. (1990), 'Using economic incentives to maintain our environment', *Challenge*, **33**(2), 42–6.

Tietenberg, T.H. (1992), *Environmental and Natural Resource Economics*, New York: HarperCollins.

Vincent, J. (1993), 'Reducing effluent while raising affluence: water pollution abatement in Malaysia', Harvard Institute for International Development, Spring.

Viscusi, W.K. (1983), *Risk By Choice: Regulating Health and Safety in the Workplace*, Cambridge, MA: Harvard University Press.

Viscusi, W.K. (1992), *Fatal Tradeoffs: Public and Private Responsibilities for Risk*, New York: Oxford University Press.

Wang, H. and D. Wheeler (1996), 'Pricing industrial pollution in China: an econometric analysis of the levy system', World Bank, Policy Research Dept, Working Paper No. 1644, September.

World Bank (1992), *World Development Report 1992: Development and the Environment*, Washington, DC: Oxford University Press.

5. To whisper in the ears of princes: laboratory economic experiments and environmental policy

Ronald G. Cummings, Michael McKee and Laura O. Taylor

1 INTRODUCTION

Over the last decade or so there have been relatively modest efforts by environmental economists to apply the tools of experimental economics to analyses of contemporary environmental policy issues. Motivation for these efforts derives from at least two considerations. First, it is often the case that data required for assessments of policy initiatives are unavailable and field trials of an initiative are not feasible.[1] In such instances one may appeal to experimental economics. When properly designed and implemented, laboratory experiments provide a powerful, low-cost mechanism for the generation of data that can be useful for policy evaluation.

A second compelling motivation for the use of laboratory experiments is the potential 'educational' benefit that can result from the use of experiments to illustrate the effects of policy initiatives – data from experiments can be used to *demonstrate* the consequences of policy alternatives to decision makers in ways that theory cannot. Many policy makers are not trained in economic theory and empirical arguments often carry more weight than the theoretical predictions alone. Absent field data, the only alternative for empirical demonstrations is laboratory experiments. Experiments may be viewed as a means of improving the decision-making process of policy makers by providing information that would be otherwise unavailable or by furthering the evaluation of decision criteria such as benefit measurement.

As noted above, a relatively modest number of environmental economists presently include experimental methods as a part of their arsenal of analytical tools. Given that training in experimental economics has only recently begun to be a part of graduate training in many universities, this is certainly understandable. We expect to see a rapid growth in the use of experimental methods by environmental economists in future years for the following, two related reasons. First, we expect to see growing recognition by environmental economists of experimental economics' promise for the *scientific* ends of generating policy-related hypotheses and data required to test these hypotheses. Second, we expect to see growing recognition by environmental economists of experimental economics' promise for achieving the more *non-scientific* ends of demonstrating, in compelling ways, the economic efficacy of policy alternatives to policy/decision makers. Our view of the potential importance of this latter motivation for the growth in economists' use of experimental methods is reflected in this chapter's title, which draws on Roth's (1986, pp. 261–6) succinct description of experimental economics' promise for 'offer[ing] the possibility of bringing scientific methods to bear on one of the traditional non-scientific vocations of economists which is *whispering in the ears of princes* who require advice about pressing practical questions whose answers lie beyond the reliable scientific knowledge of the profession'.

Thus, this chapter has two primary purposes. We wish to provide the reader with a very brief sketch of the basic methods used in experimental economics. Perhaps most importantly, we will give emphasis to precepts concerning the design and implementation of experiments that are fundamental prerequisites for meaningful expectations that environmental economists can use experiments to provide information that materially affects public policy – that is, that environmental economists can use to take advantage of what we believe will be rich opportunities for 'whispering in the ears of princes'. Our central argument in these regards will be that acceptance of results from experimental studies by 'princes' will depend in large part on the extent to which the experimental design satisfies the condition known as 'parallelism' in ways that make field applications of the experiment reasonably transparent. These issues are taken up in section 2 of this chapter.

Our second purpose will be to use our admittedly imperfect crystal ball to the end of anticipating future environmental policy issues that, in our view, offer exceptional opportunities for applications of experimental methods. We view these future 'opportunities' as falling into three general categories: the valuation of environmental amenities/damages, which is considered in section 3; policy design issues related to incentives for compliance with environmental rules and regulations, which are considered in section 4; and finally, issues related to market-based policies and privatization are taken up in section 5. Concluding remarks are offered in section 6.

2   LABORATORY EXPERIMENTS: SURVEY AND PRESCRIPTION

General Methodological Issues

Any microeconomic system consists of basic building blocks (Smith, 1982). There is an environment consisting of economic agents and 'goods' (broadly defined to include new or changed laws and regulations). There is an institution consisting of a system of property rights, rules of exchange and payoffs. There are 'outcomes' which are determined by the behaviour of agents which in turn is determined by the interactions between the environment and the institution. The essence of experimental economics is the (usually simplified*) creation of an institution*, the explicit *control of agents' preferences* and the observation of outcomes (agents' behaviour). A brief elaboration of these essential components of an economic experiment may be helpful to the reader.

The control of agents' preferences is accomplished by the use of what is referred to as 'induced preferences'. Preferences are 'induced' by a process in which the experimenter fixes the value or cost of a good for each individual agent. For example, for a 'good' which has no intrinsic value (a common requirement for experiments[2]) the 'value' of the good to a buyer is established by the experimenter's commitment to redeem any units of the good acquired by the agent at a fixed price. The buyer-agent's income then becomes the fixed redemption price minus whatever amount he or she must pay to acquire a unit of the good. The 'cost' of a unit of the good to a seller is established by the experimenter's commitment to provide the seller with a unit of the good at a fixed price. The seller-agent's income then becomes the price received from a buyer for a unit of the good minus the cost of acquiring the unit from the experimenter. The experimenter sets the redemption price (to buyers) and the acquisition price (to sellers), thereby controlling agents' preferences.[3]

The creation of an institution involves the explicit description of all contextual aspects that may 'substantively' affect an agent's behaviour – such things as property rights, rules governing exchange and payoffs (positive and negative), and information. A simple example is seen in a double-auction experiment. The relevant environment is one in which buyer-agents and seller-agents buy and sell 'units' of a good under rules wherein: information available to each agent is limited to the agent's own values/costs and posted bids and asks; payoffs to buyer-agents are straightforward: redemption value minus price paid for each unit purchased; payoffs to seller-agents are accepted bid price less acquisition cost for each unit sold.

Setting procedural issues aside,[4] the (arguably) most critical issue concerning the design of an institution turns on the extent to which the institution used in the experiment *parallels* the real-world conditions that it is intended to simulate. If policy makers are to accept as meaningful policy analysis results from laboratory experiments, both the environment and the institution used in the laboratory must closely *and obviously* establish a relationship between conditions represented in the experiment and real-world, field conditions in which the policy is intended to operate. The greater the experimenter's desire to produce results that might influence policy, the greater must be the degree of transparency for this relationship given that policy makers are likely to be unaccustomed to high levels of abstraction.

With an appropriate environment and institution, the end result of an experiment involves observations of agent behaviour. Typically, the researcher's interest is focused on how agent behaviour is affected – how it changes – given changes in institutional parameters. For example, a rules-compliance experiment focuses on how agent behaviour (compliance with the rule) changes with changes in such things as standards, the level of resources expended for rules enforcement, and/or fines and penalties.

Parallelism: How 'Real' is 'Real Enough?'

Given that policy relevance, 'whispering in the ears of princes', is an important part of the motivation that, in our view, should give impetus to the future growth in the use of experimental methods by environmental economists, the balance of this discussion of methodological issues related to experimental economics will be centred on what we described above as the most critical issue relevant for this purpose: the parallelism issue. Parallelism is a term that refers to a 'vague notion about how observations of simple laboratory phenomena can help one understand the behaviour of a complicated and changing world' (Plott, 1987, p. 193). In the most simple terms, the parallelism issue concerns the extent to which the environment and institutions in the experimental design are 'real' in terms of characterizing in a meaningful way the complicated and changing real world that is relevant for those aspects of agent behaviour under study. Two simple examples of parallelism requirements are that experimental subjects face decision costs, commensurate with rewards, in the experiments that are like those faced by agents in the real world (the field), and that subjects are provided with information equivalent to that available to agents in the field.[5] The parallelism question which the experimenter will almost always encounter in terms of the realness of his experimental design is: *how real is real enough?*

Parallelism does not require the exact replication of the field setting in the lab. Indeed, this would defeat a major advantage of laboratory investigations, that the field is simplified so that the effects on agent behaviour from changes in particular institutional features can be identified. Thus,

Plott argues that 'While laboratory processes are simple in comparison to naturally occurring processes, they are real processes in the sense that real people participate for real and substantial profits and follow real rules in doing so. It is precisely because they are real that they are interesting' (Plott, 1982, p. 1486). Having said this, the fact remains that generalizing the results of an experiment to the real world *does* require that the realness of the experimental setting be 'real enough' *vis-à-vis* essential elements of the real world.[6]

Unfortunately, however, there is no definitive, unambiguous response to the how real is real enough question. As Friedman and Sunder (1994) note, one cannot *prove* parallelism by means of deductive reasoning. That is, repeated observations of a phenomenon are not sufficient to prove that the event will continue to occur for one more time period (their example is that the sun will rise tomorrow). Rather, one can only rely on induction as a basis for *asserting* that parallelism has been satisfied. For example, suppose that we observe behavioural regularities with a given experimental design in the lab that persist when we alter the design to more closely represent the real world – for example, when we make the stakes larger (and provide greater wealth), when we make the task more complex (and provide more decision-making resources), when we make the relevant group larger (but provide focal points for equilibrium selection), or when we make the task more complex (but provide for experience and/or training). Such observations may provide a basis for asserting that parallelism has been achieved.

There are several approaches that one might take in efforts to empirically explore the parallelism issue. One approach would be to directly compare subject behaviour in a laboratory experiment with agent behaviour in the field. This approach[7] was used by Shogren, Fox and Hayes (1999) who investigated the demand for increased food safety within the context of several institutions, which included laboratory and retail markets. Some differences in agent behaviour were identified across the alternative institutions. One interpretation of these findings is that they are consistent with a finding that a part of the authors' experimental design was 'real enough' in terms of parallelism. Additional experiments of this *genre* might be particularly productive in allaying concerns that the 'artificial' setting of the laboratory *per se* may affect subject behaviour.[8]

A second approach that might be used in efforts to explore the parallelism issue would focus on the perhaps more subtle potential effects on subject behaviour associated with what might be viewed as intrinsic, or innocuous experimental conditions (a major source of concern to Smith and Mansfield, 1998). This approach, which closely follows practices used in the natural sciences, would test the extent to which behaviour obtained with a given experimental design by one set of researchers in a given laboratory is *repli-*

cated when the design is used by other sets of researchers in different laboratories.

Experimental Methods and Parallelism: Final Remarks

It is useful at this point to recall Plott's description of the value of economic experiments: 'While laboratory processes are simple in comparison to naturally occurring processes, they are real processes in the sense that real people participate for real and substantial profits and follow real rules in doing so. It is precisely because they are real that they are interesting' (Plott, 1982, p. 1486). Thus, the bulk of what experimental methods can offer as a means for allowing the environmental economist to 'whisper in the ears of princes' derives from *simplicity*. There are those, however, who reject results obtained with such simplicity as providing meaningful insights for analyses of the efficacy of public policies.

As noted above, one can never definitively prove parallelism for any given experimental design. For those to whom only *real* is 'real enough' in terms of parallelism, there is obviously nothing to argue. But the experience of experimentalists over the last two decades suggests that such a nihilistic view is not broadly shared among many decision makers and environmental economists, and their number appears to be growing. There is and, in our view, will continue to be a growing cadre of professionals concerned with environmental policy that appreciate the fundamental contribution of experimental methods to the process of applying the scientific method to the design of environmental policies. Thus, any given experiment or set of experiments can never prove the behavioural outcome of a proposed policy. An experiment can 'only' carry the burden of the scientific process – it can only *disprove* hypothesized outcomes under a set of experimental conditions. What then of the critique that the experimental 'proof' is unreliable because of a lack of parallelism? We close this section with what, in our view, is a most succinct and appropriate response to this critique, one offered by Plott in referring to his experimental tests of a particular policy model:

> The experiments were designed to check the accuracy of that model. If the model advocated because of its generality failed to be reliable in the simple case of the experimental markets, the burden of proof would presumably rest on the advocate to explain why it did not work ... If the model performs sufficiently badly in the experiment, the burden is on the model's advocate to explain why the experiments were 'special' or 'different' from the complex case in which the model is supposed to work. (Plott, 1987, p. 205)

3 PROMISING FUTURE INTERFACES BETWEEN ENVIRONMENTAL POLICY AND EXPERIMENTAL ECONOMICS: VALUING NON-PRICED GOODS

Setting the Stage: Looking to the Future

It is often essential for benefit–cost analysis that we obtain values of goods, such as environmental amenities, that are not traded in observable markets. While it may be possible to rely on indirect methods of valuation (for example, travel cost and hedonic pricing), such methods cannot be applied to a large class of environmental 'goods' of primary interest to environmental economists. In these cases, it is typically the case that researchers rely upon a survey method – the contingent valuation (CV) method – which involves the direct elicitation of values from individuals. The CV methodology involves creating a constructed market in the minds of respondents and asking them to report the price they would be willing to pay (willing to accept) for increases (decreases) in an amenity in this constructed market. The respondent must solve two (possibly interrelated) problems: value formation and value reporting. The value formation problem requires that the survey instrument induce the respondent to contemplate the good or setting and determine a maximum willingness to pay (WTP) (or minimum willingness to accept (WTA)) for the good. This cognitive task is complex since the individual is often faced with an unfamiliar setting and must factor in other demands on the budget. The value-reporting problem requires that the respondent be induced to report a willingness to pay that corresponds to his/her 'true' underlying demand for the good.

The question as to the extent to which applications of the CV method produce what they intend to produce – unbiased measures of agents' maximum willingness to pay (accept) for an increment (decrement) of an environmental good – has been and continues to be the subject of intense and often acrimonious debate. At the centre of this debate is the issue of hypothetical bias in CV surveys, and the question remains: do people respond to a hypothetical survey *as if* budget constraints were binding? Given our concern with *future* opportunities for productive uses of experimental methods by environmental economists, we choose not to revisit this debate and invite the interested reader to refer to papers by Hanemann (1994), Portney (1994) and Diamond and Hausman (1994). In what follows, attention will be focused on new and potentially innovative lines of empirical research based on experimental methods that have, in our view, considerable potential for providing environmental economists with an increasingly compelling basis for estimating the values for non-priced environmental goods.

Using Experimental Methods for Survey Design

Until fairly recently, efforts to design CV studies that might provide unbiased estimates of value for non-priced environmental goods have been limited to efforts to develop means by which values derived with a CV study might be calibrated. For example, Blackburn *et al.* (1994) and Fox *et al.* (1998) use within-sample techniques where subjects respond to hypothetical and then real valuation questions. A calibration function is then estimated which relates differences in responses obtained in the two treatments to subject characteristics. Typically, efforts to calibrate CV values were confounded by a general finding that calibration weights estimated for one particular environmental good could not be generalized to other goods. For example, Fox *et al.* (1998, p. 2) note that 'As our results show, calibration appears to be commodity-specific, and as such, (the calibration approach) must proceed on a case-by-case basis until enough evidence exists to reveal any systematic bias that can eventually lead to a general calibration function'.[9] Without predictable, stable calibration functions, this *ex-post* approach does not hold much promise for the conduct of *ex-ante* policy analysis.

A second approach, which is *ex-ante* in nature, is to directly induce subjects to provide unbiased responses to hypothetical valuation questions. Early attempts along these lines (Loomis, Gonzalez-Caban and Gregory, 1994; Neill, 1995) attempted to remove hypothetical bias by adding to the CV script brief requests that subjects consider budgetary substitutes in responding to the valuation question. While these attempts were ineffective, recent empirical inquiries based on the use of experimental methods have been introduced which suggest potentially rich lines of future research that could substantively affect the viability and credibility of the CV method, and therefore our ability to provide decision makers with more palatable (and hopefully less controversial) measures for environmental values.

Two recent works by Cummings and Taylor (1999) and Bjornstad *et al.* (1997) suggest potential future uses of experimental methods to design CV questionnaires that result in demonstrably robust, unbiased valuation responses. Both papers use as a starting point a referendum design introduced by Cummings *et al.* (1997). They take as the 'benchmark' the voting responses elicited in the referenda that involved actual payments on the part of the subjects and modify the hypothetical referenda in such a way that they generate results that are indistinguishable from the real referenda (thus assuming the real referenda are incentive compatible). Cummings and Taylor (1999) use 'cheap talk' to discuss with subjects the issue of hypothetical bias, why it might occur and how it affects responses in surveys. Using four different public goods, and several experimental designs, they find results in the *hypothetical* referenda that included the 'cheap talk' to be indistinguishable from responses in the real-payment referenda. Similarly, Bjornstad *et al.* (1997) use a 'learning design' to allow subjects to 'learn' first hand the effects of hypothetical surveys on responses (as compared to surveys involving actual payments). Again, here they find that hypothetical surveys that were part of their learning design elicited voting responses that were not significantly different from responses to the same question asked of different samples in real-payment referenda.

A second use of laboratory experiments in CV survey design uses induced value experiments as a means for investigating the causes of behavioural regularities that have been observed in field studies. Bohara *et al.* (1998) and Neilson and McKee (1998) provide examples of how the lab may be used to investigate the causes of behavioural regularities that have been observed in field studies. Bohara *et al.* (1998) examine in a laboratory setting how changes in the amount and type of information provided in CV surveys may affect valuation responses. Their results indicated that the open-ended (OE) elicitation format generates valuation responses that are sensitive to information concerning the cost and group size while the dichotomous choice (DC) elicitation format does not. Since cost and group size information are not related to individual *valuation*, Bohara *et al.* suggest that the DC format is preferred since it yields more consistent results across information provided.[10] A second example of how the lab may be used to investigate behaviour in the CV method is seen in Neilson and McKee (1998) who use the lab to investigate the relationship between WTP and WTA. They utilize a pure induced value setting to test the hypothesis that the disparity between WTA and WTP is generated by individual uncertainty in the payoffs from having the good. Their experimental evidence confirms this hypothesis, and, contrary to previous research (Coursey, Hovis and Schulze, 1987), they find that the WTP values are biased downward and the WTA values biased upward by the uncertainty.

The Future

It is important that one understands that the research cited above as examples of means by which laboratory methods might be useful in addressing some of the vexing issues in obtaining individual valuations of non-market goods is not flawless. Most, if not all, of the experimental research that has focused on the hypothetical bias question relies on the maintained assumption that the 'real' survey is incentive compatible – that payment of stated WTP induces subjects accurately and fully to reveal their preferences, and that resulting value estimates are unbiased. This assumption then justifies the author's attribution of differences observed between the hypothetical and real surveys as a 'bias'.

This assumption can be challenged on the basis of the following argument. To the extent that subjects may have incentives to free ride in 'real' surveys, there are no compelling reasons to expect symmetrical free-riding behaviour in the hypothetical survey. Thus, 'overbidding' that is reported to occur in hypothetical surveys may in fact be *under*bidding by subjects in the real surveys. While both Cummings and Taylor (1999) and Bjornstad *et al.* (1997) attempted to avoid this problem by using referenda as a valuation mechanism, it is not clear that they were successful in these regards, given that their referenda were not *closed*. In other words, provision of the public goods used in these studies was not necessarily limited to the level that would be provided by the outcome of the specific referendum in which the particular subjects were participating. The good could be provided by sources external to the group of subjects participating in the referendum. Arguably, these conditions could invite forms of free-riding behaviour, more so (perhaps) in the real surveys than in the hypothetical surveys. Taylor (1998) provides a discussion of this issue and an empirical inquiry as to the prevalence of free riding in the open referendum. While results from this empirical inquiry suggest that the effect of the open referendum is minimal, the question remains as an open issue.

The research described above is intended to suggest directions for future experimental research that may have high payoffs for the environmental economist – research results which may indeed enhance the quality of the 'whispers' of environmental economists. The challenge for future research is to develop a mechanism for valuing public goods that can be shown to be demand revealing in real payment settings *and* which can be implemented in field-CV method conditions. Laboratory (induced value) experiments will be crucial to the development of these instruments. Only when such an instrument is designed – one that is demonstrably demand revealing in a real-payment situation – may it be tested for incentive compatibility in *hypothetical* valuation situations.

4 PROMISING FUTURE INTERFACES BETWEEN ENVIRONMENTAL POLICY AND EXPERIMENTAL ECONOMICS: REGULATORY INSTITUTIONS AND COMPLIANCE

Regulatory Compliance: Opportunities for the Environmental Economist

Many environmental policies rely upon regulatory institutions that are intended to control the behaviour of firms and individuals. Such institutions are typically characterized by regulations, sanctions for non-compliance with the regulations, and an enforcement mechanism that determines the likelihood that non-compliance on the part of any given agent will be detected. As examples, the Clean Water Act and the Clean Air Act establish standards for emissions into the air and the water, provide for specific penalties for non-compliance with these standards, and charges the US Environmental Protection Agency with the responsibility for enforcing the provisions of the Act (the probability of a non-complying entity being detected is, in turn, determined by the EPA's allocation of resources to this activity).

The scope of environmental regulations has continually expanded over the last two decades, and we have every reason to expect this expansion to continue in future years. Looking forward, past experiences will surely motivate expectations for a future characterized by expanding and changing regulatory regimes for activities such as the transportation and disposal of toxic wastes, toxic materials, the disposal (burning?) of scrap tyres, food chains, ocean disposal of all classes of materials, *ad infinitum*. We feel that these expectations suggest regulatory compliance as an area of research that will become of increasing importance to decision makers and, therefore, one that will offer the environmental economist opportunities for contributing to the process of policy design. We will argue that the substance of these contributions can be materially enhanced with the use of experimental methods *if* the challenges posed by a number of difficult parallelism problems unique to compliance issues can be effectively met.

Using Experiments to Explore the Relationship between Regulatory Policy and Compliance: the Design Challenge

Notwithstanding the scope and complexity of the present regulatory system for environmental quality, and the strong likelihood that environmental regulations will be a 'growth industry' over the next several decades, there has been little research by environmental economists that has focused on the *behavioural* aspects of compliance with environmental regulations and there appear to have been no efforts to use experimental methods for this purpose.[11] This dearth of research should not be surprising given the many difficulties that one can anticipate in the design of experiments that would meet parallelism criteria for institutions that are relevant for environmental compliance.

To clarify the experimental design challenge associated with environmental compliance, we begin with a brief consideration of the following critical aspects of an experimental design that are relevant for present discussions:

1. The relationship between agent activities and outputs which are the subject of compliance must be clearly described.
2. Means for verifying, or 'auditing', elements of 1 must closely parallel field conditions.
3. Plausible mechanisms that affect expectations for audits must parallel those extant in the field.
4. The incentive structure that drives the compliance decision must be reasonably transparent and must, again, parallel those that exist in the field.

To provide perspective for our discussions, consider the following brief discussion of experiments that have focused on issues concerning tax compliance, a set of issues for which conditions (1) through (4) are readily satisfied. Such experiments rely upon the following simplified conceptual framework. Suppose that an individual receives a fixed amount of income I, and must choose how much of I he wishes to declare to the tax authorities. Declared income D is taxed at the rate t. Unreported income is not taxed; however, the individual may be audited with probability p, at which point a fine f is imposed on each dollar of unpaid taxes. If underreporting is detected, the individual's income, I_C, equals

$$I_C = I - tD - ft(I - D) \qquad (5.1)$$

while, if underreporting is not detected that income, I_N, is

$$I_N = I - tD. \qquad (5.2)$$

The individual chooses D to maximize the expected utility $EU(I)$ of the evasion gamble, or

$$EU(I) = pU(I_C) + (1 - p)U(I_N) \qquad (5.3)$$

where utility $U(I)$ is assumed to be a function only of income. This optimization generates the first-order condition

$$pU'(I_C)(f - 1)t - (1 - p)U'(I_N)t = 0 \qquad (5.4)$$

where a prime denotes a partial derivative.

From this model, the implications of increasing enforcement (higher probability and/or fines) are easily seen. In making the compliance decision, an individual faces a portfolio choice problem, with evasion as the risky, high-return asset and disclosure as the riskless asset. By reducing the return to the risky act (non-compliance) the policy maker obtains higher compliance.[12]

Now consider typical designs for experiments intended to explore various dimensions of tax compliance behaviour within the context of conditions (1)–(4):

1′. The output of interest is income. Absent substantive reasons for expecting that how income is earned will affect the compliance decision, the experiment abstracts from the income-earning process. Income is simply 'given' to subjects in the experiment.[13]

2′. Means for auditing declared income, and therefore declared taxes, are reasonably straightforward. In the experiment, a subject's 'real' income is known in the event of an audit. In the field, the tax authorities have access to matching paperwork related to income and expenses which makes 'known' an agent's income.

3′. In the field, there are millions of taxpayers' data, which are used to develop taxpayer profiles. These profiles are used to define 'ranges' for reported incomes and expenses by class of taxpayer. These established ranges are then used as a means for 'signalling' reports that warrant an audit. Taxpayers presumably are aware of baseline probabilities of an audit and, at least in general terms, of limits to reporting beyond which the probability of an audit increases. This awareness of the chance of an audit is 'paralleled' in the tax compliance experiment by simply telling subjects the probability that their report will be audited.

4′. In the main, the incentive structure that drives the compliance decision is described by equation (5.4) given above: income (utility) maximization. Imbedded in (5.4) are considerations related to such things as risk aversion. We acknowledge the potential for compliance incentives other than income. For example, the relevance of an agent's perception of how taxes are to be used was demonstrated in a set of experiments reported by Alm, Jackson and McKee (1993).

While, as demonstrated above, parallelism between laboratory and field institutions can (arguably) be reasonably attained for tax compliance experiments, this setting obviates the problems that can attend efforts to adapt these designs to issues related to compliance with environmental regulations. The following sets out examples of some of the more important issues in these regards:

1″. The production process by which inputs result in the output 'emissions' is often very complex and, perhaps most importantly, data relevant for this process may be difficult or impossible to obtain. For experiments that meaningfully parallel the field, it will generally be necessary to include the process in which agents can directly affect emissions by changes in inputs and/or technologies. Even if they are somehow simplified, the cognitive tasks required by subjects may be excessive.

2″. In the field, auditing processes exist for large, point-source emitters such as power plants – firms are required to maintain emissions measurement equipment, results from which must be reported to the environmental manager. For smaller point-source emitters, and for the wide range of emissions that come from non-point sources, meaningful auditing processes may be problematic (Segerson and Tietenberg, 1992). Until measurement mechanisms for these classes of emissions are put into place, the role of compliance experiments will be very limited.

3″. In contrast to the tax compliance case, where data from millions of agents are available for the purpose of developing signals to drive audits (and therefore the probability of an audit), the number of agents relevant for environmental compliance will be smaller – very much smaller. There are then (to our mind) no obvious means for generating plausible information concerning the probability of an emissions audit for which a parallel might be explored in the laboratory.

4″. While sanctions related to many environmental regulations will typically be applied at the level of the firm, a firm's compliance with rules and regulations may be given parallel treatment in the laboratory as being analogous to individual compliance with tax laws. The plausibility of this treatment, in terms of parallelism, relies on the extent that we (reasonably) expect that sanctions would have implications for promotion and/or job security for the individual in the firm with responsibility for making compliance decisions. These considerations may then rationalize experiments in which the compliance decision is made operational at an individual level.

Meeting the Design Challenge for Environmental Compliance Experiments

The challenges to our ability to design meaningful, 'parallel', experiments for the exploration of environmental compliance policies described above in (1″)–(4″) are certainly formidable. Equally formidable, however, are the potential payoffs for meeting these challenges in terms of significant advancements in our ability to offer to the 'ears of princes' insights regarding effective (in terms of compliance) designs for emissions policies. We conclude this chapter with our suggestions as to how one might initiate the process of meeting these design challenges.

A place to begin this process is suggested by lessons learned from tax compliance experiments. Such experiments make clear the critical importance of effective audits for high compliance rates. More specifically, for example, we know that:

- More frequent audits encourage greater compliance, although the impact of a greater probability of detection is small and non-linear. This suggests that enforcement efforts be directed in a systematic manner rather than simply increasing the frequency of inspection.
- Related to the above, conditional audits produce higher compliance rates than purely random audits.
- Many individuals overweight the probability of audit, and so comply at higher levels than predicted by expected utility theory. This may seem irrelevant to a firm that is assumed to be risk neutral but the decision to comply is made by individuals within the firms and they may be presumed to be risk averse.

Consider then policy alternatives that can have the effect of enhancing the effectiveness of environmental audits, and how experiments might be used to assess and rationalize such policies. The Toxic Release Inventory (TRI) mandated under the Emergency Planning and Community Right-to-Know Act (1986) requires that firms in certain SIC categories provide annual statements of on- and off-site emissions (or waste generation) of a large number of toxic materials. The intent of the legislation would appear to be to provide the market (investors) with information which would allow them to form a conjecture as to the potential value of the firm. Firms with poor records of toxic releases would face downward pressure on the price of their securities and would have their access to capital compromised. In theory, it sounds like an appropriate use of the market to enforce environmental standards. Hamilton (1995) finds that stock prices do reflect announcements of releases.

The problem that arises is that firms clearly have an incentive to under-report releases. In the income tax system we rely on audits for the detection of cheats, the effectiveness of which in turn is reliant on the existence of matching paperwork. The TRI Program does not provide equivalent data that allow for a strict accounting of toxic materials. This is a materials-balance issue that can be seen in the following way. A firm receives as inputs a wide variety of materials that contain toxic materials. The question becomes: what *happens* to these toxic materials? At the end of the day, these toxic materials (i) are embodied in the product produced by the firm; (ii) have been released to the environment or are contained in waste materials that are on hand or have been disposed of; or (iii) remain in the firm's inventory of input materials. Under the TRI Program, we have no way of 'auditing' the firm's reports of (ii) because there are no provisions under which we can know (i) and (iii).

A policy alternative is then immediately suggested which would result in the generation of 'matching paperwork' akin to what we have with our tax system. Firms are required to *account* for the toxic content of materials that they receive (and for which paperwork exists) as inputs, and they must report the status or disposition of such materials as described in (i)–(iii). This information might or might not affect the likelihood of an audit; it would certainly affect the likelihood that an audit would detect unreported releases. Such a reporting system coupled with an effective audit regime would increase the likelihood that firms would report honestly and the financial markets could complete their role as mechanisms to punish malfeasant firms.[14]

Laboratory experiments could be used to explore and make explicit the impact of such a reporting scheme. One would begin with an experimental setting that parallels the present TRI setting: only releases are reported. Emissions releases (for which excesses are fined at a given rate) would be observed. One would then have to establish an institution in which the broader range of reporting described above is required, and in which audits of reports occur with some probability. Reported emissions releases under this institution are observed. A comparison of the level of cheating (underreporting) in both settings would provide a measure of the efficacy of the proposed policy, and would demonstrate such efficacy in a way that (we assert) would be particularly compelling to decision makers.

5   PROMISING FUTURE INTERFACES BETWEEN ENVIRONMENTAL POLICY AND EXPERIMENTAL ECONOMICS: MARKET-BASED POLICIES AND 'PRIVATIZATION'

Overview

In motivating our view that optimal designs for *regulatory* programmes offer potentially rich opportunities for policy-relevant research in which experimental methods can play a key role, we emphasized our expectations concerning expansions in the future need for (and public interest in) enhanced schemes for environmental management. While regulatory programmes, and the associated concerns with regulatory compliance taken up in section 4, will surely be important in the mix of alternatives available to policy makers in the future, they will not represent the only alternatives that will be available. For reasons that we will discuss, we feel that this mix will increasingly include policy options that rely on market-based mechanisms, and this reliance invites particularly interesting contributions by experimental economics as a part of the process of assessing policy options.

In principle there is clearly nothing new about the idea of using market-based mechanisms to the ends of environmental management. Indeed, debate during the 1960s concerning the possible design for such mechanisms, and social implications that might be associated with their use, played an important role in the evolution of the subdiscipline of environmental economics.[15] The character of this debate has changed markedly over the last three decades, however, in terms of both breadth and depth. The contemporary reliance on market-based policies by government and non-government entities is seen in many areas. Consider species protection as an example. Policies commonly used by private and/or non-private institutions include such market-based mechanisms as the direct purchase of habitat lands,[16] 'debt-for-nature' swaps, and the use of 'offsets' as a part of land-use management.

The use of market-based mechanisms as a part of government policy is not a simple matter, however. As exemplified, to some extent, in the currently popular rhetoric concerning 'privatization', critical policy design issues arise from questions that are *institutional* in nature – questions concerning individual incentives associated with a given policy design, the likely policy outcomes and a desire to avoid unintended consequences. The importance of such issues derives from the fact that in many, if not *most*, instances the characteristics of the institutions within which government policies must operate do not satisfy fundamental institutional features of the market paradigm. This argument is made immediately apparent by considering the basic assumptions of the (competitive) market paradigm which include: many buyers and sellers, perfect information, perfect mobility (*ergo*, perfect entry and exit) and well-defined property rights.

Consider the following examples of instances in which characteristics of field institutions conflict with those assumed in the market paradigm. Western water markets are argued[17] as being good examples of the use of markets to address water-based environmental and resource-related management or allocation problems. In many cases, however, it can be argued that almost *none*[18] of the preconditions for competitive markets are met in the local water markets. Typically there is a single large buyer, often a municipality, and few sellers. Transactions costs may be substantial and factor mobility is hardly free due to the costs of moving the water to other users or uses. A second example is provided by a major problem facing agencies such as the Departments of Energy and Defense in their efforts to 'privatize' the clean-up of toxic materials on federal lands. The Request for Proposal (RfP) institution that they must use is typically characterized by a *single* buyer and (in many cases) *only two or three* sellers (bidders).[19] A third example involves the legal and legislative actions affecting environmental and resource allocation on tribal lands, which were based on the market paradigm. These have been argued to have probably failed fifth Amendment provisions for 'just compensation' due to the demonstrable lack of 'perfect mobility' in the institutional environment in which the actions were taken.[20]

Within this debate on the use of markets, the potential contribution of experimental economics is immediately obvious. Assessments of policies that rely on market-based mechanisms will require analyses of the effects on agent behaviour (and therefore policy outcomes) that arise in *different* (*vis-à-vis* the market paradigm) institutions and, of course, this is what experimental economics is all about. Thus, in terms of identifying classes of problems in which experimental research could contribute to the substance of what the environmental economist might 'whisper in the ears of future princes', an easy (and in our view accurate) response might be: all policies directed toward the use of market-based incentives.

There is one set of issues related to market-based environmental management that we wish to single out for more detailed treatment in this section, *viz*, what we have learned to date from experimental assessments of markets for emissions rights and the implications of such lessons for future experimental research. The rationale for this choice is the opportunity that we are afforded to provide the reader with a particularly illuminating example of the importance and contemporary relevance of what we described in section 2 as the fundamental methods issue in experimental economics: *parallelism*.

Experimental Assessments of Emissions Markets: What Have We Learned?

Most experimental analyses of emissions markets have focused on the provisions of the 1990 amendments to the Clean Air Act for tradable discharge permits (TDP) for sulphur dioxide (SO_2). Essential elements of these provisions and their implementation by the EPA can be briefly summarized as follows; more comprehensive summaries of markets for SO_2 permits can be found in Cason and Plott (1996). Each permit gave the owner (initially, large producers of thermal electricity) the right to emit one ton of SO_2. Once used, the permit was exhausted. Permits were allocated (in the early 1990s) on a historical basis; power producers were each awarded an initial quantity of permits based on their 1985 emissions levels. Permits, once allocated, were fungible and could be traded (under conditions described below).[21] Permits are bankable. The programme was intended to allow for a systematic reduction in the level of emissions through a planned reduction in the number of permits.

The EPA established a 'market' for emissions permits, the institutional design for which was proposed by Hahn and Noll (1982). The essential features of this institution are the following:

1. Sealed bids and asks for emissions permits are submitted to the EPA.
2. Bids received by the EPA are arrayed from highest to lowest bid (forming a demand curve); asks are arrayed from lowest to highest ask (forming a supply curve).
3. Feasible trades involve buyers and sellers that are matched by the EPA. The highest bid is matched with the lowest ask for the first trade. The second-highest bid is then matched with the second-lowest ask for the second trade, and so on until feasible trades have been exhausted.

Several policy questions concerning the EPA's adopted market institution immediately arose. As examples: will market power of participants be important? Will there be sufficient trading in this newly introduced market for the programme to accomplish its intended purpose (provide efficient prices?) What is the effect of heterogeneity of production technologies on the volume of permit trades and pricing?

Interest in these questions concerning the efficacy of the EPA auction became escalated following experience with its initial operation in 1993. Relative to pre-auction expectation, the volume of trades in the auction was *very small*, and trading prices were *much lower* than expected. These anomalies presented an ideal invitation for the use of experiments to explain them, an invitation that was quickly taken up by a number of researchers. A substantial literature evolved in which results from emissions trading experiments were reported.

Muller and Mestelman (1998) summarize this literature and pose the question: what have we learned from reported experimental research concerning emissions trading? Concern here will be limited to Muller and Mestelman's (1998) responses to this question that relate to the basic recurring theme of this chapter: *responses that centre on the issue of parallelism.*[22] The parallelism issue is most prominently seen in Cason and Plott's (1996) effort to explain the anomalies seen in the 1993 EPA auction. The design of their experiments closely followed the Hahn–Noll institution.[23] Cason and Plott's (1996) results showed that under this institution the incentives of *both* buyers and sellers were to underreveal their true values, the results being a substantial reduction in the number of trades (relative to trades that would occur with an incentive-compatible mechanism) and permit prices that were 'low' relative to a socially optimal price.[24] Since these 'results' are basically those seen in the 1993 EPA auction, Cason and Plott (1996) conclude that the EPA auction is not demand revealing and, consequently, that it provides incorrect information concerning abatement costs (the 'anomalous' results seen in 1993).

Of course, one of the basic ends sought with the use of an emissions market is price information – an approximation of competitive, market-clearing prices – information that would be expected from a market institution that is incentive compatible. Such price information would then be expected to result in socially optimal levels of investment in pollution abatement technology and then efficient, least-cost compliance with standards established by the Clean Air Act. All else equal, Cason and Plott's (1996) results suggests a failure in the EPA's market and the attendant need to redesign the auction institution.

It turns out, however, that all else may *not* be equal. Muller and Mestelman (1998) note that the EPA auction was not the only operating market in which one could trade emissions permits: at the Chicago Board of Trade, spot and futures markets for emissions permits had developed and constituted a substantial part of the total market for permits. Since the existence of this secondary market for permits was not a part of the institution used by Cason and Plott, an obvious parallelism question arises: what is the relevance of results from experiments in which subjects trade in a Hahn–Noll market institution for a 'real-world', field institution wherein agents may trade simultaneously in the (EPA) Hahn–Noll market *and* a secondary market in the Chicago Board of Trade?[25] Intuition might suggest that the existence of the secondary market would affect the Hahn–Noll market in ways that are consistent with behaviour witnessed in 1993: prices established in the secondary market would surely limit if not fix prices at which permits would trade in the EPA market; the source of supply (asks) for permits in the EPA market may have been substantially limited to those offered by the EPA (the only agent not operating in the secondary market), in which case the operation of the EPA market may have had little more effect than giving rise to an increase in the *total* (EPA and secondary) market's supply of permits, thereby driving down permit prices.

The incentive compatibility of the Hahn–Noll, and therefore now the EPA, market institution remains as an open question, as does the weight of the parallelism critique of Cason and Plott's study (Joskow *et al.*, 1998). Resolution of these issues will require experimental explorations which incorporate multiple markets and interactions between technology choice and the market for emissions permits (see Ben-David *et al.*, 1998). This issue serves to highlight the relevance of parallelism as well as pointing to potentially productive lines of future research.

5   CONCLUDING REMARKS

In this chapter we have focused attention on those areas of the frontiers of *environmental* economics in which one may find an interface with the frontiers of *experimental* economics. We have described in some detail three areas that we feel are especially suitable for the application of experimental methods to the study of environmental policy: valuation of environmental amenities/damages; compliance with environmental rules and regulations; and the transition to markets. Our intention was to demonstrate the scope of the methodology and we trust that our readers will apply their own imaginations to identify other promising areas for experimental investigation. We hope that the reader will find unarguable the case that we have attempted to make that this interface is rich with future opportunities for the environmental economist.

Our most fervent hope is that, within a context that gives emphasis to the problems of parallelism, we have succeeded in making clear the potential use of experimental methods for making manifest the policy relevance of the environmental economists' research – for 'whispering in the ears of princes'.

ACKNOWLEDGEMENTS

A very early draft of this chapter was presented the conference 'Frontiers of Environmental Economics', held at Airlie, VA, October 1998. We thank the conference participants and Jason Shogren in particular for many helpful comments and for their good-natured participation in our experiment. This chapter was written while McKee was visiting Georgia State University.

NOTES

1. This was not always the case. The 1960s was a 'hey-day' of social experimentation. Several programmes were subject to field trials. Some examples are income transfer programmes (as in the Gary, IN trials), elementary and secondary education delivery (performance contracting experiments by the Office of Equal Opportunity or OEO). More recently, ethical considerations, as well as cost, have limited the use of such trials. Laboratory experiments are often the only means remaining of obtaining real data from real human decision makers.

2. Neutrality increases the experimenter's control over subject preferences and avoids leading subjects to invoke different 'mental scripts', which may enable them to fill in (potentially) missing information in the instructions but which may also unpredictably influence their choices. It is sometimes claimed that the use of neutral instructions limits the ability to generalize from the experimental to the naturally occurring setting. In fact, however, it is not possible to generalize beyond the laboratory unless one uses neutral instructions, since the experimenter cannot control the values that subjects associate with loaded terms. This is not to say, however, that *all* experiments must be conducted with neutral terms. Indeed there may be instances that beg for the use of non-neutral terms. For example, experiments which seek to observe cultural effects on behaviour may prescribe the use of non-neutral terms precisely to enable the researcher to observe the effects of culture and/or social norms on behaviour in settings that are close to the field setting. Some examples of such research agendas are provided by work investigating cultural attitudes toward gambling, income transfers, altruism and tax compliance.

3.   There are a number of other (necessary) conditions that must be satisfied for the experi-
     menter to have 'controlled' preferences set out by Smith (1976), the more important of
     which include: *saliency* (the level of rewards received by subjects must be directly related
     to their decision); *reward (payoff) dominance* (rewards much be large enough to offset any
     subjective costs or benefits that subjects place on their participation in the experiment);
     and *privacy* (each subject must know only his or her own payoffs so that they do not
     receive any subjective value from payoffs of other subjects). The privacy condition may
     be relaxed in settings where the experimenter seeks to investigate the role of such motives
     as fairness or equity.
4.   Following Davis and Holt (1993), a few of the more important procedural conditions
     relevant for the creation of an institution include the following: the experiment should be
     administered in a uniform and consistent manner to allow replicability; the experiment
     should not be excessively long or complicated, since subjects may become bored or
     confused; subjects must believe that the procedures described to them are the procedures
     actually followed; and instructions provided to subjects should be understandable, should
     avoid the use of examples that lead subjects to anchor on certain choices that are the
     subject of the experiment, and should be phrased in neutral rather than loaded terms in
     order to mask the context of the experiment and avoid direct reference to the real-world
     phenomena under investigation. In this latter regard, the effects of language on agent
     behaviour have been the subject of a number of studies. For example, Alm, McClelland
     and Schulze (1992) investigate the effects on tax compliance behaviour of alternative
     forms of tax language.
5.   Two sources for critiques of experimental methods that are related to parallelism are the
     common use of student subjects and issues related to a subject's abilities, trained or
     untrained, to perform complex tasks that may be an integral part of the experiment. See
     Plott (1987), Smith, Suchanek and Williams (1988), and Dyer, Kagel and Levin (1989) for
     arguments and empirical evidence concerning parallelism concerns with the use of student
     subjects. Subject training issues are topics addressed by Ben-David *et al.* (1998), Muller
     and Mestelman (1998), and Harrison, McKee and Rustrom (1990).
6.   See, for example, Joskow, Schmalensee and Bailey (1998).
7.   For other notable studies of this *genre*, see also Shogren *et al.* (1994), Poe, Clark and
     Schulze (1997), Brookshire, Coursey and Schulze (1987) and Alm, Jackson and McKee
     (1992b).
8.   See, for example, Smith and Mansfield (1998) who offer the conjecture that the experi-
     mental laboratory is intrinsically an artificial setting and that generalizations to the field
     are implausible.
9.   Similar results are commonly reported in the marketing literature. For example, Louviere
     (1996, p. 170) observes that 'I think it very unlikely that one simple and generalizable
     approach to "adjusting" (stated preference) numbers will be found, despite clear evidence
     supporting strong monotonic links between stated preferences and actual choices in real
     markets ... differences in product awareness, learning, etc. ... necessarily imply that no
     one magic constant can exist across all product categories.'
10. Brown *et al.* (1996) conducted OE and DC surveys and well as OE and DC real-payment
     surveys. An important difference between Brown *et al.* and Bohara *et al.* is that Brown *et
     al.* simply compare responses with no underlying principle to test. Bohara *et al.* offer a
     theoretical underpinning, and then test it in the lab.
11. We do find efforts by environmental economists to extrapolate experimental results from
     the tax compliance literature to environmental compliance; see Segerson and Tietenberg
     (1992) and Gabel and Sinclair-Desgagné (1993). This dearth in experimental research
     related to regulatory compliance is not limited to environmental regulations. See Pagan
     (1998) for an innovative effort to explore compliance with immigration laws *via* experi-
     ments.
12. As stated above, this is a very simple model. Experiments that make use of more complex,
     realistic, institutions have been conducted by many researchers. As examples of experi-
     ments in which audit probabilities are endogenous, see Alm, Cronshaw and McKee

13. We must recognize the potential for a parallelism problem in this instance, however. This problem is described as the 'found money' problem which may arise in instances where subject decisions involving money given to them as a part of the experiment are different from decisions that they might make which involve average levels of their discretionary income.
14. This argument was suggested to the authors by Robert Ayres who argues that the TRI Program is not as effective as it might be due to the lack of a mass balance approach which would require firms to report their intake and use of toxic materials. Anything unaccounted for would be deemed to be a release. Taxpayers are placed in exactly this setting under a self-reporting tax scheme as we have in the US.
15. As early examples of this debate, see Kneese's (1962) classic work along with works by Crocker (1966) and Dales (1968).
16. Issues associated with the US Army's efforts to obtain habitat lands in markets are explored with experimental methods by Berrens and McKee (1998).
17. See Anderson (1983) and Gardner (1985).
18. See, as examples, Brajer *et al.* (1989).
19. See Dümmer, Bjornstad and Jones (1998).
20. Cummings (1991).
21. The EPA was concerned that there would be too little trading initially and mandated that each producer place 3 per cent of their permit allocation in the EPA auction.
22. We thus ignore a line of experimental research that may be of interest to many readers: experiments focused on issues related to the potential effects of market power. See, as examples, Misiolek and Elder (1989); Brown-Kruse and Elliott (1990); and Brown-Kruse, Elliott and Godby (1995).
23. In Cason and Plott's (1996) experiments, permits traded in the 'market' had capital value and were bankable.
24. See Franciosi *et al.* (1993). It should be noted that these authors do find some degree of overbidding on infra-marginal units.
25. Still another source for a potentially important parallelism question related to Cason and Plott's design concerns the initial allocation of permits to agents. Given that initial allocations were based on 1985 emissions levels, and that most power companies had necessarily reduced emissions between 1985 and the early 1990s, at which time emission permits were allocated, the initial allocations may have been 'high', thereby leading to prices that were lower than expected. This subtlety is not captured in Cason and Plott's experiments.

REFERENCES

Alm, J., B. Jackson and M. McKee (1992a), 'Institutional uncertainty and taxpayer compliance', *American Economic Review*, **82**(4), 1018–26.
Alm, J., B. Jackson and M. McKee (1992b), 'Estimating the determinants of taxpayer compliance with experimental data', *National Tax Journal*, **65**(1), 107–14.
Alm, J., B. Jackson and M. McKee (1993), 'Fiscal exchange, collective decision institutions, and tax compliance', *Journal of Economic Behavior and Organization*, **22**(3), 285–303.
Alm, J., G.H. McClelland and W.D. Schulze (1992), 'Why do people pay taxes?', *Journal of Public Economics*, **48**(1), 21–38.
Alm, J., M. Cronshaw and M. McKee (1993), 'Tax compliance with endogenous audit selection rules', *Kyklos*, **46**(1), 27–45.
Anderson, T. (1983), 'Conflict or cooperation: the case for water markets', unpub-

lished manuscript, Political Economy Research Center, Montana State University, Bozeman.

Ben-David, S., D. Brookshire, S. Burness, M. McKee and C. Schmidt (1999), 'Heterogeneity, irreversible production choices and efficiency in emission permit markets', *Journal of Environmental Economics and Management* **38**(2), 176–94.

Berrens, R. and M. McKee (1998), 'Army training bases and endangered species: an auction approach to habitat acquisition', unpublished manuscript, Department of Economics, University of New Mexico.

Bjornstad, D., R. Cummings and L. Osborne (1997), 'A learning design for reducing hypothetical bias in the contingent valuation method', *Environmental and Resource Economics*, **10**(3), 207–11.

Blackburn, McKinley, Glenn W. Harrison and Elisabeth E. Rutström (1994), 'Statistical bias functions and informative hypothetical surveys', *American Journal of Agricultural Economics*, **76**(5), 1084–8.

Bohara, A., M. McKee, R. Berrens, H. Jenkins-Smith, C. Silva and D.S. Brookshire (1998), 'The effects of total cost and group-size information on stated WTP: open ended vs. dichotomous choice', *Journal of Environmental Economics and Management*, **35**(2), 142–63.

Brajer, V., A. Church, R. Cummings and P. Farah (1989), 'The strengths and weaknesses of water markets as they affect water scarcity and sovereignty interests in the west', *Natural Resources Journal*, **29** (Spring), 489–509.

Brookshire, D.S. and D. Coursey (1987), 'Measuring the value of a public good: an empirical comparison of elicitation procedures', *American Economic Review*, **77**(3), 554–66.

Brookshire, D.S., D. Coursey and W.D. Schulze (1987), 'The external validity of experimental economics techniques: analysis of demand behavior', *Economic Inquiry*, **25**, 239–50.

Brown, T.C., P. Champ, R.C. Bishop and D.W. McCollum (1996), 'Response formats and public good donations', *Land Economics*, **72**(1), 152–66.

Brown-Kruse, J. and S.R. Elliott (1990), 'Strategic manipulation of pollution permit markets', manuscript, Laboratory for Economics and Psychology, University of Colorado, Boulder, CO.

Brown-Kruse, J., S.R. Elliott and R. Godby (1995), 'Strategic manipulation of pollution permit markets: an experimental approach', Working Paper 95–10, Department of Economics, McMaster University, Hamilton, Canada.

Cason, T. and C. Plott (1996), 'EPA's new emissions trading mechanism: a laboratory evaluation', *Journal of Environmental Economics and Management*, **30**(2), 133–60.

Coursey, D., J. Hovis and W.D. Schulze (1987), 'The disparity between willingness to accept and willingness to pay measures of value', *Quarterly Journal of Economics*, **102**(3), 679–90.

Crocker, T. (1966), 'The structuring of atmospheric pollution control systems', in H. Wolozing (ed.), *The Economics of Air Pollution*, New York: W.W. Norton, pp. 61–86.

Cummings, Ronald G. (1991), 'Legal and administrative uses of economic paradigms: a critique', *Natural Resources Journal*, **31**(2).

Cummings, R.G. and Laura Taylor (1998), 'Does realism matter in contingent valuation?', *Land Economics*, **74**(2), 203–15.

Cummings, R.G. and Laura Taylor (1999), 'Unbiased value estimates for environmental goods: a cheap talk design for the contingent valuation method', *American Economic Review*, **89**(3), June, 649–65.

Cummings, Ronald G., Steven Elliott, Glenn W. Harrison and Jane Murphy (1997), 'Are hypothetical referenda incentive compatible?', *Journal of Political Economy*, **105**(3), 609–21.

Dales, J. (1968), *Pollution, Property and Prices*, Toronto, Canada: University of Toronto Press.

Davis, D.D. and C.A. Holt (1993), *Experimental Economics*, Princeton, NJ: Princeton University Press.

Diamond, P. and J. Hausman (1994), 'Contingent valuation: is some number better than none?', *Journal of Economic Perspectives*, **8**(4), 45–64.

Dümmer, C., D. Bjornstad and D. Jones (1998), 'The regulatory environment guiding DOE's cleanup: opportunities for flexibility', draft manuscript (26 pp), The Joint Institute for Energy and Environment, Knoxville, TN, 3 September.

Dyer, D., J. Kagel and D. Levin (1989), 'A comparison of naive and experienced bidders in common value offer auctions: a laboratory analysis', *Economic Journal*, **99**(1), 108–15.

Fox, J., J. Shogren, D. Hayes and J. Kleinbenstein (1998), 'CVM-X: calibrating contingent values with experimental auction markets', *American Journal of Agricultural Economics*, **80**(3), 455–65.

Franciosi, R., R. Issac, D. Pingry and F. Reynolds (1993), 'An experimental investigation of the Hahn–Noll revenue neutral auction for emissions licenses', *Journal of Environmental Economics and Management*, **24**(1), 1–24.

Friedman, D. and S. Sunder (1994), *Experimental Methods: A Primer for Economists*, New York and Cambridge: Cambridge University Press.

Gabel, H.L. and B. Sinclair-Desgagné (1993), 'Managerial incentives and environmental compliance', *Journal of Environmental Economics and Management*, **24**(2), 229–40.

Gardner, D. (1985), 'Institutional impediments to efficient water allocation', *Policy Studies Review*, **5**(3), 353–363.

Groves, T. and J. Ledyard (1977), 'Optimal allocation of public goods: a solution to the free rider problem', *Econometrica*, **45**(6), 783–809.

Hahn, R. and R. Noll (1982), 'Designing a market for tradable emissions permits', in W.A. Magat (ed.), *Reform of Environmental Regulation*, Cambridge, MA: Ballinger, pp. 119–46.

Hamilton, J.T. (1995), 'Pollution as news: media and stock market reactions to the Toxic Release Inventory data', *Journal of Environmental Economics and Management*, **28**(1), 98–113.

Hanemann, W. (1994), 'Valuing the environment through contingent valuation', *Journal of Economic Perspectives*, **8**(4), 19–44.

Harrison, G.W., M. McKee and E.E. Rutstrom (1990), 'Experimental evaluation of institutions of monopoly restraint', in J. Kagel and L. Green (eds), *Advances in Behavioral Economics*, Vol. 2, Norwood, NJ: Ablex Publishing Co., pp. 54–94.

Joskow, P., R. Schmalensee and E. Bailey (1998), 'The market for sulfur dioxide emissions', *American Economic Review*, **88**(5), 669–86.

Kneese, A.V. (1962), *Water Pollution: Economic Aspects and Research Needs*, Washington, DC: Resources for the Future.

Kneese, A.V. (1977), *Economics and the Environment*, New York: Penguin Books.

Kneese, A.V., R.U. Ayres and R.C. d'Arge (1970), *Economics and the Environment: A Mass Balances Approach*, Washington, DC: Resources for the Future.

Loomis, J., A. Gonzalez-Caban and R. Gregory (1994), 'Substitutes and budget constraints in contingent valuation', *Land Economics*, **70**(4), 499–506.

Louviere, Jordan (1996), 'Relating stated preference measures and models to choices in real markets: calibration of CV responses', in David J. Bjornstad and James R. Kahn (eds), *The Contingent Valuation of Environmental Resources: Methodological Issues and Research Needs*, Cheltenham, UK and Brookfield, US: Edward Elgar, pp. 167–88.

Misiolek, W.S. and H.W. Elder (1989), 'Exclusionary manipulation of the market for pollution rights', *Journal of Environmental Economics and Management*, **16**, 156–66.

Muller, R.A. and S. Mestelman (1998), 'What have we learned from emissions trading experiments?', *Managerial and Decision Economics*, **19**(4/5), 225–38.

Neill, Helen (1995), 'The context for substitutes in CVM studies: some empirical observations', *Journal of Environmental Economics and Management*, **29**(3), 393–7.

Neilson, W. and M. McKee (1998), 'Value and outcome uncertainty as explanations of the WTA vs WTP disparity', unpublished manuscript, Department of Economics, University of New Mexico.

Pagan, J. (1998), 'IRCA's employer sanctions: an experiment on firm compliance and the implementation of a National ID', *Journal of Economic Behavior and Organization*, **34**(1), 87–100.

Plott, C.R. (1982), 'Industrial organization theory and experimental economics', *Journal of Economic Literature*, **20**(4), 1485–527.

Plott, C.R. (1987), 'Dimensions of parallelism: some policy applications of experimental methods', in A.E. Roth (ed.), *Laboratory Experimentation in Economics: Six Points of View*, New York: Cambridge University Press, pp. 193–219.

Poe, G., J. Clark, and W. Schulze (1997), 'Can hypothetical questions predict actual participation in public programs? a field validity test using a provision point mechanism', working paper, Department of Agricultural Economics, Cornell University, Ithaca.

Portney, P. (1994), 'The contingent valuation debate: why economists should care', *Journal of Economic Perspectives*, **8**(4), 3–17.

Roth, A.E. (1986), 'Laboratory experimentation in economics', *Economics and Philosophy*, **2**, 245–73.

Segerson, K. and T. Tietenberg (1992), 'The structure of penalties in environmental enforcement: an economic analysis', *Journal of Environmental Economics and Management*, **23**(3), 179–200.

Shogren, J., J. Fox and D. Hayes and J. Roosen (1999), 'Observed choices for food safety in retail, survey, and auction markets', *American Journal of Agricultural Economics*, **81**(5), 1192–9.

Shogren, J., S.Y. Shin, D.J. Hayes and B. Kliebenstein (1994), 'Resolving differences in willingness to pay and willingness to accept', *American Economic Review*, **84**(3), 255–70.

Sierra Club v. *Morton* (1971), 404 US 964 92 S. Ct. 331.

Smith, V.K. and C. Mansfield (1998), 'Buying time: real and hypothetical offers', *Journal of Environmental Economics and Management*, **36**(2), 209–24.

Smith, V.L. (1976), 'Experimental economics: induced value theory', *The American Economic Review, Papers and Proceedings*, **66**(2), 274–79.

Smith, V.L. (1979), 'Incentive compatible experimental processes for the provision of public goods', in V.L. Smith (ed.), *Research in Experimental Economics*, Vol. I, Greenwich, CT: JAI Press, pp. 59–168.

Smith, V.L. (1982), 'Microeconomic systems as an experimental science', *American Economic Review*, **72**(4), 923–55.

Smith, V., G. Suchanek and A. Williams (1988), 'Bubbles, crashes, and endogenous expectations in experimental spot asset markets', *Econometrica*, **56**(6), 1119–51.

Stewart, S., M. McKee, R. Berrens, A. Bohara and D.S. Brookshire (2000), 'Parallelism in the lab and the field: testing the robustness of the MCS mechanism', manuscript, University of New Mexico, Pacific Economic Review, **5**(3), 429–446.

Taylor, L.O. (1998), 'Incentive compatible referenda and the valuation of public goods', *Agricultural and Resource Economics Review*, October, pp. 132–9.

6. The firm, its procedures and win–win environmental regulations

H. Landis Gabel and Bernard Sinclair-Desgagné

> The firm in mainstream economic theory has often been described as a 'black box.' And so it is. This is very extraordinary given that most resources in a modern economic system are employed within firms, with how these resources are used dependent on administrative decisions and not directly on the operation of a market. (Coase, 1992, p. 714)

> Most production in modern economies occurs within organisations, and this production is regulated only to a limited extent by prices. ... These observations make it clear that if economists wish to understand how resources in modern economies are allocated, we must understand what goes on inside organisations. (Stiglitz, 1991, p. 15)

It has been customary among environmental economists schooled in the neoclassical tradition to assume that the link between environmental regulatory policy and the allocation of environmental resources is very simple. It is a perfectly rational and efficient black box firm, which maximizes profits given whatever technological, market and regulatory policy constraints are imposed on it. Because economists have long assumed that the firm behaves in this way, and have been content to model its behaviour as such, they saw no reason to pierce the corporate veil to understand in microanalytic detail the management processes taking place within the firm.

This tradition has had several predictable results. One was that economists concerned with environmental problems focused their attention almost exclusively on public policy instruments applicable outside the firm. This was natural since their model provided little substance to the firm, *per se*. The model was more concerned with the web of market relationships between the firm and other rational economic agents, so economists naturally believed that environmental problems were caused by some market failure.

Since by assumption environmental problems had to originate in the market, it was natural to seek to solve them by fixing the market's flaws. Economists have for several generations proselytized for the cause of public policy instruments that do so. Marketable quotas which establish property rights to environmental resources, effluent taxes which increase inefficiently low prices and legal liability for compensating victims of third-party damage are favoured instruments.[1]

A second predictable result (although not easily documented) has been that environmental damage occurred for reasons that have totally escaped policy makers' notice. Failure of organizations to coordinate behaviour can result in environmental accidents entirely independent of failures of markets. Settings apparently free of market problems are not necessarily free of environmental risk.

A final result of the neoclassical paradigm was that although managers of business firms foundered in trying to cope with the rising tide of environmental pressures, of which public policy was only one, economists had little advice to offer to them. Proffered advice came from other academics and business consultants,[2] but it lacked the rigour characteristic of economic science. In particular, there has been little rigorous analysis of how a company's environmental strategy is operationalized in the management control systems, formal and informal, that would normally convert strategy into action.

This is not a criticism of economic analysis of market failures, nor is it intended to detract from economists' well-founded enthusiasm for market-based policy instruments. Rather, the point is that the logic that looks for failed assumptions to the neoclassical model of the market should be carried into the firm. It is inconsistent, albeit convenient, to assume that markets are flawed but that firms are perfect.

Firms are, of course, exceedingly complex institutions, and profit maximization is far from trivially easy even in a context of relatively simple and stable market relationships. No reasonably large firm is run by a sole and rational chief executive – a corporate 'principal' – who maximizes the firm's value. All are run by vast numbers of employees – or 'agents' – to many of whom may be delegated a great deal of autonomy. Their activities are controlled and coordinated, however, by a set of interrelated management systems and a multitude of procedures for operationalizing the principal's objectives.[3]

The point to emphasize is that the principal does not directly make the decisions that determine the firm's performance. Rather, the process is indirect. Profit maximization must be accomplished – or attempted – via this network of necessarily imperfect systems and procedures that link the principal's objectives to the agents' actions.[4] We use the term 'management systems' broadly to include formal systems (budgeting, accounting, compensation, etc.), corporate policies, standard operating procedures (SOPs), and simpler work routines and habits, many of which may not be explicitly defined.[5] These systems are the grist of consulting firms and the management literature, they hold centre stage in business school curricula, and they preoccupy practising managers. To assume that the firm simply and perfectly maximizes profit is to assume away one of the main challenges facing its managers.

Thus, the link between environmental regulatory policy and the allocation of environmental resources is complex, multi-step, and imperfect. Designing regulatory policy is only a first step. That policy may occasionally intervene in the management systems themselves,[6] but more commonly it alters the external rules to which the corporate principal is subject. These altered rules must then induce the principal to change the management systems which play a crucial role motivating and controlling the actions of the agents. Finally, the agents must respond to the changes in the management systems, presumably in consort with the objectives of both the corporate principal and the regulatory policy maker. Any environmental impact only appears at this last step.

In these steps, there are invariably slips that break the direct link traditionally assumed between the regulator and the environment. Managers have limited attention spans, information flows imperfectly between managers and employees, and employees pursue their own objectives. All these imperfections and more cause organizational failures within the firm. As we will argue in this chapter, these organizational failures are systematic, they are in many respects similar to the market failures long studied by environmental economists, and there are instruments available to fix them analogous to the instruments available to fix markets.

Because our focus is within the firm, our analysis is not just relevant to the public policy maker. It should be obvious that organizational failures are relevant to the firm's management as well, since their manifestation is frequently unachieved profit potential. To give an example on which some of the following analysis will focus, if a firm is systematically losing money by wasting environmental resources, the firm's management would like to know it as much as, and possibly more than, the environmental policy maker.

The first objective of this chapter is to argue that designing corporate environmental policy should take an equal position on the economists' agenda to designing public environmental policy. In addition to studying the appropriate economic incentives confronting a firm (or its principal) in a decentralized market economy, environmental economists should also study the appropriate incentives facing the agents within the firm. The two areas of study are intimately linked, but they are not the same. We will show in this chapter that behind the corporate veil lie causes of systematic organizational failure that are analogous in many respects to problems of externalities in the context of market-mediated transactions. And there are management tools to mitigate these organizational failings just as there are public policy tools (for example, Pigouvian taxes, rules of civil and criminal liability, and marketable property rights) that might remedy market failings. In the lexicon of organizational economics, the causes of organizational failure include perverse incentives, hidden actions, imperfect information, strategic behaviour and moral hazard. The management tools include monitoring technologies, contract design, task allocation decisions, centralization and decentralization of authority and accounting systems, *inter alia*.

THE PARADOX OF LOW-HANGING FRUIT

> Economists … tend to regard energy efficiency like the man whose friend draws his attention to a £20 note lying on the pavement. 'It can't be', he says. 'If it were, somebody would have picked it up.'

> Every scheme to encourage investment in energy efficiency finds plenty of what the industry calls 'low hanging fruit' – projects with succulent returns. Robert Ayres, in a paper at a conference on energy and the environment in the 21st century at the Massachusetts Institute of Technology last year, drew attention to the 'energy contest' begun in 1981 by the Louisiana division of Dow Chemical, to find capital projects costing less than $200 000 with payback times of less than a year. In 1982 the contest yielded 27 projects in which Dow invested $1.7m: the return averaged 173 per cent (a payback period of about seven months). The contest continued, with more projects backed each year. In 1988 95 projects were picked, costing a total of $21.9m – and yielding an average return of 190 per cent. (*The Economist*, 1991, p. 15)

Dow's experience is not unique. The 3M company has eliminated 500 000 tons of waste and pollutants and saved $482 million in so doing and another $650 million by energy conservation since it started its 3P ('Pollution Prevention Pays') programme in 1975. The Centre for the Exploitation of Science and Technology ran an eighteen-month project in the UK to test the benefits of waste reduction and clean technologies. The project saved more than £11 million a year for the eleven participating companies, mostly from simple changes in processes that reduced inputs of water, energy and raw materials. The US Environmental Protection Agency has estimated that, if the entire country were to switch to energy-efficient lighting, its electricity bill would fall by 10 per cent and air pollution would be reduced by between 4 per cent and 7 per cent. The Agency's Green Lights Program, initiated in 1991, has helped companies switch to energy-efficient lighting to save money and the environment.

There seems to be anecdotal evidence that low hanging fruit is abundant; so abundant that Michael Porter, in an article published in *Scientific American*, claimed that

> Strict environmental regulations do not inevitably hinder competitive advantage against foreign rivals, indeed, they often enhance it. (Porter, 1991, p. 96)

That is, environmental policies are potentially win–win policies. They may prompt firms to see and pick low-hanging fruit – a harvest for both the environment and for those firms.

The significance of what has become known as the 'Porter hypothesis' is that it apparently contradicts the conventional wisdom that environmental regulations shift formerly external costs back on to firms, burdening them relative to competing firms in countries with less strict regulations. Porter has subsequently elaborated on the hypothesis with many more examples (Porter and van der Linde, 1995a,b), and others have taken up his argument, including senior officials in the US government (Gore, 1993).

The precise claim and meaning of the Porter hypothesis are unclear because Porter's original examples mix several different ways by which the hypothesis could be true. The only one that is controversial, at least to mainstream economists, is the case where regulations purportedly reduce the absolute costs of the firms subject to them. It is controversial because it requires the existence of abundant low-hanging fruit, and this in turn contradicts the neoclassical model of the firm.

If regulations are to lower the costs of firms subject to them, several conditions must be met. One is that firms are not productively efficient (they are not minimizing private costs), *ex ante*. They are operating inside a cost-efficiency frontier. Only from a starting point inside the frontier is it feasible to reduce simultaneously both social and private costs. All of this presupposes, in terms we have been using, that there is an organizational failure in the firm.

A second condition concerns the firm's behavioural response. Environmental regulations, while shifting external costs to the firm, must stimulate a sufficient improvement in productive efficiency to outweigh the internalized cost. Clearly, the existence of win–win opportunities neither ensures that strict environmental regulations will help firms find them nor that, if found, they are valuable enough to offset the internalized costs. Win–win is logically most likely in situations where the firm is far from the efficiency frontier, where the burden of the compliance cost is light, and where the shift to the frontier can be made cheaply.

A final condition that is required for the hypothesis to be interesting to academics and practitioners is that it is systematically true. One can always find some anecdotal examples to contradict the simplifying assumptions of abstract deductive models. Porter apparently believes it is systematically and commonly true, even though he qualifies his statements with words like 'may', 'often' and 'in many cases'. Yet when he uses Japan and Germany as examples to argue that strict environmental policies have helped promote their productivity growth, he is clearly making a general statement.[7]

Porter's claim has spawned a number of papers, both pro and con, in business and academic journals. Most are anecdotal, some are theoretical, and a few are empirical. As examples, Meyer (1992) claims to find some statistical evidence in the US of a positive impact of environmental regulations on economic performance. Palmer and Simpson (1993, p. 17), by contrast, find Porter's arguments 'based on unlikely assumptions and inconclusive anecdotal evidence'. Similarly, Oates, Palmer and Portney (1994, p. 21) conclude that, 'Until such time as we acquire more compelling evidence on the Porter Hypothesis, it is our sense that it should not be given much credence.' Walley and Whitehead (1994) believe that win–win opportunities exist but are rare. Jaffee *et al.* (1995, p. 159) conclude their survey paper saying, 'there is ... little or no evidence supporting the revisionist hypothesis that environmental regulation stimulates innovation and improved international competitiveness'.[8]

PROCEDURES AND ROUTINES IN COMPANIES

People are, at best, rational in terms of what they are aware of, and they can be aware of only tiny, disjointed facets of reality. (Simon, 1985, p. 302)

The lengthy and crucial processes of generating alternatives, which include all the processes that we ordinarily designate by the word 'design', are left out of the [traditional] account of economic choice. (Simon, 1987, p. 267)

The way in which the organisation searches for alternatives is substantially a function of the operating rule it has. ... The organisation uses standard operating procedures and rules of thumb to make and implement choices. In the short run these procedures dominate the decisions made. (Cyert and March, 1992, pp. 133–4)

We have already argued that the firm can be imagined as a principal who is linked to his or her agents by a network of systems and procedures. These systems, procedures and routines are key features of any organization. Cyert and March (1992) identified several types of procedures: task performing, record keeping, information handling and planning. A critical function these procedures perform is to economize on limits to time and attention which curse us all but which are assumed away in traditional neoclassical modelling.

Because neoclassical economists assumed away these limits, company systems and procedures never had any significance to them. It was left to behavioural economists to examine rational choice by decision makers with limited knowledge and computational abilities; decision makers suffering from 'bounded rationality' (see Simon, 1987).[9] This rendered management systems and procedures important to them, and, as the reader will see, our approach follows their lead.

Let us imagine a decision maker in a firm facing a flow of questions, problems, or demands for decisions, each of which must be resolved not only in isolation but in relation to other parts of the organization. Perhaps initially, in the process of learning a new job, he or she regards each event as unique and fashions a novel resolution for each. After some time, however, patterns emerge which make it possible to categorize incoming events according to standard types and to devise SOPs appropriate for resolving each type. These SOPs allow work to proceed much more quickly and efficiently, but there will be errors introduced into the work from the inevitable mismatches between the actual events and their standardized types. By refining its SOPs or creating new ones, a firm can reduce – although never eliminate – the mismatches between events and SOPs, but this will raise administrative costs.

This implies that the image of a firm setting each product's price by some idiosyncratic calculus of marginal costs and revenues is descriptively inaccurate. In reality, pricing decisions are standardized. They might be done, for example, by applying a fixed profit margin to standardized cost figures generated by a highly standardized cost-accounting system. As Cyert and March (1992, p. 124) observed, pricing decisions are 'almost as routinised as production line decisions'.

When one imagines a firm as a collection of systems, procedures and routines, it becomes clear that one can introduce a concept of productive efficiency that is similar but not identical to that of neoclassical economics. The firm devises its systems in order to minimize operating costs. Those systems are rigid, however, so that once they are installed, they can act as a constraint on the firm's objective of profit maximization. If the costs of that constraint are great enough, the firm can invest in changing the systems. Although the system constraint on profit maximization is novel, the logic of cost minimization and thus productive efficiency should be familiar to those schooled in neoclassical economics.

Less familiar is the fact that the firm constrained by its routines can make 'mistakes'. That is, the organizational constraint may prevent the firm from seeing and reacting to opportunities or threats that would be evident to an unconstrained firm.[10] This is what we call 'organizational failure'. The failure may be either an unwitting violation of the environmental laws and regulations or a missed opportunity to make a profit (that is, low-hanging fruit left unpicked). It should be clear, however, that the term 'organizational failure' does not connote that the firm is inefficient given its need for systems and procedures to economize on managerial time and attention.

Although we might suppose that the firm's systems, procedures and routines are ideal when first devised, it should be clear that with the passage of time, they will become less and less so. Relative prices change, regulatory and other environmental conditions change, and the firm's competitive situation changes. If the procedures could be changed frequently, marginally, and at negligible cost, there should be no problem. Unfortunately, that cannot be. In the short run, they are essentially fixed. Paradoxically, the procedures that increase an organization's efficiency also reduce its adaptability to changing circumstances.

The model of the insides of a firm that we have presented may be unfamiliar to traditional economists, but it is alive in the literature of organizational theory. Readers of that literature will encounter firms comprising sets of systems, the elements of which must be congruent with each other and with the external environment (Nadler and Tushman, 1997; Tushman and O'Reilly, 1996). Expressed by Kogut and Zander:

> the capabilities of the firm … rest in the organising principles by which relationships among individuals, within and between groups, and among organisations are structured. (Kogut and Zander, 1992, p. 384)

It will be explained to readers that these systems coalesce in 'quantum states' (Miller and Friesen, 1984). Tushman and O'Reilly (1996) call these 'punctuated equilibria'.

This organizational literature does not bequeath to us formal mathematical models of systems and procedures, quantum states or punctuated equilibria. However, in economics there are mathematical models of analogous phenomena: technical compatibility standards and the processes of shifting from one to another[11] (for a survey of that literature, see David and Greenstein, 1990). Explaining the analogies might help make the organizational literature comprehensible to those unfamiliar with it.

One analogy between technical standards and organizational systems is that both are a means of ensuring compatibility between different elements of a system. Technical standards ensure compatibility between software and hardware; organizational standards ensure compatibility between design, production and marketing or between the accounting system and the compensation system. Each possible outcome of the application of a set of procedures in one part of an organization (that is, each standard solution to a routine problem) must be matched with procedures in many other parts. A related analogy is that any change in one standard requires coordination with many others or behaviour will not be controlled. Miller and Friesen (1984) implicitly recognize the analogy when they explain that movement between organizational quantum states cannot be made by changing each element of the system piecemeal but only by changing all simultaneously in a quantum leap.

This implies a third analogy. A change in organizational systems will be revolutionary, disruptive, and costly. It is like a miniature paradigm revolution in science about which Kuhn (1962) wrote. It is revolutionary in that the old systems are not pushed to evolve further but are destroyed to be replaced by new ones. It is disruptive because agents must abandon traditional patterns of behaviour in which they have specific competencies and thus are of value to the firm, and they must learn new routines in their place. Clearly, agents may have a personal motive to resist this; the benefits of the change may be external to them. And it is costly. Apparent resistance to change may be more than just selfishness. Experimental evidence indicates that learning new routines is more difficult and costly when old routines must first be unlearned (Shiffrin and Schneider, 1977).

Inertia to change is a final analogy between technical standards and organizations. Inertia appears in models of conversion from an old technical standard to a new one (Farrell and Saloner, 1985, 1986), and organizational inertia is the dominant theme of organization ecology and evolutionary economics.[12] Some sources of organizational inertia arise from human traits like myopia, hubris and denial (Rumelt, 1995). Others (closer to the focus of this chapter) are 'rooted in the size, complexity, and interdependence in the organisation's structures, systems, procedures, and processes' (Tushman and O'Reilly, 1996, p. 18).

One may bemoan companies' reluctance to change systems, but one should note that this rigidity can be the penalty of success. Companies are often successful precisely because they have imbedded their routines so deep into their employees' consciousness and sub-consciousness that they become part of the company culture. To Nelson and Winter (1982), the skills and capabilities of an organization are bound up in its routines. Indeed, one could argue that some companies amount to little more than their routines and the associated brand identity. McDonald's is one obvious example: it is essentially the company's routines and the brand identity they have created that are franchised. IBM and Apple differ by much more than their product lines. Both firms succeeded for a long time in great part due to their routines, different though they were, and each eventually fell victim to the rigidity of its routines when a changing situation necessitated restructuring. General Motors is a widely cited example of a once-successful organization nearly destroyed by its inertia. In the environmental domain, The Body Shop is best known not for its products but for a set of practices that support a philosophy embodying environmental virtue.

The rigidity they introduce into a firm is not the only – and possibly not the worst – curse of systems and procedures. They may also blind the firm to the changes that make those same systems and procedures obsolete. As Cyert and March observed regarding procedures for record keeping,

> The records that are kept determine in large part what aspects of the environment will be observed and what alternatives of action will be considered by the firm. (Cyert and March, 1992, p. 126)

STANDARD OPERATING PROCEDURES AND LOW-HANGING FRUIT

> [T]here is beyond question a body of very important but unorganized knowledge which cannot possibly be called scientific in the sense of knowledge of general rules: the knowledge of the particular circumstances of time and place. It is with respect to this that practically every individual has some advantage over all others because he possesses unique information of which beneficial use might be made, but of which use can be make only if the decisions depending on it are left to him or are made with his active co-operation. (Hayek, 1945, p. 521)

> The 'facts of the case' may be directly present to the subordinate, but highly difficult to communicate to the superior. The insulation of the higher levels of the administrative hierarchy from the world of fact known at first hand by the lower levels is a familiar administrative phenomenon. ... The information needed for a correct decision may be available only to the subordinate. (Simon, 1945, p. 238)

Let us sketch a model that illustrates how the paradox of low-hanging fruit can be explicated and how public policy might be fashioned to induce the firm to harvest it. In so doing, we will build on the previous sections which discussed the paradox, procedures and routines in companies, and our notion of organizational failures.

Organizational failures in an environmental context will be of two types. The first is a choice made or an action taken with a negative risk-adjusted expected value. This could be a violation of the environmental laws or some action that entails an excessive risk of causing an environmental accident for which the firm will be liable. The second is the failure to take a legitimate and profitable action (again in terms of a suitably risk-adjusted expected value). These are organizational failures because a rational and perfect black box firm would not make these mistakes, nor would a principal interested in maximizing shareholder value. Note that the first (which we will call a type II error) is not necessarily an agent's calculated decision to break the law or risk an accident, nor is the second an agent's conscious neglect of profitable opportunities (a type I error). Rather, errors are inadvertent; they occur because information is imperfect, communication is costly and human rationality is limited.

To model these errors, one must model a decision-making process within a firm. Imagine that a corporate principal is fashioning an environmental policy[13] for the corporate agents whose actions invariably entail risk of error. The objective of the policy is to reduce the probability of these errors. The principal must choose the form of the environmental policy. Let us imagine that there are two decision variables to it. One is vigour of effort. This can be measured in terms of direct cost for training agents, for providing them with information, for staff to support them and for auditing and monitoring the agents. Specific examples of such costs might include involvement with the EPA's Green Lights programme, compliance with EMAS or ISO 14000 requirements and the cost of introducing green accounting systems. Presuming these efforts are effective, they should reduce organizational failures of both types.

The second decision variable is the constraint on agents' decision-making latitude. Two basic means are available to do this: SOPs and centralization of authority. Either one denies agents the ability to make *ad hoc* decisions. Although they are different means, they have the same consequences for the model we are developing, and we will speak from here on about SOPs. The reader may substitute centralization at will. As suggested by the quotations that introduce this section, to constrain agents' decision-making latitude may reduce the likelihood of a negligent act, but it will result in the loss of opportunity to profit from 'information ... available only to the subordinate'.

Although these two approaches are not inconsistent, they are likely to be substitutes. If agents' decision-making latitude is constrained by SOPs (or if the decisions are made closer to or even by the principal), then it is less necessary to disseminate information to agents and to audit their actions.

With this basic outline, we can model the firm as follows.[14] Agents face a flow of possible choices in their work. As regards those choices with environmental implications, some are inherently negligent. In the model following, let $P(N) > 0$ be the probability that any contemplated choice is inherently negligent, regardless of whether the agent makes the choice and regardless of whether it is detected if it does. The probability that negligence is actually committed, by contrast, is the product of $P(N)$ and the conditional probability that the firm embarks on the course of action, given that it is negligent ($P(A|N)$). We assume that $P(A|N) > 0$. *Ex post*, this may cause the firm no loss, and it may even earn a profit. Nonetheless, the expected value is negative because of the probability of detection, either by the enforcement authority's investigation or because of an actual environmental accident. The probability of detected negligence is the probability that a negligent act is committed multiplied by the conditional probability that, if committed, it is discovered ($P(S|A,N) > 0$). In this case, the firm faces a cost of compensation, perhaps environmental restitution, and punitive damages.

Not all accidents are the result of negligence, of course. It is always possible that an action that is not negligent in a legal sense can cause an accident. This probability would be given by $P(S|A,\cancel{N}) > 0$. If such should happen, the firm may have to compensate harmed parties, but this cost is naturally lower than that of a negligent accident.

Finally, the agents may inadvertently choose not to take advantage of a legitimate opportunity to save environmental resources. This is the mistake of leaving low-hanging fruit on the tree, and it entails a certain loss of the potential profit. In terms analogous to those above, $P(\bar{A}|\bar{N})$ is the probability that a legitimate course of action is not followed (a type I error).

The decision tree and the payoffs are shown below.

$$P(S|A,N) \quad P(N)P(A|N)P(S|A,N) = P(N,A,S) \quad -C_2$$

$P(A|N)$

$$P(\bar{S}|A,N) \quad P(N)P(A|N)P(\bar{S}|A,N) = P(N,A,\bar{S}) \quad \pi$$

$P(N)$

$P(\bar{A}|N)$

$$P(S|A,\bar{N}) \quad P(\bar{N})P(A|\bar{N})P(S|A,\bar{N}) = P(\bar{N},A,S) \quad \pi - C_1$$

$P(A|\bar{N})$

$$P(\bar{S}|A,\bar{N}) \quad P(\bar{N})P(A|\bar{N})P(\bar{S}|A,\bar{N}) = P(\bar{N},A,\bar{S}) \quad \pi$$

$P(\bar{N})$

$P(\bar{A}|\bar{N})$

So the firm's principal must design an environmental policy to maximize an expected return, $E(R)$

$$E(R) = \{P(N,A,\bar{S},) + P(\bar{N},A,\bar{S})\}\pi - P(N,A,S)C_2 + P(\bar{N},A,S)(\pi - C_1) - C_3 \quad (6.1)$$

where:

$P(N,A,\bar{S}) > 0$ is the probability that a negligent action is taken but not detected

$P(\bar{N},A,\bar{S}) > 0$ is the probability that a legitimate action is taken

$P(N,A,S) > 0$ is the probability that a negligent action is taken and detected

$P(\bar{N},A,S) > 0$ is the probability that a non-negligent action results in an environmental accident

C_1 is compensation and damages from a non-negligent accident

C_2 is punitive fines, damages, compensation and other costs from a negligent accident ($C_2 > C_1$)

C_3 is cost of training and monitoring agents

π is the profit earned from a legitimate action taken or a negligent action that is not detected

The expected return can be simplified by converting the joint probabilities into conditional probabilities and expressing them as the type I and II errors discussed above.

$f = P(A|\bar{N})$ is the probability that the company will make a type I error, that it will leave low-hanging fruit unpicked

$g = P(A|N)$ is the probability that the company will make a type II error; that it will take a negligent action

$m = P(S|A,\bar{N})$ is the probability that a non-negligent action results in an environmental accident

$n = P(\bar{S}|A,N)$ is the probability that a negligent action causes no accident

then,

$\alpha = (1 - n) C_2 - n\pi$ is the company's expected cost of a negligent action ($\alpha > 0$)

$\beta = \pi - m C_1$ is the company's expected benefit of a legitimate action ($\beta > 0$)

The requirement that α and β be positive implies, consistent with the text, that a rational actor would neither be purposefully negligent nor overlook a profitable action.

The expected return can now be rewritten as

$$E(R) = -P(N)g\alpha + P(\bar{N})(1 - f)\beta - C_3 \qquad (6.2)$$

The decision variables for the principal are the expenditure on training, information and monitoring, C_3, and a continuous variable X that measures the extent of SOPs controlling the agents' behaviour. A high value of X will denote extensive SOPs (or centralization). A low value, by contrast, means that the agent is empowered to make choices with few constraints. These two policy variables determine the type I and II error probabilities, f and g, with partial derivatives shown in Table 6.1.

$$f = f(C_3, X) \qquad (6.3)$$

$$g = g(C_3, X) \qquad (6.4)$$

Table 6.1   Partial derivatives

$f_c < 0$	$g_{cx} > 0$
$f_x > 0$	$f_{cc} > 0$
$g_c < 0$	$f_{xx} < 0$
$g_x < 0$	$g_{cc} > 0$
$f_{cx} < 0$	$g_{xx} > 0$

An increase in C_3 should simultaneously reduce both f and g, the company's type I and II error probabilities. By contrast, an increase in X, the extent of SOPs, should reduce type II errors but increase type I errors as agents are less able to exploit their knowledge of the uniqueness of each situation. The signs of the second derivatives are based on the idea of diminishing marginal effectiveness of the policy instruments. Presumably, steps with the greatest impact will be taken first. The assumption about the cross-partial derivatives rests on the notion that the marginal effectiveness of an instrument in reducing one error type is lessened to the extent that the other instrument has already reduced that error.

The principal will maximize $E(R)$ by varying C_3 and X. The first-order conditions can be solved for a maximum to give C_3^* and X^*, the optimal corporate environmental policy.

The manager's objective is to maximize $E(R)$ in equation (6.2) by varying C_3 and X with error probabilities implied by equations (6.3) and (6.4). First-order conditions for a maximum are

$$\partial E(R)/\partial C_3 = -P(N)g_c\alpha - P(\bar{N})f_c\beta - 1 = 0 \qquad (6.5)$$

$$\partial E(R)/\partial X_3 = -P(N)g_x\alpha - P(\bar{N})f_x\beta = 0 \qquad (6.6)$$

The two first-order conditions can be solved to give C_3^* and X^*, the profit-maximizing values of C_3 and X.

Second-order conditions required for a maximum are

$$P(N)g_{cc}\alpha + P(\bar{N})f_{cc}\beta > 0$$

$$P(N)g_{xx}\alpha + P(\bar{N})f_{xx}\beta > 0$$

and

$$\{P(N)g_{cc}\alpha + P(\bar{N})f_{cc}\beta\}\{P(N)g_{xx}\alpha + P(\bar{N})f_{xx}\beta\} - \{P(N)g_{cx}\alpha + P(\bar{N})f_{cx}\beta\}^2 > 0$$

The first two inequalities hold from our earlier assumptions. The third cannot be guaranteed, however. It simply describes a condition that must exist if there is to be a profit-maximizing equilibrium.

Comparative static analysis gives the signs shown in Table 6.2.

This model shows that by endogenizing the firm's compliance policy, we can get an insight into several phenomena not otherwise revealed. We see that starting with the positive set of probabilities laid out on the previous pages, there is always a likelihood of environmental accidents, whether negligent or non-negligent. The initial probabilities are positive because of the organiza-

Table 6.2   Signs of comparative static results for the corporation

Exogenous variable	Endogenous variable			
	C_3^*	X^*	f	g
C_1	(−)	(+)	(+)	(?)
C_2	(+)	(+)	(?)	(−)
m	(−)	(+)	(+)	(?)
n	(−)	(−)	(?)	(+)
π	(?)	(−)	(?)	(?)

tional failures discussed early in the chapter, and the company's environmental policy does not drive them to zero. C_3 is increased only until it becomes uneconomic and not until there are no longer any errors. The same is true for X. We see, as well, that there is always low-hanging fruit on the tree.

Comparative static analysis shows that an increase in the cost of accidents or the probability that negligence is detected and punished will prompt an adaptation in corporate environmental policy, and that the form of adaptation depends on the precise nature of the accident.

For example, if penalties for a negligent act are increased, the principal will adapt policy by increasing the training and monitoring of agents and by increasing the SOPs which constrain agents' discretion. This will unambiguously lower the risk of an environmental accident since both forms of corporate policy response act in the same direction. The impact on the amount of low-hanging fruit left on the tree is ambiguous, however. The reason is that the two forms of response have opposing effects on the probability of type I errors. More training, monitoring, information, support staff, green accounting, etc. will make managers more conscious of the environment generally, and they should pay more attention to low-hanging fruit as a result. But more standardized procedures will have the opposite effect. We cannot say which effect is the stronger.

The result described above will also occur if the environmental enforcement agency becomes more diligent in enforcing its policy, raising the likelihood that negligence is caught.

If we are to examine Porter's hypothesis that environmental policy may affect the likelihood that low-hanging fruit is picked, we have to examine the environmental authority's policy options. It can, of course, vary the penalties for a negligent accident or a detected violation. Let us assume that, in addition, it can determine restitution or clean-up costs and that it has the discretion to award damages to harmed parties, even if an accident was not negligent.

If more strict public environmental policy is to reduce accidents while at the same time encouraging firms to pick and profit from low-hanging fruit, then it must prompt a very specific corporate environmental policy reaction. It must first cause the firm to reduce its SOPs and thus grant more decision-making latitude to agents. Second, and simultaneously, public policy must prompt the firm to increase the training and support given to the agents to help them in their decision making. The results of comparative static analysis show that this will occur with a policy package that combines two enforcement elements: heavier penalties for negligence (higher C_3) and lower costs for the firm on the occurrence of an accident in which there was no negligence (lower C_1). In the limit, this would argue against rules of strict liability in lieu of increasing penalties for negligence.

The firm's adaptation process to this public policy change works as follows. A heavier penalty for negligence raises both C_3 and X, which reduces the probability of an accident but has an ambiguous impact on low-hanging fruit. A reduction in damages for a non-negligent accident also raises C_3 but lowers X, reinforcing the reduction in the probability of a negligent accident. The other consequence, however, is that the principal will reduce SOPs. This reinforces the impact of higher spending on training and monitoring on type I errors, and it should reduce low-hanging fruit. To conclude, the policy should reduce both the social cost of environmental accidents and the private cost of low-hanging fruit.

This does not demonstrate the Porter hypothesis, however. To do so, we must still show that the adaptation process described can increase $E(R)$, the firm's expected return. If we substitute the first-order conditions (6.5) and (6.6) into the objective function (6.2), we get the expected returns to the firm when corporate environmental policy is optimal:

$$E(R) = \{P(N)\beta f_c + 1\}g/g_c + \{-P(N)\alpha g_x\}(1-f)/f_x - C_3 \qquad (6.7)$$

We can then take the total derivative of (6.7) with respect to C_1 and C_2. If the signs are not unambiguously positive with C_1 and negative with C_2, then the Porter hypothesis is feasible. Note that we do not intend to show that strict environmental policy always enhances competitiveness. Porter did not say this; he said it 'often' did. So we do not require that the two signs be respectively negative and positive. Ambiguous signs are all we need to show that the hypothesis is feasible.

The first term to the right of the equality in (6.7) comprises the cost of negligent actions, net of gains from those that do not result in accidents and thus by assumption are not detected. The second term comprises the returns to the firm from legitimate actions, net of the cost of those that cause accidents. The final term is the cost of training and monitoring.

Not surprisingly, some of the elements of the total derivative of (6.7) are ambiguous in sign, and in composition there are offsetting impacts which render the overall signs ambiguous.[15]

We can summarize the results first with respect to an increase in fines and penalties for negligence and second with respect to a reduction in costs for non-negligent accidents. Regarding increased fines and penalties, we have the following.

1. This will have an ambiguous impact on the total cost to the firm of negligent acts. It will increase SOPs' restraint on agents' decision making, and it will increase spending on agents' training and monitoring. Both of these work in concert to reduce the frequency of negligent actions, but not necessarily enough to offset the higher cost of each single negligent act.
2. It has an ambiguous impact on the cost to the firm of low-hanging fruit since SOPs increase it while training reduces it.
3. There will be an unambiguous increase in training and monitoring cost to the firm.

A reduction in costs for non-negligent accidents will have the following consequences.

1. It will have an ambiguous impact on the cost of negligent acts since there will be more discretion for agents (fewer SOPs) coupled with increased training and monitoring. These two organizational changes have counteracting effects on the probability of a negligent act.
2. There will be a certain increase in the firm's returns from legitimate actions because both the reduction in SOPs and the increase in training reduce low-hanging fruit. This will be supported by the lower costs of non-negligent accidents noted above.
3. There will be an unambiguous increase in training and monitoring cost to the firm.

In conclusion, stricter environmental policy (interpreted here as a policy change that increases the penalties for negligence and reduces the frequency of accidents) may increase a firm's returns by reducing its absolute costs, that is, it may fit the results Porter hypothesized.

The reader should note, finally, that the firm could not have raised its profit unilaterally without the change in public policy. Although it could unilaterally mimic the increase in fines and damages for negligence, it needed the public policy maker to reduce the liability for non-negligent accidents. In other words, the firm was on an efficiency frontier prior to the policy change, an efficiency frontier that took account of the agents' imperfect information.

FURTHER INSTRUMENTS

We will discuss below several additional instruments that might be of use. This is surely not an exhaustive list, but it is our attempt to show at least some of the major alternatives.

The Compensation System

In Gabel and Sinclair-Desgagné (1993a), we explored the extent to which an incentive-based compensation system could be used to deal with a multi-task principal–agent problem. The model we presented in that paper was one in which an agent allocated a limited amount of effort between two tasks. One task earned profit for the firm and the other task reduced the risk of an environmental accident. The principal wanted to control the agent's allocation of effort between the tasks, but that allocation was not observable. The principal could only infer the agent's effort from some imperfect measure of performance on each task. So in this model, there was costless but imperfect and indirect monitoring of the variable of interest – the agent's effort. The question we posed was whether the principal should link the agent's compensation to the measure of performance on environmental risk reduction.

We found from the model that when the agent's effort constraint was not binding, then it was optimal for the principal to use an incentive wage to reward performance on environmental risk reduction. Furthermore, the slope of the optimal performance–wage schedule for either task was proportional to both the principal's eagerness to influence performance on the task and to the relative accuracy of the principal's measure of the agent's effort expended on it. In this model, monitoring technology and accuracy were exogenous.

If the agent's effort constraint is binding, however, then it may not be efficient for the principal to pay an incentive wage based on measured performance on environmental risk reduction. This rather surprising result has an intuitive rationale. If the effort constraint were binding, interaction between the principal and the agent would be limited to risk sharing, but efficient risk sharing requires that the marginal rates of substitution between the various income levels be equal. This could only be achieved if the wage schedule were invariant in the measure of risk reduction.

Auditing Non-Financial Objectives

In the model described above, monitoring was free, and its technology and accuracy were exogenous. In reality, every monitoring system is costly, and if the principal were to spend more, he or she could usually improve the system's accuracy. That is, accuracy should be endogenized. So a pertinent question to ask is how the principal should make the optimal joint decision on the level of monitoring of effort on the non-financial environmental objective and the compensation for both tasks. (Monitoring financial performance is also important, of course, but one can assume that it is done routinely irrespective of environmental concerns.)

Intuitively, monitoring would enter the principal's utility function as a cost along with the contingent wage. The principal would then maximize over the two control variables – the wage and the expenditure on monitoring. The agent's utility function would presumably be unchanged.

The benefit to the principal of greater expenditure on monitoring is that it would improve the accuracy of his or her inference of the agent's effort on environmental risk reduction. With more precision here, the principal would increase the slope of the performance–wage gradient. This would shift more of the risk of an environmental accident to the agent, and the agent would adjust by dedicating more effort to that activity, *ceteris paribus*.

A further benefit of spending more on monitoring is that it would improve the principal's assessment of whether the effort constraint on the agent was binding. As explained above, the choice of a salary system depends on this assessment. Once the quality of monitoring is endogenized, a linkage can be modelled between the cost of monitoring and the cost of a mistaken salary system.

In Sinclair-Desgagné and Gabel (1997), we used a multi-task, multi-signal principal–agent model to look at the optimal design of environmental audits and the manager's consequent allocation of effort. We showed that where managers had discretion on how to distribute their effort between standard business duties and environmental protection, the occurrence of environmental audits and the optimal wage structure should depend on the importance of the managers' prudence (or precautionary motives) relative to their aversion to risk. When prudence dominates risk aversion, environmental audits should be triggered by high financial assessments, and the wage of an audited manager should go up on average. When risk aversion dominates, however, environmental audits should be held if financial assessments are low, and the expected compensation of an audited manager should be lower than the wage when no audit occurs. These results therefore predict that environmental audits will happen more frequently when managers' attitude toward risk is strongly driven by precautionary motives, because in this case such audits constitute a reward rather than a punishment.

Internal Pricing

There are alternatives to assigning an agent multiple and potentially conflicting financial and non-financial tasks. One is for the principal to try to correct the firm's system of internal accounting prices to reflect all implicit values of the firm. If the firm were to internalize all externalities to the agent that are borne by the principal, then decentralized decision making within the firm would again be optimal to the principal. With the measure of performance on both tasks reduced to a single financial criterion, there would be no conflict between the tasks. But how could this be done?

Note that this problem is similar to, but not the same as, the familiar transfer pricing problem. The transfer pricing problem is commonly portrayed as one of finding the price for intra-firm trade that comes closest to inducing an efficient level of that trade. Presuming no exogenously available reference price, the challenge is to design an incentive mechanism to tease the correct price out of those in the firm who know it. The problem we describe here is again one of getting correct intra-firm prices, but there is no *prima facie* argument that individuals know the correct prices but have an incentive to conceal them. Rather, the principal must construct truly unknown prices (or their expected values) from data that are costly to collect.

There are many examples of companies that have attempted to improve their environmental performance via this means. Naturally, environmental audits are a frequent starting point since one of their goals is to gather data on actual and potential environmental costs facing the firm. One example is that of a European chemical producer that attempted to identify all environmental costs allocated to its overhead accounts and then to shift those costs to the products or processes that truly generated them. For example, insurance premia and legal fees incurred or expected were charged to specific production centres or products. With altered costs and product margins caused by these additional charges, production and sales managers' incentives to favour environmentally benign options increased. In a similar vein, products whose use might create future liabilities, legal or just in terms of image, could be 'artificially' burdened by accounting charges reflecting that risk (Epstein, 1996a,b,c). Feeding back through an incentive system based on profit, such products would be shunned in favour of environmentally preferable alternatives.

Another example appeared some years ago in the US steel industry. The EPA experimented with intra-firm emissions trading in the early 1980s. That allowed Armco Steel to employ linear and integer programming models

(Bodily and Gabel, 1982) to calculate the shadow price of its particulate effluents. Then the company charged its many facilities with their use value. Re-optimization earned the company a saving of $50 million annually. Although Armco dealt with emissions entitlements as an idiosyncratic experience, firms that become accustomed to emissions trading should build entitlement values into their formal cost accounting systems.

A further example of the spirit of this corporate policy is the effort of automobile producers to design models on the basis of an assumption that the makers would be responsible for repossessing the cars at the end of their lifetimes. With the costs of recovery, remanufacturing, recycling, or ultimate disposal imposed on design teams, the cars should emerge at least somewhat less environmentally pernicious. This example suggests a role for life-cycle analysis. Unlike environmental audits which look at the firm *per se*, life-cycle analysis, despite all its methodological and practical inadequacies, looks upstream and downstream at the firm. With life-cycle analysis, firms can apprise themselves of the otherwise invisible costs that they may find themselves unexpectedly bearing.[16]

Although this is a simple look at internal pricing, at a more subtle level, problems of impacted information and perverse incentives may assert themselves. For example, if intra-firm prices are 'corrected' for costs incurred by the principal but previously external to the agent, should the agent have the option to subcontract work to other firms? One can assume that there are external costs there, too, and that some of them may be borne by the principal. Under these (reasonable) assumptions, it is clear that questions of transfer pricing are not independent of questions of organizational form. Those questions could range from centralization vs decentralization of decision making all the way to integration vs specialization of the firm's activities. This suggests the relevance of work such as that of Holmström and Tirole (1991), which attempts to integrate transfer pricing and organizational form. The authors admit that their work is exploratory and at this stage cannot offer specific predictions, but the questions it poses are relevant to environmental resource management. How much flexibility should units in the firm have? Is the opportunity cost of trading outside of the firm large or small? Is monitoring of outside trading relations feasible, and, if so, at what cost?

This is not an artificial problem, and the oil industry provides an example of it. A diversified oil company could burden its shipping division with the insurable and non-insurable costs of many kinds that the corporation, as distinct from the division, would expect to incur should there be an oil spill. The intent would be to ensure a correct incentive for the shipping division to undertake risk-minimizing actions (like operating vessels with double-bottomed hulls). But once those costs were allocated, the division might decide to subcontract some of its shipping (for example, that in US waters where the legal liability for a spill is especially great) to small independent firms protected by their limited liability. Should this be permitted?

Precisely this question arose after the Exxon Valdez accident. Seeing the enormity of Exxon's legal liability and loss of reputation, Shell Oil's transport division ceased commercial tanker operations in US waters and contracted it to small shippers instead. Other oil companies refrained from following Shell's lead, and presumably employed other control systems instead. Yet a systematic model to examine these alternatives is still missing.

Horizontal Task Restructuring

Another alternative to assigning potentially conflicting profit and environmental risk reduction responsibilities to a single agent is to assign the different tasks to different agents. This, like internal accounting reforms, would obviate the problem of designing a reward system to control how one agent allocated his or her effort. In essence, the amount of effort dedicated to the different tasks is centralized with the principal, who decides on the number of agents assigned to each. But there is still the problem of how to define the tasks and how to structure the incentives for them.

Holmström and Milgrom (1991) argue that tasks for which performance is relatively easy to assess should be assigned to one manager, while tasks that are inherently difficult to monitor should be assigned to another. The former's compensation should be incentive based while the latter's should not be. It seems reasonable to assume that direct profit-making tasks are relatively easy to monitor while it is inherently difficult to monitor non-financial environmental tasks. It follows that profit and loss objectives should go to one agent while environmental performance should be the domain of another. The former should face an incentive compensation scheme and the latter not. This match between monitoring accuracy and compensation scheme is consistent with our results in the single-agent, multi-task problem referred to above.

The match is also consistent with commonly observed business practice. Firms often have line managers with profit and loss responsibility working under strong incentive salary plans based on financial measures, while staff responsible for environmental affairs have salaries de-coupled from operating profit. Under such an organizational arrangement, the environmental staff may be responsible for making capital investment decisions (with a budget allocated centrally) intended to reduce environmental effluents or risks.

Corporate Sanctions of Agents for Negligence

Segerson and Tietenberg (1992) used a principal–agent model to analyse the issue of corporate vs individual legal sanctions for violations of environmental laws. A related issue is that of corporate-imposed sanctions for agents guilty of violating company environmental policy (whether or not the violation caused environmental damage).

It is common for companies exposed to the risk of environmental liability to attempt to shift some of it to the employees whose negligent actions may incur that liability. This can be done by threatening dismissal, for example, or by stating in the employment contract that legal aid and the indemnification of fines would be denied to any employee found personally and negligently liable for an environmental accident.

In the context of a model, liability cost functions dependent on the damage caused or the seriousness of the breach of company policy would have to be specified for both principal and agent and then subtracted from their respective utility functions. Furthermore, a conditional probability of an environmental accident given the agent's action would have to be specified.

Unfortunately, if principals punish agents for mistakes, the agents may try to hide those mistakes. There are many instances in which immediate reporting of mistakes can allow the principal to mitigate both their social and private costs. In fact, prompt disclosure of environmental accidents is enshrined in the United Nations guidelines for transnational corporations (United Nations Center on Transnational Corporations, 1991). Are there ways by which a balance can be struck between a motive to punish negligence and a desire for immediate reporting?

Wathieu (1993) addressed this question in a formal principal–agent model. He showed that it was possible to set up an incentive scheme to induce self-reporting if the scheme entailed a penalty that diminished with the agent's time horizon. The penalty was always below the agent's liability constraint, and it was progressively more so with a decrease in either the agent's discount rate or the precision of the principal's ability to estimate the delay in reporting. With an increase in monitoring frequency, the size of the penalty can diminish. Rather unexpectedly, Wathieu showed that it was possible that the optimal company fine could be negative – that is, that the principal should reward the agent for reporting his or her own negligence. Despite the premium, however, the overall payoff to the agent of a mistake must still be negative (from the exogenous liability cost).

CONCLUSION AND DIRECTIONS FOR FUTURE RESEARCH

We have tried in this chapter to convince the reader that relative to spending more research time looking at market relationships between firms, there is a very high return to looking at what happens inside the firm. Many of the tools to do so exist in the repertoire of the economist, and complementary tools and concepts are on offer in other disciplines, especially organizational science. We believe that the return is more than academic. Managers are under pressure to improve the environmental performance of their companies, and our impression is that serious academic thinking about how they can do so is only beginning. Once they write the corporate policy statement to the effect that they will respect the environment and be good citizens, most managers have little idea how to proceed; little idea how to translate their goal for the company into systems of incentives and controls to achieve it. Public policy makers have profited enormously from the work of academic economists over the years. Company policy makers need help, too.

There is a great deal of anecdotal evidence suggesting that Porter revealed more than random imperfections such as exist in all organizations. Although this chapter and other papers (Cebon, 1992; DeCanio, 1993, 1994; Schmutzler, 1998; Gabel and Sinclair-Desgagné, 1998) have tried to make sense of Porter's hypothesis in academic terms, there is more research to be done, since it is unlikely that any one theory or model will satisfy the intellectually curious student of business behaviour. In particular, there is need to do more formal modelling of organizational processes to explain the seemingly inexplicable failure of firms' employees to adopt 'obvious' cost- and environment-saving technologies and practices that fall far short of being radically new. The quotation that starts the section of this chapter on 'The paradox of low-hanging fruit' and the paragraph following it still present a challenge to economists and other scholars. If this chapter stimulates some to attack that challenge, it has succeeded to the authors' satisfaction.

Beyond research on the Porter hypothesis, there are fertile fields still to cultivate. Some have been suggested here. Others can easily be imagined. Organizational design within the single-unit firm, task assignment, span of authority, degree of delegation of responsibility, compensation, organizational design for the multi-unit firm, monitoring and auditing systems, human resource management, employee training, and many more tools at the command of the corporate principal deserve the attention of researchers in environmental economics.

NOTES

1. Regulatory failure, like market failure, has also been subject to careful academic scrutiny, albeit only relatively recently. It is because of the perceived ubiquity of regulatory failure – for example, the failure of command and control environmental policies – that there is so much interest now paid to the market-oriented policies that environmental economists have been promoting (see Crandall, 1992; Gupta, Miranda and Parry, 1993; Tietenberg, 1990). Regulatory failure will not be a topic of this chapter despite its importance.

2. Good examples of work in this genre are Epstein (1996a,b,c).
3. To keep the chapter focused, we will maintain the traditional assumption that the firm's principal desire is to maximize profits. Our point of departure from neoclassical economics is to reject its assumption that the firm can be represented as a single perfectly rational decision maker.
4. For an elaboration of some of this, see Milgrom and Roberts (1992), chapter 4.
5. The notion of routines is developed in Nelson and Winter (1982) and Postrel and Rumelt (1992).
6. For example, in a Canadian case over illegal sulphur emissions, a court ordered the company, Prospec, to obtain ISO 14001 certification.
7. The obvious alternative hypothesis is that the causality is reversed; that those countries' productivity levels and wealth caused their strict environmental regulations.
8. Although the majority of economists probably dismiss the Porter hypothesis, at least as expressed here, it may have the redeeming political virtue of providing a counter argument to the business community's concern about cost of compliance with environmental regulations.
9. The behaviouralists justified their assumption with empirical observations of human behaviour and the cognitive limitations that influence it.
10. In a mathematical maximization model, this simply represents the reduced objective function value that the new constraint causes.
11. Compatibility standards are the technological or dimensional standards that allow different products to work together. Examples are standards for computer hardware and software, standards for audio or video hardware and software, automobile wheels and tyres, etc.
12. Organization ecology posits that firms cannot change in any significant way; evolutionary economics accepts that they can, albeit with great difficulty.
13. The reader should note that in this chapter, the term environmental policy is not necessarily public policy. The distinction between public and private (corporate) environmental policy will be clear in the context or it will be specified.
14. This model is adapted from Beckenstein and Gabel (1986).
15. To simplify signing the expression, we assume that all the second-order derivatives are negligible compared to the other terms. They are set to zero.
16. Of course, if all prices were correct in the first place, then there would be no need for a life-cycle analysis.

REFERENCES

Beckenstein, A. and L. Gabel (1986), 'The economics of antitrust compliance', *Southern Economic Journal*, **52**(3), 673–92.

Bodily, S.E. and H.L. Gabel (1982), 'A new job for businessmen: managing the company's environmental resources', *Sloan Management Review*, Summer, 3–18.

Cebon, P. (1992), ''Twixt lip and cup: organizational behaviour, technical prediction and conservation practices', *Energy Policy*, **20**(9), 802–14.

Coase, R. (1992), 'The institutional structure of production', *American Economic Review*, **82**(4), 713–19.

Crandall, R. (1992), 'Why is the cost of environmental regulation so high?', Center for the Study of American Business, Policy Study No. 110.

Cyert, R. and J. March (1992), *A Behavioral Theory of the Firm*, 2nd edn, Cambridge: Blackwell.

David, P. and S. Greenstein (1990), 'The economics of compatibility standards: an introduction to recent research', *Economics of Innovation and New Technology*, **1**(1), 3–42.

DeCanio, S. (1993), 'Barriers within firms to energy-efficient investments', *Energy Policy*, **21**(9), 906–14.

DeCanio, S. (1994), 'Agency and control problems in US corporations: the case of energy-efficient investment projects', *Journal of Economics and Business*, **1**(1), 105–23.

The Economist (1991), 31 August, 15.

Epstein, M. (1996a), *Measuring Corporate Environmental Performance*, Burr Ridge, IL: Irwin.

Epstein, M. (1996b), 'You've got a great environmental strategy – now what?', *Business Horizons*, September–October, 53–9.

Epstein, M. (1996c), 'Improving environmental management with full environmental cost accounting', *Environmental Quality Management*, Autumn, 11–22.

Farrell, J. and G. Saloner (1985), 'Standardization, compatibility, and innovation', *Rand Journal of Economics*, **16**(1), 70–83.

Farrell, J. and G. Saloner (1986), 'Installed base and compatibility: innovation, preannouncements, and predation', *American Economic Review*, **76**(5), 940–55.

Gabel, H.L. and B. Sinclair-Desgagné (1993a), 'Managerial incentives and environmental compliance', *Journal of Environmental Economics and Management*, **24**(3), 229–40.

Gabel, H.L. and B. Sinclair-Desgagné (1993b), 'Environmental regulation and firm structure', INSEAD Working Paper.

Gabel, H.L. and B. Sinclair-Desgagné (1995), 'Corporate responses to environmental concerns', in H. Folmer, H.L. Gabel and H. Opschoor (eds), *Principles of Environmental and Resource Economics: A Guide for Students and Decision-Makers*, Cheltenham, UK and Lyme, US: Edward Elgar, pp. 347–61.

Gabel, H.L. and B. Sinclair-Desgagné (1998), 'The firm, its routines, and the environment', in T. Tietenberg and H. Folmer (eds), *The International Yearbook of Environmental and Resource Economics 1998/1999: A Survey of Current Issues*, Cheltenham, UK and Northampton, MA: Edward Elgar.

Gore, A. (1993), *Earth in the Balance: Ecology and the Human Spirit*, New York: Penguin.

Gupta, S., K. Miranda and I. Parry (1993), 'Public expenditure policy and the environment: a review and synthesis', IMF Working Paper.

Hayek, F. (1945), 'The use of knowledge in society', *American Economic Review*, **35**, 519–30.

Holmström, B. and P. Milgrom (1991), 'Multi-task principal–agent analysis: incentive contract, asset ownership, and job design', *Journal of Law, Economics, and Organisation*, **7**, 24–52.

Holmström, B. and J. Tirole (1991), 'Transfer pricing and organisational form', *Journal of Law, Economics, and Organisation*, **7**, 201–28.

Jaffee, A., S. Peterson, P. Portney and R. Stavins (1995), 'Environmental regulations and the competitiveness of US manufacturing', *Journal of Economic Literature*, XXXIII(1), 132–63.

Kogut, B. and U. Zander (1992), 'Knowledge of the firm, combinative capabilities, and the replication of technology', *Organization Science*, **3**(3), 383–97.

Kuhn, T. (1962), *The Structure of Scientific Revolutions*, Chicago: University of Chicago Press.

Meyer, S. (1992), 'Environmentalism and economic prosperity: testing the environmental impact hypothesis', unpublished manuscript, MIT.

Milgrom, P. and J. Roberts (1992), *Economics, Organization and Management*, Englewood Cliffs: Prentice-Hall.

Miller, D. and P. Friesen (1984), *Organizations: A Quantum View*, Englewood Cliffs: Prentice-Hall.

Nadler, D. and M. Tushman (1997), *Competing by Design*, New York: Oxford University Press.

Nelson, R. and S. Winter (1982), *An Evolutionary Theory of Economic Change*, Cambridge, MA: Harvard University Press.

Oates, W., K. Palmer and P. Portney (1994), 'Environmental regulation and international competitiveness: thinking about the Porter hypothesis', unpublished manuscript, University of Maryland.

Palmer, K. and D. Simpson (1993), 'Environmental policy as industrial policy', *Resources*, Summer, 17–21.

Palmer, K., W. Oates, and P. Portney (1995), 'Tightening Environmental Standards: The Benefit-Cost or the No-Cost Paradigm?', *The Journal of Economic Perspectives* 9(4), 119–32.

Porter, M. (1991), 'America's Green Strategy', *Scientific American*, April, 96.

Porter, M. and C. van der Linde (1995), 'Green and competitive: ending the stalemate', *Harvard Business Review*, September–October, 120–34.

Postrel, S. and R. Rumelt (1992), 'Incentives, routines, and self-command', *Industrial and Corporate Change*, **1**(3), 397–425.

Rumelt, R. (1995), 'Inertia and transformation', in Montgomery (ed.), *Resource-Based and Evolutionary Theories of the Firm*, Boston: Kluwer, pp. 101–32.

Sappington, D. (1991), 'Incentives in principal–agent relationships', *Journal of Economic Perspectives*, **5**(2), 45–66.

Schmutzler, A. (1998), 'Environmental regulations and managerial myopia', unpublished manuscript, University of Zürich.

Segerson, K. and T. Tietenberg (1992), 'The structure of penalties in environmental enforcement', *Journal of Environmental Economics and Management*, **23**, 179–200.

Shiffrin, R. and W. Schneider (1977), 'Controlled and automatic human information processing: ii. perceptual learning, automatic attending, and a general theory', *Psychological Review*, **84**, 127–90.

Simon, H.A. (1945), *Administrative Behavior*, 3rd edn, New York: Free Press.

Simon, H.A. (1985), 'Human nature in politics: the dialogue of psychology with political science', *The American Political Science Review*, **79**(2), 293–304.

Simon, H.A. (1987), 'Bounded rationality', in J. Eatwell, M. Milgate and P. Newman (eds), *The New Palgrave Dictionary of Economics*, Vol. 1, London: Macmillan, p. 267.

Sinclair-Desgagné, B. (1994), 'La Mise en Vigueur des Politiques Environnementales et l'Organisation de la Firme', *L'Actualité Economique*, **70**(2), 211–24.

Sinclair-Desgagné, B. and H.L. Gabel (1997), 'Environmental auditing in management systems and public policy', *Journal of Environmental Economics and Management*, **33**(3).

Stiglitz, J. (1991), 'Symposium on organisations and economics', *Journal of Economic Perspectives*, **5**(2), 15–24.

Tietenberg, T. (1990), 'Economic instruments for environmental regulation', *Oxford Review of Economic Policy*, **6**, 17–33.

Tushman. M. and C. O'Reilly (1996), 'Ambidextrous organizations', *California Management Review*, **38**(4), 8–30.

United Nations Center on Transnational Corporations (1991), 'Transnational corporations and industrial hazards disclosure', New York: United Nations.

Walley, N. and B. Whitehead (1994), 'It's not easy being green', *Harvard Business Review*, May–June, 46.

Wathieu, L. (1993), 'Immediate self-reporting of mistakes', INSEAD Working Paper.

7. International trade and the environment: how to handle carbon leakage

Michael Hoel

1 INTRODUCTION

It is frequently argued that international trade makes it more difficult to reach an environmentally good outcome. One of the reasons often given is that international trade, and in particular internationally mobile capital, makes it difficult for the government of each country to pursue a policy which gives the environment enough attention. Typically, the argument goes something like this: in open economies with mobile capital across countries, governments will compete by offering conditions favourable to business in order to attract investment. One form such competition may take is that governments set lower environmental standards, for example through lower emission taxes, than they would without international competition. In their attempt to underbid each other with low environmental taxes, all countries end up with emissions that are higher than what is Pareto optimal for the whole group of countries.

The argument above has been studied in detail for the standard case by Oates and Schwab (1988) and others. An important conclusion is that in a competitive economy without any distortions (except for the environmental externality), and where emission taxes are used as the environmental policy instrument, there is no need for international coordination of the emission taxes. When the government of each country sets environmental taxes to maximize the utility levels of the country's consumers, we get a Pareto-optimal allocation of emissions and capital across countries.

Several important environmental problems have a transboundary dimension, that is, the environment in one country will depend on emissions in other counties. For transboundary environmental problems, the question of whether or not policies ought to be coordinated across countries has been addressed by Hoel (1991) for the case in which it is only the sum of emissions from all countries which affects the environment (the climate problem is such an example). It is shown that a system of emission quotas which are tradable between governments, and with no coordination of policies across countries, gives a (second-best) Pareto optimum provided: (a) each country is so small that its influence over the international price of emission quotas is negligible, and (b) all international prices except that of emission quotas are exogenous. Apart from these two restrictions, the conclusion that policy coordination is unnecessary is shown to hold under quite general assumptions about the objective functions of the countries' governments, the constraints on policies, and the functioning of the economies.[1] Assumption (b) is however quite restrictive. It rules out, for example, several of the cases of oligopolistic industries that compete internationally.

If the assumption that all markets are competitive is relaxed, it may no longer be true that international trade creates no problems for the design of environmental policy. There is a large literature on coordination of environmental policies under imperfect competition, including among others Barrett (1994a), Kennedy (1994), Rauscher (1991, 1994), Ulph, A. (1994) and Ulph, D. (1994). Consider, for example, the case of an imperfectly competitive industry, in which firms sell their products on an international market. For the case in which emissions from this industry are a purely national environmental problem, it has been shown, by for example Barrett (1994a), that it may be optimal for the government of each country to choose an environmental policy making marginal abatement costs lower than marginal environmental costs. This is an indirect way of subsidizing the industry, which may be optimal provided direct subsidization is ruled out. When the governments of all countries behave in this way, one may end up in a situation where all countries have more pollution than what is Pareto optimal.

For a transboundary environmental problem, in which the total emission level in each country is determined through an international agreement, a situation with too much pollution is by assumption ruled out. Also in such a situation, however, a government may find it desirable to try to use its environmental policy as a way of indirectly subsidizing the sector considered. The most obvious way would be to have, for example, a lower emission tax for this sector than for the rest of the economy. A more subtle form of an indirect subsidy would be to combine an emission tax with some form of direct regulation. For instance, in addition to a fuel tax, one could impose standards on insulation of houses and standards for fuel efficiency for cars in order to reduce the use of fossil fuels. Such a combination of policy instruments, which is not ruled out by, for example, the WTO, can in practice work in the same way as an outright differentiation of emission taxes. In order to avoid the inefficiencies associated by such differential treatment, an international environmental agreement could be supplemented with an agreement of policy coordination. This latter part of the agreement would not have to specify, for example, emission tax rates, but could specify which types of instruments should be allowed.

In the case of transboundary environmental problems, international trade and mobile capital may undermine the attempt of any particular country to improve the environment. The general point is that actions taken by a particular country (or group of countries) will in general affect equilibrium prices of internationally traded goods. This in turn may affect the production and consumption decisions of other countries, and thus emissions from these countries.

An important case of this type of mechanism, that has received considerable attention in the literature, is so-called carbon leakage. The phenomenon is related to attempts by one or more countries to reduce carbon emissions in order to slow down the climate change resulting from greenhouse gas emissions. The reason one gets carbon leakage is that international prices of fossil fuels and other goods may depend on the actions taken by the countries attempting to cut back their carbon emissions. In particular, if these countries reduce their demand for fossil fuels, international fuel prices will decline. This reduction of fuel prices will lead to an increase in fuel demand by other countries, and thus in their CO_2 emissions. In addition to this direct type of carbon leakage via the price of fossil fuels, there are also various indirect types of carbon leakages. The most important of these is via the prices of energy-intensive tradable goods. If the use of fossil fuels is reduced through a carbon tax, production of energy-intensive tradable goods will be reduced in the countries which introduce a carbon tax, thereby resulting in reduced CO_2 emissions from these countries. However, the reduced production of energy-intensive tradable goods in these countries may to some extent be counteracted by increased production of such goods in countries which have no climate policy, thus leading to increased emissions from the latter.

Several contributions to the literature discuss various aspects of carbon leakage; see, for example, Bohm (1993), Golombek, Hagern and Hoel (1995), Hoel (1994, 1996). Numerical simulations quantifying the importance of carbon leakage include Pezzey (1992a) and Kolstad, Light and Rutherford (1999), who conclude that the carbon leakage might be quite strong, while, for example, Oliveira-Martins, Burniaux and Martin (1992), Felder and Rutherford (1993), Perroni and Rutherford (1993) and Jacoby *et al.* (1997) give numerical simulations indicating that the effects are modest. The present chapter does not offer any numerical analysis of the problem of carbon leakage. Instead, it offers a detailed analysis of how one might handle carbon leakage, with explicit attention to the Kyoto agreement.

2 CARBON LEAKAGE UNDER THE KYOTO PROTOCOL

The Kyoto Protocol was signed in December 1997. It is the first international agreement specifying quantitative limits of greenhouse gas emissions for a large group of countries. This group, totalling 38 countries, consists of the so-called Annex B countries, which roughly speaking consist of the industrialized countries and the countries under transition (Russia and the East European countries). Henceforth these countries will simply be referred to as the industrialized countries. The emission limits vary from country to country, but on average the emissions from the industrialized countries over the five-year period 2008–12 must not exceed 94.8 per cent of their 1990 levels. Notice that these limits apply to the sum of greenhouse gas emissions. The composition of emissions of the different greenhouse gases is left for each country to decide unilaterally, within its overall limit. However, to simplify the subsequent discussion, we shall argue as if the emission limit applied directly to carbon emissions.

The Kyoto agreement includes formulations implying some degree of flexibility concerning the possibility of trade in emission quotas (see, for example, Barrett *et al.*, 1992, and Hoel, 1997a). Although it is not definitely decided yet, it is not unlikely that full flexibility will be permitted, so that one will have a system of tradable emission quotas among the authorities of the industrialized countries.

Ignoring carbon leakage, the economically efficient response for an individual country to the Kyoto agreement is to use domestic policy instruments that equalize marginal abatement costs across all domestic sources of emissions. This can be achieved either through a uniform domestic carbon tax, or through domestically tradable emission quotas for carbon (see, for example, Pezzey, 1992b). If the detailed rules of the Kyoto agreement turn out to allow full flexibility in the exchange of quotas between countries, an internationally given price for such quotas is likely to be established. In this case the international price of quotas should also be used domestically, through the choice of the carbon tax rate, or by linking a domestic tradable quota system to the international system. If international quota trade is not permitted, the domestic price of emissions (that is, carbon tax rate or domestic quota price) should be so high that the emission limit is reached, but not exceeded.

The brief discussion above tells us what is optimal as long as no consideration is given to carbon leakage. Notice also that carbon leakage among the industrialized countries is not an issue, since the sum of emissions is given through the agreement. However, there is a significant group of countries (basically all developing countries) that are given no quantitative emission limit through the Kyoto agreement. Carbon leakage from the industrialized countries to the developing countries is therefore an issue. Since it is the total greenhouse gas emissions from all countries which is important for climate development, it is reasonable to expect that the industrialized countries will be concerned with how large the emissions from developing countries are. In particular, the policies chosen by the industrialized countries may have an impact on the emissions in the developing countries. An argument often made is that carbon taxes should be differentiated in the industrialized countries, with low or zero taxes on energy-intensive tradable sectors. From the reasoning above, a low tax on these goods should contribute to limiting the extent of carbon leakage.

The issue of differentiating carbon taxes in order to limit carbon leakage has been treated in detail in Hoel (1996). The starting point of that paper is a situation in which a group of countries, for example, the industrialized countries, have committed themselves to cooperate. These countries are assumed to maximize their total welfare. This level of welfare depends on the consumption of all goods in the industrialized countries as well as total CO_2 emissions from *all* countries. An important conclusion in the paper is that the social optimum may be implemented by a carbon tax which is the same for all users of fossil fuels, that is, both for consumers and for all sectors using fossil fuels as an input in production (among the industrialized countries). The carbon leakage can be influenced by tariffs on the traded goods, that is, by a tax or subsidy on net imports or net exports.

This result is not surprising. There are two types of externalities within the industrialized countries, which may be internalized through appropriate taxes (or subsidies). First, there is the environmental externality of the emissions from the industrialized countries, which may be internalized through a uniform tax on the use of carbon. Second, there are externalities via the net imports of various goods, which affect the environment via the effect of the net imports on the behaviour of other countries. Obviously, it is not the industrialized countries' production or consumption of a good that affects the behaviour of the developing countries, but only the net import of the good. This externality may thus be internalized through appropriate taxes (positive or negative) on the net imports of traded goods.

It thus follows from the discussion above that tariffs are superior to a differentiation of carbon taxes if one wants to affect the degree of carbon leakage. However, it is not obvious that a set of tariffs is the best way to control the degree of carbon leakage. A more direct approach would be to try to induce the non-cooperating countries to implement policies that affect their emissions of greenhouse gases. This may be achieved through transfers from the industrialized to the developing countries, making each country of the latter group equally well off with the transfer and its climate policy as it would have been without the transfer and without the policy.

The topic of the present chapter is to analyse which of the two methods – that is, tariffs or transfer-induced policy changes, or perhaps a combination of the two – is the best way to handle carbon leakage.

I consider the industrialized countries as a group, denoted by the 'home country'. The interpretation of this is that these countries coordinate their policies in order to achieve the desired emissions from the developing countries. Acting on its own, each industrialized country is so small that the effect of its policy choice on carbon emissions from the developing countries will be negligible.

The group of developing countries is denoted by 'the foreign country'. Although these countries are thus formally treated as one country, it is not assumed that they act in a coordinated manner. On the contrary, in the analysis it is assumed that the foreign country takes all international prices as exogenous, which would be unrealistic if the developing countries had coordinated their behaviour.

3   THE FOREIGN COUNTRY

I use capital letters for variables in the foreign country, and small letters for variables referring to the home country and for variables common to the two countries. The foreign country consumes a vector $\mathbf{C} = (C_0, C_1,...,C_n)$, where C_0 is the consumption of carbon.[2] The utility level of the foreign country is $U = U(\mathbf{C})$. Net imports to the foreign country are given by the vector $\mathbf{M} = (M_0, M_1,...,M_n)$, so that the net output vector is $\mathbf{Y} = \mathbf{C} - \mathbf{M}$.

In most analyses, one is only interested in the net outputs of the goods, and not gross outputs and inputs. In such cases the net output set can be specified by a transformation function of the type $\phi(\mathbf{Y}) \leq 0$, where ϕ is increasing in each Y_i (with efficient net outputs satisfying $\phi(\mathbf{Y}) = 0$). In the present case, however, we are not only interested in net outputs of all goods, but also in the total amount of fossil fuels used as inputs. This fuel use equals carbon emissions from the production process, which is denoted by X. We therefore want to use a specification of the economy's technology which keeps track of fossil fuel inputs in production, that is, of X. For each value of X, there is a feasible set of net outputs of all goods. This may be specified by a transformation function of the type $F(\mathbf{Y},X) \leq 0$, where F is increasing in each Y_i. The derivative F_X captures the effect of using more fuel inputs in production. As long as fuel input is lower than the value which is efficient in the absence of environmental externalities, an increase in fuel use will increase the economy's ability to produce output, that is, $F_X < 0$.[3] Since $\mathbf{Y} = \mathbf{C} - \mathbf{M}$, we thus have the following equation describing efficient combinations of net outputs of all goods and carbon emissions from production

$$F(\mathbf{C} - \mathbf{M}, X) \leq 0 \tag{7.1}$$

The present analysis is static; it is therefore assumed that the foreign country cannot have a trade deficit (in the absence of any transfers). Denoting the vector of international prices by $\mathbf{p} = (p_0, p_1, \ldots, p_n)$, we thus have

$$\mathbf{pM}' \leq 0 \tag{7.2}$$

In the absence of any climate policy, the foreign country wishes to maximize its utility level subject to (7.1) and (7.2). This gives the indirect utility function

$$V(\mathbf{p}) = \max_{\mathbf{c}}\{U(\mathbf{C}) \text{ s.t. } (1) \text{ and } (2)\} \tag{7.3}$$

The maximization problem defined by (7.3) gives X and $\mathbf{M}$ as function of the international price vector

$$X = X(\mathbf{p}) \tag{7.4}$$

$$\mathbf{M} = \mathbf{M}(\mathbf{p}) \tag{7.5}$$

The functions V, X and $\mathbf{M}$ are homogeneous of degree zero in the price vector $\mathbf{p}$. Moreover, the envelope theorem implies that

$$\frac{\partial V(\mathbf{p})}{\partial p_k} = -\mu M_k(\mathbf{p}) \tag{7.6}$$

where μ is the shadow price of the trade constraint (7.2), that is the marginal utility of a money transfer E (that is with the more general constraint $\mathbf{pM}' \leq E$, we have $\mu = \partial V/\partial E$ evaluated at $E = 0$).

Consider next the case in which the foreign country receives a transfer E in exchange for limiting its total carbon emissions to L. Provided L is less than the optimal value of $C_0 + X$ in the case above, E must be positive for the foreign country to voluntarily accept this arrangement. Assuming that the foreign country will be willing to accept the deal as long as it is as least as well off with the arrangement than without it, the minimal transfer is defined by

$$E(\mathbf{p}, L, V(\mathbf{p})) = \min\{\mathbf{pM}' \text{ s.t. } U(\mathbf{C}) \geq V(\mathbf{p}), F(\mathbf{C} - \mathbf{M}, X) \leq 0, C_0 + X \leq L\} \tag{7.7}$$

The minimization problem defined by (7.7) gives $\mathbf{M}$ as a function of $\mathbf{p}$, L and $V(\mathbf{p})$:

$$\mathbf{M} = \mathbf{M}^*(\mathbf{p}, L, V(\mathbf{p})) \tag{7.8}$$

Both E and $\mathbf{M}^*$ are homogeneous of degree zero in the price vector $\mathbf{p}$. From now on we therefore normalize prices by keeping p_0 fixed throughout our analysis.

From the envelope theorem we have

$$\frac{\partial E}{\partial p_k} = M_k^*(\mathbf{p}, L, V(\mathbf{p})) \tag{7.9}$$

Notice that M_k^* measures the partial effect of a change in p_k on E. To find the total effect, we must add the effect going via $V(\mathbf{p})$. Together with (7.6) this implies

$$\frac{dE}{dp_k} = M_k^*(\mathbf{p}, L, V(\mathbf{p})) - (\mu \frac{\partial E}{\partial V}) M_k(\mathbf{p}) \tag{7.10}$$

The expression in (7.10) tells how the necessary transfer from the home country to the foreign country depends on the world market prices. Recall that the foreign country in reality consists of several countries, each taking the world market prices as given. Each country considers whether the transfer it is offered is sufficiently high for it to be willing to introduce the proposed limitation on its emissions. In equilibrium, the transfers will be just high enough for all countries to be willing to make these emission limitations. In this equilibrium there is a specific set of equilibrium prices. Each individual country takes this set of international prices as given, and considers whether or not to accept the proposed emission reduction and transfer.

In general, we cannot say much about the sign or magnitude of dE/dp_k. However, for carbon-intensive goods it seems likely that these terms are positive. The term $\mu \partial E/\partial V$ will normally be close to 1, as it is the product of the marginal effect of E on V (evaluated at $E = 0$) and the marginal effect of V on E (evaluated at the equilibrium value of E). However, M_k^* (imports *with* the climate policy) will normally differ from M_k (imports *without* any climate policy). This difference may be significant for carbon-intensive goods. For these goods we would expect the net imports to be increased as a response to the introduction of the climate policy, due to lower domestic production of these goods and given world market prices. Since the term $\mu \partial E/\partial V$ will normally be close to 1, it thus follows from (7.10) that if M_k^* is considerably larger than M_k, dE/dp_k is likely to be positive.

4   THE OPTIMAL POLICY FOR THE HOME COUNTRY

The home country consumes a vector $\mathbf{c} = (c_0, c_1,...,c_n)$, where c_0 is the consumption of carbon. The utility level of the home country is $u = u(\mathbf{c})$. Net imports to the home country are given by the vector $\mathbf{m} = (m_0, m_1,...,m_n)$ so that the net output vector is $\mathbf{c} - \mathbf{m}$. Carbon emissions from the production process are given by x. The relationship between these emissions and production is given by the constraint $f(\mathbf{c} - \mathbf{m}, x) \leq 0$. The discussion before equation (7.1) applies also to the function f.

International prices are determined by equilibrium in all goods markets, that is by

$$\mathbf{m} + \mathbf{M}^*(\mathbf{p}, L, V(\mathbf{p})) = 0 \qquad (7.11)$$

Taking L as given, this means that $\mathbf{p}$ is given by $\mathbf{p}(\mathbf{m})$. (Notice that since $\mathbf{M}^*$ is homogeneous of degree zero in $\mathbf{p}$, (7.11) only determines relative prices. As mentioned in the previous section, p_0 is therefore fixed arbitrarily.)

The home country has a target level of emissions both for itself (ℓ) and for the foreign county (L). From an environmental point of view it is, of course, only the sum $\ell + L$ that matters. However, for the present issue the allocation of $\ell + L$ into two sub-targets ℓ and L is of no importance. Given these emissions targets, the home country wishes to maximize its utility. More precisely, it wishes to maximize $u(\mathbf{c})$ subject to

$$f(\mathbf{c} - \mathbf{m}, x) \leq 0 \qquad (7.12)$$

$$c_0 + x \leq \ell \qquad (7.13)$$

$$\mathbf{p}(\mathbf{m})\mathbf{m}' + E(\mathbf{p}(\mathbf{m}), L, V(\mathbf{p}(\mathbf{m}))) \leq 0 \qquad (7.14)$$

In Appendix A it is shown that this leads to the following first-order conditions

$$\frac{u_0}{u_j} = \frac{f_0 - f_x}{f_j} \, j = 1,...,n \qquad (7.15)$$

$$\frac{f_i}{f_j} = \frac{p_i + T_i}{p_j + T_j} \quad i, j = 0, 1,...,n \qquad (7.16)$$

where

$$T_j = \sum_k m_k \frac{\partial p_k}{\partial m_j} + \sum_k \left(M_k^* - \left(\mu \frac{dE}{dp_k} \right) M_k \right) \frac{\partial p_k}{\partial m_j} \qquad (7.17)$$

or, using (7.10)

$$T_j = \sum_k m_k \frac{\partial p_k}{\partial m_j} + \sum_k \frac{dE}{dp_k} \frac{\partial p_k}{\partial m_j} \qquad (7.18)$$

Before interpreting the terms T_j, we shall see how this optimal solution may be implemented in a competitive economy.

The optimal solution may be implemented by having a uniform carbon tax τ on all carbon emissions, and a tariff T_j given by (7.17) on the import of good j ($j = 0,1,\ldots,n$).[4] For this case the consumer and producer price will be $p_j + T_j$ on good j for $j = 1,2,\ldots,n$. For carbon, $p_0 + T_0$ will be the price a producer gets from its sales of carbon, while both consumers and producers pay $p_0 + T_0 + \tau$ for their purchases of carbon. Consumers' utility maximization therefore gives

$$\frac{u_0}{u_j} = \frac{p_0 + \tau + T_0}{p_j + T_j} \qquad j = 1,\ldots,n \qquad (7.19)$$

and producers' profit maximization gives[5]

$$-\frac{f_x}{f_j} = \frac{\tau}{p_j + T_j} \qquad j = 0,1,\ldots,n \qquad (7.20)$$

It is straightforward to verify that equations (7.19)–(7.20) imply (7.15)–(7.16). In other words, the optimal solution may be achieved through a transfer to the foreign country, combined with a uniform domestic carbon tax and appropriate tariffs on imports and exports. The size of the transfer is given by (7.7), and thus depends on L, that is, on the home country's target for emissions in the foreign country. The domestic carbon tax rate is determined so that the domestic emissions constraint ℓ is met. Finally, tariffs are given by (7.17). These tariffs consist of two terms. The first term is a standard optimal tariff.[6] The second term has the following interpretation: the necessary transfer the home country has to pay in order to achieve the desired level of emissions from the foreign country depends on what the equilibrium values of the international prices are. The second term in (7.18) shows how the home country through its tariffs takes into consideration how the price effects of the tariffs also affect the transfer the country must pay.

5   CONCLUDING COMMENTS

Carbon leakage is a potential problem under the Kyoto agreement, since the developing countries have no quantitative commitments to cut back their greenhouse gas emissions. However, this does not imply that the industrialized countries ought to differentiate their carbon taxes, for example through giving energy-intensive sectors a lower carbon tax than other sectors. As shown in Hoel (1996), it is better for the industrialized countries to have the same tax for all sectors, and supplement the uniform carbon tax with appropriate import and export tariffs. It is demonstrated in Hoel (1996) that the tariff of each good consists of (a) a standard 'optimal tariff' term, and (b) a term reflecting how the import/export of the good affects emissions in the developing countries.

In the present chapter, I have also considered the possibility of inducing the developing countries voluntarily to cut back their emissions, through offering them transfers that compensate the costs their climate policy gives them. With this possibility, the appropriate tariffs are changed significantly compared with the case without such transfers. The import/export tariffs consist of two terms also in the present case. Moreover, the first term of the tariff for each good is also a standard optimal tariff in the present case. However, the second term is somewhat different in the present case than in the case with no transfers. In the present case, the second term is not directly related to how the import/export of the good affects emissions in the developing countries (as it was in the case without transfers). Instead, the second term reflects how the import/export of a good affects the transfer the home country must pay, via the effect on the equilibrium values of the international prices.

An interesting extension of the present work would be to study simulations of numerical models similar to the theoretical model presented here and in Hoel (1996). Through such simulations one could get a better idea of the qualitative and quantitative differences between the tariffs in the absence of transfers and the transfers which are supplementary to tariffs.

This chapter has focused mainly on carbon leakage in a situation where only a subgroup of all countries have emissions limits imposed on them through an international agreement. As mentioned in section 2, the whole concept of carbon leakage becomes meaningless in a situation where a Kyoto type of agreement is extended to include all countries. The present Kyoto agreement lasts only until 2012. However, the intention is to establish a similar type of agreement also for the years after 2012. Several influential countries in the Annex B group, for example, the US, are very concerned that the group of countries with emission limits should be significantly expanded in this future agreement.

There has been a significant literature addressing the question of what determines whether or not a country will voluntarily participate in an international environmental agreement of the Kyoto type.[7] Obviously, an important consideration for a country is a comparison of the situation if it participates with the situation if it chooses not to participate in the agreement. The extent to which a group of initial signatories take carbon leakage into consideration in their policy design may make a difference in the situation for a potential new signatory (see, for example, Hoel and Schneider, 1997). Moreover, if the original signatories take carbon leakage to the non-signatories into consideration, it may make a difference how they let this consideration affect their policies. The present chapter suggests that *given* the group of signatories and non-signatories, the best way to handle carbon leakage is to introduce specific import and export tariffs combined with transfers to the non-signatories in exchange for them limiting their carbon emissions. It is not obvious that this is the best policy if one takes the likelihood of the non-signatories joining the agreement at a later stage into account. Nevertheless, one could argue that the arrangement of transfers in exchange for limiting emissions is a first step towards these countries becoming formal signatories at a later stage. As future signatories of an agreement with tradable emission quotas, the present non-signatories could be given a number of quotas that is so high that their sale of excess quotas covers the costs they incur through limiting their emissions as a response to the price of quotas.

In the introduction, I gave two reasons why the presence of international trade and mobile capital might complicate the design of a good environmental policy. The reason that was the focus of the present chapter was related to transboundary environmental problems. In particular, I discussed how policies to reduce emissions in one country (or group of countries) could increase emissions in other countries. The other reason why the presence of international trade and mobile capital might complicate the design of a good environmental policy was related to imperfect competition. As mentioned in the introduction, there is a considerable literature discussing the latter issue. In most of this literature the environmental outcome is endogenously determined. However, with an international agreement of the Kyoto type, total emissions, and thus the environmental outcome, is determined through the agreement. The issue of whether or not environmental policies should be decentralized to the country level is therefore not an environmental issue, but may nevertheless be important from an economic point of view. Under the Kyoto agreement, policy design is left to the individual countries. The present chapter has argued that it may be in the interest of the signatories to let their policies be affected by the consideration of carbon leakage. If this is the case, policies must be coordinated across countries, since the effect of the policy of any individual country on the emissions of the non-Annex B countries is negligible. More generally, in a world with imperfect competition and other market failures, there may be reasons for all or some countries (for example, the EU countries) to coordinate their policies, even though total emissions from the countries are given through the agreement. I have studied one aspect of this issue elsewhere (Hoel, 1997b) for the case in which there is a market imperfection in the labour market (unemployment). However, compared with the importance and relevance for policy makers in, for example the EU countries, there has been surprisingly little research on this important issue.

APPENDIX A

Maximization of $u(c)$ subject to (7.12)–(7.14) defines the following Lagrangian

$$
\begin{aligned}
h = u(\mathbf{c}) - \alpha f(\mathbf{c} - \mathbf{m}, x) + \beta(l - c_0 - x) \\
- \gamma[\mathbf{p}(\mathbf{m})\mathbf{m} + E(\mathbf{p}(\mathbf{m}), L, V(\mathbf{p}(\mathbf{m})))]
\end{aligned}
\tag{7A.1}
$$

The first-order conditions are

$$
\frac{\partial h}{\partial c_0} = u_0 - \alpha f_0 - \beta = 0
\tag{7A.2}
$$

$$
\frac{\partial h}{\partial c_j} = u_j - \alpha f_j = 0 \quad j = 1, \ldots, n
\tag{7A.3}
$$

$$
\frac{\partial h}{\partial x} = -\beta - \alpha f_x = 0
\tag{7A.4}
$$

$$
\frac{\partial h}{\partial m_j} = \alpha f_j - \gamma \left[p_j + \sum_i m_i \frac{\partial p_i}{\partial m_j} + \sum_i \frac{\partial E}{\partial p_i} \frac{\partial p_i}{\partial m_j} + \sum_i \frac{\partial E}{\partial V} \frac{\partial V}{\partial p_i} \frac{\partial p_i}{\partial m_j} \right]
\tag{7A.5}
$$

which may be rewritten as (7.15)–(7.17), where

$$
T_j = \sum_k m_k \frac{\partial p_k}{\partial m_j} + \sum_k \left(\frac{\partial E}{\partial p_k} + \frac{\partial E}{\partial V} \frac{\partial V}{\partial p_k} \right) \frac{\partial p_k}{\partial m_j}
\tag{7A.6}
$$

Using (7.6) and (7.9), we see that (7A.6) is identical to (7.16).

NOTES

1. The reason why the outcome is only second-best and not first-best Pareto optimal is that if one had the possibility of removing some of the constraints on policies in the individual countries, or improving the functioning of domestic markets, it would generally be possible to increase welfare for all countries.
2. The simplification of only one type of fossil fuel, denoted 'carbon', is of no importance for the present analysis.
3. More precisely, $F_X < 0$ for $X < X^*(\mathbf{Y})$, where $X^*(\mathbf{Y})$ is the value of X which solves $\min_X F(\mathbf{Y},X)$. Notice also that the relationship between $\phi(\mathbf{Y})$ and $F(\mathbf{Y},X)$ is given by $\phi(\mathbf{Y}) = \min_X F(\mathbf{Y},X)$.
4. If good j is exported, we thus have an export subsidy if T_j is positive.
5. The gross output of carbon is $y_0 + x$; profits are therefore given by

$$\pi = \sum_i (p_i + T_i)y_i + (p_0 + T_0)x - (p_0 + T_0 + \tau)x = \sum_i (p_i + T_i)y_i - \tau x.$$

   Maximization of this expression subject to (7.11) gives us (7.15).
6. As shown in Hoel (1996), a similar term appears in the optimal tariffs when direct transfers to the foreign country are ruled out by assumption.
7. Among the important contributions are Barrett (1994b, 1997), Carraro and Botteon (1997), Carraro and Siniscalco (1993), Chander and Tulkens (1992, 1994, 1997) and Tulkens (1998).

REFERENCES

Barrett, S. (1994a), 'Strategic environmental policy and international trade', *Journal of Public Economics*, **54**, 325–38.

Barrett, S. (1994b), 'Self-enforcing international environmental agreements', *Oxford Economic Papers*, **46**, 876–94.

Barrett, S. (1997), 'Heterogeneous international environmental agreements', in C. Carraro (ed.), *International Environmental Negotiations,* Cheltenham, UK and Northampton, MA: Edward Elgar.

Barrett, S., M. Grubb, K. Roland, A. Rose, R. Sandor and T. Tietenberg (1992), *Combating Global Warming: A Global System of Tradable Carbon Emission Entitlements*, Geneva: UNCTAD.

Bohm, P. (1993), 'Incomplete international cooperation to reduce CO_2 emissions: alternative policies', *Journal of Environmental Economics and Management*, **24**: 258–71.

Carraro, C. and M. Botteon (1997), 'Burden sharing and coalition stability in environmental negotiations with asymmetric countries', in C. Carraro (ed.), *International Environmental Negotiations*, Cheltenham, UK and Northampton, MA: Edward Elgar.

Carraro, C. and D. Siniscalco (1993), 'Strategies for the international protection of the environment', *Journal of Public Economics*, **52**: 309–28.

Chander, P. and H. Tulkens (1992), 'Theoretical foundations of negotiations and cost-sharing in transfrontier pollution problems', *European Economic Review*, **36**, 288–99.

Chander, P. and H. Tulkens (1994), 'A core-theoretic solution for the design of cooperative agreements on transfrontier pollution', *International Tax and Public Finance*, **2**, 279–93.

Chander, P. and H. Tulkens (1997), 'The core of an economy with multilateral environmental externalities', *International Journal of Game Theory*, **26**, 379–401.

Felder, S. and T.F. Rutherford (1993), 'Unilateral CO_2 reductions and carbon leakage: the consequences of international trade in oil and basic materials', *Journal of Environmental Economics and Management*, **25**, 162–76.

Golombek, R., C. Hagem and M. Hoel (1995), 'Efficient incomplete international climate agreements', *Resource and Energy Economics*, **17**, 25–46.

Hoel, M. (1991), 'Principles for international climate corporation', in T. Hanisch (ed.), *A Comprehensive Approach to Climate Change* (CICERO, Oslo).

Hoel, M. (1994), 'Efficient climate policy in the presence of free riders', *Journal of Environmental Economics and Management*, **27**(3), 259–74.

Hoel, M. (1996), 'Should a carbon tax be differentiated across sectors?', *Journal of Public Economics*, **59**, 17–32.

Hoel, M. (1997a), 'How should international greenhouse gas agreements be designed?', in P. Dasgupta, K.-G. Maler and A. Vercelli (eds), *The Economics of Transnational Commons*, Oxford: Clarendon Press, pp. 172–91.

Hoel, M. (1997b), 'Coordination of environmental policy for transboundary environmental problems?', *Journal of Public Economics*, **66**, 199–224.

Hoel, M. and K. Schneider (1997), 'Incentives to participate in an international environmental agreement', *Environmental and Resource Economics*, **9**, 153–70.

Jacoby, H.D., R.S. Eckhaus, A.D. Ellerman, R.G. Prinn, D.M. Reiner and Z. Yang (1997), 'CO_2 emissions limits: economic adjustment and the distribution of burdens', *The Energy Journal*, **18**, 31–58.

Kennedy, P.W. (1994), 'Equilibrium pollution taxes in open economies with imperfect competition', *Journal of Environmental Economics and Management*, **27**, 49–63.

Kolstad, C., M. Light and T.H. Rutherford (1999), 'Coal markets and the Kyoto Protocol', mimeo, University of California, Santa Barbara and University of Colorado, Boulder.

Oates, W.O. and R.M. Schwab (1988), 'Economic competition among jurisdictions: efficiency enhancing or distortion inducing?', *Journal of Public Economics*, **35**, 333–54.

Oliveira-Martins, J., J.M. Burniaux and J.P. Martin (1992), 'Trade and the effectiveness of unilateral CO_2-abatement policies: evidence from GREEN', *OECD Economic Studies*, **19**, Paris, 123–40.

Perroni, C. and T.F. Rutherford (1993), 'International trade in carbon emission rights and basic materials: general equilibrium calculations for 2020', *Scandinavian Journal of Economics*, **95**, 257–78.

Pezzey, J. (1992a), 'Analysis of unilateral CO_2 control in the European Community', *The Energy Journal*, **13**, 159–72.

Pezzey, J. (1992b), 'The symmetry between controlling pollution by price and quantity', *Canadian Journal of Economics*, **25**, 983–91.

Rauscher, M. (1991), 'Foreign trade and the environment', in H. Siebert (ed.), *Economics and the Environment: The International Dimension*, Mohr, Tübingen.

Rauscher, M. (1994), 'On ecological dumping', *Oxford Economic Papers*, **46**, 822–40.

Tulkens, H. (1998), 'Cooperation versus free-riding in international affairs: two approaches', in N. Hanley and H. Folmer (eds), *Game Theory and the Environment*, Cheltenham, UK and Northampton, MA: Edward Elgar.

Ulph, A. (1994), 'Environmental policy. Plant location and government protection', in C. Carraro (ed.), *Trade, Innovation, Environment*, Dordrecht: Kluwer.

Ulph, D. (1994), 'Strategic innovation and strategic environmental policy', in C. Carraro (ed.), *Trade, Innovation, Environment*, Dordrecht: Kluwer.

8. Poverty, environment and development

Anil Markandya

1 INTRODUCTION

The literature on the nexus between poverty, environment and development is enormous. Important recent surveys include Dasgupta and Mäler (1994), Dasgupta (1996) and Duraippah (1996). In spite of these, however, even the most diligent scholar could spend several years reading the various papers, reports, books and so on that touch on these issues, and still not cover everything. The present author, while conscientious and painstaking, knows that there are bound to be gaps in what has been undertaken as background research for this chapter. A fairly large sample of the literature reveals, however, that, in terms of drawing out the main issues and in defining the research challenges, what has been reviewed provides a reasonable background. There should be few surprises in terms of major findings or 'stylized facts' in what has been omitted from the references at the end of this chapter.

There are several questions that one can sensibly ask (and that have been asked) about the linkages between the three themes of this chapter. These are summarized in Table 8.1 below and the chapter is organized around the six questions posed there. They relate to a wide range of phenomena and involve quite different ways of looking at the world. Some are comparisons of the same region or community at two different points in time. Some look at how communities evolve over time, and some compare different communities or nations at the same, or different, points in time.

In order to keep the discussion manageable, the focus in this chapter is on developing countries, although evidence from industrialized countries is quoted where it is useful for the argument. As one would expect, there are disagreements about the magnitude of the effects of some policies, or even the direction of the effects. The present chapter offers one view of how the different strands can be reconciled, and what further research is needed to advance our understanding of this important subject.

Table 8.1   Major issues in the poverty, environment and development literature

Issue	Key literature related to the issue
An increase in poverty within the community results in increased environmental degradation. Conversely, a reduction in poverty will reduce environmental degradation.	Southgate (1998), Mink (1993), De Janvry and Garcia (1988).
Other things being equal, an environment inhabited by the poor will be more degraded than one inhabited by the rich.	Jaganathan (1989), Deininger and Minten (1996), Brooks and Sethi (1997), Tietenberg (1996), Linde-Rahr (1998), Aheeyar (1998).
There have been important social changes (policies, external events) that have resulted in concurrent increases in poverty and environmental degradation in a number of developing countries.	Dasgupta (1995, 1996b), Lopez (1992, 1997), Lopez and Scoseria (1996) Heath and Binswanger (1996), Cuesta, Carlson and Lutz (1997).
A deterioration of the ambient environment hurts the poor more than the rich (and conversely).	Dasgupta (1995, 1996a), Kumar and Hotchkiss (1988), Kadekodi (1995).
Policies that change the environment can hurt the poor more than the rich (or vice versa).	Eskeland and Deverajan (1996), Brooks and Sethi (1997), Lanjouw (1997), Eskeland and Kong (1998).
Increases in economic development have a complex effect on the environment, but in the long term should help reduce poverty and improve the environment.	Grossman and Krueger (1991), Stern, Common and Barbier (1996).

2   INCREASES IN POVERTY AND CHANGES IN THE ENVIRONMENT

It is popular among policy makers in the development field to claim that poverty leads to environmental degradation. The statement is, of course, a loose one, as they do not state whether a constant level of poverty leads to a worsening environment, or whether it is increases in poverty that cause the degradation. We begin by considering the second. There are a few studies that have documented a temporal association between increased poverty and increased environmental damage. De Janvry and Garcia (1998) look at a wide variety of experiences in Latin America. They state:

> Even if the masses of rural poor are not the major agents of environmental degradation, important environmental problems in many regions of Latin America are associated with their activities ...

Other authors note a similar association (Southgate, 1988; Mink, 1993, among others). A key issue of interest is, of course, the causality. Is it increasing poverty, caused by any one of a number of factors, that results in the degradation, or is it degradation, following natural disasters or policy-induced changes, that results in increased poverty? But even before one can address that, there is a more basic question of fact. What correlation is there between *changes* in poverty and changes in the ambient environment? The literature does not pose the question in quite that way. In fact I could not find a single development-related study that had documented an increase in poverty and correlated it with a change in the ambient environment.[1] Given the central role such a hypothesis should have in this area, this is a surprising omission. Hence it cannot be said with any certainty that *increases in poverty are correlated with increases in degradation, let alone that they are the cause of the degradation.*

3   THE ENVIRONMENT OF THE POOR IS MORE DEGRADED THAN THE ENVIRONMENT OF THE RICH

This thesis implies that, in a cross-section of communities, the level of the ambient environment will be superior in a richer community than in a poorer community. Or, to be more precise, a poverty-affected community will have a more degraded environment than one that is not so affected. Some cross-section studies addressing this issue exist. Jaganathan (1989) looked at rates of deforestation and the level of poverty in West Java and land use and poverty in Nigeria. He found little evidence that poverty was a driving force in the deforestation or in the damaging changes in land use. This study, however, looked (vaguely) at the *levels* of poverty against *changes* in the environment (rates of deforestation). More recently, Deininger and Minten (1996) have studied the relationship between forest cover and poverty in the Chiapas and Oaxaca regions of Mexico. They find, using probit regressions, that the higher the level of poverty in any region, the lower the probability of a plot of land being under forest cover. The results appear well determined but do not, of course, establish causality. Nor do they establish that an increase in poverty will result in increased loss of forest cover.

At the farm level, two interesting papers that have addressed this question are Aheeyar (1998) and Linde-Rahr (1998). Aheeyar has looked at investment in soil conservation in the Mahaweli region of Sri Lanka. Investment and annual expenditures on soil conservation were analysed for different income groups, both in cash terms as well as in terms of the imputed value of labour time. As expected, the lower-income households spent less cash, but they made up for this to a large extent by higher levels of 'in-kind' expenditure on soil conservation, with the result that the aggregate level of annual expenditure on soil conservation did not show any significant relationship with the level of income. Nevertheless, the lack of cash expenditures was seen as a constraint on effective soil conservation, and an analysis of soil erosion and annual income did reveal a negative relationship between the two (again, however, without an implication of causality).

The study by Linde-Rahr looked at the farm-level determinants of reforestation in Vietnam. The factors which determine whether farmers plant trees as part of their land management activity has been looked at in a number of previous papers (Dewees, 1993; Patel, Pinkney and Jaeger, 1995). However, the direct link to incomes and poverty has not been clearly established in them. Linde-Rahr's paper is particularly interesting in that it analyses the effects of income and gender on tree planting. He finds tree planting increases with the number of female household members and decreases with female income, but decreases with the number of male household members and increases with male income. The overall implications for poverty and tree planting are not evident, but the paper is suggestive of a rather complex relationship in which gender composition will be of some importance.

The above examples are all from rural areas. For the urban environment we may think we know the answer. The slums and poor neighbourhoods are surely the most environmentally degraded parts of the towns and cities. But even here, systematic studies are not obvious in their results. The recent work by Brooks and Sethi (1997) (B&S) and other US studies (Tietenberg, 1996) have looked at community exposure to pollution or polluting activities and correlated them with the levels of poverty (among other variables). B&S find that race and poverty are both important determinants of exposure. Poverty, however, had a 'quadratic effect', so that at very high levels of poverty the exposure was lower than average but at levels above a threshold it was positive.[3] Both Tietenberg and B&S note the significance of race, so that exposure goes up as the percentage of black people in the community increases, with no threshold effects.

No such studies are available for the developing world. Were they to be undertaken, it would be interesting to know both what the situation is with respect to the urban environment as well as to the rural. Are the poorest communities the ones where the environment has been most degraded? They often have the more fragile land, but that does not mean that it is more damaged than land held by less poor people. As with much of the literature in this area, there are lots of theories but very little serious empirical data.

4   THERE HAVE BEEN IMPORTANT SOCIAL CHANGES (POLICIES, EXTERNAL EVENTS) THAT HAVE RESULTED IN CONCURRENT INCREASES IN POVERTY AND ENVIRONMENTAL DEGRADATION IN A NUMBER OF DEVELOPING COUNTRIES

Social and economic changes that impinge on the poverty–environment link are divided into those that are directly policy related (such as agricultural prices, tariffs, land tenure arrangements, etc.) and those that are related to phenomena that are less directly a function of policy – population changes, changes in institutional arrangements, etc. Lopez (1992) refers to the two as 'external' factors and 'internal' factors respectively. Although the distinction is not completely clear cut, it is useful to divide these factors in this way.

External Factors

A popular line of reasoning among researchers begins by noting that a number of undesirable agriculture-related policies have been introduced in the recent past, especially in developing countries. The consequence of these has been to increase, through a variety of channels, the degradation that is caused by poor rural communities. Lopez (1992) blames the promotion of large-scale agriculture, export-oriented forestry and major public infrastructure as the main factors. Such policies result in a permanent change in the circumstances of the poor, making it more difficult for them to retain adequate land on a secure basis. Moreover, even if the policy is subsequently reversed, or the project or programme arrested, the damage to the poor cannot be undone – there is a prevalence of hysteresis in environmental destruction. The mechanism is mainly a displacement of people to make way for the new projects or for expanded, more efficient, agriculture. The displaced often migrate to new areas, which are not suited to sustainable agriculture, and even to the extent that they could be used sustainably, the limited land rights do not encourage the migrants to use them in that way. Whether the poor are made poorer by this process remains unclear. But they certainly become more environmentally damaging in what they do.

Similar reasons are given by other scholars. De Janvry and Garcia (1988), in a review of rural poverty and environmental degradation in Latin America, were among the first to analyse the issues clearly. The proximate causes of environmental degradation by the poor are:

(a)   soil erosion by small-holders as a rational strategy of survival:
(b)   'semi-proletarianization' of the rural population and a collapse of local institutions;
(c)   deforestation as a result of migrants seeking land.

When it is asked why these developments have occurred, a number of answers are offered. Foremost among these is the claim that, in Central and South America at least, the governments pursued economic policies and strategies which are unfavourable to agriculture. The main factor was the high level of taxation ('disprotection') of the sector. This lowered the return to land, making investment in soil conservation less attractive. At the same time, subsidies to inputs such as fertilizers and pesticides, which increased the attractiveness of agriculture, rarely reached small producers. Credit subsidies, for example, which were tied to mechanization and livestock, did not help the poor. Furthermore, subsidies to mechanization reduced employment possibilities in the sector. As a result, the agricultural sector has not fulfilled the employment creation potential of the sector.

Second has been the failure of institutions to respond to the changing demographic and technological situation. Land tenure has remained concentrated and the demise of the rental market has been damaging to small farmers. Security of tenure remains a major issue for many of the poor, making investment in conservation an unattractive option. The situation has been exacerbated by what the authors call an 'anti-peasant bias' in rural institutions. Subsidized institutional credit and new technological options are not easily accessible to small-holders.

Local institutions have broken down because of the process of 'modernization and the competitive pressures it entails'. It is unclear what this means, but the examples offered show that time allocated to the maintenance of common resources in rural communities is falling. This is partly because of the poor return to conservation in the changing circumstances, and partly because new institutions are needed to ensure that the benefits of any common action can indeed be captured by the community (on this see the discussion on institutional change, below).

More recently Heath and Binswanger (1996) have gone over the same ground and come up with similar conclusions. Looking in detail at Colombia, but drawing on wider experience in rural development, they focus on the presence of too many farmers working fragile land as the cause of both increased poverty and increased degradation. When it is asked why this is happening now, the reasons given are similar to the above: the fact that modern agriculture absorbs too little labour, the subsidies for capital inputs discriminate against small farmers and the reduced scope for tenancy farming and sharecropping. The whole structure is exacerbated by the increase in the number of farmers, as the rural population increases.

The paper referred to above draws on experience in South America. For Central America, similar considerations are believed to be valid.[3] Lopez and Scoseria (1996) discuss the poverty–environment linkages in Belize, where population growth and migration from other Central American countries have increased pressure on the forest resources. Although such use of land is not the largest cause of deforestation, it accounts for about one third of the loss of forest. Why is the level as high as it is? Partly it is the need for land to accommodate more farmers, and partly the fact that methods of cultivation are land intensive. Prices of crops such as corn and beans are more attractive than those of vegetables, which are more labour intensive. If price incentives were different, land needs might be less and the damage associated with this sector correspondingly smaller.

Given the limited resources of small farmers, they need strong incentives if they are to practise sustainable agriculture.[4] The lack of secure rights to the land provides exactly the opposite: it encourages the mining of the land and moving to new areas when present plots are exhausted. In this context, however, the process of land privatization has not benefited such farmers. It requires that land be leased before purchase and the formula has resulted in higher prices per hectare for small plots than for large plots. Most farmers have not been able to afford the acquisition of land through this scheme.

Internal Factors

Population growth

Undoubtedly the most controversial of the internal factors is that of population growth. Many commentators point to the effects of increases in overall population in terms of pressure on land and increases in environmental degradation (De Janvry and Garcia, 1998; Cleaver and Schreiber, 1994; Lopez, 1992; Lopez and Scoseria, 1996 all identify an increase in the population as a contributing factor in many situations). The literature does not, however, agree on the role of population. Opposing the views of the above authors is the Boserup hypothesis (Boserup, 1965), which states that, as land becomes more scarce relative to labour, agriculture is intensified and productivity per unit area goes up. Rather than deteriorating, the land resource base improves in the process. Studies in Africa, such as Pingali, Bigot and Binswanger (1987) (Africa-wide), and Tiffen, Mortimore and Gichuki (1994) (Kenya,

Machakos district) are cited as evidence that population growth can result in improved productivity.

The issue is complicated because the studies of the Boserup hypothesis do not isolate the effects of population growth from other factors that have given rise to the success stories. In the Machakos district, for example, Tiffen *et al.* show how a situation in the 1930s, of low population and a colonial policy of restricting most of the land to white settlers, was transformed into one where yields have increased ten-fold, erosion has been arrested and the population has increased by a factor of six. The problem is to know how much of this was due to (a) the opening of land for all users, (b) investment in infrastructure, (c) access to non-farm employment opportunities, (d) technological developments that were brought in from outside the region (especially for maize) and (e) price incentives for products that were relatively environmentally benign. In other words, if the population growth had been half of what it is, would the changes in land use have been more or less environmentally beneficial?

Heath and Binswanger (1996) contrast the case of Kenya with that of Ethiopia, where areas with an increase in population density beyond 'carrying capacity' are also areas of the greatest degradation. They point out that how successfully population growth is accommodated depends on the policy framework. In other words, with the right policies, a substantial increase in population need not result in environmental degradation.

Clearly the issue of population and the environment is more complex than some analysts might suggest. In many countries, especially in Africa and Asia, rural population growth is a major contributor to environmental pressure on the land and to environmental degradation. After allowing for migration to urban areas, the population in these regions is increasing, and the Boserup effect is not evident. Not all such regions have faced an environmental deterioration, however. The examples of Machakos and others indicate that, with the right strategies, larger populations can be accommodated. But even in these areas, a lower rate of population growth might have made for a better quality of life and fewer environmental pressures.

The evidence on the effects of population on the environment is further complicated by the fact that, as urban opportunities improve, some areas of land are becoming 'depopulated'. Young men in particular are migrating to the cities, leaving behind weakened families and less allocation of labour to collective soil conservation activities. This has been a particular problem in the Andes and in Mexico (Collins, 1987). A recent NAFTA-related study on the effects of a decline in the price of corn has suggested that even more migration from rural areas will result in increased environmental pressure (Nadal *et al.*, 1998). To some extent a similar phenomenon occurred in Europe in the post-war years, when land and buildings were simply abandoned as the occupants migrated to the towns and cities. But much of this patrimony is being revived through re-migration and as tourism and other uses of land are developed.

Where rural population growth is a matter of concern, what kind of policies can one introduce to reduce the population pressure? There is considerable evidence to suggest that education (particularly of women), the level of agricultural employment and level of nutrition and the extent of civil liberty all act to reduce the levels of total fertility (Sen, 1994; Dasgupta, 1995). Policies, therefore, that act to improve these factors can be expected to reduce total fertility and, thereby, pressure on the natural resource base. Some of these will also help reduce poverty. In addition, general economic growth has been negatively associated with population growth, and it has been argued that the former will act to reduce population pressures over time. The problem with this argument, however, is that, while *average* population growth rates may decline with per capita GDP, sections of the community that depend on natural resources may find themselves locked into a cycle of poverty in which high fertility rates are maintained and that, in turn, exacerbate the pressure on the natural environment.

Dasgupta (1995, 1996b) has argued that this cycle could work in the following way. As common resource management systems break down, so individuals are more able and willing to make family size decisions that do not take full account of the social costs of child rearing, with the use of common resources treated as a free good. Over time, the natural resource base is increasingly depleted, and the family unit requires more members to achieve the same level of welfare. Thus a cycle of increasing degradation is established. The theory has some plausibility but clearly needs to be tested with real data. Such studies still need to be carried out, both to test the validity of the theory and to see how it needs to be elaborated and developed further.[5]

The dynamics of institutional change

It was noted earlier that at the heart of the environment–poverty relationship is the question of what management systems operate for natural resources and how they evolve over time. This issue has been studied in depth by Lopez (1997), Narain (1998) and others. On the evolution of institutions, there are plausible theoretical and empirical studies, which show that, contrary to some commonly held views, there is in fact an inverse relationship between rural communities' ability to cooperate in the management of common resources and the state of those resources. In other words an internal 'self-correcting' mechanism exists, which implies that institutions evolve so as to respond to a deteriorating rural environment by *increasing* the level of cooperation over common resources. In a recent paper, Narain (1998) cites some evidence for this for common forest resources in the state of Gujarat in India. The key question is what can governments do to facilitate this process of cooperation?

In a wide-ranging review Lopez identifies a number of factors that are critical for the appropriate institutional response to increasing environmental pressure. He begins by noting that neither privatization nor elaborate traditional community regulations are sufficient to guarantee that the institutional changes will be sufficient to protect the natural resource base. Privatization can be a negative factor if it leads to a 'race for property rights', if it results in the creation of landless sub-groups, and if the rights to previously communal land cannot be maintained when the land is left fallow. It can be a positive factor if it is carried out in a way that avoids these factors.[6]

What other policies can one adopt to encourage the effective evolution of the institutions, and to slow down the social and environmental change that is damaging the natural resource base? Various proposals have been made. One is through ensuring and promoting homogeneity in the affected groups and, more generally, reducing the costs of cooperation at the community level. Actions here include support through extension services, training, poverty alleviation, etc. Education is also seen as an important influence, as is gender equality.[8] These will result in a 'new order', but one that is more sensitive to the environmental constraints and the imperatives of cooperation in the management of natural resources. Another is information and public education in general. A third is legal and other government support for new and reformed property management systems. All these responses are of great importance in setting the right policy framework. Unfortunately the state of knowledge about the dynamics of institutional change, on which to base them, remains weak.

There are examples where evolution has taken place successfully in the face of increasing pressures on the resource base. One study from Nigeria (Mortimore, 1989) shows how small farmers adopted sustainable management strategies on new land even when the short-term costs of doing so were high. Another is the Kenyan study referred to above (Tiffen, Mortimore and Gichuki, 1994). It was partly the effective transformation of institutions that was responsible for the success of that case. Other examples of 'success' in institutional evolution have come from India. Taking data from Western India, Chopra and Gulati (1996) have shown that property rights have evolved in such a way as to reduce out-migration and improve the management of common resources. Similarly, Chopra and Kadekodi (1988) show how the transference of property rights from the state to village communities and from individual to 'pooled community management' has generated benefits in terms of the management of the resource base in selected Indian cases.

These are interesting and important papers, but more work needs to be done to understand the dynamics of institutional change for agricultural communities in developing countries. There is no doubt that, with the onset of major social and political changes in the post-war period, many of the systems of traditional management have broken down. If this is to be reversed, a better understanding of the dynamics and the role of environmental policy is essential.

5   A DETERIORATION OF THE AMBIENT ENVIRONMENT HURTS THE POOR MORE THAN THE RICH (AND CONVERSELY)

The general presumption among policy makers is that a declining natural environment hurts the poorest sections of society. The vulnerable are often the users of marginal resources and also the most dependent on the common resources of the community in which they live (Dasgupta, 1995, 1996a). Hence it is these groups that are most affected when deforestation, soil erosion and other negative impacts on the environment occur. This common view is probably correct, but *detailed quantitative empirical evidence* on how the poor are affected relative to the non-poor is not easy to find. There are some exceptions. Fuelwood scarcity has been shown to impose a greater cost on the poor than on the better off (for example, the time spent collecting fuelwood has a high value relative to other components of the household's income) (Kumar and Hotchkiss, 1988). Research by Kadekodi (1995) has shown that, when water shortages occur as a result of misuse or natural events, it is the poor who are the most affected. However, one cannot conclude that environmental degradation always hurts the poor more than the better off. For urban pollution problems, for example, such as outdoor air quality, the poor are more likely to live closer to highly polluted areas, but the value they place on cleaner air is lower than that of the rich. Hence a general deterioration in air quality may hurt more poor people, but each has a lower value of the benefit, implying that the change in their position *vis-à-vis* the better off is ambiguous. This is examined further in the next section.

6   POLICIES THAT CHANGE THE ENVIRONMENT CAN HURT THE POOR MORE THAN THE RICH (OR VICE VERSA)

When measures are taken to improve a degraded environment, how are the poor affected? It depends, of course, on what the measures are. Environmental regulations that increase the costs of producing certain goods can result in increased unemployment and higher prices for the goods. How they affect the poor will depend on what the goods are, what share they have in the budget of the poor, and who suffers the unemployment.

One of the more sophisticated attempts to see how changes in the quality of the environment have actually affected the poor versus the rich is the paper by Brooks and Sethi (1997). Using the same data referred to in section 2, they also look at how the changes in the Toxic Release Inventory between the date of the release of the first data set and the second (1990 and 1992 respectively) were distributed across US zip codes. Using a logit equation in which a value of 1 implied an increase in the level and 0 implied a decrease or no change, they found that jurisdiction poverty was negatively related to increases in toxic releases. The same applied to the presence of collective action and the level of voter turnout. On the other hand, a 1 per cent increase in the percentage of blacks increased the probability of a worsened release situation by 0.002. The negative sign on poverty is 'explained' in terms of lower levels of activity in poor areas. It does suggest, however, that the poor do not always fare worse as the environment changes over time. Unfortunately no such data are available for developing countries.

There are a few recent studies on the distributional impacts of environmental regulations in developing countries. Eskeland and Devarajan (1996) looked at the distribution of environmental costs for the transport sector in Indonesia and Mexico. They conclude from the data that, as expenditure on private and public transport increases as a percentage of income across quintiles, measures to reduce emissions from transport (particularly private transport) will have a progressive impact.

This has been followed by a more detailed analysis of two regions of Indonesia (Jakarta and the 'Rest of Java') by Eskeland and Kong (1998). The authors develop a measure of the 'distributional characteristics' of a policy. This is an income-weighted measure of the increase in costs for different income groups resulting from measures that increase pollution control costs, or a similar measure of the increase in benefits resulting from the improved environment that results from the same measures. Environmental regulations in the areas of energy production and use and transport are analysed in some detail. On the distributional effects of control costs the paper shows that transport policies are more 'distribution friendly' than energy policies, mainly because transport environmental controls affect the rich relatively more than do energy environmental controls. Within transport, controls on private transport have a relatively smaller impact on the lower-income groups than do controls on public transport. Within energy, gas and electricity controls have the smallest impacts on the poor, and firewood, kerosene and coal have the biggest. All these differences become much smaller, however, when the indirect effects of the control measures are taken into account – that is, when the impacts of the measures on the production costs of other commodities are allowed for.

On the benefits side the analysis is complicated by the fact that one does not know with any accuracy how the willingness to pay for the improvements changes with income. Eskeland and Kong take a range of values for the 'income elasticity of willingness to pay for environmental improvements' and estimate the distributional effects of the benefits.[8] These are roughly the same for the energy and transport regulations. With an income elasticity of demand for the benefits of 1 (a commonly assumed value) the resulting net distributional effects (taking both costs and benefits) are approximately neutral for energy and positive for transport. The lower the income elasticity of demand for the benefits, the greater are the distributional impacts of the benefits, and the greater the net benefits from both strategies.

Another study for Indonesia that has looked at the income impacts of environmental policies in a computable general equilibrium framework is that of Resosudarmo and Thorbecke (1996). They analyse the 'Blue Sky Program (BSP)' that includes a number of measures to improve air quality – such as reductions in leaded gasoline, recovery of vapour emissions, higher emissions standards for vehicles, etc. Using a social accounting matrix, to which pollution and health impacts sectors have been added, they show that the distributional outcome depends on what is assumed about reductions in output in the controlled sectors. With no change in output, there are negligible losses in incomes. With a fall in output, however, in the transportation sector, some low-income households could be worse off to the extent of 3–4 per cent. The model has a number of limitations, but the results are useful in picking out certain occupational groups and tracing through the effects of different policies on them. Such a sophisticated analysis is needed if we are to say something about the output effects of these policies elsewhere.

These results are not inconsistent with those from industrialized OECD countries, although there are some differences. The OECD experience is well covered in recent publications (OECD, 1994 and Tietenberg, 1996). Studies on air pollution distinguish between mobile and stationary sources. Control costs for mobile source pollution through vehicles tend to be regressively distributed (Harrison, 1975, 1977) in the US. The difference between the US and Indonesia and Mexico can be explained by the fact that rural car ownership is much lower in the latter two countries.[9] For stationary sources the distribution of costs is more complex to model because the incidence structure is more involved, but in essence the US studies show some regressivity of costs (Gianessi, Peskin and Wolff, 1979). The research issue here is the adoption of more sophisticated models to study the incidence effects of such measures, especially when they are adopted across a wide range of industries and result in a number of relative price changes. For water pollution Gianessi, Peskin and Wolff (1979) also found costs to be regressively distributed, in spite of the fact that part of the costs were borne by general subsidies, which come from the local/regional tax system and which are therefore (probably) mildly progressive.

On the benefits side crude estimates suggest that mobile air pollution benefits are progressive for those living in urban areas. The same does not apply, however, in suburban areas or in rural communities. Tietenberg (1996) cites some work by Asch and Seneca, who examined socio-economic data from stationary sources in three US cities and concluded that the benefits were greatest (in terms of reductions in air pollution) in the poorest areas of those cities. In the case of water regulation, however, benefits clearly favour the better off more than the poor, although the number of studies is very small. OECD (1994) found the benefits of the 1972 Water Pollution Control Act in the US to be concentrated among middle-income groups relative to the poor.

Market-based instruments, such as taxes and permits, have also been assessed for their distributional effects. Many of the studies look at instruments that have not actually been implemented; they are based on simulation results rather than historic empirical data and need to be viewed in that light. Smith (1995) has looked at the distributional effects of 'green taxes' in Britain and Germany and analysed the impacts of a carbon tax across income groups. As expected, the tax would be mildly regressive, more so in Britain than Germany. Taxes on petrol on the other hand are mildly progressive.

Comparisons between the distributional effects of taxes and of command and control instruments are not generally available for developing countries. Some work by the OECD (OECD, 1994) has looked at trading programmes for emissions and compared them (implicitly) to those of direct controls. Tradable permit schemes are generally more efficient in achieving environmental goals than command and control schemes and hence entail a smaller increase in prices. Since such price increases were found to be regressive in their impact, the smaller they are, the less the regressive impact. Furthermore, most actual schemes do not involve selling the initial allocation of permits to existing polluters but provide them free of charge. This in turn can reduce the burden on industry, compared to a tax, which is not rebated. Thus the simulation analysis carried out on US schemes has shown a net benefit to low-income households in using marketable permits compared to conventional command and control instruments. It should be noted, however, that the focus of studies of marketable permit schemes is not the distributive impacts on households, but rather the regional and industrial distributive effects.

A significant problem in environmental regulation in developing countries arises from difficulties in controlling small-scale enterprises (SSEs), because of their limited financial and human resources, and low level of technology. Regulators frequently shy away from such regulations, from fear of the effects these may have on employment and incomes of poor households.

Studies of the distributional effects of the regulation of SSEs, however, are very few. One recent attempt is Lanjouw (1997), who has analysed this sector in Ecuador. Overall, employment in the pollution-intensive SSEs is not concentrated among the poor, but among the urban, literate population. Hence to the extent that environmental regulations in the sector affect employment, they do not affect the poorest. Furthermore, estimates of the impacts of large-scale losses of employment in this sector on poverty are not large. Overall he concludes that arguments against regulation the SSEs on the grounds of increased poverty are exaggerated.

Finally there are distributive effects in developing countries arising from the regulations in developed countries. These occur through changes in the direction and composition of trade. Although there are some studies that look at the effects of environmental regulations on trade, there is little work on how these changes in trade patterns affect the distribution of income in the developing countries. The study by Verbruggen, Kuik and Benis (1998) shows, for example, how environmental export regulations in the EU have affected the exports of cut flowers from Kenya, and hence had a detrimental effect on the incomes of poor Kenyan farmers. A set of case studies on trade and the environment (Jha, Markandya and Vossenaar, 1999) also concludes that stricter environmental regulations in developed countries are having a bigger impact on the small and middle-sized enterprises in developing countries, with a *prima facie* case that perhaps the less well off are more affected than the rich. But this has not been systematically studied from the income distribution point of view.

7   INCREASES IN ECONOMIC DEVELOPMENT HAVE A COMPLEX EFFECT ON THE ENVIRONMENT, BUT IN THE LONG TERM SHOULD HELP REDUCE POVERTY AND IMPROVE THE ENVIRONMENT

There is a strand of literature (Grossman and Krueger, 1991; World Bank, 1992; Barbier, 1997) which suggests that the relationship between GDP and the quality of the environment is 'U-shaped' – that is, the quality of the environment deteriorates initially as GDP per capita increases, and then improves after a certain critical value of per capita GDP has been reached. This critical value varies with the pollutant, and indeed for some pollutants such as volatile organic compounds (VOCs) there is no 'turning point'. In fact the evidence for such a relationship is mixed, with some studies even showing an inverted 'U' curve (Stern, Common and Barbier, 1996).

This model (also referred to as the 'environmental Kuznets curve') can be looked at in conjunction with the original Kuznets curve, which postulated a deterioration in income distribution in the early stages of economic growth, followed by an improvement later. Taking the two together one would conclude that a declining environmental quality and increasing income inequality go hand in hand as part of the 'development process'. In the end things should work out fine, with improvements in both these indicators of human welfare.

Unfortunately, such a sanguine view is inappropriate and misleading from a policy viewpoint. First, some of the environmental degradation being observed, and sometimes being caused by extreme poverty, is irreversible and will never be recovered. Second, what is a long-term time-series relationship is being inferred from cross-section intercountry data. There is no reason why a particular country should follow the path characterized by a cross-section of countries. Indeed the aim should be to follow a policy based on a comparison of domestic costs and benefits of different options, taking account of their impacts on all aspects of welfare, including poverty/inequality, environmental quality, GDP and other indicators, such as those used by the UN Development Program in its *human development report* series. Although the Kuznets curve is a useful empirical regularity, its existence is of little relevance in determining such a set of policies.

8 CONCLUSIONS

This chapter has been organized as answers to a series of hypotheses about the linkages between poverty, environment and development. These hypotheses raise distinct issues and are relevant for different policy discussions. Yet the literature tends not to make these distinctions. Levels and rates of change are confused or at the least not treated differently. Measurement of effects is weak, and at times virtually non-existent. Where associations are discovered, they are general, and do not tell us about how one particular factor (for example, population growth) has affected the evolution of the social and environmental landscape in the country concerned. The area is strong on theories but weak on proper empirical literature.

In recent years some papers have started to emerge that do look at the data in a dispassionate and analytically serious way. Unfortunately most of these studies are in industrialized countries, particularly the United States. The recent interest of the World Bank in connection with the 2001 *World Development Report* has spawned a number of research efforts, which are producing some interesting and important results for developing countries. These are very much to be welcomed.

There are some interesting findings that emerge from the existing literature. In each of the areas discussed in this chapter, they point to further work in the following directions:

Increases in poverty and changes in the environment

A lot can be done to firm up the empirical understanding of how levels and changes in poverty relate to changes in environmental quality, in both urban and rural areas. Time series analyses of the linkages are very few and far between.

The environment of the poor and the environment of the rich

Again there is a need to understand how both the level and rate of change of the environment varies with poverty. It is not axiomatic that the poor will have a worse rural or urban environment, although there are strong reasons to believe that the poor are less able to protect themselves against environmental pollution. In rural areas, the environment is not necessarily deteriorating more in the poorest areas. We need to know more accurately how and where the changes are taking place.

Social changes, poverty and the environment

Where new policies are initiated, they often hurt the poor more than the rich, and thereby cause the former to damage the environment to a greater extent. Some of the papers reviewed have demonstrated this. It would make the literature more credible, however, if there were at least one paper modelling the linkages and the dynamic evolution, and testing the model against actual data. This would allow some of the effects to be quantified and better understood.

The same applies to the effects of changes in the population and the dynamics of institutional development. The papers are descriptive in their use of data and statistics and do not show the relative importance of the different factors.

Changes in the ambient environment and their effects on the poor

Again there is some evidence that the poor are most affected when deforestation, soil erosion and other negative impacts on the environment occur, but detailed studies of these effects would throw up a lot of information on the mechanisms, including coping strategies, that is simply lacking. As stated earlier, detailed quantitative empirical evidence on how the poor are affected relative to the non-poor is not easy to find.

Environmental regulations and their effects on the poor

This area has been more systematically studied than most others in the field of poverty and the environment. Until very recently most of the studies were in industrialized countries and most of them based on relatively simple models of the incidence of costs and benefits. Although the final incidence of the changes in the regulations needs more sophisticated models than have been in use to date, the evidence supports the view that, with appropriate choice of instruments, environmental regulations can achieve their environment goals without causing significant decreases in the welfare of the poor. The recent work on Ecuador, Indonesia and Mexico is a good start in analysing these problems in developing countries.

Economic development, growth and poverty
This literature is also well developed and is known as the environmental Kuznets curve. It focuses on the broad linkage between growth and environmental quality. As a statistical regularity it is interesting but it is not particularly useful for policy purposes. Even if the environment improves after a certain level of per capita income has been reached, this does not imply that a particular country should wait until that level is reached before taking corrective measures. Moreover, at the micro level, measures may well be justified to protect the poor, and what holds in terms of national statistical aggregates may mask a great deal of local degradation and poverty. If anything the focus should be on the condition of the poor in society, and how their environment changes as general development takes place.

ACKNOWLEDGEMENTS

I would like to thank the participants of the Frontiers Conference held at Airlie House, Virginia, in October 1998 for comments and suggestions that have resulted in, I think, this much-improved second draft. I would also like to thank Shelby Gerking for specific suggestions. Finally, I have benefited from parallel work that has been launched by the World Bank in preparation for its *World Development Report on Poverty, Environment and Growth-Oriented Policies*. Background papers prepared for that report have provided further details on the issues raised in this chapter. The usual caveat of author responsibility for the contents applies.

NOTES

1. One study that looks at a cross-section of US data and correlates these two variables is Brooks and Sethi (1997). I consider those results in section 6 below.
2. Low exposure for very poor communities may be explained in terms of very low levels of economic activity in these areas.
3. Scholarly 'macro' level analysis of the links between policy, poverty and the environment do not appear to be available for other regions of the world.
4. Some economists have argued that the poor pay less attention to the environment because they have higher time preference (or discount) rates. The evidence for this, however, is not strong. Pender and Walker (1990) and Cuesta, Carlson and Lutz (1997) find generally high

time preference rates among farmers, but not systematically higher ones for the poor. Furthermore, it should be noted that a high time preference rate does not necessarily imply a low level of investment in conservation.

5. Dasgupta (1996b) cites one study by Cleaver and Schreiber (1994), which produces positive correlations between poverty, fertility and environmental degradation in sub-Saharan Africa, and another by Filmer and Pritchett (1996) for Pakistan with similar results. But much more work is needed to validate this view of how these factors are related.

6. In some cases government action has been actually harmful to the effective evolution of the institutions. A case in point is the nationalization of formerly traditionally managed resources, with disastrous consequences (Bromley, 1991).

7. In this context the book by Agarwal (1994) makes a strong case for the role of women's empowerment as a factor in arresting natural resource degradation.

8. They take a range of values from 0.1 to 2. A default value of 1 is often used and a very crude estimate of the income elasticity of the willingness to pay for health benefits of 0.35 has been suggested by Krupnick *et al.* (1996), based on Mitchell and Carson (1986). But this *seriously* needs to be confirmed.

9. The US regressivity can be reduced by suitable changes in policy design. Harrison suggested, for example, that lower standards be adopted in rural areas than in urban ones. This results in a significant reduction in regressivity, because car ownership among poor households is much higher in rural areas than urban ones.

REFERENCES

Agarwal, B. (1994), *A Field of One's Own: Gender and Land Rights in South Asia*, Cambridge: Cambridge University Press.

Aheeyar, M.M. (1998), 'Small holder farmers, poverty and land degradation: evidence from Sri Lanka', Working Paper, HK/Agrarian Research and Training Institute, Colombo, hartilib@slt.lk.

Barbier, E. (ed.) (1997), 'The Environmental Kuznets Curve', Special Issue, *Environment and Development*, **3**.

Bromley, D.W. (1991), *Environment and Economy: Property Rights and Public Policy*, Oxford: Blackwell.

Brooks, N. and R. Sethi (1997), 'The distribution of pollution: community characteristics and exposure to air toxics', *Journal of Environmental Economics and Management*, **32**, 233–50.

Chopra, K. and S.C. Gulati (1996), 'Environmental degradation and population movements: the role of property rights', *Environmental and Resource Economics*, **9**(4), 383–408.

Chopra, K. and G. Kadekodi (1988), 'Participatory institutions: the context of common and private property resources', *Environmental and Resource Economics*, **1**, 353–72.

Cleaver, K.M. and A.G. Schreiber (1994), *Reversing the Spiral: The Population, Agriculture, and Environment Nexus in Sub-Saharan Africa*, Washington, DC: The World Bank.

Collins, J.L. (1987), 'Labor scarcity and ecological change', in D.P. Little, M.M. Horowitz and A.E Nyerges (eds), *Lands at Risk in the Third World: Local Level Perspectives*, Boulder, CO: Westview Press.

Cuesta, M., G. Carlson and E. Lutz (1997), 'An empirical assessment of farmers' discount rates in Costa Rica', work in progress, Environment Department, The World Bank, Washington, DC.

Dasgupta, P. (1995), 'The population problem: theory and evidence', *Journal of Economic Literature*, **33**, 1879–902.

Dasgupta, P. (1999a), 'The economics of the environment', *Environment and Development*, **1**, 387–428.

Dasgupta, P. (1996b), *Environmental and Resource Economics in the World of the Poor*, Washington, DC: Resources for the Future.

Dasgupta, P. and K.-G. Mäler (1994), 'Poverty, institutions and the environmental-resource base', World Bank Environment Paper No. 9, The World Bank, Washington, DC.

De Janvry, A. and R. Garcia (1988), 'Rural poverty and environmental degradation in Latin America: causes, effects and alternative solutions', S 88/1/L.3/Rev.2, IFAD, Rome.

Deininger, K. and B. Minten (1996), 'Determinants of forest cover and the economics of protection: an application to Mexico', Research Project on Social and Environmental Consequences of Growth-Oriented Policies, Policy Research Department Working Paper No. 10, The World Bank, Washington DC.

Dewees, P.A. (1993), 'Trees, land and labour', World Bank Environment Paper No. 4, The World Bank, Washington, DC.

Duraippah, A. (1996), 'Poverty and environmental degradation: a literature review and analysis', CREED Working Paper Series No. 8, London: IIED.

Eskeland, G.S. and S. Devarajan (1996), *Taxing Bads by Taxing Goods: Pollution Controls with Presumptive Charges*, Washington, DC: The World Bank.

Eskelund, G.S. and C. Kong (1998), 'Protecting the environment and the poor: a public goods framework applied to Indonesia', Policy Research Working Paper 1961, The World Bank Development Research Group, Washington, DC.

Filmer, D. and L. Pritchett (1996), 'Environmental degradation and the demand for children', Research Project on Social and Environmental Consequences of Growth-Oriented Policies, Working Paper No. 2, The World Bank, Washington, DC.

Gianessi, L.P., H.M. Peskin and E. Wolff (1979), 'The distributional effects of uniform air pollution', *Quarterly Journal of Economics*, **93**, 281–301.

Grossman, M. and A.B. Krueger (1991), 'Environmental impacts of a North American free trade agreement', Working Paper No. 3914, National Bureau of Economic Research, Cambridge, MA.

Harrington, W. (1981), 'The distribution of recreational benefits from improved water quality: a micro-simulation', Discussion Paper D-80, Quality of the Environment Division, Resources for the Future, Washington, DC.

Harrison, D. Jr (1975), *Who Pays for Clean Air? The Costs and Benefit Distribution of Automobile Emissions Standards*, Cambridge, MA: Ballinger.

Harrison, D. Jr (1977), 'Controlling automotive emissions: how to save more than $1 billion per year and help the poor too', *Public Policy*, **25**(4), 527–23.

Heath, J. and H. Binswanger (1996), 'Natural resource degradation effects of poverty and population growth are largely policy-induced: the case of Colombia', *Environment and Development Economics*, **1**(1), 65–84.

Jaganathan, V.N. (1989), 'Poverty, public policies and the environment', Environment Working Paper No. 24, The World Bank, Washington, DC.

Jha, V., A. Markandya and R. Vossenaar (eds) (1999), *Reconciling Trade and the Environment*, Cheltenham, UK and Northampton, MA: Edward Elgar.

Kadekodi, G.K. (1995), *Operationalising Sustainable Development, Ecology–Economy Interactions at a Regional Level*, The Netherlands: Institute for Environmental Studies.

Krupnick, A. *et al.* (1996), 'The value of health benefits from ambient air quality improvements in Central and Eastern Europe', *Environmental and Resource Economics*, **7**(4) 307–32.

Kumar, S.K. and D. Hotchkiss (1988), 'Consequences of deforestation for women's time allocation, agricultural production and nutrition in the hills of Nepal', IFPRI Research Report No. 69, International Food Policy Research Institute, Washington, DC.

Kuznets, S. (1955), 'Economic growth and income inequality', *American Economic Review*, **45**(1), 1–28

Lanjouw, P. (1997), 'Small-scale industry, poverty and the environment: a case study of Ecuador', Research Project on Social and Environmental Consequences of Growth-Oriented Policies, Policy Research Department Working Paper No. 18, The World Bank, Washington, DC.

Linde-Rahr, M. (1998), 'Rural reforestation: gender effects on private investments in Vietnam', Working Paper, Department of Economics, Gothenburg University, martin.linde-rahr@economics.gu.se.

Lopez, R. (1992). 'Environmental degradation and economic openness in LDCs: the poverty linkage' *American Journal of Agricultural Economics*, **74**, 1138–45.

Lopez, R. (1997). 'Where development can or cannot go: the role of poverty–environment linkages', *Proceedings of the Annual Bank Conference on Development Economics, 1997*, The World Bank, Washington DC.

Lopez, R. and C. Scoseria (1996), 'Environmental sustainability and poverty in Belize: a policy paper', *Environment and Development Economics*, **1**(3), 289–308.

Mink, S.D. (1993), 'Poverty, population and the environment', Environment Working Paper No. 189, The World Bank, Washington, DC.

Mitchell, R.C. and R.T. Carson (1986), 'Valuing drinking water risk reduction using the contingent valuation method: a methodological study of risks from THM and Girardia', Report for the US Environmental Protection Agency, Washington, DC.

Mortimore, M. (1989). 'The causes, nature and rate of soil degradation in the northernmost states of Nigeria and an assessment of the role of fertilizer in counteracting the process of degradation', Environment Working Paper No. 17, The World Bank, Washington DC.

Nadal, A. *et al.* (1998). 'Maize in Mexico: some environmental implications of the North America Free Trade Agreement (NAFTA)', Commission for Environmental Cooperation, Montreal, Canada.

Narain, U. (1998), 'Resource degradation, inequality and cooperation', Working Paper, Department of Agricultural and Resource Economics, University of California, narain@are.berkeley.edu.

OECD (1994), *The Distributive Effects of Economic Instruments for Environmental Policy*, Paris: OECD.

Paukert, F. (1973), 'Income distribution and different levels of development: a survey of the evidence', *International Labour Review*, **108** (September), 97–125.

Patel, S. H., T. Pinkney and W. Jaeger (1995), 'Smallholder wood production and population pressure in East Africa: evidence of an environmental Kuznets curve', *Land Economics*, **71**(4), 516–30.

Pender, J.L. and T.S. Walker (1990), 'Experimental measurement of time preference in rural India', International Crop Research Institute for the Semi-Arid Tropics (ICRISTAT), No. 97, Patancheru, Andra Pradesh.

Pingali, P., Y. Bigot and H. Binswanger (1987), 'Agricultural mechanization and the evolution of farming systems in sub-Saharan Africa', Baltimore, MD: Johns Hopkins University Press.

Resosudarmo, B.P. and E. Thorbecke (1996), 'The impact of environmental policies on household incomes for different socio-economic classes: the case of air pollutants in Indonesia', *Ecological Economics*, **17**, 83–94.

Sen, A. (1994), 'Population: delusion and reality', *New York Review of Books*, **41**(15) 62–71.

Smith, S. (1995), *'Green' Taxes and Charges: Policy and Practice in Britain and Germany*, London: The Institute for Fiscal Studies.

Southgate, D. (1988), 'The economics of land degradation in the third world', Environment Working Paper No. 2, The World Bank, Washington, DC.

Stern, D., M. Common and E. Barbier (1996), 'Economic growth and environmental degradation: the environmental Kuznets curve and sustainable development', *World Development*, **24**(7), 1151–60.

Tietenberg, T. (1996), *Environmental and Natural Resource Economics*, New York: HarperCollins.

Tiffen, M., M. Mortimore and F. Gichuki (1994), *More People, Less Erosion: Environmental Recovery in Kenya*, Chichester, UK and New York: Wiley.

Verbruggen, H., O. Kuik and M. Benis (1995), 'Environmental regulations as trade barriers for developing countries', CREED Working Paper No. 2, IIED, London.

World Bank (1992), *World Development Report*, New York: Oxford University Press.

9. Industrial ecology: wealth, depreciation and waste

Robert U. Ayres

INTRODUCTION

Materials extracted from the environment must ultimately either be embodied in durable assets or returned to the environment as wastes or pollutants. This is no longer a new insight (Ayres and Kneese, 1969). The implication is that materials-intensive economic growth cannot continue indefinitely without serious and irreversible damage to the environment, quite apart from the likelihood that, despite recent sharp price declines (attributable to the Asian economic crisis) such 'essential' resources as petroleum will not be available indefinitely at ever-declining prices (for example, Campbell, 1997; Campbell and Laherrère, 1998).

Neither is it a new idea that the availability of cheap fossil fuels (and other natural resources) has been a key driver of past economic growth: falling energy (and other raw material) prices triggered increasing demand, including many applications of mechanical power to replace human labour. This, in turn, kept real prices of natural resources and mechanical power on a continuing long-term downward trajectory, notwithstanding the exhaustion of original resource endowments in areas that were the first to be industrialized.[1]

An important growth 'engine' of the past has been the positive feedback loop involving scale economies and the so-called 'experience curve' which also keeps real costs falling and thus increases the demand for manufactured goods.[2] In fact, one of the dilemmas facing present-day governments – although largely unrecognized – has been that most of the historical growth in labour productivity has been in the manufacturing sector. Manufacturing has been the major beneficiary of both falling energy prices and the increasing scale of production and the associated returns to scale. The shift from manufacturing to services – now considerably over half of the US economy, and increasing – has sharply diluted the impact of both of these historical 'growth engines'. Meanwhile, as will be noted later, the expected productivity gains from information technology have yet to be demonstrated unambiguously in the aggregate statistics.

Environmental problems and unpaid social costs associated with all materials-energy-intensive activities have already created pressures to make materials and energy producers pay more to treat (if not reduce) wastes and pollution. These added costs are passed on to users. High-cost energy encourages users to be more efficient and to seek alternatives where possible. Many of these gains in materials/energy productivity must be achieved – in effect – by substituting labour or capital for energy or materials. (Insulating houses to reduce the need for hydrocarbon fuels would be an example; it is perfectly possible to cut the energy requirements of most buildings by 90 per cent, through careful design to utilize waste heat and solar energy (von Weiszäcker *et al.*, 1998).) Other gains can and will be achieved by extending the useful life of material products by increasing the level of re-use, repair, renovation, remanufacturing and recycling.

This set of non-new ideas, taken together, has some important economic implications that have not yet been recognized clearly. Thanks to (lack of) economies of scale, recovery, repair, renovation and recycling are inherently more labour intensive than original mass production. (This fact accounts for the current tendency to discard and replace rather than repair.) Increased re-use, renovation and remanufacturing appear to be very desirable from the standpoint of reducing unemployment. But the other side of the coin is that they also, *ceteris paribus*, reduce labour productivity.

Increasing resource productivity has a downside in the form of reduced economies of scale for the raw materials processing industries and the mass producers along the value-added chain. Moreover, the assimilative capacity of the environment is a scarce (but hitherto unpriced) resource. If this resource were correctly priced, this would *ipso facto* have a negative impact on economic growth to the extent that growth is based on cheap resources. On the other hand, since declining energy costs and economies of scale are probably less important in the service industries than in the older sectors – agriculture, mining, manufacturing and construction – higher resource prices may have less of an adverse impact on economic growth than would have been the case a generation ago.

Nevertheless, the dematerialization imperative implies that either growth must cease, or its character must change. Yet continued economic growth itself continues to be an important political and social objective. Indeed, the needs of ageing populations and increasing health-related entitlements, not to mention more investment in education, research and environmental protection, demand that economic growth should accelerate.

A stark question arises: how is future economic growth to be reconciled with higher resource prices and static or declining rates of increase of labour productivity? Is it possible? The rest of this chapter considers this question from several points of view. The most effective policy to accomplish this, in general terms, would be to use public policy to increase the relative prices of non-renewable resources (including environmental assimilative capacity), si-multaneously reducing the relative cost of labour and reducing the economic incentives to substitute resource flows for labour. In particular, dissipative uses of chemically active materials must be phased out, while durable goods must be made to last longer and provide more services during their life cycles.

One approach would be to tax resource use rather than labour and/or capital (for example, tradable consumption permits). Unfortunately, trade liberalization makes such a rational tax policy almost impossible to imple-ment at the national level. Further economic analysis of the implications of trade liberalization on tax policy is also needed, although it cannot be dis-cussed in detail here.

ECONOMIC GROWTH AND WEALTH

Economic growth is conventionally measured as increasing national income, or national output (that is, GNP) in monetary terms. GNP, in turn, is the sum of all value added by labour or capital by national entities. This aggregate is also equal (by definition) to the sum of all revenues received by the same entities as wages, dividends, interest or fees. GNP is thus interpreted as returns to labour and capital. Net national product (NNP) is GNP less depre-ciation, or capital allowance. Capital, in this case, is defined as the accumulation of net investment (investment less depreciation) over time. It does not reflect 'natural' capital.

It is standard practice to measure economic growth as increasing GNP. But GNP is really a measure of economic activity, rather than increasing wealth *per se*. In the case of individuals, households or firms, wealth consists of financial and tangible assets. The latter category includes real property, buildings, equip-ment and cultural objects and 'collectables', such as works of art. These assets, valued at market prices or (in the case of equipment) initial cost less deprecia-tion, constitute 'book value'. There is another accounting category for 'good will' in business, to account for the market value of a viable enterprise over and above its book value. Brand names, franchises and the like fall into this cat-egory. Finally, to calculate net equity, debts and receivables must be subtracted from, or added to, the total of other assets.[3] In practice, equity in proprietorships, partnerships and firms with non-traded securities cannot be valued directly. Valuations are imputed by the Federal Reserve Bank by means of a so-called 'flow-of-funds' model that balances assets and liabilities.

It is tempting to extend this scheme to the national level. Indeed, calcula-tions of national wealth were a standard feature of the annual *Economic*

Report of the President to the Congress of the United States until the early 1990s (CEA, 1992). Tangible wealth for households (including non-profit institutions) was subdivided into real property (land and structures) and consumer durables, mainly automobiles. Tangible wealth for government consisted of infrastructure, buildings, vehicles and military equipment. However, in the case of business, no separate estimate of tangible wealth was made. Instead, it was included in business equity, subdivided between incorporated and non-incorporated businesses. Since business equity is ultimately a financial asset of households (albeit ownership is largely indirect, through a maze of other financial institutions), it seemed unnecessary to subdivide business equity into tangible and financial components.[4]

National wealth, thus calculated, showed a satisfying long-term annual growth (see Table 9.1). However, the standard scheme omitted two important items. One was expected future earnings from labour, which can be equated to the present value of the stock of skills, knowledge and institutional structures – whether embodied in individuals, organizations or in society as a whole – that enables workers to perform economically valuable services. This effectively constitutes 'human capital' and should be counted as national wealth. In reality, it is the basis on which many hard-headed lenders are eager to provide credit to individuals, even students without jobs, and on which governments are able to calculate future tax revenues and guarantee future payments of interest on debt, or social security and health care for individuals.

The discounted present value of expected future earnings by workers bears somewhat the same relation to financial wealth as payments to labour (that is, wages) bear to payments to capital (that is, dividends and interest) in the national accounts. Putting it another way, if financial wealth can be regarded as the present value of future returns to tangible and/or financial capital, then there should be a corresponding term representing the present value of future returns to labour, or 'human capital'. To do the calculation, of course, human capital must be valued quantitatively.

The second omission of the standard scheme for calculating national wealth is the various forms of 'natural capital' – from forests, minerals, fisheries, fresh water, topsoil and biodiversity to climate – that provide essential services to the economy. The monetary value of some of these services is obviously very difficult to estimate. (To do a better job at this is surely one of the chief challenges of environmental economics for the next decade, as emphasized by several other authors in this volume.) It should not be forgotten, in this context, that natural wealth also delivers welfare (that is, income) directly to individuals in the form of environmental services. Most of this welfare is not included in financial income, nor can the eco-services be purchased for money except in a few cases where it is possible to use money to buy access

Table 9.1 National wealth, based on national accounts data, 1945–92 (1987 $)

	1945	1950	1955	1960	1965	1970	1975	1980	1985	1989	1990	1992
1 Real estate, owner occupied ([a])	554.4	838.8	1162.6	1413.5	1583.3	1882.9	2361.7	3348.3	3569.1	4254.1	4023.5	
2 Consumer durables	309.4	512.6	671.0	734.1	808.7	1016.5	1141.0	1329.5	1462.5	1764.9	1775.3	1817.7
3 Corporate equity ([b])	746.7	633.4	1221.1	1499.0	2175.0	1984.8	1220.8	1517.8	1975.9	2387.0	2043.9	2984.9
4 Non-corporate business equity	1265.1	1351.1	1398.8	1468.6	1563.8	1564.6	1898.5	2655.4	2349.9	2403.6	2311.3	1845.8
5 Other equity ([c])	1488.0	1103.6	1195.6	1344.1	1630.2	1911.7	2151.1	2423.9	3562.9	4549.5	4447.4	5117.0
6 Subtotal, tangible reproducible private wealth ([d])	939.1	1449.8	1963.9	2319.1	2625.1	3186.9	3830.1	5050.7	5427.9	6441.0	6207.4	7763.9
7 Subtotal, private financial wealth	3499.8	3088.0	3815.5	4311.8	5368.9	5461.1	5270.4	6597.1	7888.6	9340.1	8802.6	9947.7
8 Total private wealth	4438.9	4537.8	5779.4	6630.8	7994.0	8647.9	9100.5	11647.9	13316.6	15781.0	15009.9	17711.6
9 Gov't tangible reproducible assets ([e])						1873.0	2059.9	2206.8	2364.2	2582.8	2537.0	2587.0
10 Federal gov't net financial assets	−1495.3	−924.5	−865.0	−794.3	−775.3	−702.4	−755.7	−825.9	−1513.0	−2039.5	−2186.2	−2441.4
11 State and local gov't net financial assets	−5.4	−18.6	−90.0	−158.2	−192.4	−232.4	−182.5	−93.9	−63.2	−91.2	−110.5	−184.0
12 Subtotal gov't net financial assets	−1498.8	−941.3	−952.9	−950.0	−964.6	−931.6	−931.8	−910.7	−1567.1	−2120.5	−2286.9	−2590.1
13 Subtotal national wealth, excluding row 9	2940.1	3596.5	4826.5	5680.8	7029.4	7716.4	8168.6	10737.2	11749.5	13660.5	12723.0	15121.5
14 Total of above including row 9						9589.4	10228.5	12943.9	14113.7	16243.3		17708.5

Notes:
[a] Including owned by non-profit institutions.
[b] Market value of securities, where available.
[c] Credit market instruments, life insurance and pension reserves, security credit and miscellaneous assets, net of liabilities.
[d] Includes wealth held by households and non-profit institutions (for example, churches, universities, foundations, etc.).
[e] Including infrastructure, buildings, vehicles, military equipment, etc.

Source: Data from *Statistical Abstract of the US*, 1991, table 762.

to them, for example, by buying a house on a hill where the air is cleaner and the view is better than in the adjoining valley.

In any event, such services should be included, in principle, in personal income and – of course – in the present value of expected future income. However, the component of personal income that is omitted from standard calculations is the component that cannot be attributed to human capital, but only to natural capital. So the omission is not a crucial one for our present purposes.

Unfortunately, failure to include natural capital in the system of national accounts (SNA) has led many politicians (and economists) into a thoroughly misleading habit of treating income from the sale of natural resources like lumber and minerals as 'rents' – part of national income – while failing to make any compensating allowance for the reduction in asset stocks.[5] To correct for this failure was a part of the UN's motivation for developing a satellite system of environmental and economic accounts (SEEA), as a step towards a 'green' SNA (OECD, 1991a). Unfortunately, the effort seems to have stalled in the US and UN for political reasons, as well as for inherent problems (for example Harris, 1996). However, such accounts have been constructed for Japan (Nakamura and Oda, 1996) and are currently being constructed for China (UNU/IAS, 1999).

An issue closely related to the problem of quantification of natural capital is the argument between 'strong' versus 'weak' sustainability. Advocates of the 'weak' version believe that produced capital (and goods) can be a reasonable substitute for most natural capital and services derived therefrom. It follows that sustainability implies non-decreasing total capital, that is, the sum of the three separate components (for example, Solow, 1974, 1986, 1992; Hartwick, 1977; Pearce and Atkinson, 1993). To the extent that the services in question are recreational or aesthetic amenities, there is a valid argument for weak sustainability. (For instance, a holographic picture or movie of a beautiful mountain panorama or sporting event may be a good enough substitute for actually travelling to the spot, at least for many people.) Similarly, to the extent that the natural capital in question is utilized as a raw material for manufacturing, the potential for technological substitutes is generally plausible.

But to the extent that the environmental services in question are necessary for the long-run survival of human life on the planet – and climatic stability, stratospheric ozone, biodiversity, pollination, disposal and recycling of dead biomass and the nutrient cycles are among those services – the case for weak sustainability is unconvincing (for example, Ayres, Hourcade and Helioui, 1998). Technology offers no plausible substitutes for many of these environmental services, and inadequate substitutes for others (such as nitrogen fixation). The 'strong sustainability' criterion implies that the natural capital providing such services should not be allowed to decline beyond a critical threshold level. What that level should be is a matter of dispute.

However, while further comment on these topics is certainly relevant to environmental economics and industrial ecology, it is beyond the scope of this chapter. What is relevant here is two facts. First is the fact that environmental assets are, in principle, an important (albeit unquantified) part of national wealth. And, second, the environmental component of national wealth is evidently being degraded by economic activity, especially in the area of land use, materials extraction and processing. The extent of annual degradation is hard to measure quantitatively, although estimates have been attempted in several countries in recent years (Repetto, 1985a,b; Repetto *et al.*, 1989; Sedjo, 1992; Smil, 1996; UNU/IAS, 1999). However, the sign of the change – the fact that the stock of natural capital is declining – is undisputed. In fact, it is clearly evident. (The single contrary indicator is the fact that temperate and boreal forests in the Northern hemisphere appear to be increasing [Kauppi *et al.*, 1992].)

Under either sustainability criterion, total national wealth cannot be allowed to increase unless other forms of capital increase enough to compensate for environmental degradation. Under strong sustainability, of course, the latter cannot be allowed to continue indefinitely. Under the weak criterion, it is only the total that matters. So far this is straightforward arithmetic. Given that environmental capital is depreciating, what is the implication for produced capital? Can increasing human capital alone counterbalance decreases in the other two categories? Intuition suggests that this is not likely, either in the short term or in the long term.

The reason is that human capital, as measured by future earning capacity, cannot easily be disconnected from physical capital precisely because labour productivity owes so much to capital investment and the substitution of capital for labour. In short, though resource flows are underappreciated and human capital is critical, GDP remains tightly linked to the stock of physical capital. In short, if output is to continue to grow, as we postulate, the stock of produced physical capital must continue to grow in market value, if not in mass.

Tangible capital assets belonging to households are now a significant component of national wealth. Moreover, a major part of financial assets – another component of national wealth – consists of expected future returns to tangible capital assets belonging to businesses. Valuation of tangible (produced) capital is a problem, however. Financial wealth has intrinsic value in the marketplace because it is fungible – it can be used to purchase any service that is available and it can be reasonably presumed that each consumer will optimize in terms of her own preferences.

On the other hand, physical capital, including structures and durables of all kinds, is non-fungible or at best only partially fungible. A house cannot be used for transportation. A road has little or no value for any other purpose, and so forth. This is of no consequence as long as there are efficient markets for all these forms of capital. One can sell the house and use the proceeds to buy a car, or vice versa. However, there are always very significant transaction costs in such markets; in some cases, there are no secondary markets at all, except for scrap value. A bridge or tunnel going nowhere cannot be sold as such. Highly specialized manufacturing machinery or equipment has no value to others if either the product or the process is obsolete. Most clothing, furniture and furnishings are so individualized as to be unsaleable, or only at prices far below cost. (Antiques and works of art are the exceptions that prove the rule.) Garage sales do not constitute an efficient market.

A question similar to the one raised at the end of the last section now arises: how can the *value* of tangible physical asset stocks be increased if the *quantity* of raw materials and energy consumed by the economy must decrease rather drastically (as environmental constraints require)? One part of the answer is that to increase the market value of such capital goods, they must be made more fungible. This, in turn, implies being more flexible, more modular, more transportable, more easily disassembled for renovation, upgrading or remanufacturing and less rather than more specialized. Such goods must also be made more productive, at the same time. Finally, they must be made to last longer.

One of the fundamental problems associated with information technology (IT) is that, while computers *per se* are extremely flexible, most software is not. Moreover, the dominant producers of software strive constantly to make their old products obsolete – and, therefore, worthless. Since most IT investments flow into software, the implication (increasing capital depreciation) is clear.

DISSIPATION AND DEMATERIALIZATION

There is a significant literature on material use and dematerialization at least since the 1980s (Tilton, 1986; Labys and Waddell, 1988; Herman, Ardekani and Ausubel, 1990; Considine, 1991; von Weiszäcker, Lovins and Lovins, 1998). However, it is fair to say that virtually all of this literature deals with improvements in properties of materials that permit size reduction or miniaturization. The electronics industry and the substitution of glass fibres for copper telephone wire are the two star examples, although one can point to significant and continuing technology-driven weight reductions in many other categories of products, including outdoor clothing, automobiles, aircraft, diesel engines, etc.

A key point is the following: whereas structural materials *embodied* in long-lived tangible assets obviously contribute directly to wealth, there is no such direct link between *dissipative intermediate* material flows and wealth creation. On reflection, it is clear that some, but not all, intermediates are converted into other goods. For tax purposes (that is, estimating depreciation) the difference between an intermediate good and a capital item is essentially a matter of re-usability and useful lifetime. There is a large class of intermediates that is dissipated in use rather than transformed. Fuels, lubricants, cleaning agents, coatings, solvents, pesticides, fertilizers and packaging materials are only the most obvious examples. Such dissipative flows are equivalent to assets that depreciate totally during a single use.

In fact, dissipative intermediate materials contribute a great deal to pollution and environmental harm. It should be noted, too, that they also add spurious value to other goods and services when their unnecessary use is mandated by governments for job-creation purposes. In Western Europe a large number of people and vehicles are employed by driving schools that add much to the cost but little to the skills of the drivers. Accident rates in Europe stubbornly remain above US levels. Similarly, in Japan many people are employed in cleaning, polishing and waxing the floors and walls of public buildings whether they are dirty or not. In many cases dissipative materials add nothing to wealth *per se* but they do add significantly to costs and environmental harm.

At first sight this statement may seem hard to justify. Surely dissipative intermediates provide services, which add to and/or preserve value. For instance lubricants and surface coatings *reduce* wear; detergents and solvents *remove* dirt, etc. This is true. But the point is that the service function in question often does not inherently require dissipation. In principle, most lubricants, solvents, detergents and even packaging materials could be recovered and re-used. Fertilizers could also be conserved and recycled by changing agricultural practices (e.g., manuring land). Some pesticides can be reduced or eliminated by integrated pest control techniques. In other words, some materials that are normally dissipated could be regarded as potential capital assets that happen to be very wastefully used.

On the other hand, this is not true for fuels, bleaches, some pesticides or for many process chemicals. In these cases the service function is, indeed, associated with the dissipation. And, in these cases the dissipation is also inherently pollution. Thus there is a double-barrelled argument for reducing or eliminating dissipative uses of materials, especially chemically active ones.

Returning to the restricted domain of tangible man-made capital, it is worth recapitulating a point made previously. The difference between a capital asset and an intermediate good in the economy is essentially that a capital asset is re-usable, whereas an intermediate good is immediately converted into something else, either another good or a waste.[6]

Evidently the monetary value of tangible produced wealth is strongly dependent on (1) the existence of efficient secondary markets or, failing

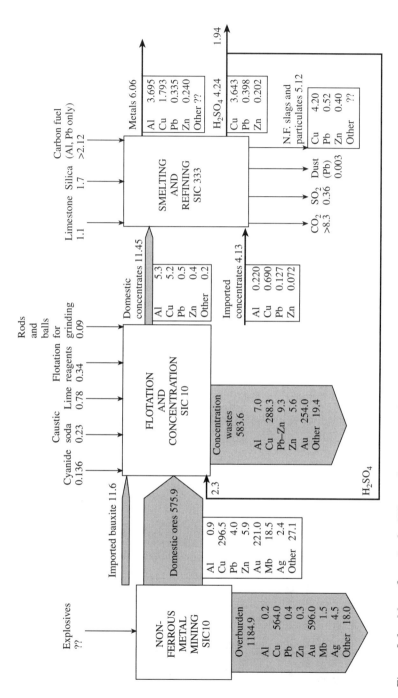

Figure 9.1   Mass flows in the US non-ferrous metals sector, 1993 (MMT)

223

Table 9.2 Recycling savings multipliers (tonnes/tonne product)

	Iron/steel	Aluminium	Copper	Lead	Zinc
Ore per cent	*52.8% Fe*	*17.5% Al*	*0.6% Cu*	*9.3% Pb*	*6.2% Zn*
Major source	*[USS, 1971]*	*[Parsons, 1977]*	*[Gaines, 1980]*	*[PEDCo-Pb 1980]*	*[PEDCo-Zn 1980]*
Energy used (gJ/t)	22.4	256	120	30	37
Water flow in/out (t/t)	79.3	10.5	605.6	122.5	36.0
Material inputs					
Air	1.9	0.3	1.6	4.4	5.8
Solids	17.3	11.0	612.1	126.2	55.8
Total material inputs	19.2	11.3	613.7	130.6	61.6
Material outputs					
Product	0	0	0	0	0
Byproducts	0.2	0.1	1.0	6.7	4.9
Depleted air	1.5	0.2	1.3	1.2	2.4
CO_2	0.5	0.8	0.02	0.03	0.03
SO_x	0.01	0.06	1.47	0.005	0.01
Other gaseous material	1.18	0.002	0.15	0.28	0.03
Potential recycle	0.6	n.a.	3.2	0.1	0.5
Overburden	12.5	0.6	395.4	72.5	37.3
Gangue	1.1	6.1	211.0	44.6	16.3
Other solid material	1.5	1.4	0.1	2.5	0.1

Sludges, liquids	0.1	1.9	0.1	2.6	0.1
Total material outputs	19.2	11.2	613.7	130.5	61.6

Notes:
Major by-products include SO_2 used for sulphuric acid production and saleable offgas.
Depleted air = air from which all oxygen has been taken for combination with other materials.
Potential recycle includes slag, scrap, etc. potentially usable in the process chain, but not used.
Overburden = that portion of solid material extracted during the mining process which is not part of the ore.
Gangue = that portion of the ore extracted during beneficiation which is not part of the concentrate.
Sludges and liquids do not include dilution water.

Sources: Source for aggregate energy values: Forrest and Szekely (1991). The materials/energy costs of producing this energy are not considered in this table. Source for water flow values: Lübkert *et al.* (1991). Source for overburden and gangue percentages: Adriaanse *et al.* (1997). Other sources used: Battelle (1975); Bolch (1980); Davis (1971, 1972); Lowenbach *et al.* (1979); McElroy and Shobe (1980); Masini and Ayres (1996); PEDCo-Cu (1980); Thomas (1977); Watson and Brooks (1979).

that, (2) the assumed rate of depreciation of durable goods (as determined by the tax authorities). Obviously the real value of tangible produced wealth may be lower or higher than the value for tax purposes. But it is dependent on the real rate of depreciation. It follows that cutting the rate of real depreciation of durables would increase the rate of accumulation of tangible wealth as well as financial wealth derived therefrom. On the other hand, reducing or eliminating the use of dissipative intermediates would be a net gain if non-dissipative alternatives could be found. Suppose, for purposes of argument, that all intermediate flows of materials that are not embodied in final products (that is, materials that are 'used up' and dissipated within the production process) could be either recovered and re-used over and over, or magically eliminated by process changes, *without affecting the quantity or quality of durable goods and tangible assets.* Suppose, too, that durable goods became even more productive (of services to users) and even more durable. Suppose, finally, that after one 'life' they could be renovated or remanufactured indefinitely (as most old houses in Western Europe are). All of these changes would sharply increase the output of the economy per unit of material input. They would simultaneously constitute a major *dematerialization* of the economy.

From the environmental perspective, dematerialization – by conserving value-added and by reducing dissipative uses of materials – has enormous benefits in terms of reducing the need to extract and process primary materials. It is, after all, the mining, concentrating and refining processes that generate the vast bulk of industrial wastes and pollutants. Recovery and re-use of a ton of copper wire or lead batteries not only saves significant value-added, it also saves hundreds of tons of mine waste, explosives and fuel used in mining, chemicals used in concentration, arsenic and other toxic heavy metals that would otherwise be mobilized and dispersed via dust or slag, and so forth. To illustrate, an overview of the US non-ferrous metals sector is shown in Figure 9.1.

In view of the long-term consumption trends discussed later, it is important to note that the environmental impact of non-ferrous metals production is disproportionately large in comparison with other materials. It is relevant to compare primary extraction with recycling in terms of the life cycle of the metal. This means counting all inputs and outputs for each ton of metal that is recycled *vis-à-vis* a ton of metal that is mined, concentrated, smelted and so on. The comparison, which also allows for the materials consumed in the recycling process, is shown in Table 9.2. For instance, on the input side, one tonne of recycled iron eliminates the need for extracting and processing 17.3 tonnes of ores (including overburden), limestone, coal, etc. For copper the corresponding figure is 612 tonnes. For uranium, silver, gold and platinum the amounts saved by recycling are nearly astronomical. On the output side

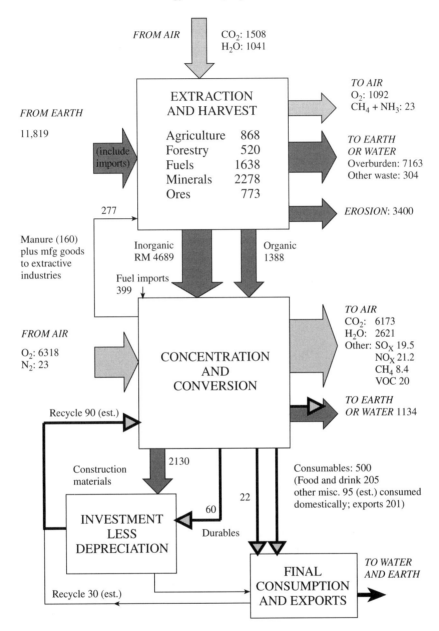

*Figure 9.2   The US economic system as a whole from a mass flow
perspective, 1993 (MMT)*

there are comparable savings, mainly of wastes and pollutants (because in-puts and outputs must balance).

It is illuminating to view the economic system as a whole from a mass flow perspective. This overview is shown in Figure 9.2 for the US in 1993. It is convenient to distinguish three stages of materials processing, namely extrac-tion and harvest, 'conversion', and final consumption, including investment in durable goods and structures. Disregarding air, water, earth moved but not otherwise processed, and biomass residues left on the land, inputs to the conversion stage include 1.388 billion tonnes of biomass harvested by hu-mans or farm animals, 1.992 billion tonnes of hydrocarbon fuels consumed (including oil imports), 771 million tonnes of metal ores and 2.278 billion tonnes of non-metallic minerals. Recycled materials, mainly metals and pa-per, amounted to 90 million tonnes. The conversion stage also consumed roughly 11 billion tonnes of atmospheric oxygen for fuel combustion to pro-duce heat and electric power, most of which is consumed in the production of goods and services. (Atmospheric nitrogen is ignored, both as an input and output, except for the small amount that is oxidized to NO_X.) No attempt has been made to quantify inputs of water that is only used as a diluent or coolant, although it is worth noting that water flows dwarf all others in mass terms.

Outputs of the conversion stage, in this picture, included 5.465 billion tonnes of carbon dioxide, 7.990 billion tonnes of water vapour, 90 million tonnes of other air pollutants, such as methane, VOCs, SO_2 and NO_X. Solid wastes and solids dissolved or suspended in water amounted to 1.42 billion tonnes. Useful outputs included 70 million tonnes of agricultural chemicals, 2.130 billion tonnes of construction materials, 60 million tonnes of producer durables (machinery and equipment), 22 million tonnes of consumer durables (mainly cars and appliances), 205 million tonnes of food and beverages (not including added water) plus 95 million tonnes of other consumer goods, such as cleaning agents, household chemicals, paint, paper products and packag-ing materials. All fuels were assigned to the conversion sector for convenience.

Almost all of the non-metallic minerals (sand, gravel, limestone, gypsum) are used for construction materials and these are environmentally harmless, both in their original and final forms (concrete, brick, tile, glass, plaster, etc.). If one subtracts the chemically inactive materials from both inputs and out-puts of the 'conversion' stage, the picture becomes very much starker. The conversion process waste flows, *not* including carbon dioxide and water vapour, amounted to over 1.5 billion tonnes (dry weight), as compared to a total final mass of farm chemicals and consumables of all kinds amounting to about 370 million tonnes including food and beverages. The solid and other conversion wastes included air pollutants, mineral concentration wastes, ash, agricultural and pulp wastes and chemical wastes. The bulk of this mass (like mine waste, slag and ash) was not chemically reactive as such. But most of it was sufficiently contaminated by toxic or other dangerous materials to be considered hazardous.

HISTORICAL PERSPECTIVE: IS THE ECONOMY DEMATERIALIZING?

There is a widespread assumption among economists that, as the economy becomes more and more service oriented, it dematerializes more or less automatically. For example, it is fairly well known that the energy/GDP ratio for the US economy peaked in the 1920s and has been declining ever since. The mass of energy carriers (fuels) consumed per unit of GDP has also been declining, more or less along the same trajectory (Figure 9.3).

With regard to other materials, the trends are mixed. The category of (finished) construction materials consumed (including steel) does show a significant and nearly continuous drop in mass per unit of GDP since 1905, except for a brief rise in the late 1930s and again in the early post-war years (Figure 9.4). The mix has changed significantly, of course. In the early years of the century it was dominated by lumber. In recent years the mix has been more diverse. For non-ferrous metals and miscellaneous non-metallic materi-

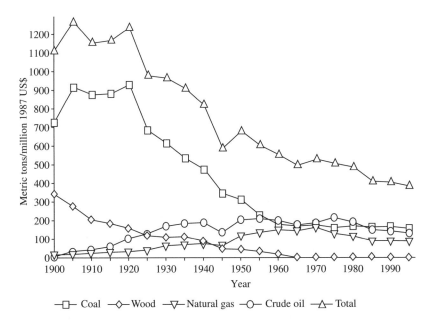

Figure 9.3   Fuels: apparent consumption (mass/GDP: USA 1900–1995)

als, however, the trends are less clear. Total consumption of non-ferrous metals per unit of GDP rose very gradually and irregularly to a peak in 1965; since then it has declined by a third (Figure 9.5). In the case of non-metallic materials (sulphur, plastics, paper, rubber) the overall production trend is up, not down (Figure 9.6). Consumption data are difficult to find, but the overall trend probably does not differ significantly.

In summary, fuel consumption per unit of GDP has declined markedly, along with consumption of construction materials. However, the part of the economy that urgently needs to be dematerialized is *not* the construction sector, which mainly utilizes chemically inactive materials and generates very little harmful pollution.[7] The need for dematerialization is acute, however, in the part of the economy that produces everything else (and that consumes enormous quantities of fossil fuels and other dissipative intermediates in the process).

The term 'dematerialization' may have been coined to reflect the intensity of use per unit of economic output. In this sense, there are favourable trends in regard to several categories, notably fuels. As a producing machine it can be argued that the economy is dematerializing. But the trend is quite different when materials consumption is considered, especially on a per capita basis.

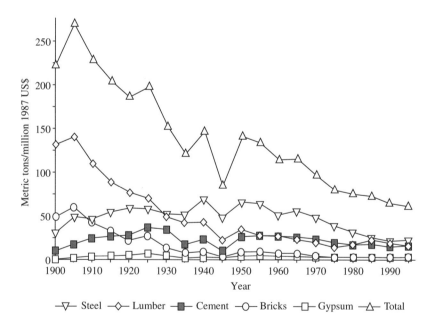

Figure 9.4   Construction materials: apparent consumption (mass/GDP: USA 1900–1995)

Overall consumption is on a rising trajectory (except for the depression) in virtually every category. In the case of fuels (Figure 9.7*)*, there has been a dramatic shift in the mix, from coal and wood to oil and gas – although coal has recovered somewhat since the low point in 1960. In the case of construction materials, consumption per capita in 1995 is nearly the same as it was in 1905 (Figure 9.8*)*. There was a depression-related dip and a post-war peak, but no obvious long-term trend. As regards non-ferrous metals (Figure 9.9) and other non-metallic materials (Figure 9.10), the per capita consumption trend is sharply rising.

It is clear from the data that the economy as a whole is not spontaneously dematerializing in any environmentally significant sense, although only a few categories of materials are rapidly rising in importance. To change the material consumption trends of our society, and to tilt them sharply downward, policy changes will clearly be necessary.

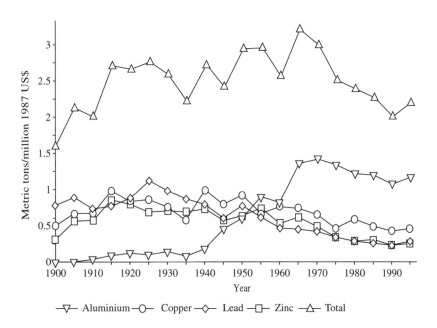

Figure 9.5   Non-ferrous metals: apparent consumption (mass/GDP: USA 1900–1995)

GROWTH, DEPRECIATION AND TECHNOLOGICAL CHANGE

All models of economic growth assume a production function whose arguments are tangible capital (K) and labour (L). More recently energy E and materials M have been included by some modellers (Berndt and Jorgenson, 1973; Jorgenson, Christensen and Lau, 1973; Berndt and Wood, 1975), albeit only in monetary terms. Because it is difficult to measure capital stock directly, either in monetary or physical terms, it is assumed that capital accumulation is determined by the integral over time of investment (usually equated with savings) less depreciation. The rate of real depreciation is also difficult to measure, as already noted. In corporate accounts it is defined rather arbitrarily by the tax authorities (or the legislature) for purposes of calculating the fraction of earnings that can be retained free of corporate income tax to reinvest. In national accounts the so-called 'capital allowance' – currently around 10 per cent of GNP – is the sum of all such tax-sheltered earnings. (It is allowable depreciation, rather than savings by householders, that is the major – almost the only – source of investment into the corporate sector of the US economy.)

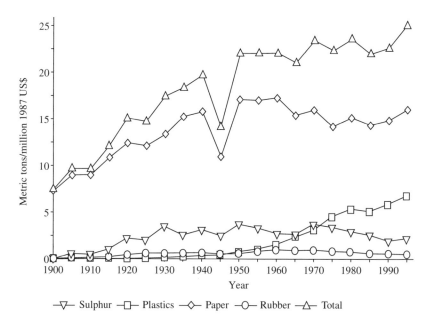

Figure 9.6   Miscellaneous other materials: production (mass/GDP: USA 1900–1995)

While the rate of depreciation of tangible physical capital is impossible to measure accurately and difficult to estimate even at the micro level, aggregate depreciation is evidently a real loss to the economy. An asset that depreciates in a day is no asset at all. An asset that *appreciates*, such as an orchard or a vineyard or a growing forest, or an old master, or stock in a growth company, or land in a city centre, is best of all. But the main point is this: the greater the real rate of depreciation, the less the real rate of economic growth, *ceteris paribus*. Depreciation of man-made capital assets is, of course, an immediate source of material waste and environmental pollution. A second interesting point is that most natural assets *do not* depreciate when left undisturbed by man. If they do depreciate, like topsoil, forests, fisheries, biodiversity or mineral reserves, it is because of human activity. Moreover, produced tangible assets, like buildings, equipment or infrastructure, invariably depreciate at some rate and must be replaced at some rate by human activity, whereas natural assets (other than mineral resources) normally replace themselves. *It follows that the more national income is based on man-made assets, the greater the fraction of (produced) national income that must be reserved for replacing those assets as they depreciate.*

In fact, the US economic growth rate, in conventional GNP terms, has declined markedly since 1973. The average from 1947 to 1973 was 2.85 per

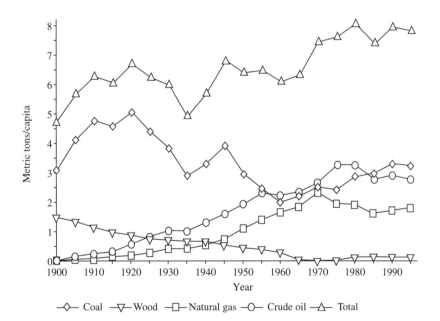

Figure 9.7   Fuels: apparent consumption (mass/capita: USA 1900–1995)

cent per annum. From 1973 through 1992 it averaged only 1.1 per cent per annum.[8] (Since then it has bounced back up to nearly 3 per cent but nobody knows how long the current boom can continue.) To be sure, there are several competing theories to explain the growth slowdown, no single one of which is generally accepted.[9] Given the general confusion about causes, it is not unreasonable to suggest that part of the observed decline can be traced to accelerating depreciation – and thus a reduced rate of real tangible capital accumulation – across the whole economy.

There is anecdotal evidence suggesting that the average rate of depreciation of both structures and tangible capital equipment may have increased significantly over the last century. The most important components of productive capital in 1900 were long-lived structures, railroads (including rolling stock), bridges, canals, harbours, tunnels, dams and mines. A 50-year lifetime, corresponding to 2 per cent annual depreciation, was not an unreasonable assumption for economists to make.[10] Today many business structures are designed and built of relatively flimsy materials to facilitate replacement after 20–30 years, railroads have been largely supplanted by highways and trucks (with 10–15-year lifetimes) and more and more investment is going into computers, information processing equipment and software – 35 per cent by

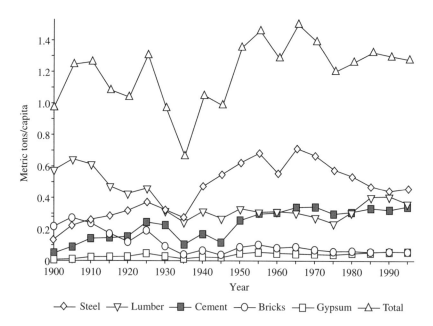

Figure 9.8   Construction materials: apparent consumption (mass/capita: USA 1900–1995)

some estimates – with even shorter (3–5 years) useful lifetimes in some cases. It is hard to estimate the average, but 25 years' lifetime (4 per cent depreciation) might even be conservative for producer capital in today's economy, although houses and infrastructure do last much longer.

Setting aside this interesting historical speculation, which might be worthy of some future researcher's attention, it is important to note that some kinds of depreciation are not even included in the national accounts, although they may qualify for tax exemption by extractive industries. This applies to exhaustible natural resources, such as oil and gas, minerals deposits and forests. Owners are generally allowed to deduct a depreciation allowance from revenues before tax, even though the original resource cannot be recreated. In effect, the law assumes that profits from the sale of natural resources can be (and will be) reinvested in another sort of capital stock that is equally productive.

But there are still other depreciable environmental resources that do not qualify for depreciation allowances, either because of, or despite, the fact that they can neither be recreated or substituted for by man. Fisheries, topsoil and biodiversity are examples. Clean air, fresh water, the carbon, oxygen and nitrogen cycles, benign climate and the stratospheric ozone layer are others. These resources, too, are being depreciated at an accelerating rate.

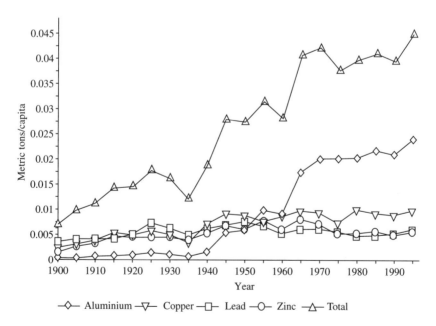

Figure 9.9   Non-ferrous metals: apparent consumption (mass/capita: USA 1900–1995)

The economy adds value to materials. It does so by refining, combining, shaping, forming, assembling, finishing and otherwise embodying information in them (for example, Ayres, 1994a, chapter 9). Some of this added value (that is, embodied information) is lost each year, due to wear and tear (for example, of shoes, tyres, bearings, cutting tools), corrosion – largely due to acid pollutants, such as NO_X and SO_2 – and to various natural processes. Cutting the rate of real depreciation in the economy (irrespective of 'allowable' depreciation for tax purposes) would result in faster economic growth. A decrease in the real capital depreciation rate (say, from 4 per cent to 3 per cent per annum) would automatically increase the rate of capital accumulation and thus the real economic growth rate.

If promoting growth of real tangible wealth is our objective, it is worthwhile examining some of these depreciation mechanisms and searching for ways to reduce the loss of value-added. Thus, while the strategy of repair, reuse, renovation and remanufacturing is more labour intensive than mass production and replacement, it has a less obvious economic virtue of conserving value-added.

The question at the end of the first section can now be answered, at least in principle. One can imagine a set of technological changes that make it possi-

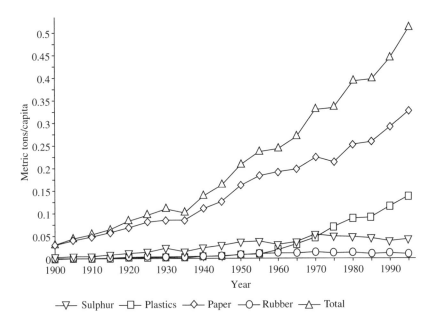

Figure 9.10   Miscellaneous other materials: apparent consumption (mass/ capita: USA 1900–1995)

ble to accomplish two things. One of them is to reduce the rate of depreciation – hence increase the rate of accumulation – of tangible produced wealth (consisting of durable material goods). The second part of this strategy must be to cut down sharply on the use of inherently dissipative materials, especially hydrocarbon fuels. This is the primary strategy for reducing the environmental impact of economic growth, because most of the chemically active non-structural materials extracted and processed by the economy, as it now operates, are actually dissipative. This means they are converted into wastes as soon as they are used.

The second part of the overall strategy is relatively familiar in the environmental literature. It is a major part of what is often called 'clean' or 'non-waste' technology or 'pollution reduction', all of which concern process change to reduce wastes and pollution. The substitution of non-polluting energy sources (such as wind or solar power) would be obvious examples. The first part of the strategy, however, is the one that permits tangible wealth to continue to accumulate even as materials flux and pollution are reduced. The objective must be to conserve value-added by renovation and remanufacturing of durable goods, which are the only material products that truly constitute wealth (by generating immaterial services to final consumers).

To summarize the two intertwined themes of the preceding discussion: (1) to achieve economic development and environmental salvation requires radical 'dematerialization' of the economy; and (2) this strategy has two fundamental material-related elements, *viz. repair, re-use, renovation and remanufacturing* and *elimination of dissipative intermediates* (especially fossil fuels) to the maximum possible extent. The economics of the first part of the dual strategy has been discussed qualitatively: namely *conservation of value-added* (to permit growth without relying on economies of scale in mass production). There is a clear need for much more theoretical modelling and empirical work to clarify the issues, of course.

The question now arises: is it possible to achieve the second part of this dual strategy without unacceptable economic costs? Or even at negative cost? The answer depends on whether the necessary technological evolution – away from hydrocarbon dependence – will occur automatically in response to current market forces or not. If market forces are *not* likely to be effective in the near term (due to well-known market failures and externalities), the answer turns on whether there exists a significant potential for 'free lunches' and 'double dividends'. If the economy truly is on an equilibrium growth trajectory, in the sense that R&D and other investments are now close to optimal – in terms of the existing markets – then only a major (and unlikely) change in the political climate will suffice to bring about the necessary changes. This issue is extremely controversial, of course, because it raises fundamental questions about widely used neoclassical economic models.

ON ECONOMIC DISEQUILIBRIUM AND FREE LUNCH

To restate two of the critical questions at issue: is there any hope that non-carbon energy technologies can replace carbon-based technologies *without* interference by government? And, if not, is there any hope that such interference could be economically beneficial and growth enhancing (as well as environmentally necessary)? Or must we assume, as the US Congress does, that cutting carbon consumption will necessarily be growth inhibiting? Needless to say, this belief has been strongly influenced by lobbyists supported by a number of economists using long-term general equilibrium models that, in turn, assume that the economy is already on an optimal growth path.[11] It follows automatically, from this assumption alone, that any interference by government must *ipso facto* reduce option-space and thus be growth inhibiting. As regards the first question, it is clear that most of the sustainability indicators currently point in the wrong direction. The carbon-based energy industry is extremely well entrenched and it has all the advantages of scale, experience and political influence. Alternative technologies may eventually have their day without help from government. But the process will take many decades unless it is significantly accelerated by government policy. As regards the second question, however, the economic models on which policy advice is being given are based on a very questionable set of assumptions. I believe that these assumptions have not received adequate scrutiny.

This issue has recently been clarified by several papers that address the problem in terms of induced technological change (ITC) and 'crowding-out' (Grubb, Chapuis and Duong, 1995; Goulder 1995; Goulder and Schneider 1996). The last authors acknowledge that the gross costs of CO_2 reduction policies based on ITC depend on whether or not there are 'serious prior inefficiencies in the R&D market'. This issue is obviously crucial to the conclusion.

It is well known that a number of 'bottom–up' (engineering) studies have claimed the existence of very large opportunities for cost saving while cutting energy consumption – known as 'free lunches' or 'double dividends'. These studies give many examples, together with detailed explanations (in many cases) of the barriers preventing their adoption. See, especially, Lovins and Lovins (1981, 1997); Krause, Bach and Kooney (1992); Krause *et al.* (1993); Ayres (1994b); von Weizsäcker, Lovins and Lovins, (1998). It is also well known that most economists have not taken these claims very seriously (see Palmer *et al.*, 1995). Similar claims have been made by Porter and others on the basis of more top–down arguments (Porter 1991; Porter and van der Linde, 1995; Hourcade and Robinson, 1996; Ayres, Hourcade and Heliou, 1998).

These claims are typically dismissed on the (theoretical) argument that 'if such opportunities really existed, they would be exploited by cost-minimizing entrepreneurs'. The fact that this has not occurred is usually explained in terms of 'hidden costs'. The possible origins of such costs within a firm have been explored recently at a theoretical level by Gabel and Sinclair-Desgagné (Gabel and Sinclair-Desgagné 1995, 1998) (also in this volume, Chapter 6). The possibility of plausible institutional reasons why firms might not take advantage of such apparent double-dividend opportunities has not been tested empirically. Clearly economic statistics cannot throw much light on the matter. This subject is one that deserves more serious attention, especially in business schools.

The other way to approach the question is to seek direct evidence of disequilibrium. One indicator is the extent to which R&D investment is related to returns. In principle, technologies with a recent history of rapid cost reduction are the ones offering high returns, and should therefore attract the most investment. Conversely, technologies with a recent history of negative returns (cost increases) should discourage investment. Thus, it is curious that in the energy field, the technology that has long attracted the bulk of government investment is nuclear power, although the recent returns appear to be zero or negative. The other large past consumer of government R&D funding has been coal gasification and shale liquefaction. Both have failed economically. Meanwhile wind power and photovoltaic power – both of which are non-carbon-based energy technologies – have demonstrated radical and continuing cost reductions with minimal R&D investment. At first glance, this suggests that the R&D market is indeed very inefficient and casts doubt on the viability of the 'crowding-out' hypothesis.

Other indicators of disequilibrium include underemployment of labour and underutilization of produced capital (for example 'capacity'). Obviously, the whole subject needs much more (and more open-minded) attention from economists. Admittedly, reliable data on returns to R&D are difficult to obtain. But this should not excuse unwillingness to make the effort.

In my own view, there is sufficient and sufficiently strong historical evidence to support the thesis that reducing option-space – far from reducing the rate of productivity increase – can have, and frequently has had, a very positive impact on economic growth. I believe, in short, that 'necessity is (indeed) the mother of invention'. And when the invention (or innovation) is a radical one, in Schumpeter's sense, it can have enormous consequences in terms of opening up many new possibilities. This is not the place to discuss the point in great detail (it would require a book-length monograph) but a few recent examples should at least make it clear that the 'induced technology' thesis cannot be dismissed lightly.

- The extreme scarcity of land in Japanese cities led Toyota to develop the 'just in time' process in the 1960s and 1970s which eliminated most warehouses and made Toyota the world's most efficient automobile manufacturer. It has also revolutionized the automobile manufacturing industry worldwide.

- Concern about the ozone layer, together with threats of tighter regulation, has led chemical companies to develop a new class of refrigerants; it has also led some users of chlorinated hydrocarbon solvents to develop alternative non-polluting cleaning techniques; large-scale spray-painting processes based on the use of solvents have been largely replaced by either hot dip or electrostatic schemes that sharply reduce wastes. In fact UNEP has collected many examples of profitable 'clean technologies', most of which qualify as 'double dividends' in the usual sense (UNEP, 1994).

- The California 'zero emissions' law, requiring that a certain percentage of vehicles sold in Los Angeles should be based on non-carbon propulsion systems, has had a remarkable catalytic effect on the automobile industry. While all-electric cars based on storage batteries alone are now widely regarded as a niche technology at best (though some might differ), the result has been to launch a serious competition between two other propulsion technologies. One of them is the so-called hybrid-electric propulsion system which uses a small constant-speed internal combustion engine to drive a generator, using stored battery power for acceleration. Toyota has already introduced such a model. The other is the fuel cell-based system now under serious development by Daimler-Chrysler and several other big firms.

I hope that this list is long enough to make the point. It is true enough that not every major technological innovation can be traced to a real shortage. The telephone and the electric light exploited latent, rather than actual, demand. It is arguable that they did not replace a direct competitor, although the electric light did compete with gas lighting in cities and this competition induced major innovations in the latter before the substitution became final. More to the point, I strongly believe that serious efforts to limit the output of CO_2 would actually be quite beneficial, in that they would accelerate the introduction of photovoltaic (PV) cells, fuels cells and – ultimately – hydrogen-based energy technologies that are known to be technically feasible but are (currently) rather far from economic competitiveness (Ayres and Axtell, 1996; Ayres and Frankl, 1998). However, this, too, is a topic that leads well beyond the limited scope of the present chapter.

TRADE POLICY VERSUS TAX POLICY IN EQUILIBRIUM

Up to this point I have not discussed policy implications of industrial ecology (IE) or of the dematerialization imperative. The IE perspective would touch, at least peripherally, on a great many policy-related topics. It is impossible to cover them all here. However, one topic in particular deserves special note, namely the conflict between trade policy and tax policy.

The situation can be summarized briefly. Trade policy seeks to reduce trade barriers, including tariffs. The economic justification for this objective is that protectionism encourages inefficiency and keeps prices high whereas free trade *ceteris paribus* encourages production efficiency and benefits consumers through lower prices. There is no need to cite the enormous body of theoretical literature supporting this proposition, even though the empirical evidence is not nearly so compelling as the classical theory.

However, there is also a very compelling case for taxing 'bads' and reducing the tax burden on 'goods'. Much of the discussion has dealt with relatively minor cases, such as cigarettes and alcoholic beverages. But, in view of the foregoing evidence, it seems clear that it would be desirable to tax the use of environmental waste assimilative capacity. Given the obvious administrative difficulties of calculating or imposing such a tax, the second-best approach would be to tax the consumption of material inputs that contribute to pollution. If chemically inert structural materials (and perhaps food) were exempted, this would mean taxing the consumption of chemically active resources, such as fuels, metals and non-food organic materials, while reducing or eliminating the taxes on labour. The tax could be imposed at the source and based on the exergy content of every material used in commerce. It would then be incorporated in the price of every product or service along the value-added chain.

The economic justification of the resource tax would be to alter the price relationships in favour of labour, as against material resources that ultimately contribute to pollution. By raising the effective cost of resources and reducing the effective cost of labour (holding the total tax burden constant), producers would be encouraged to employ more labour and fewer energy-containing resources. The result, in time, would be to encourage material conserving technological innovation and accelerate dematerialization.

Unfortunately, the practical application of this idea would depend upon imposing border adjustment taxes on all imported products manufactured outside the country, while simultaneously refunding the tax on exports. Otherwise the adverse impact on competitiveness (in some industries) could be disastrous. Fear of such an impact on the part of industry would certainly mobilize political opposition to the tax, and the rules of the World Trade Organization (WTO) might forbid it absolutely. There is a potential conflict between trade liberalization and resource taxation.

Yet, in a general equilibrium sense, even without the border adjustments, the trade impacts might not be catastrophic. This would be the case if (and only if) the cuts in labour overheads compensated for higher resource costs. Obviously, if a resource-based tax were to replace labour taxes on the national level, the end result would be to favour information-intensive industries consuming few material resources and more labour, *vis-à-vis* resource-intensive industries. There is an obvious need for detailed quantitative analysis of various policy scenarios, especially making use of computable general equilibrium (CGE models).

CONCLUSIONS AND RESEARCH NEEDS

It is difficult to conclude a chapter such as this. I have touched on a number of important economic issues that also clearly fall within the domain of industrial ecology. There are a number of areas where more research is needed. From the economic point of view, the most important new idea may be that changing times require new growth models based on more sophisticated theory. Certainly the new growth theory must adequately reflect the importance of declining energy/raw materials costs as drivers of past growth.

The new theory must also enhance our detailed understanding of the implications of the approaching end of this era, notably the fact that future growth must depend increasingly on conservation of value-added and reduction of depreciation losses. The substitute for declining energy/raw material costs, as an 'engine' of growth, must be accelerated technological change in other areas, perhaps based largely on applications of information technology. The new growth theory must also explicitly reflect the role of economic disequilibrium, such as underemployment of labour and capital (partly due to technological change itself) and its impact on the rate and direction of innovation. In this context, there is a need to develop more sophisticated measures of disequilibrium.

However, the devil is in the details, and there are a host of peripheral details to be explored. For one thing, the continuing conflict between theory-based 'top–down' models and engineering-based 'bottom–up' approaches needs to be reconciled. At the 'top–down' end there is a need to develop models that reflect disequilibrium conditions and that permit disaggregation and exploration of several different types of 'double dividends' and the conditions (scenarios) under which they can occur.

At the empirical 'bottom–up' end of the research spectrum there is a need for assembling data on past and recent technological innovations, and for detailed analysis of the reasons for success or failure. It is increasingly important to either confirm or deny the theoretical assumption that technologies are selected by a Darwinian 'survival of the fittest' mechanism, which would support the notion of economic growth along an optimal path. But there are other possibilities (as in biological evolution) in which case accidents, luck, non-economic factors or path-dependence (for example, returns to adoption) might turn out to be important or even dominant. If this is the case, it would follow that there is a significant potential for double dividends or even 'free lunches'. It would also tend to support the so-called Porter hypothesis.

Again, if the existence of significant double-dividend potentials is confirmed by this kind of research, it would also undermine the 'hidden-cost' hypothesis. In that case, there would be a need for deeper research into organizational theory, game theory and the potential for organizational restructuring to induce greater cooperation and less competition among individuals and units within the organization. In other words, there is a need to explore organizational ways of inducing managers to act in the interest of the firm, just as there is a need to explore governmental policies for bringing the interests of the firm and the interests of society – including long-term sustainability – into coincidence.

The potential for conflicts between trade liberalization policy (or at least its implementation by WTO) and the use of taxes or tradable permits to shift the relative prices of labour and resources at the national level has also been mentioned as a topic requiring more attention from theorists. Also, the sheer magnitude of the international monetary flows resulting from joint implementation via exchangeable permits could be significantly greater than the magnitude of the 'petrodollar' flows into OPEC countries in the late 1970s and early 1980s. Those flows caused serious dislocations. This issue needs attention from theorists.

From the industrial ecology perspective, the major message of this chapter must be two-fold. First, it is important to recognize a kind of 'master equation', namely that depreciation equals waste and waste equals pollution. The second contribution of an IE perspective is that value-added conservation specifically means extended product life, enhanced recovery, renovation and remanufacturing of durables. It also implies gradual elimination of industrial processes involving dissipation of intermediates, *especially* combustion of fossil fuels.

Clearly there are a number of specific issues requiring both theoretical and empirical work by economists and engineers (in the broad sense) working together. For instance, a comprehensive dematerialization scenario would involve extensive industrial restructuring (eco-restructuring). It is impossible to calculate a priori the impact of such a restructuring on aggregated financial wealth. The financial value of stocks in resource-based firms – for example, oil companies – for instance, would decline. But other stocks (in remanufacturing enterprises, for instance) would increase in value. What can be said, however, is that tangible wealth and the utility of real final services consumed by households would be unaffected (by definition). Meanwhile the real disservices resulting from environmental pollution would be abated considerably, and the rate of degradation of natural environmental capital would correspondingly decrease.

Once again, the details are crucial and much more research is needed to evaluate environmental losses in monetary terms. To give only one example, the rapid industrial development of China has caused massive air and water pollution, resulting in serious health problems in many cities. Moreover, northern China is dry and water tables are falling, which has given rise to proposals for large-scale water diversion projects. Yet more water for the north will mean less water for the lower reaches of the Yangtze, resulting in less dilution for industrial pollutants and a variety of related problems. Benefit–cost considerations arise at every turn in this situation, and many – if not most – of them involve comparing quantitative costs and losses with non-quantifiables, not even mentioning 'quality of life'.

Indeed, China may be the first country where the distinction between 'strong' and 'weak' sustainability has practical and immediate importance. For instance, if natural capital is not substitutable by man-made capital, how much of the watershed of the upper Yangtze should be left forested? How much industrial pollution can be safely put into the watershed without adversely affecting future generations? Such questions will arise with increasing frequency and will require economists to develop measures more sophisticated than the Pearce–Atkinson criterion that is currently in vogue.

NOTES

1. The long-term downward trend has been well documented, especially by a number of studies conducted by Resources for the Futures Inc. (for example, Barnett and Morse, 1962; Potter and Christy, 1968; Smith and Krutilla, 1979). However, exhaustion does happen. There is no tin or copper left to mine in Cornwall. For that matter, there is very little (except coal) left worth mining anywhere in Western Europe, except the North Sea. There is no petroleum left to pump from Western Pennsylvania or Ohio or Indiana or Southern California, etc.
2. The literature is extensive. For a useful summary see Argote and Epple (1990).
3. Financial wealth consists of money, marketable securities, partnerships, bank deposits, receivables, insurance policies, etc.
4. A difficulty in quantification arises from the fact that liquid assets are financial, not tangible. But financial wealth can rise and fall for a number of reasons, some of which are not very well understood. The decline of Japanese financial wealth since 1989 and that of the rest of East Asia since 1997, while US financial wealth was doubling (or more) illustrates this point well enough. Nevertheless, the bulk of financial wealth still rests on a tangible, material basis. Information may be increasingly important, but only a very small fraction of total wealth (as yet) can be attributed to 'pure' information, such as stored data, chemical formulae, blueprints, or computer software.
5. This problem, and some of its implications, has been pointed out by a number of authors (for example, Hueting, 1980; Repetto *et al.*, 1989; Ahmad, el-Serafy and Lutz, 1990).

6. In this regard Georgescu-Roegen introduced a useful distinction between '*funds*' and '*flows*' (Georgescu-Roegen, 1979). Capital is a fund, whereas intermediates are flows.
7. The cement industry is a partial exception, since the older plants are notorious for generating large quantities of particulates and modest quantities of carbon dioxide. However, the cement industry is also a potential sink for otherwise hard-to-dispose-of wastes, such as rubber tyres, which can be burned for fuel without emitting sulphur dioxide or other metallic pollutants.
8. This decline has been termed 'the Solow paradox' because of a published comment by Solow (1987) to the effect that increasing investment in computers and software had not led to increased labour productivity. This 'paradox' led to a major OECD conference (OECD, 1991b).
9. The four main contenders have been characterized as: (1) mismeasurement, (2) mismanagement, (3) diffusion delay and (4) 'the capital stock theory'. The mismeasurement theory suggests that productivity has in fact improved, but that it does not show up in the statistics because much of it is hidden in product quality and performance. The mismanagement theory is that investment in information technology has in fact been a waste of money. The diffusion delay theory says that the economic benefits of information technology are real enough, but take a long time to be manifest in the productivity statistics. The capital stock theory is relevant: it says, in effect, that IT still constitutes a small percentage of total invested capital (11.7 per cent for all information processing equipment and only 2 per cent for computers *per se* in 1993) mainly due to the fact that (i) large-scale investment is still a relatively recent phenomenon, so accumulation is still not very large and (ii) both equipment and software depreciate much faster than conventional capital equipment and infrastructure (for example, Sichel, 1997).
10. For an instance, see Wolff (1995).
11. For comprehensive recent surveys of the models and their underlying assumptions, see Azar (1996); Repetto and Austin (1997); Azar and Dowlatabadi (1998).

REFERENCES

Adriaanse, Albert, Stefan Bringezu, Allen Hammond, Yuichi Moriguchi, Eric Rodenburg, Donald Rogich and Hemut Schütz (1997), *Resource Flows: The Material Basis of Industrial Economies*, Washington, DC: World Resources Institute, with Wuppertal Institute, Germany, National Ministry of Housing, Netherlands and National Institute for Environmental Studies, Japan.
Ahmad, Yussuf J., Saleh el-Serafy and Ernst Lutz (eds) (1990), *Environmental Accounting for Sustainable Development*, Washington, DC: World Bank.
Argote, Linda and Dennis Epple (1990), 'Learning curves and manufacturing', *Science*, **247** (February), 920–24.
Ayres, Robert U. (1994a), *Information, Entropy and Progress*, New York: American Institute of Physics.
Ayres, Robert U. (1994b), 'On economic disequilibrium and free lunch', *Environmental and Resource Economics*, **4**, 435–54. (Also INSEAD Working Paper 93/45/EPS.)
Ayres, Robert U. and Robert Axtell (1996), 'Foresight as a survival characteristic: when (if ever) does the long view pay?', *Journal of Technological Forecasting and Social Change*, **51**(1), 209–35. (Also INSEAD Working Paper 93/83/EPS.)
Ayres, Robert U. and Paolo Frankl (1998), 'Toward a nonpolluting energy system', *Environmental Science and Technology*, September.
Ayres, Robert U. and Allan V. Kneese (1969), 'Production, consumption and externalities', *American Economic Review*, June. (AERE 'Publication of Enduring Quality' Award, 1990.)

Ayres, Robert U., Jean-Charles Hourcade and Khalil Helioui (1998), 'Theoretical and empirical background of the double dividend perspective', *Integrating Technology Diffusion Micro Models for Assessing Sustainable Development Policy Options (IMAD)*, Chapter Part I: 1–91 (Project ENV4-CT96-0292), Commission of the European Communities: Directorate-General for Science, Research & Development, Brussels, October.

Ayres, Robert U., Jeroen C.J.M. van den Bergh and John M. Gowdy (1999), 'Viewpoint: weak versus strong sustainability: economics, natural science and cons', *Environmental Values*, forthcoming.

Azar, Christian (1996), 'Technological change and the long-run cost of reducing CO2 emissions', Working Paper (96/84/EPS), INSEAD, Fontainebleau, France, July.

Azar, Christian and Hadi Dowlatabadi (1998), 'A review of technical change in assessments of climate policy', draft for *Annual Review of Economics*, **24**.

Barnett, Harold J. and Chandler Morse (1962), *Scarcity and Growth: The Economics of Resource Scarcity*, Baltimore: Johns Hopkins University Press.

Battelle–Columbus Laboratories (1975), 'Evaluation of the theoretical potential for energy conservation in 7 basic industries', (PB-244-772), Battelle–Columbus Laboratories, Columbus, OH, June. (Prepared for US Federal Energy Administration.)

Berndt, Ernst R. and Dale W. Jorgenson (1973), 'Production structure', in *US Energy Resources and Economic Growth*, Ford Foundation Energy Policy Project, October, Washington, DC.

Berndt, Ernst R. and David O. Wood (1975), 'Technology, prices, & the derived demand for energy', *Review of Economics and Statistics*, **56**(3), August, 259–68.

Bolch, William E. Jr (1980), 'Solid waste and trace element impacts', in Alex E.S. Green (ed.), *Coal Burning Issues*, Gainesville, FL: University Presses of Florida, chapter 12, pp. 231–48.

Campbell, Colin J. (1997), *The Coming Oil Crisis*, Brentwood, UK: Multi-Science Publishing & Petroconsultants.

Campbell, Colin J. and Jean H. Laherrère (1998), 'The end of cheap oil', *Scientific American*, **278**(3), March, 60–65.

CEA (Council of Economic Advisors) (1992), *Economic Report of the President Together with the Annual Report of the Council of Economic Advisors*, Washington, DC: United States Government Printing Office.

CEA (Council of Economic Advisors) (1996), *Economic Report of the President Together with the Annual Report of the Council of Economic Advisors*, Washington, DC: United States Government Printing Office, February.

Considine, T. (1991), 'Determinants of the material intensity of use', *Land Economics*, **67**, 99–115.

Davis, W.E. (1971), *National Inventory of Sources and Emissions: Mercury, 1968* (APTD-1510), Leawood, KS: W.E. Davis & Associates, September (for EPA, Research Triangle Park, NC).

Davis, W.E. (1972), *National Inventory of Sources and Emissions: Barium, Boron, Copper, Selenium and Zinc 1969 – Copper, Section III* (APTD-1129), Leawood, KS: W.E. Davis & Associates, April (for EPA, Research Triangle Park, NC).

Forrest, David and Julian Szekely (1991), 'Global warming and the primary metals industry', *Journal of Metallurgy*, **43**, December, 23–30.

Gabel, H. Landis and B. Sinclair-Desgagné (1995), 'Corporate responses to environmental concerns', in H. Folmer, H.L. Gabel and H. Opschoor (eds), *Principles of Environmental and Resource Economics: A Guide for Students and Decision-Makers*, Cheltenham, UK and Lyme, MA: Edward Elgar, pp. 347–61.

Gabel, H. Landis and B. Sinclair-Desgagné (1995), 'The firm, its routines, and the environment', in T. Tietenberg and H. Folmer (eds), *The International Yearbook of Environmental and Resource Economics 1998/1999: A Survey of Current Issues*, Cheltenham, UK and Lyme, MA: Edward Elgar.

Gaines, Linda L. (1980), 'Energy and material flows in the copper industry', Technical Memo, Argonne National Laboratory, Argonne, IL, 1980. (Prepared for the United States Department of Energy.)

Georgescu-Roegen, Nicholas (1979), 'Myths about energy and matter', *Growth and Change*, **10**(1).

Goulder, Lawrence H., 'Effects of carbon taxes in an economy with prior tax distortions: an intertempororal general equilibrium analysis', *Journal of Environmental Economics and Management*, **29**(3), November, 271–97.

Goulder, Lawrence H. and Stephen H. Schneider, 'Induced technological change, crowding out, and the attractiveness of CO2 emissions abatement', Draft, Institute for International Studies, Stanford University, Palo Alto, CA, October.

Grubb, Michael, T. Chapuis and M. Ha Duong (1995), 'The economics of changing course: implications of adaptability and inertia for optimal climate policy', *Energy Policy*, **23**(4/5), 417–32.

Harris, D. (1996), 'Commentary and critique of "Accounting for Mineral Resources: Issues & BEA's Initial Estimates"', *Non-Renewable Resources*, **5**, 7–21.

Hartwick, J.M. (1977), 'Intergenerational equity and the investing of rents from exhaustible resources', *American Economic Review*, **67**, 972–4.

Herman, Robert, Simiak Ardekani and Jesse H. Ausubel (1990), 'Dematerialization', *Journal of Technological Forecasting and Social Change*, **38**(4), 333–48.

Hourcade, Jean-Claude and J. Robinson (1996), 'Mitigating factors: assessing the costs of reducing GHG emissions', *Energy Policy*, **24**(10/11), 863–73.

Hueting, Rofie (1980), *New Scarcity and Economic Growth: More Welfare through Less Production?*, Amsterdam: North-Holland.

Jorgenson, Dale W., Lauritz R. Christensen and Lawrence J. Lau (1973), 'Transcendental logarithmic production frontiers', *Review of Economics and Statistics*, **55**(1), February, 28–45. (Also available in the series 'Reprints in Economic Theory and Econometrics', Department of Economics, Harvard University.)

Kauppi, P., Mielikainen and Kuusula (1992), 'Biomass and carbon budget of European forests, 1971 to 1990', *Science*, **256**, 311–14.

Krause, Florentin, W. Bach and Jonathan Kooney (1992), *Energy Policy in the Greenhouse*, London: Earthscan.

Krause, Florentin, with Eric Haites, Richard Howarth and Jonathan Koomey (1993), 'Cutting carbon emissions: burden or benefit? The economics of energy-tax and non-price policies', in *Energy Policy in the Greenhouse*, **2**(1), International Project for Sustainable Energy Paths, El Cerrito, CA.

Labys, W. and L. Waddell (1988), 'Commodity life cycles in US materials demand', *Resources Policy*, **15**, 238–53.

Lovins, Amory B. and L. Hunter Lovins (1981), *Energy/War: Breaking the Nuclear Link*, New York: Harper & Row.

Lovins, Amory B. and L. Hunter Lovins (1997), *Climate: Making Sense & Making Money*, Snowmass, CO: Rocky Mountain Institute, 13 November.

Lowenbach, William A. and Joyce S. Schlesinger (1979), 'Arsenic: a preliminary materials balance' (EPA-560/6-79-005), Lowenbach & Schlesinger Associates, Inc., McLean, VA, March (for EPA, Washington, DC).

Lübkert, Barbara, Y. Virtanen, M. Muhlberger, I. Ingham, B. Vallance and S. Alber

(1991), 'Life cycle analysis: international database for ecoprofile analysis (IDEA)', Working Paper (WP-91-30), International Institute for Applied Systems Analysis, Laxenburg, Austria.

Masini, Andrea and Robert U. Ayres (1996), 'An application of exergy accounting to four basic metal industries', Working Paper (96/65/EPS), INSEAD, Fontainebleau, France, September.

McElroy, A.D. and F.D. Shobe (1980), 'Source category survey: secondary zinc smelting and refining industry' (EPA-450/3-80-012), Midwest Research Institute, Kansas City, MO, May 1980 (for EPA, Research Triangle Park, NC).

McGannon, H.E. (ed.) (1971), 'The making, shaping and treating of steel', United States Steel Corporation, Pittsburgh PA.

Nakamura, Yoichi and Katsuki Oda (1996), 'Green GDP of Japan for 1985 and 1990: trial estimates of integrated environmental and economic accounting', Working Paper 8, United Nations University Institute of Advanced Studies, June.

Organization for Economic Cooperation and Development (1991a), *The State of the Environment*, OECD, Paris.

Organization for Economic Cooperation and Development (1991b), *Technology & Productivity: The Challenge for Economic Policy*, OECD, Paris.

Palmer, Karen, Wallace E. Oates and Paul R. Portney (1995), 'Tightening environmental standards: The benefit–cost or no-cost paradigm', *Journal of Economic Perspectives*, **9**(4), 119–32.

Pearce, David W. and Giles Atkinson (1993), 'Capital theory and the measurement of sustainable development: an indicator of weak sustainability', *Ecological Economics*, **8**, 166–81.

PEDCo-Environmental (1980a), 'Industrial process profiles for environmental use: primary copper industry' (PB81-164915, EPA-600/2-80-170), PEDCo-Environmental, Cincinnati, OH, July (for IERL, Cincinnati, OH).

PEDCo-Environmental (1980b), 'Industrial process profiles for environmental use: primary lead industry' (PB81-110926, EPA-600/2-80-168), PEDCo-Environmental, Cincinnati, OH, July (for IERL, Cincinnati, OH).

PEDCo-Environmental (1980c), 'Industrial process profiles for environmental use: primary zinc industry' (PB80-225717, EPA-600/2-80-169), PEDCo-Environmental, Cincinnati, OH, July (for IERL, Cincinnati, OH).

Porter, Michael (1991), 'America's competitiveness strategy', *Scientific American*, April.

Porter, Michael E. and Claas van der Linde (1995), 'Green and competitive', *Harvard Business Review*, September–October, 120–34.

Potter, Neal and Francis T. Christy, Jr, *Trends in Natural Resource Commodities*, Baltimore: Johns Hopkins University Press.

Radian Corporation (1977), 'Industrial process profiles for environmental use: primary aluminum industry' (PB281-491, EPA-600/2-77-023y), Radian Corporation, Austin, TX, February (for IERL, Cincinnati, OH).

Repetto, Robert (1985a), 'Natural resource accounting in a resource-based economy: an Indonesian case study', 3rd Environmental Accounting Workshop, UNEP and World Bank, Paris, October.

Repetto, Robert (ed.) (1985b), *The Global Possible: Resources, Development & the New Century*, New Haven, CT: Yale University Press.

Repetto, Robert and Duncan Austin (1997), *The Costs of Climate Protection: A Guide for the Perplexed*, Washington, DC: World Resources Institute.

Repetto, Robert, William Macgrath, Michael Wells, Christine Beer and Fabrizio

Rossini (1989), *Wasting Assets: Natural Resources in the National Income Accounts*, Washington, DC: World Resources Institute.

Sedjo, Roger (1992), 'Temperate forest ecosystems in the global carbon cycle', Washington, DC: *Ambio*, **21**, 274–7.

Sichel, Daniel E. (1997), *The Computer Revolution*, Washington, DC: Brookings Institution Press.

Smil, Vaclav (1996), 'Environmental problems in China: estimates of economic costs', East–West Center Special Report (5), East-West Center, Honolulu, HA, April.

Smith, V. Kerry and John Krutilla (eds) (1979), *Scarcity and Growth Revisited*, Baltimore: Johns Hopkins University Press.

Solow, Robert M. (1974), 'The economics of resources or the resources of economics', *American Economic Review*, **64**.

Solow, Robert M. (1986), 'On the intergenerational allocation of natural resources', *Scandinavian Journal of Economics*, **88**, 141–9.

Solow, Robert M. (1987), 'Growth theory and after', Lecture, Nobel Prize in Economics, Nobel Foundation, Stockholm, 8 December.

Solow, Robert M. (1992), *An Almost Practical Step Towards Sustainability*, Washington, DC: Resources for the Future.

Thomas, J.A.G. (1977), *Energy Analysis*, Boulder, CO: Westview Press.

Tilton, John E. (1986), 'Beyond intensity of use', *Materials and Society*, **10**, 245–50.

UNU/IAS (1999), Lo Fu-Chen (Project Director), 'Sustainable development framework for China: summary report', Draft Report, United Nations University Institute of Advanced Studies, Tokyo, February.

United Nations Environment Programme Industry & Environment (1994), 'Cleaner production', *UNEP Industry & Environment*, **17**(4), October–December; special issue.

Von Weizsäcker, Ernst-Ulrich, Amory B. Lovins and L. Hunter Lovins (1998), *Factor Four: Doubling Wealth, Halving Resource Use*, London: Earthscan.

Watson, John W. and Kathryn J. Brooks (1979), 'A review of standards of performance for new stationary sources-secondary lead smelters' (MTR-7871), MITRE Corp., McLean, VA, January.

Wolff, Edward N. (1995), 'Technological change, capital accumulation, and changing trade patterns over the long term', *Structural Change & Economic Dynamics*, **6**(1), March, 43–70.

10. Ecosystems as lotteries

Thomas D. Crocker and Jason F. Shogren

1 INTRODUCTION

The connections and conflicts among private land uses, collective environmental protocols, and ecosystem geographies are much talked about, and yet few studies have explored their interaction. This chapter frames this nexus of private action, collective constraints, and ecosystem services by depicting ecosystems as lotteries. Ecosystem lotteries reflect our view that the odds and outcomes of good/bad states of nature are in part determined by private choices collectively constrained by environmental protocols defined by outside experts. Understanding the uncertainties and risk embedded in the private–collective–ecosystem nexus is crucial for more effective environmental policy. To see why, follow our thread of logic.

Major private land uses include the production of timber, food, minerals, housing space and other extractive, ecosystem-altering activities. Governments worry about how these activities might affect the odds that private land will continue to provide amenity and life support services to society. Perceived tensions between private interests in extractive activities and collective interests in maintaining ecosystem services have spawned a myriad of public regulatory agencies and collective protocols.

Collective protocols define a new set of constraints on private land use that serve either to take rents from or give rents to private land. New protocols institutionalize a public policy reorientation toward the risks and benefits of preservation (see, for example, Shogren, 1998a, on 'The West' in the United States), an uncertain and frequently contested reorientation often justified by vague references to the notion of 'sustainable development'. The need to define sustainability in some coherent way has stimulated institutional and technological innovations by raising the demand for specialized insight from biologists, chemists, economists, engineers and lawyers. These specialists often interpret sustainability as a union of 'clean' technical fixes and a progressive integration of their favoured collective protocols into private land-use practices. These fixes and protocols present private landowners with new incentives and constraints on their extractive practices.

As a consequence, new ecosystem geographies or landscapes emerge which redefine the odds of good and bad states of nature under which we all operate – ecosystems as lotteries. So whose environmental values are actually being encoded in these new regulated ecosystem lotteries? Can the encoding be explained by the high drama suggested by the popular spectacle of the extractive private landowner versus the preservationist outsider environmental specialist? What are the interactions between private landowners and environmental regulators and specialists who determine ecosystem lotteries? Addressing these questions is important because not only do people have preferences over outcomes, they have preferences over the lotteries themselves.

Existing models of economic–ecological system interactions and the management problems these interactions pose focus mainly on their aggregated, intertemporal and known features: other than the influence of the passage of time upon a known sequence of events, one state of the world is as desirable as any other (for example, Barbier and Burgess, 1997). Despite this characterization of the world, these intertemporal models provide considerable enlightenment about the mediating behavioural interactions of economic and ecological systems. Elbasha and Roe (1996), for example, give insight into the requirements for environmental sustainability by constructing a growth model which allows the economic system to change the structure and the context of natural processes (for example, making a forest into a desert) which, in turn, can alter the way that the economic system organizes itself. Nordhaus (1994) provides a worthy empirical example of using mediating behavioural interactions to link economies and ecosystems. His Dynamic Integrated Model of Climate and Economy (DICE) adapts Ramsey's (1928) economic growth model to have the economy generate CO_2 climate-affecting emissions while maximizing the present value of social welfare, which is made a function of consumption. The emissions that current production and consumption create accumulate in the atmosphere, increasing global temperatures and causing subsequent environmental damages which reduce production, thereby ultimately provoking declines in consumption.

There are, however, more specific features of these mediating behavioural interactions between economic and ecological systems not easily accommodated within a restricted, highly aggregated intertemporal framework (Crocker and Tschirhart, 1992). When the chosen land-use practices of the private landowner are the focus of public concern, grappling with these interactions requires attention to additional core features of the private landowner's decision problem. In particular the existence of private landowner and outside specialist and regulator uncertainty about world states and the presence of complex heterogeneous economic and ecological geographies seem incompatible with a known, aspatial world. Capturing these readily observed patterns of interactions requires an underlying analytical structure which represents spatial and uncertainty differences between and among landowners, outside specialists and regulators. That is, grasping the connections and conflicts among the private–collective–ecosystem nexus demands attention to the uncertainty features of spatial interactions, features that the economics literature has not entirely neglected but features that probably have not been given their due if measured by their prominence in the biological literature.

Uncertainty most obviously enters because the private landowner's choices about the type (the extensive margin) of his land uses usually entails his commitment to specific actions, which may be difficult or impossible to adjust for months or years. The durability or irreversibility of the owner's land-use decisions mean he is unable to respond easily to new information subsequent to his land-use commitment. When he commits, he foregoes his options to make other commitments (Dixit and Pindyck, 1994). The owner must make his decisions without knowing how a specific combination of biotic and abiotic ecosystem components, capital and location will translate into his fortunes. His uncertainty arises from several features whose impacts he cannot unequivocally know prior to his land-use decisions: what collective environmental protocols will be and how they will be applied to him; how the ecosystem on his land works; and the effects adjacent landowner decisions and exogenous natural events will have upon the uses he selects.

The discrete nature of land-use decisions is another frequently unacknowledged influence upon ecosystem geographies. Examples of discreteness at the extensive margins of land and ecosystem choice abound – whether to dam a stream, to build a road through an uninhabited forest, to place a trophy home on a ridge top, to introduce an exotic species into an ecosystem, and to follow or not to follow an outsider-imposed environmental protocol. Preferences may also cause discreteness: the landowner's choice may be between the current configuration of the ecosystem on his land and his most preferred of the feasible alternative configurations.[1] Similarly, transactions costs, such as getting the permission of outsiders to change uses that do not vary with land use, may cause lumpiness. These costs encourage the landowner to stick to current land uses instead of adopting a slightly different use. Discrete choices at the intensive margin include technological choices, such as the use or non-use of skidders and tree harvesters in logging operations and the adoption of less or more environmentally benign pesticide types in farming enterprises.

In the next section of this chapter, we present a model which embodies the uncertainty and discrete choice features of the landowner's decision problem. We explore how the interaction of private actions and public environmental protocols affects the landowner's value function for reducing uncertainty in the presence of discrete uses. A third section evaluates the implications of a private land-use decision problem involving discreteness and uncertainty for the impact of outsider-imposed land-use regulations upon ecosystem

geographies. The fourth section briefly reviews the small technical economics literature which considers how landscapes are formed, suggests how the
model set forth in this chapter complements this literature and indicates some
research opportunities. A summary concludes the chapter.

2 VALUING ECOSYSTEMS AS PROTECTION AGAINST RISK

Consider a model of a landowner's *ex-ante* valuation of the risk to his fortunes
that the impacts of the ecosystem on his land hold for him. The different
ecosystem states that he fosters may be viewed as alternative protection technologies which lessen the likelihood (self-protection) or the severity (self-
insurance) of untoward events having their origins off his land (Ehrlich and
Becker, 1972). For brevity, we refer to these alternative natural hedging technologies as natural protection. For example, an undisturbed forest ecosystem
diffuses economic risks from weather events by stabilizing many environmental processes, notably by acting as a sponge that soaks up moisture before
releasing it at regular rates. Wetlands also buffer the economy from natural and
man-made shocks by tempering fluctuating water levels from tides, precipitation and runoff, and providing water purification and habitat services. People
purchase open space adjacent to their existing property to add to and to protect
the ecological services that their property provides them.

We build upon Arnott and Stiglitz's (1988) model of moral hazard to develop
a static framework which shows that a non-convexity often exists in this owner's *ex-ante* willingness to pay a premium for natural protection.[2] The natural
protection premium is defined as the monetary consequences for him of voluntarily restricting his access to and use of property. He hobbles the exercise of
his property rights, as measured by access, obligations and responsibilities, in
order to decrease his likelihood of damages from lessened protection services.[3]

Suppose the owner confronts the prospect of two mutually exclusive and
jointly exhaustive ecosystem states. Let w represent monetary wealth, and
let $U_0 \equiv U(w)$ represent the utility he would receive under the good ecosystem state where he allows the ecosystem to serve its natural protection
function by buffering him from exogenous market and natural shock events.
Assume $U_0' > 0$ and $U_0'' > 0$, where primes denote derivatives of functions.
Let $EU_1 \equiv \int_a^b U_1(w - D) \mathrm{d}F(D; \xi)$ represent the expected utility he would receive under the bad ecosystem state in which the ecosystem might fail to
serve its protection function, where $D < w$ is the money equivalent of any
damages suffered due to the failure.

The likelihood of a failure in this bad state is given by the cumulative
distribution $F(D; \xi)$ bounded over the compact support $[a, b]$. Let $\xi \geq 0$

represent an index of damage riskiness such that an increase in ξ creates a first-order stochastic dominant shift in the distribution of damages, $F_\xi < 0$, where a letter subscript indicates a derivative taken with respect to the subscript. Increases in the index of damage riskiness are due to a loss of ecosystem resilience, an ecological measure of the perturbation that a natural asset can endure before being shifted into another state (Holling, 1986). Assume $EU_1' \equiv \int_a^b U_1'(w-D)\,dF(D;\,\xi) > 0$ and $EU_1'' \equiv \int_a^b U_1''(w-D)\,dF(D;\,\xi) < 0$; and $E\tilde{U}_1' \equiv \int_a^b U_1(w-D)\,F_\xi(D;\,\xi)dD < 0$. This last expression refers to the expected utility consequence of a first-order stochastic dominant shift in the distribution of damages.

Let p^i and $(1-p^i)$ be the probabilities that the good or the bad ecosystem states are realized. Allow the owner to influence these odds by prudence over how he uses his land. Let s^i be the opportunity costs in utility terms of this self-restraint, where $i = H, L$ represents high (H) and low (L) levels of self-restraint, such that $s^H > s^L$ and $p^H > p^L$.[4] Self-restraint involves combinations of the intensity with which a given management practice is applied to a given area of land and the share of a land ownership to which a given management practice is applied.

Require the owner to choose one of two self-restraint alternatives, though our framework only demands that he choose one alternative from among what could be a near-continuum. His choice between the two, self-restraint alternatives affects the utility loss he will suffer from a given level of riskiness. Let the owner's expected utility, V^H and V^L, from the high and low levels of self-restraint, be written as

$$V^H \equiv p^H U_0(w) + (1-p^H)EU_1(w-D) - s^H \qquad (10.1)$$

and

$$V^L \equiv p^L U_0(w) + (1-p^L)EU_1(w-D) - s^L. \qquad (10.2)$$

Note that the expected utility opportunity cost, s^i, of self-restraint is assumed separable from the expected utility benefits of self-restraint and to be wealth independent. We thereby avoid treating this opportunity cost as a money amount that may affect the marginal rates of substitution between goods in the two ecosystem states (Shogren and Crocker, 1991a).

Figure 10.1 illustrates the owner's indifference curves in wealth–risk space for the high self-restraint case. The slope of the indifference curves is

$$\left.\frac{\partial \xi}{dw}\right|_{V^H} = -\left[\frac{EU_1'}{E\tilde{U}_1'} + \frac{p^H}{(1-p^H)}\frac{U_0'}{E\tilde{U}_1'}\right] > 0 \qquad (10.3)$$

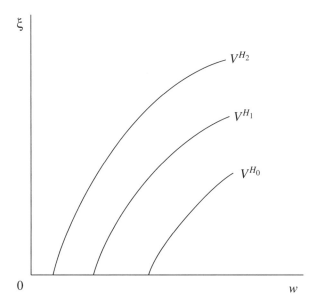

Figure 10.1   High self-restraint indifference curves

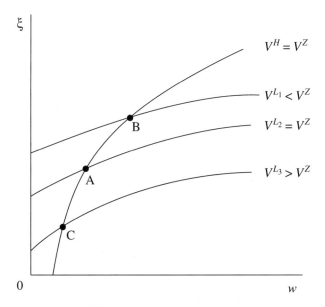

Figure 10.2   High and low self-restraint indifference curves

because riskiness is undesirable and wealth is desirable. Lower indifference curves are therefore more preferred. Note that the owner's willingness to trade off risk for wealth given high self-restraint exceeds in absolute magnitude his willingness given low self-restraint

$$\frac{d\xi}{dw}\bigg|_{V^H} = -\left[\frac{EU_1'}{E\tilde{U}_1'} + \frac{p^H}{(1-p^H)}\frac{U_0'}{E\tilde{U}_1'}\right] > -\left[\frac{EU_1'}{E\tilde{U}_1'} + \frac{p^L}{(1-p^L)}\frac{U_0'}{E\tilde{U}_1'}\right] = \frac{d\xi}{dw}\bigg|_{V^L} \quad (10.4)$$

This implies, as Figure 10.2 shows, that the slope of the high self-restraint indifference curves exceeds the slope of the low self-restraint curves. That is, a low self-restraint owner needs more wealth to accept more risk if he is to maintain constant utility than if he used high self-restraint. This occurs because a higher level of self-restraint generates a higher objective probability that the good ecosystem state will result, that is, $p^H > p^L$, and that the risk of untoward realizations will therefore be less.

Manipulating equations (10.1) and (10.2), we see that the comparative levels of expected utility depend on the relative magnitudes of the benefits $(U_0 - EU_1)$ and costs $[(s^H - s^L)/(p^H - p^L)]$ of self-restraint

$$V^H \underset{<}{\overset{>}{=}} V^L \quad \text{as} \quad (p^H - p^L)(U_0 - EU_1)\underset{<}{\overset{>}{=}}(s^H - s^L). \quad (10.5)$$

The expected utilities of high and of low self-restraint are equal if the net benefits of high versus low self-restraint, $(p^H - p^L)$ $(U_0 - EU_1)$, equal their net utility opportunity costs, $(s^H - s^L)$. For a given level of wealth, if an owner perceives trivial, if any, real damages from loss of natural protection, the difference in utility between ecosystem states approaches zero, $(U_0 - EU_1) \rightarrow 0$, and the expected utility of low self-restraint will most likely exceed the expected utility of high self-restraint, $V^H - V^L$. Also, if the owner believes that his self-restraint has a trivial impact on the likelihood of damages, $p^H \approx p^L$, then $V^H < V^L$. Alternatively, if he perceives large potential damages, or that his self-restraint has a significant impact on the likelihood of a good ecosystem state, the opposite holds, $V^H > V^L$.

In Figure 10.2 the intersection of the two expected utility curves, $V^H = V^{L_2}$ (point A), is where the landowner is indifferent between the two levels of self-restraint. This intersection also represents a switching point between low and high self-restraint. To see this, let $V^H = V^L = V^Z$ at point A. If we move to greater wealth and riskiness, say to point B, while holding the expected utility of high self-restraint constant, the owner prefers high self-restraint because $V^H = V^Z > V^{L_2}$. The relative expected utility of low self-restraint declines because wealth has not increased sufficiently at B to compensate for the increased riskiness associated with low self-restraint at that point. Low self-restraint at B places the individual on V^{L_1}, where $V^{L_1} < V^{L_2}$.

But with a move to lower wealth and lower riskiness, say from point A to point C, the owner prefers low self-restraint because $V^{L3} > V^H = V^Z$, that is, the reduction in riskiness with the good ecosystem state is not enough to compensate for the loss of wealth. By switching from high to low self-restraint in the move from A to C, the owner obtains a higher utility level, $V^{L3} > V^{L2}$, whereas if he had maintained high self-restraint his utility level would be unchanged. Now the expected utility of low self-restraint is greater than for high self-restraint as the owner reduces opportunity costs in response to the lower riskiness.

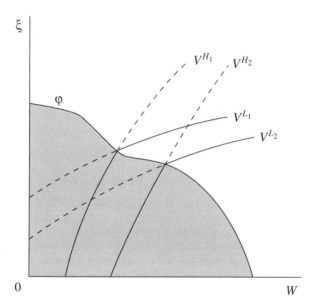

Figure 10.3   Switching locus

In Figure 10.3, the downward-sloping line, φ, represents the locus of switching points between low and high self-restraint. Inside the shaded area, the owner uses low self-restraint and outside the area he chooses high self-restraint. The scalloped-shaped utility curves of Figure 10.3 represent different levels of his non-convex expected utility in wealth and risk of damages; the degree of non-convexity will be greater the greater the difference in the slopes of the high and the low self-restraint indifference curves.

3   POLICY IMPLICATIONS OF THE NON-CONVEX WILLINGNESS TO PAY FOR NATURAL PROTECTION

Now suppose the person must value a collectively provided prospective increase in the likelihood that the good ecosystem state of secure natural protection will be realized with 100 per cent certainty. His *ex-ante* willingness to pay, R^i, for the collectively provided guarantee of natural protection given high and low self-restraint is written as

$$U(w - R^H) = V^H \text{ and } U(w - R^L) = V^L \qquad (10.6)$$

From equations (10.1), (10.2), (10.5) and (10.6) we can now compare the two levels of willingness to pay to secure these risk-reduction services

$$R^L \overset{\geq}{\underset{<}{}} R^H \text{ as } (p^H - p^L)(U_0 - EU_1) \overset{\geq}{\underset{<}{}} s^H - s^L \qquad (10.7)$$

Again the owner's comparative willingness to pay is determined by the relative benefits and costs of high and low self-restraint. The slope of the willingness-to-pay function given low self-restraint exceeds the slope of the function given high self-restraint

$$\frac{dR^H}{d\xi}\bigg|_{V^H} = -(1-p^H)\frac{E\tilde{U}'_1}{U'_0} < -(1-p^L)\frac{E\tilde{U}'_1}{U'_0} = \frac{dR^L}{d\xi}\bigg|_{V^L} \qquad (10.8)$$

Figure 10.4 illustrates that the *ex ante* willingness-to-pay function for natural protection is also non-convex given the relative benefits and costs of self-restraint. Assuming a constant wealth level, an owner chooses low over high self-restraint when damage risks are small, and vice versa when damage risks are large. The owner's value function is represented by the dashed lower envelope of the willingness-to-pay curves, R^H and R^L.

Why should policy makers care about a non-convex value function for natural protection? The short answer is that policy makers who ignore this scalloped function will affect environmental outcomes by producing a greater likelihood of overproviding natural protection that truncates opportunities to create lotteries to smooth preferences over states of nature.

Consider these two points in detail. Starting with the overprovision of natural protection, let the policy maker be characterized as a naive pessimist or optimist. A pessimist believes the owner will always exercise low self-restraint; an optimist believes he will always use high self-restraint. Both are naive in that they unaware of the non-convex value function.

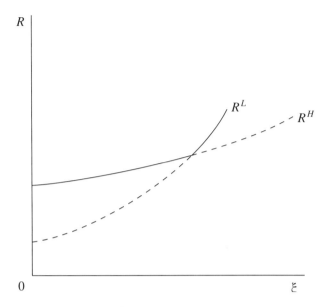

Figure 10.4 Non-convex willingness to pay

We illustrate the overprovision issue by focusing our discussion on the standard case that compares marginal benefits with marginal costs, that is, marginal willingness to pay, $\bar{R}^H$ and $\bar{R}^L$. Note that the marginal willingness to pay retains the scalloped property. Figure 10.5a shows the case with relatively low societal marginal benefits derived from the ecosystem subsidy, that is, they lie to the left of the switching point. A naive pessimist selects the optimal level of ecosystem care that he wants the owner's property to provide to society by equating the societal marginal benefits with the owner's scalloped value function, point *b*. Here ignoring the non-convex value function causes no inefficiency – the pessimist anticipated low self-restraint and was correct. But a naive optimist who presumes high self-restraint overprovides ecosystem care, point *c*; and overreduces ecosystem risk, ξ', relative to the optimal level, ξ^*. In contrast, Figure 10.5b shows the opposing case of relatively large marginal benefits. Here the roles are reversed: a naive optimist finds the optimal ecosystem care, point *d*; while a naive pessimist provides too much ecosystem care, point *e*, and too little risk, $\xi'' > \xi^{**}$.

Neglect of the non-convex value function leads to excessive provision of natural protection. But the source of inefficient provision does not follow the common drone heard from those promoting ecosystem conservation. This inefficiency arises not from market failure, but from government failure.

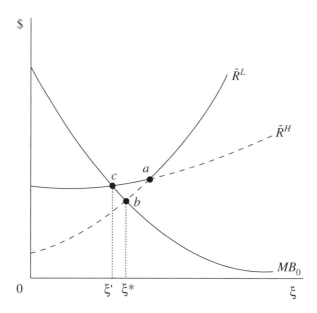

Figure 10.5a   Optimistic regulator

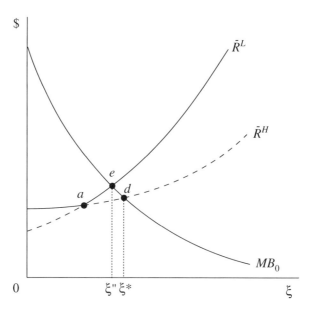

Figure 10.5b   Pessimistic regulator

Markets that fail to account for non-excludable benefits have too little protection of ecosystem services; government regulators failing to acknowledge a non-convex value function impose too much protection. Inefficient protection arises from too much investment in collective risk reduction. The excess originates in policy-maker neglect of the private actions of the people who own and live on the land that provides these natural protection services for the rest of society.[5]

Excessive investment in ecosystem protection is reminiscent of the overstrenuous protective actions that happen when transferable negative externalities exist (Bird, 1987). A transferable externality occurs when a person protects himself by transferring a risk through time or space to another generation or location. Policies that allow unilateral transfers rather than encouraging cooperative resolutions will result in excessive expenditures on self-protection.[6] Again government failure can occur in the presence of a market failure. This suggests an interesting trade-off to explore in future work on the devolution to local control – locals may increase efficiency because of better knowledge about private self-restraint, but locals may also reduce efficiency because of poorer insight about the regional or global nature of transferable externalities. A balance must be struck between superior local knowledge of local behaviour and global consequences.

The above mistakes would not occur if policy makers developed lotteries that would smooth (or convexify) the two value functions – our second policy implication. To see this, we return to total valuations to frame our thinking. By smoothing we mean a policy that uses a lottery which transforms the scalloped value function into one well-behaved function with all the desirable properties expected by economic theory.[7] We illustrate this implication by showing that land-use policies, whether federal or local, which provide landowners opportunities to participate in gambles can increase land-use specialization and thus spatial heterogeneity. More specialization implies that even greater losses are associated with generic federal policies that fail to sort landforms by damage risks. The non-convex value function and the undiscriminating policy tool used are the ultimate causes of the increased spatial heterogeneity. Smoothing replaces the losses from ignoring the non-convex value function by the losses from an increased likelihood of imperfect landform sorting, given that sorting mistakes become more likely as heterogeneity increases.

To see this, allow the impact of an owner's self-restraint on damage risk to be uncertain, again in the sense that more uncertainty creates a first-order dominant shift in damage risk. Drought, for example, may reduce the protection that owner self-restraint offers against fire and flood. Consider an owner who initially confronts a damage risk near or equal to point A in Figure 10.6. This owner welcomes access to any activity or lottery that tempers the non-

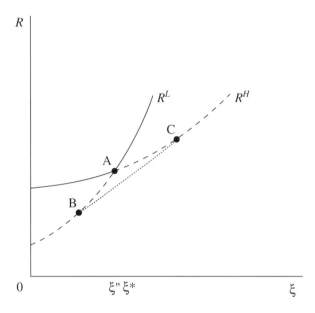

Figure 10.6   Smoothing willingness to pay

convexity of his willingness-to-pay function, or, as with actuarially fair insurance, fully smooths his preferences. With fair insurance, for example, the owner will be better off with any combination of damage risks on the chord connecting B on R^L and C on R^H than he will be by practising a level of self-restraint entailing any damage risk in the neighbourhood of A.

The chord connecting B and C shows that the lottery permits a lower outlay to achieve any expected level of damage risk lying between B and C. Thus the owner prefers the lottery to a more certain world. That is, he behaves as if he is a risk lover rather than a risk averter (Ng, 1965). Moreover, contrary to the traditional result in which fair insurance makes total valuations equal, this treatment equates the marginal rather than total valuations (Bergstrom, 1996). Ultimately the owner who makes this bet will realize either damage risk B or C and appear as a risk averter. His risk preference defined on land use is endogenous.

The size of the gain which the chord between B and C offers the owner is independent of his wealth. Even if the realization of B or C affects the owner's income or relative prices such that the dashed envelope of the R^L and R^H lobes is shifted, the kinked property persists, given that the owner chooses only a single self-restraint alternative. If the owner loses his bet and realizes C, he practises high self-restraint; if he wins his bet and realizes B, he chooses low self-restraint. Only if the damage risk interval between B and C is empty or if his *ex-ante* damage risk is less than B or greater than C will the owner initially act as a risk averter and refuse to make a bet. In these instances, he will already have settled upon a given damage risk and its associated least-demanding level of self-restraint.

Now consider multiple owners who have identical *ex-ante* non-convex willingness-to-pay functions and who can bet on damage risks. Suppose some owners bear damage risks that are distributed within the B to C interval in Figure 10.6. The closer the initial risk is to A, the more a person gains from betting on the realization of either B or C rather than adopting a level of self-restraint that guarantees a given damage risk. Some will lose (C) and adopt high self-restraint; others will win (B) and practise low self-restraint. Even though owners may initially be similarly situated on identical non-convex willingness-to-pay functions, any opportunities to smooth will produce heterogeneous joint distributions over space of damage risks (ecosystem configurations) and management (self-restraint) practices. A non-convex willingness-to-pay function thus implies that the observed mosaic of ecosystem configurations can be the joint result of natural landscape variations and economic choices that multiple owners make in response to what were originally identical damage risks among them. Smoothing can accentuate already existing differences in ecosystem configurations among areas; it also concentrates degradation at selected locations rather than distributing degradation evenly over space (Helfand and Rubin, 1994).

Policy decisions can influence property owners' choices to appear as risk lovers or risk averters, and can thus affect the spatial distribution of ecosystem configurations. Presume, for example, that federal drought or flood insurance is unavailable to low self-restraint owners. Low self-restraint management practices would thus entail higher utility opportunity costs. The R^L function in Figure 10.6 would then shift to the left and point A would move to a lower damage risk. These movements would alter the risk-damage interval over which risk-loving behaviour is desirable. The interval would be shifted to the left and the fair insurance line would be flattened, implying that owners have less to gain than before by being risk lovers.

The question remains of who supplies the lotteries that allow owners to temper their valuation of non-convexities or even to smooth them fully. Private and public insurance against natural disasters could do so, though restrictions to inhibit moral hazard and adverse selection discourage actuarial fairness. Federal drought and flood insurance is a worthy example, as are plans to provide local public goods supported by current property taxes. These public measures create lotteries of land uses in that these activities create givings and takings of property rights and infrastructure which are unevenly distributed across a locale. Property owners must make their self-restraint decisions more or less behind a veil of ignorance. They obligate themselves *ex ante* to a lottery for immobile public goods and location-specific property rules the values of which will be capitalized into only some owners' land. Regardless of whether an owner is a lucky or unlucky beneficiary of public largess or imposition, he must still pay property taxes and these taxes can be viewed as a gambling debt.

In general, the complex ways in which both federal and local policies use the economic gains from smoothing to encourage self-restraint and to manipulate the intensive and the extensive margins of land use make problematic broad, sweeping statements about the appropriate jurisdictional loci of *ex-ante* natural resources and environmental policies. Nevertheless, one can unequivocally say that environmental regulations which set damage thresholds discourage smoothing, and thus increase the justification for generic policy. For example, an owner cannot make a bet involving a damage risk greater than B in Figure 10.6 if environmental regulations prohibit risk levels greater than B. Moreover, the tighter the threshold, the greater the likelihood that no lottery can be constructed which will allow smoothing to occur. Recall that policy makers who disregard the non-convex value function encourage overprovision of ecosystem care and too low a level of damage risk. It then follows that any allowed damage threshold following from this policy-maker neglect also discourages smoothing and thereby foregoes the economic gains smoothing produces.

4　SOME RESEARCH OPPORTUNITIES

Ecologists and geographers with ecological interests dominate both positive and normative treatments of the structure of landscapes. Even though standard ecological discussions of landscape structure (for example, Naveh and Lieberman, 1984) call for integrating the biological, economic and spatial aspects of ecological problems, rarely do the models ecologists use to guide their empirical inquiries and policy recommendations have any economic content whatsoever.[8] The sizes and configurations of landscapes are held to be the overriding influences in determining the long-term dynamics of the ecosystem of interest (Wilson, 1992). If any formal attention is paid to the services of these sizes and configurations, it is only to their biology. Even then, ecologists disagree on the tightness and the length of spatial habitat linkages necessary to achieve a particular ecosystem state.

The debate turns on the extent to which differences in size and configuration affect the population dynamic effects of the species' interactions (Strong *et al.*, 1984). Integration of economic analysis into the debate requires admission that observed differences in landscapes are functions of natural science parameters and the extractive activities and self-restraint decisions of individual landowners and users. Alternatively stated, the expectations on the basis of which people make land-use decisions which affect ecosystems will differ across individuals with their preferences and the relative marginal productivities of their self-restraint efforts, even though the properties of the phenomena triggering these efforts may apply equally to everyone. It follows that to assess the structure of landscapes solely in natural science terms may be highly misleading: landowner treatments of ecosystems are endogenous and may thus vary systematically in observed landscape size and configuration data (Daly, 1968; Crocker, 1984). Economic parameters enter as determinants of ecosystem geographies just as these geographies shape landowner extractive activities and self-restraint decisions.

Though the form of their models is different, Antle and Just (1991) and Crocker and Tschirhart (1992) provide comparative static frameworks in which the joint distribution of natural science and economic parameters is shown to be essential to understanding the interactions of ecosystem components and their responses to alternative regulatory policies. Sanchirico and Wilen (1999) have recently shown how the joint determination concept is necessary to account for the existence of landscape patchiness and for heterogeneity and linkages among landscape patches. Swallow and his co-authors have followed with a series of papers in the context of jointly determined systems in landscapes. They separately consider non-convexities in extractive activities (Swallow, Parks and Wear, 1990), spatial interactions of the tree stands in a forest (Swallow and Wear, 1993), efficient design of the number, size, shape and juxtaposition of conservation reserves (Swallow, 1996a), trade-offs between mobile renewable and immobile non-renewable resources within the same landscape (Swallow, 1996b), and simultaneous spatial and temporal optimization of tree stands in a forest ecosystem (Swallow, Talukdar and Wear, 1997). Expectations about states of the world are always fulfilled for all of the agents in these papers. Albers (1996) treats many of the same issues as the Swallow *et al.* papers and performs a sensitivity analysis for a planner confronted with two probability-weighted ecosystem states. Both Swallow *et al.* and Albers disregard the spatial implications of non-convexities in preferences for land uses. As in Helfand and Rubin (1994), Vincent and Brinkley (1993), and in the previous section of the current chapter, encouragement rather than discouragement of landscape heterogeneity is the general policy prescription in this work.

Another strand of spatially explicit work involving ecosystems and non-point pollution appears in the technical economics literature. Non-point source pollution is characterized by regulator uncertainty about who did what to the ecosystem and by great spatial variation in the economic efficacy of alternative economic and technological control instruments (Griffin and Bromley, 1982). Given that non-point pollution contributions to ecosystems are driven in part by stochastic weather phenomena, the landowner also confronts uncertainty about the potential contributions of his land-use practices, his 'ecological footprint', both within and beyond his ownership boundaries.

These features cast doubt on the universal appropriateness of spatially undifferentiated standard economic instruments based upon taxes or tradeable permits for emissions. The efficiency properties of quantity rationing instruments such as input controls (Baumol and Oates, 1988), price rationing instruments such as input taxes (Sergerson, 1988), and property right alternatives such as environmental bonds (Herriges, Govindusamy and Shogren, 1994) have been assessed. Again, though none of this work recognizes the joint determination of economic and ecological systems or non-convexities in preferences for environmental states, all of it suggests public environmental policies which encourage rather than discourage specialization in land uses across sites (Babcock *et al.*, 1997).[9]

But results calling for public policies which promise specialization leave unanswered questions of how it is to be achieved. More specialization may increase the likelihood of incomparable land uses among sites. The 'how' thus involves landscape design issues of the economic efficiency and the equity of the location of particular uses, the size, shape and juxtaposition of use sites, and the numbers of sites within a particular ecosystem. Explicit economic criteria do not now exist to identify simultaneously the properties of solutions to all these dimensions of the design problem. At least intuitively, an extension of standard modelling frameworks would seem capable of specifying these criteria, though the non-convexities and uncertainties prominent in land-use decisions would surely complicate matters. Of course, when these criteria are developed, economists must still ascertain the incentive and informational properties of alternative public policy instruments to implement the criteria.

5   CONCLUDING COMMENTS

While adding more states of nature, non-separable utility and more levels of self-restraint can complicate our model of ecosystems as lotteries, these intricacies would reinforce our message – the non-convex value function for ecosystem risk-reduction services is a missing market that leaves wealth on the table. The imperfectly informed federal regulator who steps into the void is likely to overprotect the ecosystem by reducing damage risk by more than is justified by the corresponding benefits. Overprotection creates an environmental threshold or quantity constraint (for example, safe minimum standard, maximum daily dose) that truncates both private and public opportunities to fill the void with lotteries that smooth preferences across states of nature.

Truncation reduces specialization in land use, and thus removes the potential gains from trade that arise from specialization (Smith, 1937; Ricardo, 1951; Tiebout, 1956). But while the general public might lose out, the regulator does itself a favour by making a mistake. Less specialization means more justification exists for generic policy for all land areas. Power remains centralized because regulated areas are more homogeneous, and thus generic policies are more likely to be justified and tolerated. The federal regulator keeps power with more errors, stricter thresholds, fewer lotteries and less specialization.

Eventually, the deadweight losses of such mistakes will trigger reform toward devolution of such policies (Becker, 1983). Private landowner and public land-use regulator ecosystem care efforts interact. Regulator failure to account for this interaction causes inefficient environmental policies. The regulator can relax an environmental threshold by loosening the quantity constraint or by granting more exemptions, for example, 'safe harbours' and 'no-surprise' policies in habitat conservation plans for endangered species protection. When the constraints loosen, both private agents and public agencies can then construct lotteries to overcome the regulator's initial error about the non-convex value function for ecosystem services. Lotteries lead to more specialization in land use, and less justification for generic federal policy. This creates a new role for regulators – as creators of public lotteries for private action or as facilitators of the creation of private lotteries to smooth preferences and capture the wealth previously left on the table. Future research exploring efficient institutional designs of lotteries for ecosystem care seems most worthwhile.

ACKNOWLEDGEMENT

Comments of a referee and the editors have improved an earlier version of the chapter. Senior authorship is shared.

NOTES

1. An economist reader of an early draft of this chapter complained that it would be the unusual landowner who 'controls an entire ecosystem'. However, Tandley (1935) defines an ecosystem as any assemblage of abiotic and biotic components making up an interdependent system. Therefore, according to the ecologist Reiners (1995), 'one can use the ecosystem concept to describe ... a specific representation of a general ecosystem type, such as a prairie relic consisting of only a few acres along a railroad in Iowa' (p. 12).
2. Empirical evidence for non-convex preferences with respect to the aesthetic dimensions of the natural environment exists (see Crocker, 1985, Green and Tunstall, 1991 and Schulze *et al.*, 1983, for example). These studies, as well as the limited theoretical work on non-

convex preferences (for example, Balcer, 1980; Henry, 1972; Starr, 1969; Anderson and Francois, 1997), all presume that the state-of-the-world has been revealed.

3. Lessened natural protection services originate from several sources of market failure, often due to ill-defined property rights (for example, Adelman *et al.*, 1992). First, reduced natural protection arises from public ownership of large areas of land with open access property right regimes and little government capacity to manage the land. Second, institutional constraints can create a system where alternatives to ecosystem destruction are difficult to find. For example, 'use it or lose it' water laws provide a limited opportunity set from which to choose alternatives to current practices. Third, land tenure is insecure in many countries since the locals in remote rural areas have little or no influence over national laws, policies, social changes and economic forces. Lack of secure land tenure provides little incentive to maintain the habitat necessary for natural protection. Land-tenure insecurity promotes excessive resource extraction. The local residents have little incentive to conserve if they are unsure their kin will have access to the same land. Fourth, a divergence in the temporal objectives of the management agencies and the local population – the long-term communal benefits of conservation versus the short-term individual benefits that encourage development – can create problems.

4. The assumption of $s^H > s^L$ implies that natural protection and commercial and industrial development are substitutes in the sense that greater self-restraint increases utility opportunity costs. But the two would be complements in the much less frequent but perfectly plausible case where the highest commercial use is the preservation of many features of a 'pristine' ecosystem. Certainly the advertising of upscale rural land subdivisions frequently tries to communicate this complementarity.

5. Suppose the policy maker is aware of the scalloped value function. Now the threat of suboptimal ecosystem protection arises if the marginal benefits curve of the subsidy from nature is unknown (Weitzman, 1974). The relative elasticities of marginal benefits and costs affect the wedge between perceived high self-restraint and realized low self-restraint.

6. See Shogren and Crocker (1991b). The discussion applies equally well to a bet with more than two independent potential realizations. Such realizations can be linearly combined to yield a bet with two realizations having equal expected utility for a given income level.

7. See Winkler (1989) for a discussion on randomization through lotteries to smooth non-convex functions. Also see Zeckhauser (1973) on using lotteries to establish a common utility unit for a town park.

8. Hof and Joyce (1992) is an exception.

9. Nevertheless, case studies (Helfand and House, 1995; Fleming and Adams, 1997) do exist showing that the costs for a planner to acquire the information which allows him to optimally differentiate sites can be greater than the benefits.

REFERENCES

Adelman, I., C. Morris, H. Fetini and E. Golan-Hardy (1992), 'Institutional change, economic development, and the environment', *Ambio*, **21**, 106–10.

Albers, H. (1996), ' Modeling ecological constraints on tropical forest management: spatial interdependence, irreversibility and uncertainty', *Journal of Environmental Economics and Management*, **30**, 73–94.

Anderson, S. and P. Francois (1997), 'Environmental cleanliness as a public good: welfare and policy implications of nonconvex preferences', *Journal of Environmental Economics and Management*, **34**, 256–74.

Antle, J. and R. Just (1991), 'Effects of commodity program structure on resource use and the environment', in R. Just and N. Bockstael (eds), *Commodity and Resource Policies in Agricultural Systems*, Berlin: Springer-Verlag.

Arnott, R. and J. Stiglitz (1988), 'The basic analytics of moral hazard', *Scandinavian Journal of Economics*, **90**, 383–413.

Babcock, B., P. Lakshminarayan, J. Wu and D. Ziberman (1997), 'Targeting tools for purchasing environmental amenities', *Land Economics*, **73**, 325–39.

Balcer, Y. (1980), 'Equilibrium in an exchange economy with non-convex preferences: a simple approach', *Journal of Economic Theory*, **23**, 236–42.

Barbier, E., and J. Burgess (1997), 'The economics of tropical land use options', *Land Economics*, **73**, 174–95.

Baumol, W. and W. Oates (1988), *The Theory of Environmental Policy*, New York: Cambridge University Press.

Becker, G. (1983), 'A theory of competition among pressure groups for political influence', *Quarterly Journal of Economics*, **98**, 371–400.

Bergstrom, T. (1996), 'Soldiers of Fortune?', in W. Heller, R. Starr and D. Starett (eds), *Essays in Honor of Kenneth J. Arrow, vol. 2 Equilibrium Analysis*, Cambridge: Cambridge University Press, pp. 149–73.

Bird, J. (1987), 'The transferability and depletability of externalities', *Journal of Environmental Economics and Management*, **14**, 54–7.

Crocker, T. (1984), 'Scientific truths and policy truths in acid deposition research', in T. Crocker (ed.), *Economic Perspectives on Acid Deposition Control*, Boston, MA: Butterworth Publishers, pp. 65–80.

Crocker, T. (1985), 'On the value of the condition of a forest stock', *Land Economics*, **61**, 244–54.

Crocker, T. and J. Tschirhart (1992), 'Ecosystems, externalities and economies', *Environmental and Resource Economics*, **2**, 551–67.

Daly, H. (1968), 'On economics as a life science', *Journal of Political Economy*, **76**, 392–406.

Deblinger, R. and R. Jenkins, Jr (1991), 'Preserving coastal biodiversity: the private, nonprofit approach', *Coastal Management*, **19**, 103–13.

Dixit, A. and R. Pindyck (1994), *Investment Under Uncertainty*, Princeton, NJ: Princeton University Press.

Ehrlich, I. and G. Becker (1972), 'Market insurance, self-insurance, and self-protection', *Journal of Political Economy*, **80**, 623–48.

Elbasha, E. and T. Roe (1996), 'On endogenous growth: the implications of environmental externalities', *Journal of Environmental Economics and Management*, **31**, 240–67.

Fleming, R. and R. Adams (1997), 'The importance of site-specific information in the design of policies to control pollution', *Journal of Environmental Economics and Management*, **33**, 347–58.

Green, H. and S.M. Tunstall (1991), 'The evaluation of river quality improvements by the contingent valuation method', *Applied Economics*, **23**, 1135–46.

Griffin, R. and D. Bromley (1982), 'Agricultural runoff as a nonpoint externality: a theoretical development', *American Journal of Agricultural Economics*, **70**, 37–49.

Hardin, R. (1993), 'Trusting individuals, trusting institutions', in R. Zeckhauser (ed.), *Strategy and Choice*, Cambridge, MA: Harvard University Press, pp. 185–209.

Helfand, G. and B. House (1995), 'Regulatory nonpoint source pollution under heterogeneous conditions', *American Journal of Agricultural Economics*, **77**, 1024–32.

Helfand, G. and J. Rubin (1994), 'Spreading versus concentrating damages: environmental policy in the presence of non-convexities', *Journal of Environmental Economics and Management*, **27**, 84–91.

Henry, C. (1972), 'Market games with indivisible commodities and nonconvex preferences', *Review of Economic Studies*, **39**, 73–6.

Herriges, J., R. Govindasamy and J. Shogren (1994), 'Budget balancing incentive mechanisms', *Journal of Environmental Economics and Management*, **27**, 275–85.

Hof, J. and L. Joyce (1992), 'Spatial optimization for wildlife and timber in managed forest ecosystems', *Forest Science*, **38**, 489–508.

Holling, C. (1986), 'Resilience of ecosystems: local surprise and global change', in W. Clark and R. Munn (eds), *Sustainable Development of the Biosphere*, New York: Cambridge University Press.

Naeem, S., L. Thompson, S. Lawler, J. Lawton and R. Woodfin (1994), 'Declining biodiversity can alter the performance of ecosystems', *Nature*, **368**, 734–7.

Naveh, Z. and A. Lieberman (1984), *Landscape Ecology*, Berlin: Springer-Verlag.

Ng, Y.-K. (1965), 'Why do people buy lottery tickets? Choices involving risk and the indivisibility of expenditure', *Journal of Political Economy*, **73**, 530–35.

Nordhaus, W. (1994), *Managing the Global Commons: The Economics of Climate Change*, Cambridge, MA: MIT Press.

Ramsey, F. (1928), 'A mathematical theory of saving', *Economic Journal*, **38**, 543–59.

Reiners, W. (1995), 'Ecosystems of the Great Plains: scales, kinds, and distributions', in S. Johnson and A. Bouzaher (eds), *Conservation of Great Plains Ecosystems: Current Science, Future Options*, Boston, MA: Kluwer Academic Publishers.

Ricardo, D. (1817), *Principles of Political Economy and Taxation*, reprinted in P. Sraffa and M. Dobb (eds) (1951), *The Works of David Ricardo*, Cambridge, MA: Cambridge University Press.

Sanchirico, J. and J. Wilen (1999), 'Bioeconomics of spatial exploitation in a patchy environment', *Journal of Environmental Economics and Management*, **37**, 129–50.

Schelling, T. (1980), 'The intimate contest for self-command', *The Public Interest*, **60**, 94–118.

Schulze, W., D. Brookshire, E. Walther, K. MacFarland, M. Thayer, R. Whitworth, S. Ben-David, W. Malm and J. Molnar (1983), 'The economic benefits of preserving visibility in the national parklands of the southwest', *Natural Resources Journal*, **23**, 18–32.

Segerson, K. (1988), 'Uncertainty and incentives for nonpoint pollution control', *Journal of Environmental Economics and Management*, **15**, 88–9.

Shogren, J. (1998a), 'Do all the resource problems in the west begin in the east?', *Journal of Agricultural and Resource Economics*, **23**, 309–18.

Shogren, J. (ed.) (1998b), *Private Property and the Endangered Species Act: Saving Habitats, Protecting Homes*, Austin, TX: University of Texas Press.

Shogren, J. and T. Crocker (1991a), 'Risk, self-protection, and ex ante economic value', *Journal of Environmental Economics and Management*, **20**, 1–15.

Shogren, J. and T. Crocker (1991b), 'Cooperative and noncooperative protection against transferable and filterable externalities', *Environmental and Resource Economics*, **1**, 195–214.

Smith, A. (1776), *An Inquiry into the Nature and Causes of the Wealth of Nations*, reprinted in E. Cannan (ed.) (1937), *The Wealth of Nations*, Modern Library Edition, New York, NY: Random House.

Starr, R. (1969), 'Quasi-equilibria in markets with non-convex preferences', *Econometrica*, **37**, 25–8.

Strong, D., Jr, D. Simverloff, L. Abele and A. Thistle (eds) (1984), *Ecological*

Communities: Conceptual Issues and the Evidence, Princeton, NJ: Princeton University Press.

Swallow, S. (1996a), 'Ecosystem issues in ecosystem management: an introduction and overview', *Agricultural and Resource Economics Review*, **25**, 83–100.

Swallow, S. (1996b), 'Resource capital theory and ecosystem economics: developing nonrenewable habitats with heterogeneous quality', *Southern Economic Journal*, **63**, 106–23.

Swallow, S. and D. Wear (1993), 'Spatial interactions in multiple use forestry and substitution and wealth effects for a single stand', *Journal of Environmental Economics and Management*, **25**, 103–20.

Swallow, S., P. Parks and D. Wear (1990), ' Policy relevant non-convexities in the production of multiple forest benefits', *Journal of Environmental Economics and Management*, **19**, 264–80.

Swallow, S., P. Talukdar and D. Wear (1997), 'Spatial and temporal specialization in forest ecosystem management under sole ownership', *American Journal of Agricultural Economics*, **79**, 311–26.

Tansley, A. (1935), 'The use and abuse of vegetational concepts and terms', *Ecology*, **16**, 284–307.

Tiebout, C. (1956), 'A pure theory of local expenditures', *Journal of Political Economy*, **64**, 416–24.

Vincent, J. and C. Brinkley (1993), 'Efficient multiple use forestry may require land-use specialization', *Land Economics*, **69**, 370–76.

Weitzman, M. (1974), 'Prices vs. quantities', *Quarterly Journal of Economics*, **41**, 477–91.

Wilson, E. (1992), *The Diversity of Life*, Cambridge, MA: Belknap Press.

Winkler, G. (1989), 'Intermediation under trade restrictions', *Quarterly Journal of Economics*, **104**, 299–324.

Zeckhauser, R. (1973), 'Determining the qualities of a public good – a paradigm on town park location', *Western Economic Journal*, **11**, 39–60.

11. Corporate governance in the presence of major technological risks

Marcel Boyer and Bernard Sinclair-Desgagné

1 INTRODUCTION

Most analysts and forecasters of the new economy adopt an optimistic view of technology. Together with globalization, technology is seen as the main engine of economic growth. It lies at the heart of the 'knowledge-based economy'. And it provides comforting answers to the advocates of pessimistic scenarios based on climate change, natural resource depletion, endangered species and overpopulation.

Technology, however, does not only yield benefits. The other side of the coin is that, first, technology itself often produces new hazards, such as industrial accidents and pollution.[1] Secondly, by increasing the power of mankind over nature, technology also exacerbates the impact of human errors, as the deadly gas leak at Bhopal, the Exxon-Valdez oil spill and the threat of extensive destruction posed by modern warfare dramatically illustrate. Finally, technology often increases the extent of damages linked to natural events. This was shown in the Durunqa disaster of 1994, in Egypt, when over 100 people were killed by floods that destroyed a petroleum storage facility and carried burning oil into the heart of the town (Smith, 1996, p. 266), and also in the January 1998 ice storm that hit southern Québec, provoking a huge blackout which left more than 3 million electricity-dependent people without heat and power in the middle of the Canadian winter.

Several institutions and management systems have therefore progressively been designed and implemented in order to control technological risks and enhance the net benefits associated with technological development.[2] There is a sense, however, that the situation might not be improving as much nor as fast as it should. Economic agents seem to be lagging behind. According to Shrivastava (1986), for instance, amongst the 28 major industrial accidents of this century that have resulted in more than 50 casualties, half have occurred since 1977 and three happened in the year 1984 alone. There is therefore an urgent need for the elaboration and implementation of creative approaches for dealing with technological risks. In this field, moreover, society cannot afford to rely only on trial and error and learning by doing. Demand is then high for sound theoretical research and rigorous modelling.

This chapter focuses on the economic analysis of corporate means for alleviating major technological risks. Private and public corporations are the main developers and users of large-scale technologies; it is also through their activities and outputs that most disasters attributable solely or partly to technology happen. Under mounting pressure from governments, shareholders, the public in general and their own employees, they currently spend huge sums of money to shelter themselves and their stakeholders against the occurrence of technological catastrophes. This is true not only for firms in traditionally exposed and regulated sectors, such as chemicals or nuclear energy, but also for an increasing number of firms engaged in the service industry (which comprises more than 40 per cent of the activity in the most advanced economies).[3] Our two-fold objective now is to present some current economic theory that concerns corporate risk management and to point out what might be valuable topics for future theoretical and policy research.

The chapter unfolds as follows. The next section explains the concept of major technological risk. Section 3 discusses one feature of the corporate landscape that has a significant impact on firms' strategy and the decisions taken by corporate boards of directors: the extent of corporate liability. Particular attention will be devoted to the new rules of environmental liability which apply to financial creditors and banks. Section 4 presents some internal mechanisms for implementing corporate policies towards technological risks, such as stakeholders' involvement and selective audits. Section 5 sketches some policy implications. Section 6 outlines a research agenda and concludes the chapter.

2   CHARACTERISTICS OF MAJOR TECHNOLOGICAL RISKS

Risk and uncertainty are unavoidable features of human life. They have therefore received considerable attention in the social and behavioural sciences, including economics. Traditional studies of risk and uncertainty, however, do not capture very well those situations involving catastrophic risks. The main reason is that such situations are characterized by small probabilities of potentially disastrous events, hence they belong to an area where economic behaviour remains hard to grasp using conventional means. Hundreds of laboratory experiments have now shown that decision making in the presence of rare outcomes often runs counter to the common predictions of economic theory.[4] Moreover, the very size of the potential losses forbids several of the usual institutional assumptions which underlie economic analysis and modelling.[5]

In their account of global environmental externalities, Chichilnisky and Heal (1992) suggest a characterization of catastrophic risks that has already proved useful for understanding the failure of traditional economic approaches to risk, such as insurance.[6] First, catastrophic risks are difficult to measure. Their attached probabilities, being very small, cannot be estimated through empirical frequencies (unlike actuarial probabilities) and must be derived indirectly in ways that are often controversial. Their associated outcomes might also be difficult to list and describe, and it is usually impossible to agree *ex ante* on an evaluation of the damages that would hold *ex post*. Second, such risks are essentially collective. The occurrence of a bad outcome would always affect a large number of people; in other words, individual losses are correlated. Finally, catastrophes are dreadful events from which it might be impossible to recover, even to a modest extent; they entail a significant degree of irreversibility.

Major technological risks (MTRs) naturally pertain to the category of catastrophic risks. One peculiar feature which justifies a specific treatment is that, unlike purely natural disasters such as earthquakes or landslides, MTRs are man-made and therefore endogenous to human activity (see Smith, 1996, chapter 13). Most researchers, furthermore, would confine MTRs to production activities or decisions, which exclude other endogenous catastrophes, such as bank runs and financial collapse, war, large riots, starvation or epidemics due to cultural traits and shared consumption habits. One last distinction is that MTRs comprise latent and diffuse risks associated for instance to long-term exposure to hazardous substances, in contrast with most other catastrophic risks which rather involve some punctual disastrous event concentrated in time and space.

To summarize, MTRs emanate from production activities and decisions, they are often diffuse, difficult to assess precisely, and characterized by small probabilities of large collective and irreversible losses. We shall now turn to some new developments surounding the corporate governance of those risks.

3   THE CORPORATE LANDSCAPE

Many external factors influence corporate strategy and governance, amongst which are the competitive environment, what is perceived to be the firm's mission, the available resources and the regulatory and legal background. As far as technological and environmental risks are concerned, the last is probably the aspect of the corporate landscape that has the greatest impact on the board's agenda and decisions. This section therefore discusses the recent evolution of corporate environmental liability and outlines a model based on Boyer and Laffont (1997) that captures the logic behind it.

3.1 The Extent of Responsibility

The polluter pays principle is a widely accepted rule to allocate responsibility for environmental damages. Application of this principle, however, is not straightforward for the following reasons: first, it is often difficult to identify the polluter; second, insurance contracts are often invalidated by some clauses the polluter fails to satisfy; and, finally, polluting firms are subject to limited liability. In order to alleviate those problems that delay and affect the compensation of victims, governments have created special funds financed by taxation (such as Fipa and Superfund) and have introduced new regulations extending responsibility for clean-up beyond the firm's legal borders.[7]

The best-known example of such regulations is perhaps CERCLA – the 1980 Comprehensive Environmental Response, Compensation and Liability Act (and its amendments) – in the United States. It specifies that parties responsible for clean-up costs following some environmental accident can be the current but also the past owners and operators of the firm. In many instances, furthermore, the courts have determined that the firm's creditors could be seen as operators, especially when they were involved in the supervision and monitoring of the firm's activities.[8]

The extent of creditors' responsibility, however, is not fixed and the drawing line is still moving. In the case of *US* v. *Mirabile* in 1985, for example, the Mellon Bank was found liable for damages but the American Bank and Trust and the Small Business Administration, who were also involved in financing the firm, were not: the court's verdict was based on the fact that the Mellon Bank was significantly more involved in supervising the operations of the firm. In the case of *US* v. *Maryland and Trust* in 1986, the court found the bank, which held a mortgage on the property, liable for clean-up costs, on the basis that at the time the pollution damage was discovered the bank was the owner of the facility it had purchased at the foreclosure sale. Finally, in the case of *US* v. *Fleet Factors Corporation* in 1990–91, the bank was found liable for clean-up costs on the basis that its participation in the financial management of the firm gave it an 'ability to influence' the overall management of the firm even if the bank was not directly involved in the operations.[9]

In the last case, the court explicitly rejected the allegation that its current decision would most likely make banks reluctant to provide loans to some industries and would ultimately raise the cost of financing. The court stressed that it wished rather to encourage lenders to monitor and supervise more closely their borrowers' environmental policies and practices while basing lending decisions upon sound environmental processes. The court's own wording reads as follows:

> Our interpretation of the exemption may be challenged as creating disincentives for lenders to extend financial assistance to businesses with potential hazardous waste problems and encouraging secured creditors to distance themselves from the management actions, particularly those related to hazardous wastes, of their debtors. As a result the improper treatment of hazardous wastes could be perpetuated rather than resolved. These concerns are unfounded. Our ruling today should encourage potential creditors to investigate thoroughly the waste treatment systems and policies of potential debtors. If the treatment systems were inadequate, the risk of CERCLA liability will be weighed into the terms of the loan agreement. Creditors, therefore, will incur no greater risk than they bargained for and debtors, aware that inadequate hazardous waste treatment will have a significant adverse impact on their loan terms, will have powerful incentives to improve their handling of hazardous wastes. Similarly, creditors' awareness that they are potentially liable under CERCLA will encourage them to monitor the hazardous waste treatment systems and policies of their debtors and insist upon compliance with acceptable treatment standards as a prerequisite to continued and future financial support. Once a secured creditor's involvement with a facility becomes sufficiently broad that it can anticipate losing its exemption from CERCLA liability, it will have a strong incentive to address hazardous waste problems at the facility rather than studiously avoiding the investigation and amelioration of the hazard.

This statement raises many issues, from assessing the real impact of this judgment on subsequent loans and banking practices to determining the extent of bank responsibility that best encourages the prevention of disasters. Those issues are not only relevant for public policy but also for corporate boards, who need to understand precisely the main forces driving the evolution of regulation and jurisprudence on matters of responsibility. The following subsection will now briefly sketch how the matter of bank liability was recently modelled and analysed.

3.2 Bank Liability under Moral Hazard

Consider a two-period model involving a regulator, a risk-neutral firm and a risk-neutral bank. In each period the firm faces an investment opportunity that costs F and yields a low revenue π_L with probability θ or a high revenue π_H with probability $(1 - \theta)$. Denote the expected profit as $\bar{\pi} = \theta\pi_L + (1 - \theta)\pi_H$. To keep the analysis simple, revenues are assumed to be independent across periods. The firm can affect the probability of some catastrophic damage $d > \pi_H$ through its choice of effort $e \in \{L,H\}$. High effort reduces this probability to the level $p_H < p_L$, but it costs $\psi_H > \psi_L$. Effort is expended in period 1 and the accident may occur or not in period

2. Making the highest effort is socially optimal (in a first-best sense) provided $\psi_H - \psi_L < (p_L - p_H)d$. However, effort cannot be observed by either the bank or the regulator.

At the beginning of period 1, the bank and the firm negotiate a two-period loan contract. This contract specifies, for loans of size F at the beginning of each period, reimbursements R_L (respectively R_H) if revenues at the end of period 1 are low (high), and reimbursements R^L (respectively R^H) at the end of period 2 if revenues in this period are low (high). The bank will be willing to provide such a loan as long as its expected profit is non-negative. If there is no insurance and the firm's profit is taken away in case of an accident, the bank lends if and only if[10]

$$\theta R_L + (1-\theta)R_H + (1-p_e)[\theta R^L + (1-\theta)R^H] \geq 0 \qquad (11.1)$$

When an accident occurs, the firm must pay for the damages up to the maximal amount made possible by its limited liability, that is up to π_H $(< d)$.[11]

The firm chooses a high effort if and only if it finds it profitable to incur the cost ψ_H, that is:

$$(1-p_H)[\pi - (\theta R^L + (1-\theta)R^H)] - \psi_H \geq (1-p_L)[\pi - (\theta R^L + (1-\theta)R^H)] - \psi_L,$$

or equivalently $\theta R^L + (1-\theta)R^H \leq \pi - \dfrac{\psi_H - \psi_L}{p_L - p_H}$ $\qquad (11.2)$

The reimbursement constraints of the firm are also given by

$$R_L \leq \pi_L, R_H \leq \pi_H$$
$$R^L \leq \pi_L - R_L + \pi_L, R^H \leq \pi_H - R_H + \pi_L \qquad (11.3)$$

and the participation or individual rationality constraint can be written as

$$\bar{\pi} - \theta R_L - (1-\theta)R_H + [(1-p_e)(\bar{\pi} - \theta R^L - (1-\theta)R^H) - \psi_e] \geq 0 \quad (11.4)$$

The regulator maximizes social welfare under the constraints (11.2), (11.3) and (11.4). There is an assumed cost of public funds $(1 + \lambda)$, $\lambda > 0$, which multiplies the bank's profit and the net cost of disaster $(\bar{\pi} - d)$, but not the (unobservable) firm's net benefit, in the social welfare function.[12] Distortions (with respect to first-best) due to moral hazard appear when some informational rent Γ is given up to the firm which expends high effort. The (second-best) social optimum entails $e = H$ if and only if

$$(p_L - p_H)d \geq \psi_H - \psi_L + \frac{\lambda}{1+\lambda}\Gamma \qquad (11.5)$$

and the optimal investment rule is:

- if $e = H$, then the bank should invest in both periods provided

$$2\pi - 2F - p_H d - \psi_H - \frac{\lambda}{1+\lambda}\Gamma \geq 0 \qquad (11.6)$$

- if $e = L$, then the bank should invest in both periods provided

$$2\pi - 2F - p_L d - \psi_L \geq 0 \qquad (11.7)$$

The bank, however, maximizes its own expected profit subject to (11.2), (11.3) and (11.4). On the one hand, it undervalues the cost of disaster at $p_H\overline{\pi}$ instead of $p_H d$, which leads it to lend too much and to induce less effort than optimal. On the other hand, it values at Γ the rent left to the firm whilst socially this rent has value $(\lambda/(1 + \lambda))\Gamma$, which makes it lend too little but also encourages effort to a lesser degree. Introduction of a positive share δd, $0 < \delta \leq 1$, of damages in the bank's objective function can contribute to align the bank's actions with the regulator's goals and social welfare. Let

$$\delta_1 = \frac{\psi_H - \psi_L + \Gamma}{(p_L - p_H)d}, \quad \delta_2 = \frac{2\pi - \psi_H - 2F - \Gamma}{p_H d}, \quad \delta_3 = \frac{2\pi - \psi_L - 2F}{p_L d}$$

be respectively the smallest responsibility level which makes the bank induce high effort, the highest responsibility level for which the bank would finance the project provided $e = H$, and the highest responsibility level at which the bank would still invest with $e = L$. The last is larger than 1 if the project is socially valuable with $e = L$ and less than 1 otherwise. It can be shown that, if $\delta_1 < \delta_2$, the second best is implemented with partial responsibility of the bank at the level δ_1. If $\delta_1 > \delta_2$, however, partial responsibility cannot induce the appropriate effort level without killing the project. In this case, if it is socially optimal to run the project (that is, $\delta_3 > 1$), then the second best can only be achieved with two instruments, say bank partial liability combined with a subsidy for financing the project.

3.3   Other Considerations

The above section did not cover the whole story, of course. Besides moral hazard, adverse selection always constitutes a major problem.[13] Moreover, extending liability to lenders may affect the firm's capital structure and may modify the commitment constraints in financial contracting, with significant implications for the treatment of MTRs. Several studies have recently addressed this complex issue. For instance, Feess and Hege (1998) show that both strict liability and lender liability lead to distortions in the capital structure which itself generates an inefficiently low care level. Their results call for a different regulation strategy, namely mandatory insurance coverage for environmental risks, which can be underwritten either by an insurer, a lender or another institution. According to Dionne and Spaeter (1998), however, the level of prevention may be too high if indeed the investment in care is financed, together with investment in a 'green' technology, from borrowed funds which will not be paid back if a major accident occurs. Extending liability to banks increases the face value of debt (banks do charge the firm for the social insurance of potential victims) and thus increases the probability of bankruptcy; it may therefore increase the firm's chosen care level by reducing the expected cost of prevention. In a dynamic contracting set-up, finally, Gobert and Poitevin (1998) find that extended liability relaxes the bank's self-enforcing constraint and leads to better risk sharing for the firm; this, however, reduces the firm's incentives to invest in environmental risk reduction.

4   THE IMPLEMENTATION OF STRATEGY

Traditional business strategy focuses more on the content of strategy than on the organizational means for achieving it. This is unfortunate, especially when dealing with major technological and environmental risks, since an organization is not a single-minded entity but rather a complex network of interpersonal relationships whose coordination is a non-trivial task.

This task is undertaken successfully, for example, in the so-called 'high-reliability organizations'. Roberts (1990) defines those organizations as ones where 'performance reliability rivals productivity as a dominant goal'. She suggests to identify such organizations using the following test: 'How often could this organization have failed with dramatic consequences? If the answer to the question is many thousands of times the organization is highly reliable.'

In most organizations, however, the hierarchy of goals remains unclear, and this leaves some freedom for weighing various implementation methods. In their study for the Royal Society of London, Warner *et al.* (1992) list a set of considerations that could be useful in sorting out the various approaches to implementation. In this section we examine two of these considerations which seem to occur most often, using a general multiple-task principal–agent model. The first one relates to where corporate risk management should lie between narrow and broad participationism. In other words, what are the benefits and costs of involving all stakeholders instead of just the shareholders?[14] It is shown in subsection 4.1 that one of the costs of bringing in more stakeholders might be a decrease in the power of incentives. The second consideration relates to the opportunity cost of dealing explicitly with technological risk. Is there some complementarity between technological risk management and other business functions, or is a strict trade-off to be made? Subsection 4.2 presents a simple mechanism based on selective audits that would enhance synergies and complementarities.

4.1 Broad versus Narrow Participationism

Consider the one-period contractual relationship between K principals, labelled $\alpha = 1,\ldots,K$, and an agent. The agent must allocate his effort between tasks $t = 1,\ldots,m$; effort is then an m-dimensional vector $\mathbf{a}$ where each component a_t belongs to $\mathbb{R}$ and denotes the amount of effort (or attention) spent on task t. No principal can observe the agent's effort directly. The agent's performance is summarized by a vector of noisy signals $\mathbf{s} = (s_1,\ldots,s_L)$ where $s_i \in S_i = \{1,\ldots,J_i\}$. Those signals are linked to the agent's effort vector through the conditional likelihood function $p(\mathbf{s}|\mathbf{a})$, which is positive and twice continuously differentiable in $\mathbf{a}$ at every $\mathbf{s}$.

The agent is risk averse, with positive, strictly concave, strictly increasing and three times differentiable Von Neumann–Morgenstern utility index $u(\cdot)$ defined over monetary payoffs. His cost of effort is given by the positive, strictly convex and twice continuously differentiable function $c(a)$. This function may exhibit strict substitutability (supermodularity) in efforts, that is: $c_{rt} > 0$ for all components $r \neq t$.[15]

The principals are risk neutral. Each principal α's expected revenue conditional on observing s is given by $R^{\alpha}(s)$, where $R^{\alpha}(\cdot)$ is an increasing function. The principals wish, therefore, to influence the agent's effort allocation through an incentive contract. We shall examine two extreme scenarios. In the first one, the principals fully cooperate and behave as a single principal who offers the agent a wage schedule $w(\mathbf{s})$. In the second case, the principals behave non-cooperatively and commit separately to contracts $w^{\alpha}(\mathbf{s})$, $\alpha = 1,\ldots,K$.

As usual, a contract will be called optimal if it maximizes the principals' net benefit under incentive compatibility and participation constraints. To compute such a contract we will replace the incentive compatibility constraints by a finite set of inequalities involving the first-order derivative of the agent's expected utility. This so-called 'first-order approach' is guaranteed to work under the following assumptions (Sinclair-Desgagné, 1994).

Assumption 1 [MLRP] For all t and all $\mathbf{a}$, $p_t(s|a)/p(s|a)$ is increasing in s.

$$\text{Let } Q(j_h, s_{-h}|a) = \sum_{s_h=j_h}^{J_h} p(s_h, \mathbf{s_{-h}}|a) \quad (j_h = 1,\ldots,J_h).$$

Assumption 2 (Generalized SDC) For at least one index h, the partial derivatives $Q_t(j_h,\mathbf{s_{-h}}|a)$ are positive at every effort vector $\mathbf{a}$ and performance levels $(j_h, \mathbf{s_{-h}})$.

Assumption 3 (Generalized CDFC) For at least one index h, the matrix $[Q_{rt}(j_h,\mathbf{s_{-h}}|a)]$ of second-order derivatives is negative semi-definite at every $\mathbf{a}$, j_h and $\mathbf{s_{-h}}$.

Assumption 4 The Lagrange multipliers associated with the first-order conditions are strictly positive.

Assumption 5 A solution to the optimization problem exists.

When the principals cooperate, the optimal contract solves the following problem

$$\underset{w(s),a}{\text{maximize}} \sum_{\text{all } s} p(s \mid a)\left(\sum_{\alpha=1}^{K} R^\alpha(s) - w(s)\right), \text{ subject to}$$

$$\text{for } t = 1,\ldots,m : \sum_{\text{all } s} p_t(s \mid a)u(w(s)) - c_t(a) \geq 0 \tag{11.8}$$

$$\sum_{\text{all } s} p(s \mid a)u(w(s)) - c(a) \geq U^*$$

Let λ_t $(t = 1,\ldots,m)$ and μ be the Lagrange multipliers associated with the first-order-derivative conditions and the participation constraint respectively. The optimal wage schedule must then satisfy the (necessary and sufficient) Kuhn–Tucker conditions

$$\text{for all } s, \quad \frac{1}{u'(w(s))} = \mu + \sum_{t=1}^{m} \lambda_t \frac{p_t(s \mid a)}{p(s \mid a)}. \tag{11.9}$$

Hence

$$\text{for all } s: \ w(s) = \psi(\mu + \sum_{t=1}^{m} \lambda_t \frac{p_t(s\,|\,a)}{p(s\,|\,a)})$$

(11.10)

$$\text{where } \psi(\cdot) = (\frac{1}{u'(\cdot)})^{-1}$$

Note that $\psi'(\cdot) = 1/(1/u'(\psi(\cdot)))' = u'(\psi(\cdot))/\rho(\psi(\cdot))$, where $\rho(\cdot) = -u''(\cdot)/u'(\cdot)$ is the coefficient of absolute risk aversion. The wage gradient, which captures the strength of incentives, can then be approximated as

$$\Delta_h^{col} = w(s_h, \mathbf{s_{-h}}) - w(s_h - 1, \mathbf{s_{-h}}) \approx \frac{u'(\cdot)}{\rho(\cdot)} \sum_{t=1}^{m} \lambda_t \left(\frac{p_t(s_h, \mathbf{s_{-h}}\,|\,a)}{p(s_h, \mathbf{s_{-h}}\,|\,a)} \right. \\ \left. - \frac{p_t(s_h - 1, \mathbf{s_{-h}}\,|\,a)}{p(s_h - 1, \mathbf{s_{-h}}\,|\,a)} \right)$$

(11.11)

Clearly (all things equal) the effect of a higher coefficient of risk aversion is to dampen the Δ_hs and therefore the power of incentives.

Let us now compare this situation with what obtains under the non-cooperative scenario. In this case, each principal α (= $1,\dots,K$) would offer the agent a contract that solves the following problem

$$\underset{w^\alpha(s),a}{\text{maximize}} \sum_{\text{all } s} p(s\,|\,a)(R^\alpha(s) - w^\alpha(s)), \text{ subject to}$$

$$\text{for } t = 1,\dots,m : \sum_{\text{all } s} p_t(s\,|\,a)u(w^\alpha(s) + \sum_{k \neq \alpha} w^k(s)) - c_t(a) \geq 0 \quad (11.12)$$

$$\sum_{\text{all } s} p(s\,|\,a)u(w^\alpha(s) + \sum_{k \neq \alpha} w^k(s)) - c(a) \geq U^*$$

Proceeding as before, let λ_t^α ($t = 1,\dots,m$) and μ^α be the Lagrange multipliers associated with the first-order-derivatives conditions and the participation constraint of this problem. Principal α's wage schedule will then be a solution to the equations

$$\text{for all } s: \ \frac{1}{u'(w^\alpha(s) + \sum_{k \neq \alpha} w^k(s))} = \mu^\alpha + \sum_{t=1}^{m} \lambda_t^\alpha \frac{p_t(s\,|\,a)}{p(s\,|\,a)} \quad (11.13)$$

A similar set of conditions must hold for every principal. Therefore, at the equilibrium (assuming it exists), summing up expression (11.13) over α yields

$$\text{for all } s: \frac{1}{u'(w(s))} = \frac{1}{K} \sum_{\alpha=1}^{K} (\mu^\alpha + \sum_{t=1}^{m} \lambda_t^\alpha \frac{p_t(s \mid a)}{p(s \mid a)} \qquad (11.14)$$

where $w(s) = \sum_\alpha w^\alpha(s)$. The wage gradient is now approximately equal to

$$\Delta_h^{\text{non-coop}} \approx \frac{u'(\cdot)}{K\rho(\cdot)} \sum_{\alpha=1}^{K} \sum_{t=1}^{m} \lambda_t^\alpha \left(\frac{p_t(s_h, \mathbf{s_{-h}} \mid a)}{p(s_h, \mathbf{s_{-h}} \mid a)} - \frac{p_t(s_h - 1, \mathbf{s_{-h}} \mid a)}{p(s_h - 1, \mathbf{s_{-h}} \mid a)} \right) \quad (11.15)$$

Comparing this expression with the one obtained in (11.11), and supposing that $\sum_\alpha \lambda_t^\alpha \leq \lambda_t$ for all t, it appears that the effect of submitting an agent to several principals whose goals may conflict is as if the agent's risk aversion were multiplied by a factor equal to the number of such principals. The strength of the incentives put on the agent must then decrease in proportion.[16]

4.2 Complementarism versus Trade-offism

Let us now consider the question whether implementing some strategy towards a reduction of technological risk could raise the firm's financial performance. In their seminal paper on the multiple-task principal–agent problem, Holmström and Milgrom (1991) show that:

(i) 'when there are multiple tasks, incentive pay serves not only to allocate risks and to motivate hard work, it also serves to direct the allocation of the agents' attention among their various duties'.
(ii) 'the desirability of providing incentives for any one activity decreases with the difficulty of measuring performance in any other activities that make competing demands on the agent's time and attention'.

They then suggest two methods to alleviate the strict trade-off that a heavily solicited agent necessarily makes between tasks. One is to reduce the dilution of effort by putting explicit restrictions on some activities. This is an obvious purpose of the procedures and constraints that firms impose on employees in order to regulate risk. Another possible means is to re-group tasks and define jobs in such a way that each agent's job includes tasks that differ as little as possible in their measurement characteristics; the intensity of incentives for a given job should then increase with the ease of measuring performance on that job.

The approach underlying these methods amounts to altering the agent's opportunity cost of effort on the various tasks. In recent articles we take the other route, which consists of changing the way agents are compensated.[17] The alternative (or rather complementary) control and reward scheme that we propose can be described as follows. Consider an agent whose job includes two tasks, A (say a short-term business one) and B (one dealing with the long-run and major technological risks).

- Let task A performance be routinely monitored, whilst performance on task B can be audited.
- The principal commits to making an audit contingent on observing high performance on task A.
- The agent's expected utility is higher when an audit takes place than when no audit occurs.
- However, if an audit yields a bad assessment of performance on task B, then the agent's *ex post* compensation is inferior to what it would have been if no audit had taken place.

The intuitive reason why this scheme could help overcome trade-offism is straightforward. Take an agent who is not too risk averse. Under the above scheme such an agent should seek to be audited. He would then be led to spend more effort on task A, in order to increase the likelihood of showing high performance on this task and triggering an audit. But since there is no benefit to being audited if performance on task B is ultimately assessed to be low, he would be led to work harder on task B as well. This means that the respective efforts expended on tasks A and B have now become complementary, as far as compensation is concerned. If this complementarity is strong enough, it might counterbalance the fact that efforts on tasks A and B are substitutes in the agent's cost function. In this case, the strict trade-off between tasks emphasized by Holmström and Milgrom (1991) would vanish.

This incentive scheme will now be formalized as follows. Using the framework of the previous section, let there be only two possible signals $i = 0$, $1,...,I$ and $j = 0$, $1,...,J$, and denote the effort devoted to tasks A and B as a and b respectively. We make the following additional assumption on the likelihood function.

Assumption 6 $p(i,j|a,b)$ is separable with respect to efforts, that is: $p(i,j|a,b) = p_i(a) \cdot q_j(b)$.

Let the principal be risk neutral. She cannot observe the agent's efforts directly. Instead, she routinely gathers signal i, and she may get the additional assessment j through an audit. Such an audit costs $K \geq 0$. Her expected revenue conditional on observing i and j is given by $R(i,j)$, where $R(\cdot,\cdot)$ is an increasing function. She can commit to a contract which includes a conditional probability m_i of making an audit, a wage schedule s_i in case no audit occurs, and contingent wages w_{ij} when an audit takes place. For a given allocation, noted $[s_i, w_{ij}, m_i;a,b]$, her expected net benefit is then

$$V(s_i,s_{ij},m_i;a,b) = \sum_{i,j} p_i(a)q_j(b)[m_i(R(i,j)-w_{ij}-K) \\ +(1-m_i)(R(i,j)-s_i)] \tag{11.16}$$

In this context, the agent's expected utility becomes

$$U(s_i,w_{ij},m_i;a,b) = \sum_{i,j} p_i(a)q_j(b)[m_iu(w_{ij}) \\ +(1-m_i)u(s_i)]-c(a,b) \tag{11.17}$$

Let the cost function exhibit strict substitutability (supermodularity) in efforts, that is: $c_{ab} > 0$.

The principal now wishes to regulate the agent's effort supply on each task. What matters is not only the respective levels of these supplies, but also their interaction. The latter is captured (locally) by the cross-partial derivative U_{ab} of the agent's expected utility defined in (11.17). The inequality $U_{ab} < 0$ exhibits strict trade-offism: inducing greater effort on one task would cause substitution away from the other task, so raising incentives on task A would decrease the average performance on task B. This corresponds to the situation most commonly encountered in the literature. On the other hand, when $U_{ab} > 0$, efforts are complementary, so the agent would not work harder at the margin on one task without expending more effort on the other task as well. Such a win–win situation seems difficult to achieve, however, because the agent's cost of effort $c(a,b)$ entails that increasing effort on one task always raises the marginal cost of effort on the other task. But suppose it is possible to have selective audits. Taking the cross-partial derivative of (11.17) with respect to a and b, we have

$$U_{ab}(s_i,w_{ij},m_i;a,b) = \sum_{i,j} p_i'(a)q_j'(b)m_i[u(w_{ij})-u(s_i)]-c_{ab} \tag{11.18}$$

By assumption 1, the derivatives $p_i'(a)$ and $q_j'(b)$ are negative for low values of i and j and positive for high values of i and j. The cross-partial derivative U_{ab} might now be made positive with the following auditing scheme:

- set $m_i > 0$ if and only if $p_i'(a) > 0$;
- for all i, let $[u(w_{ij}) - u(s_i)]$ have the same sign as $q_j'(b)$.

Under this scheme, audits are triggered by high assessments of performance on task A, and the wage after an audit is undertaken is higher (resp. lower) than the wage when no audit took place if performance on task B is found to be good (resp. bad). This corresponds precisely to the audit scheme described at the beginning of this subsection.

Now, one may wonder whether and when such a scheme turns out to be optimal. Formally, an optimal contract must be a solution to the problem

$$\underset{s,w,m;a,b}{\text{maximize}}\ V(s_i, w_{ij}, m_i; a, b),$$

subject to

incentive compatibility (a,b) maximizes $U(s_i, w_{ij}, m_i; a, b)$

(11.19)

participation $U(s_i, w_{ij}, m_i; a, b) \geq U^*$

The following standard proposition can be derived using the first-order approach.

Proposition 1 *The wage schedules s_i and w_{ij} are non-decreasing in the signals i and j. Moreover, $w_{ij} < s_i$ when j is low and $w_{ij} > s_i$ when j is high.*

Now, one original feature of the above audit scheme is that the agent should want to be audited. In general, this might only happen at a significant cost to the principal that would outweigh the benefits: the agent being risk averse, the expected wage when an audit takes place but before audit results are known might have to be a lot higher than the wage received if there had been no audit. Observe, however, that the agent can protect himself against the additional risk entailed by the threat of an audit in two ways. One is to try to lower as much as possible the probability that an unfavourable audit conclusion occurs; this behaviour is associated with risk aversion. Another means is to seek and guarantee for oneself the highest expected income; this approach corresponds to the agent's so-called precautionary motives. By offering the agent a wage which is higher on average under an audit than the wage received if no audit occurs, the principal relies on the latter behaviour. This strategy might work at a reasonable cost provided the agent's precautionary motives dominate sufficiently his aversion to risk.

To make the latter statement precise, let us recall that the agent's degree of risk aversion can be measured by the coefficient of absolute risk aversion $\rho(z)$ $= -u''(z)/u'(z)$. Let us also introduce the coefficient of absolute prudence, noted $p(z) = -u'''(z)/u''(z)$, which can be shown to capture the strength of the agent's precautionary motives.[18] The statement that precautionary motives 'dominate' risk aversion in some sense can now be made a formal assumption.

Assumption 7 $\forall z \in \mathbb{R}_+ : p(z) > 3 \, \rho(z).$

Utility functions belonging to the well-known hyperbolic absolute risk aversion (HARA) class, that is functions of the form

$$u(z) = \frac{1-k}{(2-k)A}[Az+B]^{(2-k)/(1-k)} \quad \text{with} \quad A > 0$$

satisfy this assumption when $k > 3$. Note also that

$$\frac{\rho'(z)}{\rho(z)} = \frac{d}{dz} \ln\left(\frac{-u''(z)}{u'(z)} \right) = \frac{u'''(z)}{u''(z)} - \frac{u''(z)}{u'(z)} = \rho(z) - p(z)$$

Therefore, absolute risk aversion is decreasing – an intuitive assumption that has received strong empirical support – if and only if $p(z) > \rho(z)$; and we have $p(z) > 3 \, \rho(z)$ if absolute risk aversion decreases fast enough.

This assumption is now sufficient to show that the principal finds it optimal to offer the agent a compensation which yields a higher expected utility than the one obtained if no audit takes place.

Proposition 2   *Under assumption 7, for all i and b:* $\Sigma_j q_j(b) u(w_{ij}) > u(s_i).$

This result is key to showing that audits in the present case are upper-tailed, that is, that they are triggered by high performance assessments on task A. According to the next proposition, if the probability of occurrence of an audit is positive at performance level i and 0 at i', then $i' < i$. Hence, when the cost of audit K is neither too large nor too small, audits only occur at high values of i.

Proposition 3   *If $m_{i'} = 0 < m_i$, then we must have that $i' < i$.*

The above propositions convey the important message that there is no unavoidable trade-off between increasing firm competitiveness and dealing with major technological risk. There is always a range of plausible circumstances where the appropriate use of selective audits, provided they are well defined and not too costly, generates synergies between tasks, allows stronger incentives to be deployed and creates therefore a win–win situation.

5   SOME POLICY IMPLICATIONS

The above analyses have several ramifications for public policy. A major trend nowadays in public policy towards technological risks is, for instance, the active promotion of appropriate management systems. In the United States, since (at least) the delivery to Congress of the Review of Emergency Systems in 1988, it is believed that the prevention of accidental releases requires an integrated approach that considers technologies, operations and management practices. This has led the Environmental Protection Agency to propose several regulations on risk management planning (RMP), the final one being promulgated in 1996. According to it, the basic elements of RMP include an integrated prevention programme to manage risk and an overall management system to supervise the implementation of this programme. The latter entails the use of periodic safety audits to ensure that procedures and practices are being followed (see Er, Kunreuther and Rosenthal, 1998). Risk management planning, however, is always subject to moral hazard. Therefore, the regulator cannot avoid the issue of incentives for implementing an effective RMP. Section 3 makes it clear that those incentives will depend on the extent of corporate liability and on the way prevention expenses are financed. Section 4.2 points out, furthermore, that selective upper-tailed audits might do a better job than periodic audits at reconciling public safety with other business considerations. Implicit in the latter result is that the cost of carrying safety audits should remain reasonable. In a manner analogous to what happens for technical standards, the regulator can also contribute significantly to lowering that cost, by accelerating the adoption of common (and comparable) practices for the conduct of audits and the selection of auditors.

Another recurrent issue in the regulation of major technological risks is the involvement of stakeholders in the assessment, prevention and mitigation of such risks. In many countries, new hazardous facilities are subject to mandatory public hearings, and existing ones must comply with mandatory rules for public disclosure of risk. Whilst such an approach can certainly be justified based on ethical and fairness considerations, the analysis of section 4.1 makes it clear that new institutional arrangements might have to be set in order to compensate for a loss in the power of incentives.

6   CONCLUDING REMARKS AND DIRECTIONS FOR FUTURE RESEARCH

Corporate governance comprises two main subjects, one dealing with how corporate boards endorse the firm's strategy according to their own reading of the business environment, the other with how corporate strategy is implemented. This chapter addresses those two subjects from the viewpoint that the firm is subject to major technological risks. In this context, the feature of the business environment that seems most important is the extent of corporate responsibility in case of a disaster. Section 3 focused on this issue and presented a model that is useful in apprehending the evolution of regulation concerning the liability of banks. Two implementation criteria were discussed next in section 4: the degree of stakeholders' participation in supervising the firm's operations and the avoidability or not of a strict trade-off between technological risk prevention and short-run financial objectives. Using various versions of the multiple-task principal–agent model, it was shown, first, that the cost of involving more stakeholders in technological risk management might be a decrease in the strength of incentives, and second, that the introduction of upper-tailed risk audits might reconcile short-run business performance and technological risk mitigation.

The chapter suggests various avenues for future research. First, the characterization of major technological risks that is defined in section 2 needs to be refined. What precisely makes a technological risk major? Answering this question would help managing the trade-off underlying network industries (that is, power, transportation, water and telecommunications), for instance, where the risk of general failure must be weighed against the benefits attributable to size.

A second avenue would be to study further the evolution of regulation concerning corporate liability, and also the development of new insurance markets and institutions for sharing major risks. From the corporate viewpoint, this would constitute an exercise in positive economics that should prove quite useful for making sense of a rather hilly corporate landscape.[19]

Finally, section 4 above hints at eventual normative contributions dealing with other implementation dilemmas, such as a carrot-and-stick approach versus a forgiving one, or an engineering (ergonomics) approach to risk management versus a sociological and psychological one (see Warner *et al.*, 1992). The current analysis also requires further work. Although the above selective audit scheme seems robust, the stated conditions which guarantee its optimality are only sufficient ones and are too strong. Finding minimal conditions would be a welcome contribution, for it would increase the range of possible win–win situations, and thus the incentives for business to be proactive in the prevention of major technological risks.

ACKNOWLEDGEMENTS

We wish to thank Tom Crocker, H. Landis Gabel, Erwann Michel-Kerjan, Tom Tietenberg, Carel Vachon and especially our discussant, Howard Kunreuther, for valuable discussions and comments. Sinclair-Desgagné acknowledges financial support from a Strategic Grant by the Social Sciences and Humanities Research Council of Canada.

NOTES

1. What is particularly worrisome is that several of the hazards created by the adoption of new technologies are often unforeseeable. For instance, in a 1983 report the National Research Council of the United States estimated that the damages on human health had been formally identified for only 7000 chemicals over a total of 5 million substances. And the gap is growing, due mainly to the pace of innovation, the complexity of new products and the increasing costs of research.
2. For complete surveys, see Warner *et al.* (1992) and Lees (1996).
3. A vivid example is provided here by the year 2000 bug.
4. Camerer and Kunreuther (1989) provide a nice overview of the experimental evidence.
5. That financial markets would keep operating, for instance, or that insurance and labour contracts would remain enforceable.
6. For an exhaustive and up-to-date presentation of new remedies to insurance market failures, see Chichilnisky (1998).
7. One should not underestimate the political economy of these new regulations. For a formal political economy account of market-based vs command and control approaches to environmental regulation, see Boyer and Laffont (1999).
8. See Olexa (1991) and Strasser and Rodosevich (1993) for discussions of the meaning and limits of the security interest exemption rule in view of the apparently conflicting interpretations by the courts.
9. For details and discussions surrounding those legal cases, see the *Journal of Environmental Law*, **1**: 145–51.
10. Boyer and Laffont (1997) examine the introduction in this model of a competitive insurance sector. They show that their main results are robust to this generalization. The reader interested in this issue may also see Freeman and Kunreuther (1997).
11. The firm has no equity. Limited liability is what is focused on.
12. This cost comes essentially from distortions due to taxation: it costs $(1 + \lambda)T$ to raise T through taxes. The value of λ is non-negligible and considered to be of the order of 0.3 in developed countries or more in developing ones.
13. See Boyer and Laffont (1997) for a discussion of adverse selection.
14. This question reaches far beyond the management of technological and environmental risks. To the interested reader we recommend Tirole (1999).
15. The subscripts $_r$ and $_t$ denote partial derivatives with respect to components r and t of a respectively.
16. Dixit (1996, 1997) recently derived a similar result in the Holmström–Milgrom framework.
17. See Sinclair-Desgagné and Gabel (1997) and Sinclair-Desgagné (1999) for further discussion of the upcoming assumptions and results, and for formal proofs.
18. For further discussion and a rigorous derivation of this coefficient, see Kimball (1990).
19. The value of positive economics for general economic decision making is nicely demonstrated in the introduction of Lazear (1995).

REFERENCES

Boyer, Marcel and Jean-Jacques Laffont (1996), 'Environmental protection, producer insolvency and lender liability', in Anastasios Xepapadeas (ed.), *Economic Policy for the Environment and Natural Resources*, Cheltenham, UK and Northampton, MA: Edward Elgar, pp. 1–29.
Boyer, M. and J.-J. Laffont (1997), 'Environmental risks and bank liability', *European Economic Review*, **41**(8), 1427–59.

Boyer, M. and J.-J. Laffont (1999), 'Towards a political economy of the emergence of environmental policy', *Rand Journal of Economics*, **30**, 137–57.

Camerer, C. and H. Kunreuther (1989), 'Decision processes for low probability events: policy implications', *Journal of Policy Analysis and Management*, **8**(4), 565–92.

Chichilnisky, Graciela (1998), 'The economics of global environmental risks', in Tom Tietenberg and Henk Folmer (eds), *The International Yearbook of Environmental and Resource Economics 1998/1999*, Cheltenham, UK and Northampton, MA: Edward Elgar, pp. 235–78.

Chichilnisky, G. and G. Heal (1992), 'Global environmental risks', *Journal of Economic Perspectives*, **7**(4), 65–86.

Dionne, Georges and Sandrine Spaeter (1998), 'Environmental risk and extended liability: the case of green technologies', working paper, HEC, Montréal.

Dixit, Arinash K. (1996), *The Making of Economic Policy: A Transaction-Cost Politics Perspective*, Cambridge, MA: MIT Press.

Dixit, A.K. (1997), 'Power of incentives in private versus public organizations', *American Economic Review*, **87**(2), 378–82.

Er, J., H.C. Kunreuther and I. Rosenthal (1998), 'Utilizing third-party inspections for preventing major chemical accidents', *Risk Analysis*, **18**(2), 145–53.

Feess, Eberhard and Ulrich Hege (1998), 'Lender liability, capital structure and mandatory coverage', working paper, University of Frankfurt and Tilburg University.

Freeman, Paul K. and Howard Kunreuther (1997), *Managing Environmental Risk through Insurance*, Boston, MA: Kluwer.

Gabel, H. Landis and Bernard Sinclair-Desgagné (1995), 'Corporate responses to environmental concerns', in Henk Folmer, H. Landis Gabel and Hans Ops'hoor (eds), *Principles of Environmental and Resource Economics*, Cheltenham, UK and Brookfield, VT: Edward Elgar.

Gobert, Karine and Michel Poitevin (1998), 'Environmental risks: should banks be liable?', CIRANO Working Paper 98s-39, Montréal.

Holmström, B. and P. Milgrom (1991), 'Multitask principal–agent analyses: incentives contracts, asset ownership, and job design', *Journal of Law, Economics and Organization*, **7** (special issue), 24–52.

Kimball, M.S. (1990), 'Precautionary savings in the small and in the large', *Econometrica*, **58**(1), 53–73.

Lazear, Edward P. (1995), *Personnel Economics*, Cambridge, MA: MIT Press.

Lees, Frank P. (1996), *Loss Prevention in the Process Industries*, Oxford: Butterworth Heinemann.

National Research Council, Committee on the Institutional Means for Assessment of Risks to Public Health, Commission of Life Sciences (1983), *Risk Assessment in the Federal Government: Managing the Process*, Washington, DC: National Academy Press.

Olexa, M.T. (1991), 'Contaminated collateral and lender liability: CERCLA and the new-age banker', *American Journal of Agricultural Economics*, **73**(5), 1388–93.

Roberts, K.H. (1990), 'Some characteristics of one type of high reliability organization', *Organization Science*, **1**(2), 160–76.

Shrivastava, Pankaj (1986), *Bhopal*, New York: Basic Books.

Sinclair-Desgagné, B. (1994), 'The first-order approach to multi-signal principal–agent problems', *Econometrica*, **62**(2), 459–65.

Sinclair-Desgagné, Bernard (1999), 'How to restore higher-powered incentives in multitask agencies', *Journal of Law, Economics and Organizations*, **15**, 418–22.

Sinclair-Desgagné, B. and H.L. Gabel (1997), 'Environmental auditing in management systems and public policy', *Journal of Environmental Economics and Management*, **33**(3), 331–46.

Smith, Keith (1996), *Environmental Hazards*, London: Routledge.

Strasser, K.A. and D. Rodosevich (1993), 'Seeing the forest for the trees in CERCLA liability', *Yale Journal on Regulation*, **10**(2), 493–560.

Tirole, Jean (1999), 'Corporate governance', 1998 Presidential address to the Econometric Society.

Warner, Sir Frederick *et al.* (1992), *Risk: Analysis, Perception and Management*, London: The Royal Society.

12. Strategies for dealing with large-scale natural and environmental risks

Howard Kunreuther

1 INTRODUCTION

What alternative strategies are appropriate for reducing losses and providing protection against natural and environmental hazards which can create potentially catastrophic losses to individuals, firms and society? New scientific knowledge and recent developments in information technology offer the possibility of estimating the risks of these hazards more precisely than in the past and utilizing these data for developing more effective programmes for coping with losses from these events.

This chapter emphasizes the importance of combining market mechanisms such as incentives and insurance with regulations and standards (for example building codes) in developing risk management strategies for natural and environmental risks. Particular attention will be given to the challenges and opportunities of utilizing benefit–cost analysis in the evaluation process.

The next section contrasts normative and descriptive choice behaviour by individuals and managers regarding low-probability events. To illustrate these concepts, I focus on the specific example of reducing losses and providing protection against natural hazards. The concluding section of the chapter proposes ways of extending benefit–cost analysis to incorporate behavioural factors that influence people's choice processes.

2 NORMATIVE MODELS AND DESCRIPTIVE FEATURES OF CHOICE

Consider the following questions that face individuals, firms and society today with respect to investing in measures to reduce losses from environmental and natural hazards:

- Can one reduce the consequences from catastrophic accidents to a firm by purchasing insurance and/or investing in some risk-reducing meas-

ures? Section 112R of the Clean Air Act requires chemical facilities to
develop and implement risk management programmes for preventing
the occurrence and mitigating the consequences of such releases and
share these prevention plans with the public.[1]

- What steps can be taken by firms to reduce pollution? The long-run
  benefits from less pollution can be measured in terms of reduction in
  illnesses, fatalities and a cleaner environment. These benefits may
  exceed the upfront costs of making this investment.[2] For example,
  developing better sewage treatment facilities will improve water quality over a long period of time (Freeman, 1990). Investing in better
  quality underground storage tanks for storing gasoline at stations involves upfront costs to the owner of the facility. Such an investment
  promises to yield benefits in future years by reducing groundwater
  contamination that now occurs from an existing poorly constructed
  tank (Boyd and Kunreuther, 1997).
- What protective actions can residents take in hazard-prone areas to
  reduce their losses from natural disasters? For example, bolting one's
  house to a foundation reduces the chances of damage from an earthquake. It involves an upfront expenditure to strengthen the house but
  yields benefits over the life of the structure. Purchasing earthquake
  insurance provides the policyholder with financial protection against a
  disaster loss for a fixed period of time (normally one year) in return for
  a premium to the insurance company.

Normative Models of Choice

In determining what actions an individual or firm should take to reduce their
losses from environmental and natural hazards, there are generally three
elements that need to be considered:

- The chances that the event will occur. For simplicity assume that there
  is one event such as a catastrophic accident or natural disaster that has
  a probability p of occurrence
- The resulting loss L associated with this event
- The cost C associated with protection that reduces this loss from an
  accident or disaster to $L' < L$.

There are two types of protective measures that can be considered: *insurance*
and *mitigation*. Insurance requires the individual to pay an annual premium,
which reduces the potential financial loss from L to L'. A risk-neutral individual will want to purchase insurance coverage whenever $C < p (L - L')$. If
the person is risk averse then one must determine the utility U associated

with the person's final wealth with and without insurance cover. In this case the person will want to invest in insurance whenever

$$pU(W - C - L') + (1 - p)U(W - C) > pU(W - L) + (1 - p)U(W)$$

The more risk averse an individual is, the more willing she will be to purchase an insurance policy at a price C, everything else remaining equal (Arrow, 1971).

Mitigation measures are similar to insurance except that there is an upfront cost of the investment and the benefits are normally accrued over a longer period of time. One then utilizes an appropriate discount rate d to convert these benefits back to the present. If a firm invests in a measure which reduces the environmental consequences of an accident, then the expected benefits need to be calculated over the length of time that the measure is in place. If an individual invests in a structural measure to make his house safer against earthquakes, then the benefits of the measure are accrued over the length of life of the house.

More specifically, the expected discounted benefits of a measure if an individual is risk neutral is simply

$$E(B) = \sum_{t=1}^{T} (L - L')/(1 + d)^t$$

If $E(B) > C$, then the person should adopt the measure; otherwise she should not.[3]

Descriptive Features of Choice

There is a growing empirical literature that suggests that individuals and firms do not obtain the relevant data and/or undertake the types of computations implied by normative models of choice, such as maximizing expected utility or comparing expected benefits with costs (Kahneman and Tversky, 1979; Thaler, 1991, 1992). There is a large empirical literature illustrating the types of biases and heuristics that individuals use in estimating the likelihood of events occurring (Kahneman, Slovic and Tversky, 1982). Below we list a number of factors which lead people to behave in ways which differ from normative models of choice.[4]

Misperception of the risks

Individuals often misperceive the probability that certain events will occur. If an event is highly salient because of media coverage, then there is often a tendency to overestimate its chance of occurrence. For example, most people perceive the likelihood of deaths from highly reported disasters, such as fires and homicide, to be much higher than those from events such as diabetes and breast cancer that are rarely reported in the media (Combs and Slovic, 1974). Judged probability of events increases by unpacking items that are part of a general category. In a study with 120 Stanford undergraduates, Tversky and Koehler (1994) found that subjects estimated the combined probability of dying of specific natural causes (that is, heart disease, cancer, other natural causes) to be 1.26 times higher than if subjects were simply asked what is the probability of dying from a natural cause. Unpacking unnatural causes into the categories accident, homicide and other unnatural causes led to an estimate 1.66 times higher than when the category 'unnatural causes' was presented to subjects.

Past experience may also play an important role in influencing individuals' perception of the probability of an event occurring. If one recently suffered a loss from a flood or earthquake, then one is more likely to view the event as more likely than before the disaster (Kunreuther *et al.*, 1978) The availability bias, whereby the chances of various events happening is based on familiarity with these events, may help explain this behaviour (Tversky and Kahneman 1973).

'It cannot happen to me'
For low-probability events individuals may behave as if they view the probability to be zero. Some individuals may relate their perceived probability of a disaster (p) to a threshold level (p^*), which they may unconsciously set. If they feel $p < p^*$ then they do not worry about the consequences at all. They behave as if the event 'will not happen to me' and take no protective actions.

The contingent weighting model proposed by Tversky, Sattath and Slovic (1988) provides a useful framework for characterizing individual choice processes with respect to adopting protective measures. In this descriptive model, individuals make trade-offs between the dimensions associated with alternatives, such as probability and outcomes. The weights they put on these dimensions are contingent, because they may vary depending on the problem context and the way information is presented. People often weight these dimensions differently than would be suggested by normative models of choice, such as expected utility theory.

It is easy to see why the 'it will not happen to me' strategy violates the tenets of expected utility theory or benefit–cost analysis. Instead of weighting the outcome from an event by its perceived probability of occurrence, individuals who utilize a threshold model treat low probabilities as having a zero chance of occurrence. They do not even consider the consequences from events which they treat as impossible, when, in fact, they may actually occur. Homeowners who follow this decision process will have no interest in adopting loss reduction measures because they do *not* think about the consequences of a disaster.

The decision to ignore events where $p < p^*$ may be justified by individuals by claiming that there is a limited amount of time available to think about protecting oneself against hazards. Setting a threshold level p^* enables people to devote their attention to events that are a source of worry and concern. Such a rule is also easy to explain and justify to others because of its simplicity.

High discount rates

With respect to investment in mitigation measures where the benefits are accrued over time, persons may have a very high discount rate so that the future benefits are not given much weight when evaluating the protective measure. Loewenstein and Prelec (1992) provide an analytical review of behavioural inconsistencies associated with discounted utility (DU) theory. They propose a model whereby intertemporal choices represent deviations from an anticipated status quo or a reference point, and the discount function is hyperbolic, rather than exponential.

The Loewenstein and Prelec model appears to explain a number of choices which contradict DU predictions, such as the reluctance of individuals to incur the high immediate cost of energy-efficient appliances in return for reduced electricity charges over time (Hausman, 1979; Kempton and Neiman, 1987). A recent paper by Ahlbrecht and Weber (1997) compares the cases of certainty and risk for intertemporal choices through experiments involving lotteries. They show that the discount rate is sensitive to the type of elicitation procedure utilized.

Reframing the problem

Presenting information to individuals in different forms may have different impacts on their perception of the risk. For example, if individuals utilize threshold models of choice with $p^* = 1/75$ for determining whether to worry about the flood problem, then they will assume that a disaster will not happen to them if their estimate of their house being damaged by rising water is $p = 1/100$. Suppose that this homeowner was told that the chances of experiencing at least one damaging flood within the next 25 years was 0.22. Then he might pay attention to the event and decide to take protective action.

This reframing of probabilities has been used to increase voluntary seatbelt use. The chance of a fatality on an average car trip is extremely low (about 0.00000025) which is well below most people's threshold. But over a lifetime of driving the probability of fatality is 0.01. In one study 39 per cent of the respondents said they would use seat belts when given lifetime probability figures compared to only 10 per cent when provided with a single trip probability (Slovic *et al.*, 1978).

Presenting the information on probabilities in different formats may also lead to choices by individuals which would not be predicted by normative theories. In a very interesting controlled experiment, where subjects could 'win' a sum of money if they drew a red jelly bean, subjects frequently elected to draw from a bowl that contained a greater absolute number (for example, 7 in 100) than from a bowl with fewer red beans but better odds (for example, 1 in 10). If subjects were told they would lose money if a red bean was drawn, many followed the reverse pattern by choosing the bowl with fewer red beans but a higher chance of losing (Denes-Raj and Epstein, 1994). A recent study asked forensic psychologists and psychiatrists to judge the likelihood that a patient would harm someone within six months of being discharged from a hospital. A patient was judged to pose a higher risk if the likelihood was derived from a frequency scale (for example, 10 out of 100) than if derived from a probability scale (for example 10 per cent). The different reactions to probability and frequency appear to be due to the more frightening images evoked by frequencies (Slovic, Monahan and MacGregor, 1999).

Another way to reframe the problem is to focus on the consequences of an event so that individuals want to undertake protective measures rather than saying to themselves that 'it won't happen to me'. Consider the problem of getting individuals to wear seat belts. In the US most states impose a fine for not wearing a seat belt. The problem is that the law is often not enforced or in some states a motorist cannot be fined unless stopped for other violations, such as speeding. Furthermore, the fine is often relatively small so that individuals may not be concerned about having to pay it. A more promising approach for encouraging seat-belt use is practised in many European countries. Drivers and passengers are told that if they have an accident and are not wearing a seat belt, their medical insurance will not pay their hospital expenses. Fear of not obtaining insurance payments leads many people to wear a seat belt when they otherwise might not.

Role of emotions
Judgments of riskiness are based on dimensions other than probability and monetary losses (for example, hospital expenses if one is injured in an accident). Dimensions such as fear and dread have been shown to be very critical to people's risk perception (Slovic, 1987). For example, in a study undertaken a few years ago the public was very concerned with the risks associated with hazardous waste, yet scientific experts felt it posed a relatively small risk. On the other hand, radon and climate change were virtually ignored by the public while the experts felt they were some of the biggest risk problems (*Science*, 1990).

Kahneman, Wakker and Sarin (1997) bring affect and feelings into the picture by distinguishing between two types of utility: decision utility and experienced utility. *Decision utility* is inferred from observed choices or elicited willingness to pay and is used to explain choices. It characterizes the way benefit–cost analysis or expected utility theory evaluates different alternatives. It is an outcome-oriented approach. The term *experienced utility* is associated with the philosopher Jeremy Bentham and refers to the pleasure and pain associated with different acts. Kahneman *et al.* (1997) show through a series of experiments that people behave in a way that is inconsistent with how economists treat rationality from a decision utility perspective.[5]

With respect to protective behaviour, Hogarth and Kunreuther (1995) found that people often buy warranties because they want to have 'peace of mind' or 'reduce their anxiety'. Factors such as probability of the object being damaged or needing repair often do not influence their decision. Hsee and Kunreuther (2000) have found that if individuals have a strong affection for an object that they have purchased (for example, a painting or vase) they will pay considerably more for insurance than if they do not have any particular feeling for the item. Finuciani *et al.* (1998) suggest that this affect may serve as a cue for judgments of risk and benefit as well as probability.

Ambiguity

Ambiguity or vagueness about probabilities is an attribute that is ignored in normative models of choice, such as expected utility theory or benefit–cost analysis, but which seems to affect choices people make. Consider the normative models of choice regarding the adoption of insurance or mitigation measures. Suppose the probability of loss p is not known exactly but instead has a distribution $f(p)$ with expected value p^*. Under normative models of choice, the expected probability p^* is all that matters.

Empirical evidence suggests that ambiguity does make a difference in people's willingness to pay to protect themselves against a risk as well as firm's decisions on how much to charge for protection. In a series of empirical studies, sophisticated subjects (including actuaries and underwriters) indicated an aversion to ambiguity for low-probability events. When subjects were asked to play the role of insurer, they showed an aversion to ambiguity that was even greater than when they played the role of consumer interested in purchasing coverage (Hogarth and Kunreuther, 1989). The greater ambiguity aversion of insurers helps explain the failure of private insurance markets in recent years against ambiguous risks such as environmental pollution, earthquake losses and nuclear power plant accidents. The premium that insurers want to charge is likely to be much higher than potential clients are willing to pay and/or state insurance commissioners will allow to be charged.

Summary

The above empirical evidence suggests that policies for dealing with low-probability–high-consequence events must take into account a set of behavioural factors which are not considered in standard normative models of choice. The probability of an event occurring and its potential consequences are appropriate factors for analysing the cost-effectiveness of mitigation measures and the prices that should be charged for insurance. However, they may not be the deciding factors with respect to the actions taken by those who face the risk. Some individuals are likely to use rules of thumb such as 'it will not happen to me' and hence tune out of the event. Others may be fearful or anxious and hence want to take protective measures. Often past experience plays a role in determining the factors which influence a person's or firm's decision processes. Those who have gone through a disaster or know of others who have suffered losses are more concerned with protection than those who have been unscathed by the event.

3   NATURAL DISASTERS: AN ILLUSTRATIVE EXAMPLE

This portion of the chapter focuses on the problem of how we can develop meaningful public policies for reducing the losses from natural disasters and providing protection to the victims of these events. By focusing on a specific example one can better appreciate the importance of understanding the decision processes of individuals in developing programmes that can achieve their desired impacts. The concepts and principles discussed below are also appropriate for examining environmental and technological disasters.

Nature of the Problem

The financial costs of natural disasters are on the societal radar screen. Until recently these events received relatively little notice except in the immediate aftermath of a catastrophic earthquake, flood or hurricane. Since 1989 the cost of natural disasters has been rising at an alarming rate. During that time, 11 catastrophes have cost the nation more than $1 billion each. Hurricane Andrew in Florida (1992) and California's Northridge earthquake (1994) together cost the federal government $28 billion, more than its combined annual expenditures on aiding higher education, pollution control and running the federal court system (Emerson and Stevens, 1995).

   Property owners in hazard-prone areas are experiencing greater difficulty today in acquiring insurance and are paying considerably more for it. Moreover, these conditions will become much worse if insurers continue to withdraw from the marketplace. Overbuilding and high real-estate prices in the Atlantic and Gulf Coast hurricane-prone areas have, until recently, been facilitated by relatively inexpensive and readily available property insurance. Commercial development has followed the population's movement to coastal areas, and this has increased the potential economic losses from natural disasters.

The requests by insurers for significantly higher rates and the desire on their part to reduce the number of policies in hazard-prone areas threaten to deflate property values and hurt the economies of these regions. More specifically, many residents living in hurricane-prone areas may not be able to afford insurance premiums based on the actual risk. If they are forced to purchase cover to maintain their mortgage, they may have to sell their homes. Purchasers will offer a lower price than in the past because of the higher insurance costs they will be forced to incur.

The *natural disaster syndrome* is a term which links the lack of interest by those at risk in protecting themselves against hazards and the resulting significant financial burden on society, property owners, the insurance industry and municipal, state and federal governments when severe disasters do occur. More specifically, most homeowners, private businesses and the public sector do not purchase insurance voluntarily or adopt cost-effective mitigation measures to reduce potential losses from future disasters. A significant amount of damage could be averted if more stringent wind and seismic building codes were adopted and/or existing ones enforced. Serious consideration should also be given to reducing damage through more effective land-use control measures (Kunreuther and Roth Sr, 1998; Burby, 1998).

Multiple Stakeholders

Any hazard-prone area has a set of interested parties concerned with the impact of hazards on their well-being. The interaction of these different parties with each other depends upon formal and informal institutional arrangements, the type of information presented to them and the programmes and policies in place. The values and agendas of these parties may differ from each other, as illustrated by the following somewhat oversimplified characterization of their concerns:

- *Homeowners and renters* Residing in a safe structure while still enjoying pleasant surroundings and a nice view (for example locating near a river bank).
- *Commercial enterprises* Being able to continue operations after a disaster (i.e. avoiding business interruption) due to the disaster.
- *Banks and financial institutions* The ability of the property owner to

continue making payments after a disaster on the mortgages while still
remaining competitive.
- *Construction industry* Building affordable housing which is safe enough.
- *Insurance and reinsurance industry* Offering protection against the
  losses from natural disasters using rates based on risk while being
  mindful of the financial impact that a catastrophic disaster will have on
  their balance sheets.
- *Environmental groups* Preserving environmental quality and the appropriate balance of the ecosystem in both the long and short run.
- *Municipalities* Designing safe communities that are sufficiently resilient after a disaster so that they do not have to rely on enormous
  amounts of state and federal aid.
- *State and federal disaster agencies* Building disaster-resistant communities so that they will not have to pay large amounts of state and
  federal aid after a disaster.

A change in any given policy or programme has to be carefully structured
to reflect the interaction between these different stakeholders and their nested
decision structure (Kleindorfer, Kunreuther and Schoemaker, 1993). To illustrate, consider the challenges associated with reducing disaster losses through
mitigation measures.

Relatively few *homeowners* adopt loss-reduction measures even if they are
inexpensive and promise to yield sufficient benefits to justify the cost (Palm,
1995). One solution to this problem is to inform individuals of the dangers of
living in specific areas. Other stakeholders have good financial reasons *not* to
implement this measure. *Real-estate agents* have no reason to provide prospective buyers with information on the hazards associated with living in a
particular structure that fails to meet the building code. They are supported
implicitly by the *current property owner* who wants to sell his home at as
high a price as possible. Furthermore, prospective buyers may have little
interest in knowing about the design of the structure if they are not aware of
the risks associated with future disasters.

Role of Mitigation in Natural Disasters

Cost-effective risk-mitigation measures (RMMs) are defined as ones for which
the discounted expected benefits over the life of the property are greater
than the upfront investment costs of the measure and other related expenses.
In theory, all of the interested parties concerned with natural disaster losses
should view such RMMs favourably. The property owner should see this as
an attractive investment that will increase the value of his residence or business. The insurer should be able to provide attractive premium reductions to

the property owner on his policy to reflect the decreased expected future losses from natural disasters. Banks and financial institutions should feel that they are at a lower risk of default by the property owner following a major disaster. The contractor and developer should find it easier to sell a property that is better designed against hazards even if it costs more than one which is relatively unsafe. Public sector agencies at the state, local and federal levels should celebrate the lower need for disaster assistance due to the reduced losses from future disasters.

The reality is somewhat different. Few property owners voluntarily adopt mitigation measures; nor do insurers provide incentives for these investments through premium reductions which reflect the decreased expected future claims payments. Housing values do not appear to reflect the benefits of mitigation measures, perhaps because people do not want to be reminded that they live in a hazard-prone area. Banks do not normally require these measures as a condition for a mortgage. As a result, developers and contractors have no economic incentive to build safer structures, since it means incurring costs that they feel will hurt them competitively because the RMMs are undervalued by the potential buyers. For example, interviews with structural engineers concerned with the performance of earthquake-resistant structures indicate that they have no incentive to build structures that exceed existing codes. They have to justify these expenses to their clients and would lose out to other engineers who did not include these features in their design (May and Stark, 1992). Hence the public sector has to bear a larger portion of the disaster losses than if these measures had been adopted.

Let us turn to the empirical data. After Hurricane Andrew in Florida in 1992, most residents in hurricane-prone areas appear not to have made improvements to existing dwellings. A July 1994 telephone survey of 1241 residents in six hurricane-prone areas along the Atlantic and Gulf Coasts revealed that 62 per cent indicated that they had not installed protective measures, such as hurricane shutters or roof bracing, either before or after Hurricane Andrew (Insurance Institute for Property Loss Reduction, 1995).

Measures such as strapping a water heater at a cost of under $75 can significantly reduce damage by preventing the heater from toppling during an earthquake and causing a fire (Levenson (1992). The expected benefits from such a measure greatly exceed the costs in quake-prone regions and yet even these loss-reduction investments are not being adopted. A 1989 survey of 3500 homeowners in four California counties subject to earthquakes revealed that only between 5 and 9 per cent of the respondents in each of these counties reported adopting any loss-reduction measures (Palm *et al.*, 1990). A follow-up survey by Palm and her colleagues in 1993 revealed that between 20 and 25 per cent of the homes in two counties affected by the 1989 Loma Prieta earthquake (Santa Clara and Contra Costa) had bolted their house to

the foundation. Less than 10 per cent of homeowners in two southern counties in the survey who had not suffered damage from Loma Prieta (Los
Angeles and San Bernadino) had undertaken this measure (Palm, 1995).

These data imply that individuals do not believe that investing in the RMM
will increase their residences' property value sufficiently for them to incur the
upfront costs. With respect to their decision processes, many people have
short time horizons and/or severe budget constraints that either reduce their
perceived net benefits from RMMs or simply prevent them from making the
investment (Kunreuther, 1996).

Controlled Experiments on Protective Measures

To gain insight into individuals' decision processes with respect to RMMs
and to determine how much an individual is willing to pay for investing in
such measures, a set of controlled experiments was conducted in Pennsylvania and California (Kunreuther, Onculer and Slovic, 1998). For example,
individuals participating in this survey were asked to specify the maximum
they were willing to pay (WTP) for bolting the structure to its foundation. In
the first scenario they were told that they planned to reside in it for exactly 5
years and that the expected annual reduction in damage from the RMM was
approximately \$500.[6] The second scenario was identical to the first except
they were told that they expected to live in the house for exactly 10 years.

Table 12.1 presents the distribution of these WTP figures for 84 students at
the University of Pennsylvania. Half of these students were *not* told the cost

Table 12.1   *Distribution of maximum willingness to pay (WTP) (%
individuals in each category)*

	Price not given		Price given = \$1500	
	5 years	10 years	5 years	10 years
\$0–\$500	5%	5%	7%	4%
\$501–\$1000	7%	7%	16%	16%
\$1,001–\$1500	45%	17%	43%	44%
\$1,501–\$2000	31%	36%	16%	19%
\$2,001–\$2500	5%	14%	3%	0%
\$2,501–\$3000	5%	14%	3%	0%
\$3000 up	2%	7%	12%	17%
	Number of subjects = 42		Number of subjects = 42	

Source: Kunreuther, Onculer and Slovic (1998).

of installing the RMM and the other half were told that the price of installing the RMM was $1500. A risk-neutral person should be willing to pay as much as $2085 if their annual discount rate was 10 per cent and they expected to live in their house for 5 years. The data in Table 12.1 reveal that only 12 per cent of the individuals would be willing to pay over $2000 for the measure if the price was not given and they expected to live in the house for 5 years. The proportion in this category increases to 18 per cent for the group who were given a price of $1500.

When the time horizon is lengthened to 10 years the maximum WTP for a risk-neutral investor facing an annual discount rate of 10 per cent increases to $3380. Yet only 7 per cent of the subjects who were *not* given the price chose to spend more than $3000; the percentage increases to 17 per cent for this group when the price was specified to be $1500. These results suggest that RMMs may need to be very cost effective indeed if they are to be adopted through normal private choice without regulation.

Similar findings emerged from a survey of 252 individuals visiting the Exploratorium Museum in San Francisco. Now three different time horizons (*T*) for residing in the house were utilized: 5 years, 10 years and 20 years for obtaining the maximum WTP when the price of the quake RMM was given at $1500. As in the earlier experiment, a significant proportion of the respondents had either high effective discount rates (the mean value varied between 67 per cent and 74 per cent depending on the values of *T*)[7] or did not change their maximum WTP as the time horizon for residing in the house was increased. For the case where the length of time in the house was extended from 5 to 10 years, 45 per cent of the subjects did not change their expressed WTP for the protective measure (Kunreuther, Onculer and Slovic, 1998). The large group of individuals who maintained the same WTP as the time horizon was changed may have done so because they could not afford to pay more and/or they believed that the cost of the RMM would be fully capitalized in the selling price of the property.

Taken together with earlier studies on individuals' behaviour on low-probability–high consequence events as described in section 2, these results suggest that some property owners are reluctant to invest in cost-effective RMMs because they do not make the implied trade-offs between spending money now in return for potential benefits over time. Private developers may do nothing to change this behaviour. Those constructing and selling homes may believe (perhaps correctly) that they are unable to recover the costs of RMMs in increased selling prices for the structures. Insurers and regulators may need to provide additional incentives and/or building codes so that these cost-effective measures will be adopted.

3   PROPOSED PROGRAMME FOR HAZARD MANAGEMENT[8]

What are the appropriate roles of the private and public sectors in financing the cost of recovery from large-scale natural disasters? To the extent that private insurance markets provide protection against catastrophe risk, policy makers must decide how these markets should be regulated. They must also determine the role of land-use regulations and building codes and the extent to which private choice and incentives will guide hazard-mitigation efforts. Within the realm of public choice, decisions also must be made with respect to the delegation of authority among the different levels of government and its agencies. In evaluating these options policy makers must consider how various government actions affect the behaviour of firms and individuals in responding to catastrophe risk.

Current natural disaster policy places a large financial burden on all tax-payers after a disaster occurs. Under the Stafford Disaster Relief and Emergency Assistance Act of 1988, the federal government provides funds to cover at least 75 per cent of the costs of rehabilitating public facilities (US Congress, 1995). For catastrophic events, such as Hurricane Andrew in 1992 and the Mississippi Floods of 1993, the federal government covered the entire cost of the repairs of public facilities; 90 per cent of these costs were covered after the Northridge earthquake, with the remainder financed by the State of California. Thus, it is not surprising that there has been little interest by most municipalities in investing in loss-reduction measures for their facilities; city officials probably assume that damage will be covered by federal or state funding. For the same reason a number of local governments have shown little interest in adopting mitigation measures or purchasing insurance against losses to their buildings (Burby, 1992).

With respect to the private sector, the federal government offers low-interest loans to uninsured and underinsured disaster victims through a Small Business Administration (SBA) disaster loan programme. Under the current arrangement homeowners and businesses suffering damage from a disaster can obtain a low-interest loan to aid their recovery. The interest rate varies between 4 per cent and 8 per cent. These programmes can be costly to taxpayers if many such loans are provided at below-market rates. During the period from 1977 through 1993, the SBA loaned approximately $21 billion to disaster victims (US Congress, 1995).

The challenge society faces today is how to promote investments in cost-effective risk-mitigation measures (RMMs), while at the same time placing more of the burden of recovery on those who suffer losses from natural disasters. This section outlines a programme for managing large-scale disasters which relies on market mechanisms, standards and regulations. For the programme to be successful, a number of stakeholders from the private and public sectors need to work together. These include insurance and reinsurance firms, financial institutions, investment bankers, and the building and real-estate communities as well as government agencies at the local, state and federal levels.

Improving Estimates of Risk

All these interested parties will benefit from improved estimates of the risk associated with specific hazards. To illustrate, consider insurers and reinsurers. By obtaining better data on the probabilities and consequences of disasters, they will be able to set their premiums more accurately and tailor their portfolios to reduce the chances of insolvency. The improved information should enable insurers more accurately to determine their needs for protection through reinsurance or capital market instruments. More accurate data on risk also reduce the asymmetry of information between insurers and other providers of capital. Investors are more likely to supply additional capital as they become increasingly confident in the estimates of the risks of insured losses from natural disasters.

Auditing and Inspecting Property

One way to determine the ability of a structure to withstand the impact of natural disasters is to inspect the property carefully. A careful appraisal of the structure is expensive. To date, such audits have been undertaken primarily on commercial risks where the insurer has absorbed the cost of the audit through its large premium base with the policyholder. On the residential side, the success of such a programme requires the support of the building industry, of realtors and of a cadre of inspectors, well qualified to provide accurate information on the condition of the property.

Banks and financial institutions could require that structures be inspected and certified against natural hazards as a condition for obtaining a mortgage. This inspection, which would be a form of buyer protection, is similar in concept to termite and radon inspections normally required when property is financed.[9] If cost-effective risk-reduction measures were incorporated in building codes, banks could provide a seal of approval to each structure that meets or exceeds these standards.

Role of Building Codes

Building codes mandate that property owners adopt mitigation measures. Such codes may be desirable when property owners would otherwise not adopt cost-effective RMMs because they misperceive the benefits from adopting the RMM and/or underestimate the probability of a disaster occurring. For example, suppose the property owner believes that the losses from an earthquake to the structure are $20 000 and the developer knows that it is $25 000 because the building is not well constructed. There is no incentive for the developer to relay the correct information to the property owner because the developer is not held liable should a quake cause damage to the structure. If the insurer is unaware of how well the building is constructed, then this information cannot be conveyed to the potential property owner through a premium based on risk. Inspecting the building to see that it meets building codes and then providing it with a seal of approval provides accurate information to the property owner.

If these property owners were forced to cover their own disaster losses, then one might contend that they should be left to their own designs, since they would have only themselves to blame for not taking preventive action. However, as pointed out in the introduction, all taxpayers bear some of the costs of restoring damaged property through low-interest federal loans and grants. Hence there is an economic justification for all citizens to design structures to be safer.

Cohen and Noll (1981) provide an additional rationale for building codes. When a building collapses it may create externalities in the form of economic dislocations and other social costs that are beyond the economic loss suffered by the owners. These may not be taken into account when the owners evaluate the importance of adopting a specific mitigation measure. For example, if a building topples off its foundation after an earthquake, it could break a pipeline and cause a major fire that would damage other homes that were not affected by the earthquake in the first place. In other words, there may be an additional annual expected benefit from mitigation over and above the reduction in losses to the specific structure adopting this RMM. All financial institutions and insurers that are responsible for these other properties at risk would favour building codes to protect their investments and/or reduce the insurance premiums they charge for fire cover following earthquake.

If a family is forced to vacate their property because of damage that would have been obviated if a building code had been in place, then this cost also needs to be taken into account when determining the benefits of mitigation. In addition to these temporary food and housing costs, the destruction of commercial property could cause business interruption losses and the eventual bankruptcy of many firms. The impact on the fabric of the community and its economic base from this destruction could be enormous (Britton, 1989). In a study estimating the physical and human consequences of a major earthquake in the Shelby County/Memphis, Tennessee area, Litan *et al.* (1992, pp. 65–6) found that the temporary losses in economic output stemming from damage to workplaces could be as high as $7.6 billion. This figure was based on the magnitude of unemployment and the accompanying losses in wages, profits and indirect 'multiplier' effects.

Providing Economic Incentives for Mitigation

Insurers could provide financial incentives in the form of lower premiums, lower deductibles or increased coinsurance to encourage the adoption of cost-effective RMMs. If budget constraints prevent a property owner from investing in mitigation measures, then insurers should consider having a bank or other financial institution provide funds through a home improvement loan with a payback period coterminous with the life of the mortgage.

Consider the following example, where the cost of an RMM on a piece of property in earthquake-prone country is $1500. If the seismologists' best estimate of the annual probability of an earthquake is $p = 1/100$, and the reduction in loss from investing in the RMM is $27 500, then the expected annual benefit is $275. A 20-year loan for $1500 at an annual interest rate of 10 per cent would result in payments of $145 per year. If the annual insurance premium reduction reflected the expected benefits of the RMM (that is, $275), then the insured homeowner would have lower *total* payments by investing in mitigation than by not undertaking the measure.

Many poorly constructed homes are owned by low-income families who are uninsured. They cannot afford the costs of mitigation measures on their existing structure or are unable to incur the costs of reconstruction should their house suffer damage from a natural disaster. Equity considerations argue for providing this group with low-interest loans and grants so that they can either adopt cost-effective RMMs, or relocate to a safer area. Since low-income victims are likely to receive federal assistance to cover uninsured losses after a disaster, subsidizing these mitigation measures can also be justified on efficiency grounds.

Broadening Protection against Catastrophic Losses

New sources of capital from the private and public sectors could provide insurers, reinsurers and government with funds against losses from catastrophic events. They range from capital market instruments to insurance pools to federal solutions.

With respect to capital market solutions, in the past couple of years investment banks and brokerage firms have shown considerable interest in developing new financial instruments for protecting against catastrophic risks. Their objective is to find ways to make investors comfortable trading new securitized instruments covering catastrophic exposures, just like the securities of any other asset class. In other words, catastrophe exposures would be treated as a new asset class (Insurance Services Office, 1999).

In June 1997 the insurance company, USAA, floated act-of-God bonds that provided them with protection should a major hurricane hit Florida. A two-year catastrophe (CAT) bond was put together by Swiss Re Capital Markets and Credit Suisse First Boston in July 1997. The loss triggers were tied to California insurance industry earthquake losses based on the Property Claims Insurance index for the state. Since that time there have been a number of other CAT bonds issued in Japan and other countries. (For more details see the Insurance Services Office, 1999.)

Turning to the role of the public sector, Lewis and Murdock (1996) developed a proposal that the federal government offer *catastrophe reinsurance contracts*, which would be auctioned annually. The Treasury would auction a limited number of excess-of-loss (XOL) contracts covering industry losses between $25 billion and $50 billion from a single natural disaster. Insurers, reinsurers and state and national reinsurance pools would be eligible purchasers.

Another proposed option is for the government to provide protection against catastrophic losses. Governments could purchase CAT bonds from either the private sector or organizations such as the World Bank to obtain the needed capital to cover these large losses. In countries where there is an active private insurance industry, insurers would be assessed for premium charges in the same manner that a private reinsurance company would levy a fee on insurers for providing protection to them against large losses.

4   EVALUATING ALTERNATIVE STRATEGIES USING BENEFIT–COST ANALYSIS

Benefit–cost analysis (BCA) is the standard technique for evaluating alternative programmes and strategies. Suppose one wanted to evaluate whether imposing a building code for structures in an earthquake-prone area would be a desirable policy. The two alternatives would then be:

Alternative 1:   No building code.
Alternative 2:   Impose a building code.

If one were to use BCA as an evaluative technique, one would determine the benefits and costs for each affected individual and then aggregate across all the relevant individuals to determine which one of the alternatives would be most desirable from a societal point of view. This section poses some challenges in utilizing BCA for comparing alternative programmes and suggests a set of process issues that need to be considered when undertaking a BCA.

Challenges in Using BCA

Estimating the risks of specific events (for example, earthquakes)

There is often considerable uncertainty and ambiguity regarding the estimates of the likelihood of disasters of different magnitudes and intensities as well as the resulting direct damage to structures and indirect costs of disruption. It is important in any BCA to understand the range of estimates and undertake sensitivity analysis to see how the mitigation measures perform under a wide range of estimates.

Capturing all the costs and benefits

There are considerable difficulties in specifying all the benefits and costs associated with specific alternatives. The principal issues are related to technological externalities (for example, if a building topples off its foundation after an earthquake, it could break a pipeline and cause a major fire which would damage other homes that were not affected by the earthquake in the first place) and second-order effects (for example, disruption of businesses and the life of the community as a result of damage to property from a disaster).

Distributional issues

Most BCA studies produce an aggregate net benefit number without providing different interested parties with information on how they are affected. By identifying the distribution of impacts across individuals and groups, each stakeholder can learn how they personally will fare if a particular option is chosen as well as the impact that such a choice will have on society as a whole. Furthermore, policy makers have a much clearer idea as to which groups are likely to support each option and who will be opposed to it. They can then make the trade-off between pushing for a policy which maximizes the net present value (NPV) of social benefits but may be difficult to implement due to distributional considerations and alternatives that are second-best using the social benefit criterion but are viewed as more desirable from a political vantage point because of distributional considerations.

Specification of values for non-quantitative attributes or goods

The contingent valuation methodology (CVM) is fraught with problems in trying to determine willingness to pay for certain goods.[10]

Dealing with the future

Normally BCA uses a constant discount rate over time but there have been arguments raised by economists and philosophers that for impacts that occur further in the future declining discount rates should be used to reflect the concern for future generations. Some philosophers have even argued that the social discount rate should be zero (that is, non-discounting), so that future events are given the same weight as current events.[11]

Process Issues Associated with Using BCA

BCA assumes that individuals behave rationally and maximize their expected utility. If individuals exhibit a set of biases and utilize simplified decision rules when dealing with specific choice situations, these need to be recognized in the analysis. In addition, one may want to consider attributes that have not traditionally been part of a BCA and recognize that certain trade-offs may be viewed by individuals as inappropriate.

Incorporating emotions into a BCA

As pointed out in section 2, affect and feelings appear to play a role in how people make decisions regarding protective measures. The importance of incorporating emotions into a BCA cannot be overemphasized. If people have concerns such as fear and dread in their perception of different alternatives, as Slovic (1987) and others have shown, then these attributes should be part of any BCA. By taking this step we will have gone a long way to understanding why past experience and future expectations are important ingredients in any comparison of alternatives.

Anderson (1993) makes the point that when it comes to issues associated with health, safety and the environment, simply providing compensation to individuals will not fully capture their concerns. People may have intrinsic attitudes toward their surrounding environment, such as awe and admiration of nature and/or beauty, which cannot be translated into monetary terms should the environment be despoiled. For many individuals facilities that pose health and safety risks raise significant moral objections that we cannot simply counteract with money. Calabresi and Bobbitt (1978) interpret this effort on the part of society to preserve the belief that life is 'special'.

Trading off money for health or safety

In many situations people feel that it is illegitimate to obtain money in return for an increased risk associated with one's health or safety. An example of this negative attitude toward compensation was observed when the federal government offered the Western Shoshone Tribe compensation to resolve a land dispute. In 1979, a court awarded the tribe $26 million as 'just compensation' for the federal government's seizure of deeded land in southern Nevada (including the Nevada Test Site and the proposed Yucca Mountain repository site). However, the tribe refused to accept the award on the grounds that they had an obligation to maintain their claim to the lands.

Tribal members have argued that the testing of nuclear weapons and the disposal of nuclear waste inflict irreparable harm upon their ancestral lands; from their standpoint, relinquishing the tribe's claims would constitute an abdication of their obligation to the land, the spirits that reside there and future generations. As such, the tribe has continued to refuse the compensation award, even though it would provide major economic benefits to tribal members (the award was placed in escrow and is now valued at approximately $60 million, or about half a million dollars for each member) (Easterling and Kunreuther, 1995). Opposing another site in California, one Native American said, 'For us to have this unnatural project in a natural land that is sacred to us just doesn't go. I'd rather have a nice drink of clean water than a pocket full of gold' (Baron, 1998).

5   SUGGESTIONS FOR FUTURE RESEARCH

There are a number of directions for future research to better understand how key interested parties deal with large-scale risks and to suggest ways for improving behaviour.

Understanding Uncertainty

There is a need to incorporate uncertainty into the analysis. Rather than just providing point estimates of the probability and potential losses from accidents, environmental risks and natural disasters, it would be useful to provide bounds or confidence intervals surrounding these values and then undertake sensitivity analyses as to how robust certain proposed strategies are. How can one better characterize the uncertainties in determining the probability of disasters of different magnitudes and the vulnerability of structures from these events? Are hazard- and loss-estimating modelling approaches sufficiently reliable and valid measures to guide the insurance underwriting decision process? What information does the insurance industry want to assess risks better, and how does the industry anticipate obtaining this information in the near future?

Encouraging Adoption of Cost-effective Mitigation Measures

How can one determine what are cost-effective mitigation measures? How does one evaluate the benefits (indirect/direct) from mitigation? Can we utilize past experience and engineering studies on building performance to evaluate the cost-effectiveness of mitigation with sufficient precision that they can be incorporated into building codes?

Individuals are often not interested in voluntarily adopting mitigation measures because they believe the disaster will not happen to them. Hence they need to be convinced through a package of economic incentives and requirements to adopt these measures. What types of economic incentives such as insurance premium reductions, lower deductibles, and/or higher limits of insurance coverage are likely to be attractive to policyholders to encourage them to adopt mitigation measures? What would be the most effective ways of providing subsidies to low-income families to encourage them to adopt cost-effective risk-mitgation measure (RMMs)?

When will it be necessary to require that individuals adopt specific RMMs and how can this be implemented? Today banks and financial institutions do not have in place standard procedures for issuing mitigation loans which are tied into their property. Furthermore, the competitive nature of the mortgage business does not encourage them to promote measures unless it is a financially attractive package. Hence one must understand more fully what incentives are needed for banks to require mitigation loans and insurance as a condition for a mortgage. When will insurers require mitigation as a condition for an insurance policy?

Future research also needs to look more closely at the role that well-enforced building codes could play in helping to reduce future losses. Given the limitations of individuals in collecting and processing information on risks coupled with technological externalities and second-order effects, there appears to be a need for well-enforced building codes to deal with losses from large-scale disasters. How can the construction industry be convinced that it is in their best interest to build safer houses even when a building inspector is not down their back? What empirical studies are necessary for determining the magnitude of the social costs and externalities that could be reduced through well-enforced building codes?

Towards a Broader Theory of BCA

There is a need for a broader theory of BCA to evaluate different alternatives. The elements of such a theory noted below should be more fully developed through future research and empirical analysis:

- Specify a broad and imaginative set of options including the status quo.
- Identify the different interested parties and their concerns. By understanding the goals and objectives of each of the parties, one can take into account both equity and distributional issues at the outset.

- Determine the attributes which are of concern to each of the interested parties. By using techniques such as value-tree analysis (see von Winterfeldt, 1987) one can see what factors are important to each of the stakeholders and how much weight they place on them. In this way one can contrast how different stakeholders view the world.

- Incorporate the decision processes of the key stakeholders into the analysis. This requires one to understand what information individuals collect on risk and the heuristics or rules of thumb they utilize as well as the types of process attributes that are of concern to them.

- Use an evaluation process that recognizes the limitations of contingent valuation approaches for determining WTP. For example certain trade-offs may be found to be unacceptable to certain parties and need to be considered as part of the process (cf. Shoshone tribe's refusal to accept compensation in exchange for a nuclear waste facility). The procedure proposed by Gregory *et al.* (1993) which utilizes multi-attribute utility theory and value trees should be examined as an alternative to CVM.

- Undertake sensitivity analysis to see how robust certain alternatives are to changes in the parameters as well as other factors (for example, process variables). One may be able to justify an alternative by showing that it is desirable over a wide range of these values.

ACKNOWLEDGEMENT

Partial support from NSF Grant # 524603 is gratefully acknowledged.

NOTES

1. The April 1998 issue of *Risk Analysis* is devoted to an analysis of the challenges of implementing section 112R of the Clean Air Act Amendments and its implications for behaviour by chemical firms affected by this regulation as well as the Environmental Protection Agency charged with enforcing this provision.
2. Although pollution from faulty facilities is normally not considered as a low-probability event (and may even be a certainty if the plant is poorly constructed), the potential consequences to many individuals may be quite severe but perceived by them to have a low probability of occurrence.
3. One could undertake a similar analysis of the trade-offs between the costs and benefits of mitigation if a person is risk averse by introducing a utility function into the picture as in the case of insurance. The qualitative results are identical to the risk-neutral case. For more details see Kunreuther, Onculer and Slovic (1998).
4. See Camerer and Kunreuther (1989) for more detailed descriptions of many of these features, with illustrative examples from consumer behaviour, firm and government decision making.
5. See Lowenstein *et al.* (1999) for a summary of the literature which shows that emotional reactions to risky situations often diverge from cognitive assessments of those risks.

6. The expected annual reduction in damage was specified in the following manner. The reduction in damage from preventing the house from toppling off its foundation is $20 000. The risk-mitigation measure (RMM) is assumed to reduce the annual probability of an earthquake causing the structure to topple off its foundation from 1/20 to 1/40. Hence the expected annual benefits of the RMM are approximately (1/20–1/40) $20 000 = $500.
7. These high discount rates are consistent with empirical findings on the reluctance of individuals to incur the high immediate cost of energy-efficient appliances in return for reduced electricity charges over time (Hausman, 1979; Kempton and Neiman, 1987).
8. This section draws heavily on Kunreuther and Roth Sr (1998), chapter 9.
9. These kinds of inspections are not routinely undertaken by banks today, even though it is in their interest to know as much about the risk as possible to protect their mortgages.
10. For a more detailed discussion of these issues see the special issue of *The Journal of Economic Perspectives* (Fall, 1994) devoted to contingent valuation.
11. See Boardman *et al.* (1996, chapter 5) for a discussion of the issues associated with selecting the social discount rate(s). For empirical evidence on declining social discount rates as the time horizon extends into the future in the context of savings lives today rather than in the future see Cropper, Aydede and Portney (1992).

REFERENCES

Ahlbrecht, Martin and Martin Weber (1997), 'An empirical study on intertemporal decision making under risk', *Management Science*, **43**, 813–26.
Anderson, Elizabeth (1993), *Value and Ethics in Economics*, Cambridge, MA: Harvard University Press.
Arrow, Kenneth (1971), *Essays in the Theory of Risk Bearing*, Chicago: Markham.
Baron, Jonathan (1998), *Judgment Misguided*, New York: Oxford University Press.
Boardman, Anthony *et al.* (1996), *Cost–Benefit Analysis: Concepts and Practice*, Upper Saddle River, NJ: Prentice Hall.
Boyd, James and Howard Kunreuther (1997), 'Retroactive liability or the public purse?', *Journal of Regulatory Economics*, **11**, 79–90.
Britton, Neil R. (1989), 'Community attitudes to natural hazard insurance: what are the salient facts?', in John Oliver and Neil R. Britton (eds), *Natural Hazards and Reinsurance: Proceedings of Sterling Offices College*, Lidcombe, NSW: Cumberland.
Burby, Ray (1992), *Sharing Environmental Risks*, Boulder, CO: Westview Press.
Burby, Ray (ed.) (1998), *Cooperating with Nature*, Washington, DC: Joseph Henry Press.
Calabresi, Guido and Philip Bobbitt (1978), *Tragic Choices*, New York: Norton.
Camerer, Colin and Howard Kunreuther (1989), 'Decision processes for low probability events: policy implications', *Journal of Policy Analysis and Management*, **8**, 565–92.
Cohen, Linda and Roger Noll (1981), 'The economics of building codes to resist seismic shocks', *Public Policy*, Winter, 1–29.
Combs, Barbara and Paul Slovic (1974), 'Causes of death: biased newspaper coverage and biased judgments', *Journalism Quarterly*, **56**, 837–43, 849.
Cropper, Maureen, Sema Aydede and Paul Portney (1992) 'Rates of time preference for saving lives', *American Economic Review: Papers and Proceedings* (May), 469–72.
Denes-Raj, Veronika and Seymour Epstein (1994), 'Conflict between intuitive and

rational processing: when people behave against their better judgment', *Journal of Personality and Social Psychology*, **5**, 819–29.

Easterling, Doug and Howard Kunreuther (1995), *The Dilemma of Siting a High-Level Nuclear Waste Repository*, Boston: Kluwer Academic Publishers.

Emerson, Bill, and Ted Stevens (1995), 'Natural disasters: A budget time bomb', *Washington Post*, 31 October, p. A13.

Finuciani, M.L., A. Alhakami, P. Slovic and S.M. Johnson (1998), 'The affect heuristic in judgments of risks and benefits', working paper, Decision Research.

Freeman, Myrick (1990), 'Water pollution policy', in Paul Portney (ed.), *Public Policies for Environmental Protection*, Washington, DC: Resources for the Future.

Gregory, Robin *et al.* (1993), 'Valuing environmental resources: a constructive approach', *Journal of Risk and Uncertainty*, **7**, 177–97.

Hausman, Jerry (1979), 'Individual discount rates and the purchase and utilization of energy-using durables', *Bell Journal of Economics*, **10**, 33–54.

Hogarth, R.M. and H. Kunreuther (1989), 'Risk, ambiguity and insurance', *Journal of Risk and Uncertainty*, **2**, 5–35.

Hogarth, R.M. and H. Kunreuther (1995), 'Decision making under ignorance: arguing with yourself', *Journal of Risk and Uncertainty*, **10**, 15–36.

Hsee, Christopher and H. Kunreuther (2000), 'The affection effect in insurance decisions', *Journal of Risk and Uncertainty*, **20** (2), 141–160.

Insurance Institute for Property Loss Reduction (1995), 'Homes and hurricanes: public opinion concerning various issues relating to home builders, building codes and damage mitigation', Boston, MA: IIPLR.

Insurance Services Office (1999), 'Financing catastrophe risk: capital market solutions', New York, NY: Insurance Services Office.

Kahneman, Daniel and Amos Tversky (1979), 'Prospect theory: an analysis of decision under risk', *Econometrica*, **47**, 263–91.

Kahneman, Daniel, Paul Slovic and Amos Tversky (1982), *Judgment Under Uncertainty: Heuristics and Biases*, New York: Cambridge University Press.

Kahneman, Daniel, Peter Wakker and Rakesh Sarin (1997), 'Back to Bentham: explorations of experienced utility', *Quarterly Journal of Economics*, May, 304–77.

Kempton, Willett and Max Neiman (eds) (1987), *Energy Efficiency: Perspectives on Individual Behavior*, Washington, DC: American Council for an Energy Efficient Economy.

Kleindorfer, Paul, Howard Kunreuther and Paul Schoemaker (1993), *Decision Sciences: An Integrative Perspective*, New York: Cambridge University Press.

Kunreuther, Howard (1996), 'Mitigating disaster losses through insurance', *Journal of Risk and Uncertainty*, **12**, 171–87.

Kunreuther, Howard and Richard Roth Sr (eds) (1998), *Paying the Price: The Status and Role of Insurance Against Natural Disasters in the United States*, Washington, DC: Joseph Henry Press.

Kunreuther, Howard, Ayse Onculer and Paul Slovic (1998), 'Time insensitivity for protective measures', *Journal of Risk and Uncertainty*, **16**, 279–99.

Kunreuther, Howard *et al.* (1978), *Disaster Insurance Protection*, New York: Wiley.

Levenson, Leo (1998), 'Residential water heater damage and fires following the Loma Prieta and Big Bear Lake earthquakes', *Earthquake Spectra*, **8**, 595–604.

Lewis, Christopher and Lewis Murdock (1996), 'The role of government contracts in discretionary reinsurance markets for natural disasters', *Journal of Risk and Insurance*, **63**, 567–97.

Litan, Robert, Frederick Krimgold, Karen Clark and Jayant Khadilkar (1992), *Physical Damage and Human Loss: The Economic Impact of Earthquake Mitigation Measures*, New York: Insurance Information Institute Press.

Loewenstein, George and Drazen Prelec (1992), 'Anomalies in intertemporal choice', *Quarterly Journal of Economics*, **107**, 573–97.

Loewenstein, G.F., E.U. Weber, C.K. Hsee and E.S. Welch (1998), 'Risk as feelings', Working paper.

May, Peter and Nancy Stark (1992), 'Design professions and earthquake policy', *Earthquake Spectra*, **8**, 115–32.

Palm, Risa (1995), *Earthquake Insurance: A Longitudinal Study of California Homeowners*, Boulder, CO: Westview Press.

Palm, Risa, Michael Hodgson, R. Denise Blanchard and Donald Lyons (1990), *Earthquake Insurance in California: Environmental Policy and Individual Decision Making*, Boulder, CO: Westview Press.

Science (1990), 'Counting on Science at EPA', 10 August, pp. 9–11.

Slovic, Paul (1987), 'Perception of Risk', *Science*, **236**, 280–85.

Slovic, Paul, Baruch Fischhoff and Sarah Lichtenstein (1978), 'Accident probabilities in seat belt usage: a psychological perspective', *Accident Analysis and Prevention*, **10**, 281–5.

Slovic, Paul, John Monahan and Donald MacGregor (1999), 'Violence risk assessment and risk communication: the effects of using actual cases, providing instruction and employing probability vs. frequency formats', working paper, Decision Research.

Thaler, Richard (1991), *Quasi-Rational Economics*, New York: Russell Sage.

Thaler, Richard (1992), *The Winner's Curse*, Princeton, NJ: Princeton University Press.

Tversky, Amos and Daniel Kahneman (1973), 'Availability: a heuristic for judging frequency and probability', *Cognitive Psychology*, **5**, 207–32.

Tversky, Amos and Derek Koehler (1994), 'Support theory: a nonextensional representation of subjective probability', *Psychological Review*, **101**, 547–67.

Tversky, Amos, Samuel Sattath and Paul Slovic (1988), 'Contingent weighting in judgment and choice', *Psychological Review*, **95**, 371–84.

US Congress (1995), *Federal Disaster Assistance. Report of the Senate Task Force on Funding Disaster Relief*, Washington, DC: US Government Printing Office.

von Winterfeldt, Detlof (1987), 'Value tree analysis', in Paul Kleindorfer and Howard Kunreuther (eds), *Insuring and Regulating Hazardous Materials: From Seveso to Bhopal*, Berlin, Springer-Verlag.

13. Resilience and sustainability

Charles Perrings

1 SUSTAINABLE DEVELOPMENT

At its most general, development may be thought of as the evolution of an economic system and the environment by which it is supported. Many of the most significant advances in the economic analysis of the process stem from the realization that the economy and its environment are jointly determined, and that the dynamics of the joint system are highly sensitive to the size and rate of growth of the economy relative to its environment. Development implies a process of evolutionary change: a process that has all the dynamical properties of complex systems. It is characterized by path dependence, sensitivity to initial conditions, non-linearities and discontinuous change around threshold values for both environmental resources and ecological functions. For any economy there are many possible states: that is, there are many equilibria. The sustainability of any particular state (or any particular development path) depends on the properties of the stability domain corresponding to that state.

The economic literature on the concept and implementation of sustainability includes two main approaches. The first is associated with the welfarist tradition in philosophy. It assumes that the appropriate way to represent human preferences for future consumption is through the intertemporal welfare function, and the appropriate way to discuss sustainability is via the optimal consumption path for a given intertemporal welfare function (Dasgupta, 1995; Dasgupta and Mäler, 1995). These authors admit that sustainability concepts may have a role in identifying consumption paths that might satisfy the Koopmans axioms but be ethically indefensible. However, they otherwise reject most research on the problem.

The welfarist approach implicitly denies that preferences for sustainability may be reflected in preferences over the 'rules of the game'. Instead it identifies intertemporal preference structures that yield, through present value optimization, sustainable consumption paths. Chichilnisky argues that qualifying intertemporal welfare functions are those in which neither the present nor the future plays a dictatorial role in the choices made by society

(Chichilnisky, 1996, 1997; but see Asheim, 1996). The Chichilnisky criterion replaces the discounted integral of utilities with a maximand involving two terms: one reflecting a discounted stream of utilities and the other reflecting the limiting behaviour of utility (the sustainable utility level). The key feature of the criterion is that it requires that alternative consumption paths be ranked both by reference to the present value of a utility stream, and by reference to the capacity of the system to deliver benefits in the very long run (Heal, 1998).

Implicitly, the Chichilnisky criterion supposes that discount rates are non-constant. The notion that preferences may be time varying is also implicit in recent work on the endogeneity of preferences, and is at least consistent with the empirical evidence offered in support of the so-called environmental Kuznets curve (EKC) (Grossman and Krueger, 1993, 1995; Seldon and Song, 1994; Shafik, 1994; Panayotou, 1995, 1997; Rayner and Bates, 1997; Antle and Heidebrink, 1995). If preferences are not independent of the state of nature, they may be expected to evolve with development. Perrings (1989) proposed that rates of time preference vary with the level of real income, and showed that people in subjective poverty who chose to dissave in order to maintain real consumption levels implicitly discount at very high levels. Recent empirical studies of the links between rates of time preference, income and wealth, and investment in conservation technology confirm this. Pender and Walker (1990) and Pender (1996) in studies in rural India found rates of time preference to be inversely related to wealth. Holden, Shiferaw and Wik (1998) investigated the relation between rates of time preference, poverty and conservation in Indonesia, Zambia and Ethiopia. They found that rates of time preference amongst rural households are generally high, and increase with poverty in both assets and income. They concluded that poverty is a disincentive to invest in environmental protection. Following the work of Tversky and Kahneman (1991), the relevance of reference-dependent preferences for the economics of the environment has been examined both theoretically and experimentally by Munro and Sugden (1997) and Bateman *et al.* (1998).

The second broad approach to the problem is concerned with the identification of constraints that are sufficient for sustainability. This approach is argued by Pezzey (1997) to be loosely associated with the 'resourcist' tradition in philosophy. It seeks the set of rights and obligations that will support the sustainable use of resources. For example, Howarth (1997) appeals to Kantian moral rules to justify adoption of a 'strong sustainability' constraint. In utility terms, Pezzey (1997) classifies such work according to the following criteria according to whether it yields utility levels that are:

- non-declining over time ($dU/dt > 0$ always);

- not exceeding the maximum constant level of utility ($du/dt \leq U_t^m$ always);
- not below some prescribed minimum ($dU/dt \geq U^s$ always).

He defines these as, respectively, sustained, sustainable and survivable development. In physical terms, the work includes the strong sustainability constraints associated with Turner and Pearce (1993) and supported by Howarth.

The most widely explored sustainability constraints, however, are those associated with the investment rule identified by Hartwick (1977, 1978) to satisfy the 'Rawlsian' maximin of utility sustainability criterion proposed by Solow (1974). The rule – that net investment in the sense of Dixit, Hammond and Hoel (1980) is non-negative – has been adapted to take account of international trade effects (Asheim, 1996; Hartwick, 1995) and capital gains (Peskin, 1989; Mäler, 1991; Vincent, Panayotou and Hartwick, 1997), but the general sense remains. A necessary condition for consumption to be sustainable over time is that investment should be maintained at a level that at least compensates for the depreciation of assets, including natural assets. Most empirical studies of investment relative to the Solow criterion have focused on depletion issues where there is a ready analogue to the depreciation of produced capital (Repetto *et al.*, 1991; van Tongeren *et al.*, 1993; Pearce and Atkinson, 1993; Vincent, 1997).

This chapter discusses advances in understanding the sustainability of development against this background. It focuses on advances that stem from the application of the ecological concept of system resilience in environmental economics. It happens that scale effects, discontinuities and ecosystem resilience have also driven some of the most important developments in the field of ecological economics (Costanza, Perrings and Cleveland, 1997; Turner, Perrings and Folke, 1997). The chapter accordingly crosses these fields. Its aim is to construct a way of thinking about the problem that helps to identify fruitful areas for further work in the field.

2   THE EMPIRICAL EVIDENCE

The empirical evidence on the relation between per capita income (as a proxy for development) and indicators of environmental quality (as a proxy for environmental sustainability) is summarized in the literature on the EKC (Barbier, 1997). This literature has identified an inverted U-shaped relation between income and a range of environmental indicators including emissions of sulphur dioxide (Grossman and Krueger, 1993, 1995; Seldon and Song, 1994; Shafik, 1994; Panayotou, 1995, 1997), particulates and dark matter

(Grossman and Krueger, 1993), nitrogen oxides and carbon monoxide (Seldon and Song, 1994) and carbon dioxide and CFCs (Cole, Rayner and Bates, 1997). Grossman and Krueger (1995) have also found a Kuznets relation involving various indicators of water quality, including faecal coliform, biological and chemical oxygen demand and arsenic. Panayotou (1995) and Antle and Heidebrink (1995) have found the same general relation between deforestation rates and per capita income, while Coles, Rayner and Bates (1997) have extended it to include energy use and traffic volumes. The evidence does not all run in the same direction. Volumes of municipal waste have been found to be a strictly increasing function of per capita income (Shafik, 1994; Coles, Rayner and Bates, 1997) and there are conflicting results on solid particulates (Grossman and Krueger, 1995) and carbon dioxide (Shafik, 1994). Nevertheless, the broad direction of the evidence to date favours the EKC.

Four main explanations for the EKC have been offered in the literature. Two focus on change in the sectoral composition of economies (Panayotou, 1997) and technology (de Bruyn, 1997). A third focuses on the link between income and the demand for environmental quality (McConnell, 1997). A fourth identifies it as evidence of the effect of environmental constraints to growth (Arrow *et al.*, 1995; Dasgupta, 1996). This last argues that what matters is not the absolute level of per capita emissions or depletion, but aggregate emissions or depletion relative to the assimilative or carrying capacity of the environment. Where environmental constraints are not binding there is little incentive to reduce emissions or the depletion of environmental resources. At low levels of income the scale of the economy relative to its environment may be small, and the environmental impacts of consumption may lie within the assimilative or carrying capacity of the environment. But as incomes rise the scale of the economy relative to its environment will also tend to rise, and assimilative or carrying-capacity constraints may become binding. In this case, if pollution and other forms of environmental deterioration are not 'delinked' from consumption, then consumption growth will be constrained by the environment's limited capacity to absorb the effects of consumption.

The connection with the concept of resilience is the following. Economic growth inevitably has environmental consequences. Whether those consequences are sustainable depends on whether they threaten the resilience of the ecological systems on which economic activities depend. As a first approximation, this may be measured by an index of the level of pollution or depletion relative to the assimilative or carrying capacity of the ecological system concerned. This indicates whether a system is operating near the limits imposed by its environment. There is at least the potential for collapse if further stress or shocks to the system may induce an irreversible change, as is the case with biodiversity loss, soil erosion, depletion of some aquifers or desertification. This reflects the notion that the sustainability of activities that stress ecological systems depends on some measure of the capacity of those systems to absorb stress and shocks. The literature yields many candidate measures for this property including stability, persistence, resistence, non-vulnerability, stochastic return time and resilience (Tinch, 1998). The property that most closely connects with the idea of sustainability as conservation of opportunity is resilience.

3   RESILIENCE AND SUSTAINABILITY

Stress is generally measured by the level of demand on the carrying or assimilative capacities of the system. An increase in stress makes the system more susceptible to exogenous shocks or changes in environmental conditions. One measure of resilience is the magnitude of disturbance that can be absorbed before a system flips from one state to another (Holling, 1973).[1] It is an index of the capacity of a system to retain productivity following disturbance. Specifically, if the dynamics of some renewable resource, $x(t)$, are denoted by $dx/dt = f(x(t))$, $f:X{\rightarrow}X$, where X is the state space of the system and $f(\bullet)$ is the growth function for $x(t)$. If x^* is an equilibrium of this equation, it is stable if all solutions close to x^* remain close, and is asymptotically stable if all solutions close to x^* tend to x^*. If $X'' \subset X$ is the closed bounded subset of X that contains all such points, $x(t)$, in the basin of x^*, such that $|x(t) - x^*| < \psi$ for all t, a Holling measure of the resilience of $x(t)$ is the maximum perturbation that can be sustained without causing the system to leave the ψ neighbourhood of x^* (Dalmazzone and Perrings, 1997).

For example, in ecology and ecotoxicology assimilative capacity refers either to an ecosystem's ability to return to the original equilibrium following some pollution event, or the capacity of an ecosystem to absorb pollution without degrading some notion of biological integrity (Westman, 1985). One refers to limits of the ecosystem's capacity to cleanse itself of waste materials. The other refers to the quantity of waste that can be absorbed before triggering different levels of response. It reflects the view that there are three response 'zones':

- where no adverse effects are noted and where a change in concentration is not accompanied by a change in response;
- where a change in concentration is accompanied by a change in response, usually increasing with increasing concentration; and
- where the system has 'peaked out' and changes in concentration produce no changes in response.

Assimilative capacity in this sense is equivalent to critical load. It is the waste burden that can be absorbed before provoking a defined response. This is how the term has frequently been used in environmental economics. The gap between current and critical loads is equivalent to a measure of resilience if the defined response involves the probability of a fundamental change of state/productive potential.

It has subsequently been argued that this measure, and the concept behind it, offers a useful way to address the sustainability not just of ecological systems, but of jointly determined ecological economic systems as well (Common and Perrings, 1992; Perrings, 1998; Levin *et al.*, 1998). Indeed, the approach has implications for the way we think about the dynamics of any stochastic, evolutionary system. Levin *et al.* (1998) argue that sustainability as a concept is more pertinent in stochastic systems away from equilibrium than in deterministic systems at equilibrium. Like Common and Perrings (1992) they equate it with the capacity of the system to function over a range of environmental conditions without losing its self-organization. A reduction in resilience implies a narrowing of the range of environmental conditions over which a system can function. The approach changes how the environmental effects of economic development are modelled and analysed in two different ways. First it affects the treatment of density dependence. Second it affects the treatment of risk.

Density dependence, hysteresis and field effects

Most biological growth functions assume density dependence – the fact that the rate of growth of the stock depends on its size. This has been reflected in bioeconomic models used in resource economics for more than three decades (Clark, 1990) and has begun to be reflected in models of 'stock' pollution (Pethig, 1994). However, most density-dependent bioeconomic models assume the global stability of the stock. The maximum carrying or assimilative capacity in Lotka–Volterra models, for example, is a stable equilibrium. The problem identified by Arrow *et al.* (1995), however, is that increasing levels of pressure on environmental resources are often more likely to induce a system 'collapse' or transition to a state characterized by lower levels of productivity than to bring about an automatic error correction.

Aoki (1995, 1996) has identified effects in preference formation in economic systems that involve a very particular form of density dependence. Field effects, such as speculative bubbles, imply that people's beliefs or expectations are sensitive to the proportion of the population sharing those same beliefs or expectations. He argues that beliefs are conditioned by the level of uncertainty about alternative states, and that they affect the transition rates between states. Field effects are important precisely because they lead to the concentration of activities, expectations or beliefs that may lock the system into a particular technology or set of preferences (Perrings, 1998). While this makes the system more stable in the sense that there is less variation in behaviour, it also makes it more sensitive to shocks. This is analogous to the point made by Holling (1986) that as terrestrial ecosystems approach the climax state (carrying capacity) they become more 'brittle'. The system becomes more not less sensitive to the exogenous shocks – it becomes what he describes as 'an accident waiting to happen'.

Technological lock-in and social customs are both examples of field effects that tend to retard change, but make the system more brittle. Customs codified into law or reinforced by institutions can, for example, prevent societies from containing even quite small shocks. While the environmental effects of institutional rigidities have been exhaustively studied by environmental economists, little has been done on field effects of the Aoki type (although recent examples such as the BSE scares in Britain have provided an incentive to do the work). I suspect that this is largely due to the fact that environmental economists, like other economists, are also locked into the standard assumptions about the exogeneity of preferences, technology and environmental conditions.

An application that includes both density dependence (in a biological sense) and field effects in expectations is provided in new work in epidemiological economics. Myers (1997) has recently suggested that one of the principal effects of environmental degradation in low-income countries is an increase in the migration of people from one area to another. He refers to the phenomenon of 'environmental refugees'. There are many implications of an increase in rates of rural–rural and rural–urban migration, and one is the spread of infectious disease. Building on standard economic growth models and the epidemiological models of Anderson and May (1982), Delfino and Simmons (2000) model the dynamics of tuberculosis where economic growth changes the risk of contracting the disease.

The propensity of a system to flip from one equilibrium or persistent state to another is associated with a common property of non-linear dynamical systems – hysteresis. Hysteresis in the state dynamics implies that a system that flips from one state to another at some value of the control may require a very different value of the control to return it to the original state. A related set of papers at the frontiers of environmental, resource and development economics alike builds on work by limnologists on shallow lakes that may exist in either dystrophic or eutrophic states (Carpenter and Cottingham, 1997; Carpenter and Pace, 1997). Carpenter, Ludwig and Brock (1999) and Mäler, Xepapadeas and de Zeeuw (2000) model the optimal management of dynamical shallow lake systems involving multiple attracting states for certain values of both parameters and controls.[2]

They also consider the regulatory implications of the propensity of this model to flip between equilibria, and to become trapped by hysteresis. Because shallow lakes can flip suddenly from one state to another as a result of pollution run-off 'events', it is difficult for any regulatory agency to observe the signals of an impending change in time to take action to avert it. In a managed system, the dynamics of the resource are revealed through the response of the state variables to the controls. The closer the system is brought to the boundaries of the stability domain, the higher is the risk of an unanticipated irreversible or only slowly reversible change as the system flips from a higher-productivity state to a lower-productivity state. The same phenomenon makes it difficult to devise a decentralized regulatory system involving taxes or charges. Once the system has flipped to an undesirable state, taxes or user fees would have to be such as to drive run-off well below the original levels and to hold them there in order to overcome the hysteresis effect.

The implications for regulation and management of hysteresis effects of this sort have yet to be explored, but there is reason to believe that they are both widespread and have significant welfare effects. The shallow lake example is a metaphor for a much more general set of problems associated with the degradation of ecological systems. Systems ranging from coral reefs to semi-arid savannas have been observed to behave in very similar ways. From a regulatory perspective the problem is precisely that bifurcation points may not been seen before they are reached. The observable level of environmental quality does not generally offer a reliable indicator of the system's relative position with respect to thresholds. Moreover, the conditions under which ecosystems respond to increasing stress without suffering an irreversible or near irreversible loss appear to be fairly restrictive.

In practice, environmental policy in cases of this sort is focused on the identification of bounds on allowable activities. In many cases these are fixed by reference to criteria such as health and safety, critical loads, assimilative and carrying capacity and so on. Indeed, the establishment of bounds on economic activity is the way in which the natural sciences generally inform environmental policy. Such bounds have been argued to protect the boundaries between observed and unobserved states of nature (Dalmazzone and Perrings, 1997). An alternative approach is beginning to be seen in the theory of managing cyclic dynamical systems. Holling (1986) describes ecosystem behaviour in terms of the sequential interaction between four system functions: exploitation or colonization of disturbed ecosystems; conservation as biomass accumulates; creative destruction where an abrupt change caused by external disturbance releases energy and material that have accumulated during the conservation phase; and reorganization where released materials are mobilized to become available for the next exploitative phase. Resilience is measured by the effectiveness of the last two system functions. It is crucial to the ability of the system to satisfy 'predatory' demands for ecological services over time, and to cope with both sustained stress and shock.

This sequence of processes has been interpreted by Batabayal (1998a, b) as a renewal cycle. The important feature of the cycle is that it is driven by shocks or events. Batabayal considers the case where the shocks to an ecological system are a function of its management. Pulse fishing or clear-cut felling are the most obvious examples, but any resource management regime that involves discrete actions may be considered to involve shocks to the system. Since shocks can induce the last two phases of the Holling four-box cycle, they can determine the length of that cycle. Fire-managed systems are a good example. The dynamics of fire-driven systems, whether grasslands or forests, depend on the impact of fire. This in turn depends on the fuel load. If fire is suppressed despite the build-up of fuel load it can, when it does occur, trigger a fundamental change in state. The management of fire regimes is very much the management of the length of a Holling cycle. Batabayal (1998b) applies the renewal reward cycle to this problem to identify the optimal length of an economic use cycle in terms of the frequency of managed events, the marginal cost of those events and the costs of 'closing' the cycle.

Resilience, diversity and risk
The link between the resilience of systems and the probability of their collapse or change of state is reflected in the literature on the analysis and management of environmental risk. Although deterministic bioeconomic models for the optimal utilization of natural resources generate sustainable (steady-state) solutions, they necessarily ignore inherent or environmental stochasticity in the modelled relationships, and in trophic or competitive interactions. Randomness has been incorporated into such models via assumptions of stochasticity in model parameters (Ludwig, Walker and Holling, 1997), density-dependent risk of collapse (Reed, 1988; Tsur and Zemel, 1994; Tinch, 1998) or as random catastrophe. Density-dependent risk of collapse includes both the existence of a density-dependent hazard function (Reed, 1979, 1988) or thresholds which, if reached, trigger the immediate collapse of the stock (Tsur and Zemmel, 1994, 1997). A density-dependent threshold implies that increasing stress on the system raises the probability that it will flip from one state to another, and so corresponds well with a measure of resilience in the sense of Holling. The implications of this for the optimal management of natural resource stocks have been considered by Tinch (1998), but the implications for the management of susceptible systems have not.

The link between resilience, diversity and risk reflects the fact that in many cases, the link between stress and the loss of resilience in managed systems is a change in the mix of species in the system (Perrings *et al.*, 1995; Perrings, 1995). This link has been closely studied in ecology against the backdrop of a long-standing dispute about the relation between the complexity of ecological systems, their diversity and their stability (May, 1973; Elton, 1975), and an alternative proposition that diversity supports not stability, but resilience (Holling, 1973, 1986) and ecosystem functioning (Vitousek and Hooper, 1993; McNaughton, 1993). Experimental research of grasslands has now shown that ecosystem productivity increases significantly with plant biodiversity (Tilman, Wedin and Knops, 1996). This is because the main limiting nutrient, oil mineral nitrogen, is utilized more effectively the greater the diversity of species. These results have led to the proposition that the sustainability of soil nutrient cycles and so of soil fertility increases with biodiversity.

More generally, the resilience of any ecosystem with respect to variation in environmental conditions depends upon the existence of species capable of supporting the key ecological functions as conditions vary. Deletion of a species important under some conditions will have little effect on ecosystem functioning if there are other species capable of stepping in as substitutes. If there are no substitutes, however, the deletion of some species can trigger a fundamental change from one ecosystem type to another – from forest to grassland, or grassland to a shrubby semi-desert, for example (Westoby, Walker and Noy Meir, 1989). The importance of the mix or diversity of species for the resilience of ecosystems lies in the fact that species which are 'redundant' in one set of environmental conditions may be critically important in other environmental conditions. Resilience has been shown to depend on the functional diversity of species supporting critical structuring processes (Holling *et al.*, 1995).

The significance of this for resource-based development is that agroecosystems – ecological systems whose species mix is transformed for the purpose of agriculture – may be especially sensitive to species deletion precisely because they are already simplified by the exclusion of competitor or predator species (Conway and Barbier, 1990; Conway, 1993). The specilization gains from simplification of agroecoystems typically involve a reduction in the resilience of the system. The costs of a reduction in resilience include, for example, the cost of the herbicides, pesticides, fertilizers, irrigation and other inputs needed to maintain output in the simplified system. They include the cost of relief where output fails, relocation where soils or water resources have been irreversibly damaged, rehabilitation where damage is reversible and insurance against crop damage by pest or disease. If the system loses resilience and flips from one state to another, they include forgone output under the new state.

Perrings and Walker (1995, 1997) have modelled the dynamics of stochastic fire-driven rangelands as a function of the mix of broad classes of species, and find them to be more sensitive to price fluctuations the less 'diverse' the systems. But, although agricultural and resource economists routinely evaluate changes in productivity induced by changes in management regime, there have as yet been few attempts to estimate the loss of resilience in real agroecosystems. Perrings and Stern (1998) estimate the resilience of semi-arid rangelands as a stochastic trend using an approach developed to model the impact of technological progress (Slade, 1989; Harvey and Marshall, 1991).

Taking the case of Botswana they estimate changes in the latent productivity of the range, subject to both natural disturbances (rainfall deficits) and economic shocks (affecting offtake prices and the cost of livestock holdings). They find that if the system is not resilient, the use of either price- or cost-based incentives can induce a switch from one equilibrium state to another. If the system is resilient, the implications of the difference in impulse responses is that intervention in herd maintenance costs is likely to be more effective than intervention in offtake prices.

4   MODELLING RESILIENCE

The literature discussed in this chapter supports the notion that sustainability requires constraints on the current allocation of resources – that it requires specification of the 'rules of the game'. But this simply reflects the fact that intertemporal preferences are not formed in a vacuum. They are context dependent. Preferences are formed alongside the rules that constrain them. This section considers how resilience, institutional conditions or the 'rules of the game' and sustainability may be formally integrated.

Let the time behaviour of the system be described by some recursive function involving a finite number of resources denoted by $X_t = (x_{1t}, \ldots, x_{nt})$, and let I be the state space, $i \in I$ defining a state within I – the state of nature. Decision makers are assumed to allocate resources through actions, $a \in A$, where A is a subset of I. These actions describe the consumption and production activities of economic agents. They affect the probability attaching to each state of nature. That is, we can identify a probability transition matrix, $P(a)$, whose elements give the transition probability between states as a function of the consumption and production activities of decision makers. These activities are, in turn, determined by behavioural rules that translate observations on the state of nature into purposive action. A familiar example of such a behavioural rule is profit maximization. Given observations on the relative scarcity of resources via the price system, application of this rule determines the optimal combination of inputs in production. Such behavioural rules are referred to as 'policies', and are denoted u_t. The state space model of this system is then defined by

$$X_t = F(X_{t-1}, u_t)$$

Policies of this sort may be stationary or non-stationary. If a policy is stationary, the behavioural rule is insensitive to the state of the system. That is, u_t: $I \to A$, and the process $(X_t)_{t \geq 0}$ will be Markov with transition probabilities $p_{ij}{}^u = p_{ij}(u(i))$. If a policy is non-stationary, the behavioural rule will be sensitive to the state of the system: u_t: $I^{t+1} \to A$, $t = 0,1,2,\ldots$ In both cases the policy determines the probability law(s) for the process $(X_t)_{t \geq 0}$. We may express the probability law associated with policy u in the form

$$P^u(X_{t+1} = i_{t+1} \mid X_0 = i_0, \ldots, X_t = i_t) = p_{i_t, i_{t+1}}(u_t(i_0, \ldots, i_t)).$$

where $P^u(\cdot)$ is the probability law associated with the policy, and $u_t(i_0, \ldots, i_t)$ is the policy.

There are in fact several reasons why it may not be unreasonable to think about policies as stationary processes. The most important of these is that policies are to a large extent determined by the institutional conditions – the 'rules of the game' – within which they are made. That is, institutional conditions determine the logic of optimizing behaviour in a way that makes the decision maker's behaviour fully predictable once the institutional conditions are given. The logic of open access, for example, ensures that decision makers will choose to use resources up to the point where total revenue and costs are equal, and so on. The implication of this is that for given institutions we can identify the long-term probabilistic evolution of the system. This does not stop us from thinking about the effects of changes in institutions or rules. Indeed, it offers a very natural and structured way of doing this. A change in institutions induces a change in policies and hence the probability laws of the system.

For present purposes I take the policy to be to maximize a measure of discounted net benefit. That is, associated with some policy in state i, $u_t(i)$, there is a discounted net benefit, $v(i, u_t(i)) = v_i(u_t(i))$. Specifically, the expected discounted net benefits from the policy is

$$V^u(i) = E^u \sum_{t=0}^{\infty} v(x_t, u_t(x_0, \ldots, x_t))$$

The value function for $\{u_t\}$ starting from state i is $V^*(i) = \max_u V^u(i)$. At time $t + 1$

$$V_{t+1}(i) = \max_u \{v(i, u_t(i)) + \sum_{j \in I} P_{-ij}(u_t(i)) v_t(j)\}$$

Now if v_i and p_{ij} are continuous for all i and j, the set $\{u_t(i): v_i(u_t(i)) \leq \upsilon\}$ is compact for all i, t, and $\upsilon < \infty$; and $p_{ij}(u_t(i)) = 0$ for each i, for most j, and for all $u \in O_u$, where O_u is the control set, then it can be shown that $V_\infty(i) = V^*(i)$.

The advantage of thinking about the development or evolution of an economy–environment system in this way is that it makes it easy to identify the resilience of the system in a given state. The ways in which decision makers can influence the process $(X_t)_{t \geq 0}$ depends on the structure of the system. If the time path for the state variables, x_t, given u_t, is

$$x_t = f_t(x_0, u_1, \ldots, u_t)$$

then the set of all states in I that are reachable from x_0 at time t by the control is defined by

$$A^t(x_0) = \{f_t(x_0, u_1, \ldots, u_t) : u_k \in O_u, 1 \leq k \leq t)$$

and the set of all states reachable at any time in the future is $A^\infty(x_0)$.

The controlled process $\{X_t\}_{0 \leq t \leq T}$ is Markov (λ, P) if and only if for all $i \in I$

$$P^u(X_0 = i_0, X_i = i_i, \ldots, X_t = i_T) = \lambda_{i0} p_{i0i1} p_{i1i2} \cdots p_{iT-1iT}$$

and

$$P_i^u(X_t = j) = P^u(X_{t+k} = j \mid X_k = i) = p_{ij}^{(t)}$$

where $P_i^u(X_t = j)$ is the conditional probability that $X_t = j$ given that it is initially in state i. In other words, the process is Markov (a) if X_0 has distribution λ_{i0}, and (b) if for time $t \geq 0$, given $X_t = i$, the distribution of X_{t+1} is independent of $X_0, \ldots, X_{t-1}$. That is, the current state of the system fully reflects its history, and its future evolution depends only on the current state together with the set of transition probabilities, $p_{ij}^{(t)}$. The transition probability, $p_{ij}^{(t)}$, is the conditional probability that the system will be in state j at time t given that it is initially in state i. That is, it is the t-step transition probability from state i to state j. This turns out to be sensitive to the structure of the matrix of transition probabilities, P. To see this, let π_{it} be the probability that the system will be in state i at time t. The probability that it is in any one of n possible states at that time may then be summarized by the vector π_t. Since the transition probabilities conditional on the state of the system at time t are given by P^t, π_t evolves according to the recursive relation, $\pi_t = \pi_0 P^t$. That is, it reflects the structure of the tth power of the matrix of transition probabilities.

It is useful to distinguish between transient and recurrent states. States that are revisited are said to be recurrent. More particularly, a state, i, is said to be recurrent if $P_i^u(X_t = i$ for infinitely many $t) = 1$, and is said to be transient if $P_i^u(X_t = i$ for infinitely many $t) = 0$. Recurrent states are either occupied permanently or revisited periodically, transient states are left after some finite time and never revisited thereafter. It is quite natural to associate recurrent states with the long-term equilibria of a system, and transient states with far-from-equilibrium positions. Transient states correspond to zero entries in P^t as $t \to \infty$.

To relate this to the concept of resilience, recall that the term was used by Holling (1973) to denote the capacity of a system to remain in some state in the face of external shocks. It is frequently measured by the size of the disturbance the system can absorb before flipping from one stability domain to another. Now the transition probabilities just described define the probability that a system in one state, and subject to some disturbance regime, will change to another state. This is exactly what the Holling measure requires. However, this measure is much more general than the Holling measure. It defines the transition probability from one state to another state whether or not that other state lies in a different stability domain. In the special case where P is both irreducible and aperiodic the system will have a unique globally stable equilibrium – it has only one stability domain. Suppose that the system is associated with an invariant distribution, π, then if λ is any other distribution and $(X_t)_{t \geq 0}$ is Markov (λ, P):[3] $p_{ij}^{(t)} \to \pi_j$ as $t \to \infty$ for all i and j. That is, the probability that the system is in any state converges to that distribution. In the case where P is irreducible, the transition probabilities of the system may be said to be equivalent to Holling-resilience measures.

In the more general case where P is reducible, the state space may be partitioned into classes or groups of communicating states. Classes of states are those in which each state may be reached from every other state in the same class. In other words, if P is reducible the system has multiple equilibria. Take the simple case where the state space may be partitioned into two disjoint sets only: A and $\tilde{A}$. $\tilde{A}$ is the complement of A in I, and corresponds to an isolated block on the principal diagonal of the probability transition matrix written in normal form. That is, it is possible for the system to move from a state in A to a state in $\tilde{A}$, but not vice versa. We assume that the two sets of states are not equally desirable, and that we can define the following value functions: $\{V_i: i \in A\}$ and $\{W_i: i \in \tilde{A}\}$. The expected net benefits of the control policy that determines the probability law for this system is then

$$Z_i^u = E^u\left[\sum_{t < \tau} v(x_t, u_t(x_0, \ldots, x_t)) + w(x_\tau)I_{\tau < \infty}\right]$$

in which τ is the expected time before the system reaches a state in $\tilde{A}$. It is referred to as the 'hitting time' of $\tilde{A}$. Because absorption into $\tilde{A}$ is irreversible, the consequences of reaching $\tilde{A}$ can be summarized by its value at the boundary. This makes $\tilde{A}$ analogous to a terminal state.

We can now identify two measures of Holling resilience. The first is the conditional probability that the system will be in state $j \in \tilde{A}$ at time t given that it is initially in state $i \in A$: the t-step transition probability from a state in one stability domain to a state in another stability domain, $p_{ij}^{(t)}$. This measure is defined for a given time, t. The second is the 'hitting time' just referred to. More particularly, if P is reducible and $\tilde{A}$ is an absorbing state, the vector of hitting probabilities τ_i^A is an indirect measure of Holling resilience of the transient state i with respect to $\tilde{A}$.[4] This measure gives the expected time before the system converges on $\tilde{A}$ from some state in A, given some disturbance regime.

If resilience is measured by the probability that a system will flip from one stability domain to another, then it follows trivially that a sufficient condition for a system to be infinitely resilient is that the limiting probabilities do not depend on the initial probabilities. The limiting probabilities will only be independent of the initial probabilities if P is irreducible, has a dominant eigenvalue of 1, and that there are no other eigenvalues equal to 1. Resilience in this sense is only an issue if the matrix of transition probabilities is reducible, implying that the system has multiple equilibria. If P is reducible (a) the system may, in the limit, occupy any one of a finite number of closed classes; (b) it is sensitive to initial conditions and (c) it is path dependent (the key properties of complex systems generally). In this case, the limiting transition probabilities of the chain depend on the initial state, i. The future evolution of the system depends on where it starts.

The central element in this way of thinking about sustainability is the idea is that the evolutionary potential of an economy–environment system is limited by institutional conditions – or the 'rules of the game'. The evolutionary possibilities of a system are summarized in the matrix of transition probabilities, P, which reflects a probability law P^u. The probability law in turn depends on the control policy applied, and the control policy is driven by the set of institutional conditions. In other words, institutional conditions determine the control set, the decision maker's objectives, and the admissible policies and actions. Since the literature already addresses the way in which property rights determine economic decisions, this idea is already familiar. The argument here is that for a given set of institutional conditions, a given disturbance regime and a given state of nature, it may be possible to estimate the probability that the system will converge by some finite time on some other state of nature. The connection with the notion of sustainability is direct. If the transition probabilities are known, it is possible to estimate either the time the system occupies a particular state (the sustainability of that state) or the time to convergence on any other state (the time to sustainability). It is also possible, through the transition probabilities themselves, to estimate the robustness of the system under a particular disturbance regime to change in any particular direction.

5   CONCLUSIONS: IMPLICATIONS FOR FUTURE RESEARCH

The chapter aims to draw out the implications of an approach to sustainability that builds on the ecological concept of resilience using a Markov framework. It suggests that the development implies a process of evolutionary change that has all the usual dynamical properties of complex systems: path dependence, sensitivity to initial conditions, non-linear and often discontinuous change around threshold values for both environmental resources and ecological functions. For any economy–environment system there are many possible states (equilibria) and many development paths associated with those states. The resilience and hence sustainability of the system in any one state depends on the way it is used – the control policy applied.

For most economies the process of development has involved a sequence of states. Indeed, early development theory was all about the transition between equilibria – about escaping from states associated with low levels of well-being and moving towards states associated with higher levels of well-being. Strategies for sustainability, in the sense of this chapter, is about enhancing or protecting the resilience of the system in desirable states and reducing the resilience of the system in undesirable states (poverty traps, subsistence or semi-subsistence equilibria and the like). This is a view that accords with the resourcist take on sustainability.

I have suggested that it is possible to think about such systems as being driven by a probability law that reflects both the underlying dynamics of a set of environmental (biogeophysical) processes and a set of institutionally determined 'policies'. I have also suggested that we can analyse the evolution of the system in terms of the impact of different probability laws and so different institutional conditions. Indeed, it makes it possible to compare the long-run implications of different institutional conditions in terms of the sustainability or resilience of the system under each.

The implications for future research on the problems of the resilience and sustainability of particular states or regimes are immediate. Real economy–environment systems are not characterized by globally stable equilibria, far-sighted agents who form rational expectations about the future evolution of the systems, complete markets and so on. Real systems generally involve states that are only partially observable and controllable, decision processes that are adaptive, that involve learning and that include the conflicting objectives of distinct groups of agents each of which acts strategically.[5] The transition probabilities associated with different institutional conditions, technologies, preferences and states of nature are generally uncovered through experience, and are often surprising to decision makers. The agenda for research is just to identify the 'transition probabilities' associated with specific institutional conditions, and to weight those probabilities in terms of social objectives.

In some respects this leads on to familiar ground for environmental economists. It requires, for example, an understanding of the incentive effects of different institutional conditions. It also requires identification of the (general) equilibria and convergence paths associated with particular 'policies' or controls, and conditional on a given initial state. In other respects, however, it demands some rather radical extensions to the scope of environmental economics research.

The first of these relates to the set of system observers used by decision makers. In a decentralized market system it is clearly important to understand the sensitivity of decisions to variations in prices, which are the main system observers. But where markets are incomplete or function poorly the observers tend to be much more than the set of relative prices and price-like mechanisms (taxes, subsidies, penalties and the like). Consumers and producers alike respond to a wide range of indicators other than prices. Some indicators are direct observations on the physical stocks and flows associated with non-marketed environmental processes. They provide the means to track unanticipated environmental change or to monitor anticipated change. Others, often termed sustainability indicators, are proxies for the kind of measures discussed in this chapter: transition probabilities, residence or hitting times. Decision makers use indicators of this sort in lieu of more conventional measures of actual or potential scarcity. Environmental economists already pay some attention to the quality of measures of scarcity. The valuation literature, for example, is designed to obtain measures that more closely approximate the social opportunity cost of resource use than market prices. But little attention has been paid by environmental economists to the quality of non-price measures of scarcity or potential scarcity (sustainability) that are used by decision makers, or how those indicators are used in the decision process. Where markets are incomplete the analysis of decentralized decisions is certainly incomplete too if it leaves out the formation and role of non-market system observers. This is an area of legitimate concern for environmental economists, even though it takes them beyond the conventional limits of the field.

The second extension to the scope of environmental economics research suggested by this approach concerns the modelling of the system dynamics. A suitable state space representation of an economy and its supporting environment requires specification of the dynamics of both economic and natural resources, and the interactions between them. This is already acknowledged in bioeconomic models of renewable resource use. But, in cases where the resilience of the system is an issue, it also requires specification of the probabilistic convergence on the system equilibria, conditional on the starting state. This is acknowledged in some of the preliminary modelling work on hysteresis effects in shallow lakes referred to earlier in this chapter. It is also reflected in some of the modelling work undertaken on co-evolutionary systems in the field of ecological economics. But there is a very long way to go before we have effective dynamical models of economy–environment interactions, and even longer before we identify effective ways of calibrating and estimating such models.

As a last word, both of these extensions to the environmental economics research agenda imply the need to step outside the traditional boundaries of economics as a discipline. Neither is possible without engaging with other social and natural scientists. This uncomfortable fact is likely to mean that they will remain off the research agenda for most environmental economists. Institutionally, it is likely to depend on the development of interdisciplinary research groups supported by interdisciplinary doctoral programmes. The costs of an agenda of this sort are therefore likely to be quite high, but the potential payoffs are surely higher still.

ACKNOWLEDGEMENT

Thanks are due to Adam Rose for helpful comments on an earlier version of this chapter.

NOTES

1. A second definition of resilience refers to the properties of the system near some stable equilibrium (i.e. in the neigbourhood of a stable focus or node). This definition, due to Pimm (1984), takes the resilience of a system to be a measure of the speed of its return to equilibrium following perturbation. The two measures are related (Dalmazzone, 1998).
2. In the simplest case the problem is taken to be to maximize

$$\int_0^\infty e^{\rho t} U(L, P) dt$$

    subject to

$$\frac{dP}{dt} = L - sP + r\left[\frac{p^2}{p^2 + m^2}\right]$$

$$P(0) = P_0$$

    where P is phosphorous in suspended algae, L is phosphorous loading from the watershed, s is losses to sediment, other organisms or outflow, $r[\cdot]$ is internal loading, and $U(\cdot)$ is concave in (L,P), increasing in L and decreasing in P. Depending on the parameter values, this can yield an s-shaped curve for phosphorous loading, each branch of which is associated with one of the two states described.

3. Moreover, if P is irreducible and has an invariant distribution, π, then every state is recurrent and the expected return time for each state, $E_i\sigma_i$, is equal to $1/\pi_i$ for all i.
4. It is possible for the system to evolve from one state to another in the same closed class, but not to another state in any other class, and not to a transient state. It is also possible for the system to evolve from one transient state to at least some other transient states, or from a transient to an absorbing state. It is therefore quite natural to think of the switch from a transient state to an absorbing state in any closed class as irreversible.
5. Dejon *et al.* (1996) attempt to model the interactive behaviour of multiple classes of agent in a Markov framework.

REFERENCES

Anderson, R.M. and R.M. May (1982), *The Population Dynamics of Infectious Diseases: Theory and Applications*, London: Chapman and Hall.

Antle, J.M. and G. Heidebrink (1995), 'Environment and development: theory and international evidence', *Economic Development and Cultural Change*, 43(3), 603–25.

Aoki, M. (1995), 'Economic fluctuations with interactive agents: dynamic and stochastic externalities', *Japanese Economic Review*, 462, 148–65.

Aoki, M. (1996), *New Approaches to Macroeconomic Modeling*, Cambridge: Cambridge University Press.

Arrow, K., B. Bolin, R. Costanza, P. Dasgupta, C. Folke, C.S. Holling, B.-O. Jansson, S. Levin, K.-G. Mäler, C. Perrings and D. Pimentel (1995), 'Economic growth, carrying capacity, and the environment', *Science*, 268, 520–21.

Asheim, G.B. (1996), 'Ethical preferences in the presence of resource constraints', *Nordic Journal of Political Economy*, 23, 55–68.

Barbier, E.B. (1997), 'Introduction to the Environmental Kuznets Curve', special issue, *Environment and Development Economics*, 2(4), 357–67.

Batabayal, A.A. (1998a), 'The concept of resilience: restrospect and prospect', *Environment and Development Economics*, 3(2), 235–39.

Batabayal, A.A. (1998b), 'Aspects of the management of cyclical ecological–economic systems', mimeo, University of Utah.

Bateman, I., A. Munro, B. Rhodes, C. Starmer and R. Sugden (1998), 'A test of the theory of reference-dependent preferences', *Quarterly Journal of Economics*, 112 (2): 479–505.

Carpenter, S. and K. Cottingham (1997), 'Resilience and restoration of lakes', *Conservation Ecology* (online publication of the Resilience Alliance), www.consecol.org, 1 (1) article 2.

Carpenter, S. and M. Pace (1997), 'Dystrophy and eutrophy in lake ecosystems: implications of fluctuating inputs', *Oikos*, 78, 3–14.

Carpenter, S., D. Ludwig and W.A. Brock (1999), 'Management of eutrophication in lakes subject to potentially irreversible change', *Ecological Applications*, 9 (3), 751–71.

Chichilnisky, G. (1996), 'An axiomatic approach to sustainable development', *Social Choice and Welfare*, 13, 231–57.

Chichilnisky, G. (1997), 'What is sustainable development?', *Land Economics*, 73(4), 467–91.

Clark, C.W. (1990), *Mathematical Bioeconomics*, New York: Wiley.

Cole, M.A., A.J. Rayner and J.M. Bates (1997), 'The Environmental Kuznets Curve: an empirical analysis', *Environment and Development Economics*, **2**(4), 401–16.

Common, M. and C. Perrings (1992), 'Towards an ecological economics of sustainability', *Ecological Economics*, **6**, 7–34.

Conway, G.R. (1993), 'Sustainable agriculture: the trade-offs with productivity, stability and equitability', in E.B. Barbier (ed.), *Economics and Ecology: New Frontiers and Sustainable Development*, London: Chapman and Hall.

Conway, G.R. and E.B. Barbier (1990), *After the Green Revolution: Sustainable Agriculture for Development*, London: Earthscan.

Costanza, R., C. Perrings and C. Cleveland (eds) (1997), *The Development of Ecological Economics*, Cheltenham, UK and Northampton, MA: Edward Elgar.

Dalmazzone, S. (1998), 'Economic activities and the resilience of ecological systems: a stochastic approach', mimeo, Environment Department, University of York.

Dalmazzone, S. and C. Perrings (1997), 'Resilience and stability in ecological economic systems', Environment Department, University of York, mimeo.

Dasgupta, P. (1995), 'Optimal development and the idea of net national product', in I. Goldin and L.A. Winters (eds), *The Economics of Sustainable Development*, Cambridge: Cambridge University Press.

Dasgupta, P. (1996), 'The economics of the environment', *Environment and Development Economics*, **1**(4), 387–428.

Dasgupta, P. and K.-G. Mäler (1995), 'Poverty, institutions and the environmental resource base', in J. Behrman and T.N. Srinivasan (eds), *Handbook of Development Economics*, 3(A), Amsterdam: Elsevier.

de Bruyn, S.M. (1997), 'Explaining the Environmental Kuznets Curve: structural change and international agreements in reducing sulphur emissions', *Environment and Development Economics*, **2**(4), 485–503.

Dejon, B., F. Graef, H.-J. Meier and J. Novotny (1996), 'Dynamic stochastic choice modelling of disequilibrium in an economy', in W.A. Barnett, G. Gandolfo and C. Hillinger (eds), *Dynamic Disequilibrium Modelling*, Cambridge: Cambridge University Press, pp. 365–94.

Delfino, D. and P. Simmons (2000), 'Infectious diseases as invasives in human populations', in C. Perrings, M. Williamson and S. Dalmazzone (eds), *The Economics of Biological Invasions*, Cheltenham, UK and Northampton, MA: Edward Elgar, pp. 31–55.

Dixit, A., P. Hammond and M. Hoel (1980), 'On Hartwick's rule for regular maximin paths of capital accumulation and resource depletion', *Review of Economic Studies*, **XLVII**, 551–6.

Elton, C.S. (1975), 'The Ecology of Invasions by Animals and Plants', London: Chapman and Hall.

Grossman, G.M. and A.B. Krueger (1993), 'Environmental impacts of the North American Free Trade Agreement', in P. Garber (ed.), *The US–Mexico Free Trade Agreement*, Cambridge, MA: MIT Press.

Grossman, G.M. and A.B. Krueger (1995), 'Economic growth and the environment', *Quarterly Journal of Economics*, **110**(2), 353–77.

Hartwick, J.M. (1977), 'Intergenerational equity and the investing of rents from exhaustible resources', *American Economic Review*, **66**, 972–4.

Hartwick, J.M. (1978), 'Investing returns from depleting renewable resource stocks and intergenerational equity', *Economics Letters*, **1**, 85–8.

Hartwick, J.M. (1995), 'Constant consumption paths in open economies with exhaustible resources', *Review of International Economics*, **3**(3), 275–83.

Harvey, A.C. and P. Marshall (1991), 'Inter-fuel substitution, technical change and the demand for energy in the UK economy', *Applied Economics*, **23**, 1077–86.

Heal, G. (1998), *Valuing the Future: Economic Theory and Sustainability*, New York: Columbia University Press.

Holden, S.T., B. Shiferaw and M. Wik (1998), 'Poverty, market imperfections and time preferences: of relevance for environmental policy?', *Environment and Development Economics*, **3**(1), 105–30.

Holling, C.S. (1973), 'Resilience and stability of ecological system', *Annual Review of Ecological Systems*, **4**, 1–24.

Holling, C.S. (1986), 'The resilience of terrestrial ecosystems: local surprise and global change', in W.C. Clark and R.E. Munn (eds), *Sustainable Development of the Biosphere*, Cambridge: Cambridge University Press.

Holling, C.S., D.W. Schindler, B.W. Walker and J. Roughgarden (1995), 'Biodiversity in the functioning of ecosystems: an ecological primer and synthesis', in C.A. Perrings, K.-G. Mäler, C. Folke, C.S. Holling and B.-O. Jansson (eds), *Biodiversity Loss: Ecological and Economic Issues*, Cambridge: Cambridge University Press, pp. 44–83.

Howarth, R.B. (1997), 'Sustainability as opportunity', *Land Economics*, **73**(4), 569–79.

Levin, S.A., S. Barrett, S. Aniyar, W. Baumol, C. Bliss, B. Bolin, P. Dasgupta, P. Ehrlich, C. Folke, I.-M. Gren, C.S. Holling, A.-M. Jansson, B.-O. Jansson, D. Martin, K.-G. Mäler, C. Perrings and E. Sheshinsky (1998), 'Resilience in natural and socioeconomic systems', *Environment and Development Economics*, **3**(2), 222–34.

Ludwig, D., B.H. Walker and C.S. Holling (1997), 'Sustainability, stability and resilience', *Conservation Ecology*, **1**(1), 7.

Mäler, K.-G. (1991), 'National accounts and environmental resources', *Environmental and Resource Economics*, **1**, 1–15.

Mäler, K.-G., A Xepapadeas and A. de Zeeuw (2000), 'The economics of shallow lakes', mimeo, Beijer Institute, Stockholm.

May, R.M. (1973), *Stability and Complexity in Model Ecosystems*, Princeton: Princeton University Press.

McConnell, K.E. (1997), 'Income and the demand for environmental quality', *Environment and Development Economics*, **2**(4), 383–99.

McNaughton, S.J. (1993), 'Biodiversity and function of grazing systems', in E.D. Schulze and H.A. Mooney (eds), *Biodiversity and Ecosystem Function*, Berlin: Springer, pp. 361–84.

Munro, A. and R. Sugden (1997), 'A theory of general equilibrium with reference-dependent preferences', mimeo, School of Economic and Social Studies, University of East Anglia.

Panayotou, T. (1995), 'Environmental degradation at different stages of economic development', in I. Ahmed and J.A. Doelman (eds), *Beyond Rio: The Environmental Crisis and Sustainable Livelihoods in the Third World*, London: Macmillan Press.

Panayotou, T. (1997), 'Demystifying the Environmental Kuznets Curve: turning a black box into a policy tool', *Environment and Development Economics*, **2**(4), 465–84.

Pearce, D.W. and G.D. Atkinson (1993), 'Capital theory and the measurement of sustainable development: an indicator of "weak" sustainability', *Ecological Economics*, **8**, 103–8.

Pender, J.L. (1996), 'Discount rates and credit markets: theory and evidence from rural India', *Journal of Development Economics*, **50**, 157–96.

Pender, J.L. and T.S. Walker (1990), 'Experimental measuring of time preference in rural India', Report No. 97, ICRISAT, Andra Pradesh.

Perrings, C. (1995), 'Ecological resilience in the sustainability of economic development', *Economie Appliquée*, **48**(2), 121–42.

Perrings, C. (1998), 'Resilience in the dynamics of economy–environment systems', *Environmental and Resource Economics*, **11**(3–4), 503–20.

Perrings, C., K.-G. Mäler, C. Folke, C.S. Holling and B.-O. Jansson (eds) (1995), *Biological Diversity: Economic and Ecological Issues*, Cambridge: Cambridge University Press.

Perrings, C. and D. Stern (2000), 'Modelling the resilience of agroecosystems: rangeland degradation in Botswana', *Environmental and Resource Economics*.

Perrings, C. and B.H. Walker (1995), 'Biodiversity loss and the economics of discontinuous change in semi-arid rangelands', in C. Perrings, K.-G. Mäler, C. Folke, C.S. Holling and B.-O. Jansson (eds), *Biological Diversity: Economic and Ecological Issues*, Cambridge: Cambridge University Press, pp. 190–210.

Perrings, C. and B.H. Walker (1997), 'Biodiversity, resilience and the control of ecological–economic systems: the case of fire-driven rangelands', *Ecological Economics*, **22**(1), 73–83.

Peskin, H.M. (1989), 'Accounting for natural resource depletion and degradation in developing countries', Environment Department Working Paper 13, World Bank, Washington, DC.

Pethig, R. (1994), *Valuing the Environment: Methodological and Measurement Issues*, Dordrecht: Kluwer Academic Publishers.

Pezzey, J.C.V. (1989), 'Economic analysis of sustainable growth and sustainable development', Environment Department Working Paper 15, World Bank, Washington, DC.

Pezzey, J.C.V. (1997), 'Sustainability constraints versus "optimality" versus intertemporal concern, and axioms versus data', *Land Economics*, **73**(4), 448–66.

Pimm, S.L. (1984), 'The complexity and stability of ecosystems', *Nature*, **307**, 321–6.

Reed, W.J. (1979), 'Optimal escapement levels in stochastic and deterministic harvesting models', *Journal of Environmental Economics and Management*, **6**, 350–63.

Reed, W.J. (1988), 'Optimal harvesting of a fishery subject to random catastrophic collapse', *IMA Journal of Mathematics Applied in Medicine and Biology*, **5**, 215–35.

Repetto, R., W. Cruz, R. Solórzano, R. de Camino, R. Woodward, J. Tosi, V. Watson, A. Vásquez, C. Villabos and J. Jiménez (1991), 'Accounts overdue: natural resource depletion in Costa Rica', World Resources Institute, Washington, DC.

Seldon, T.M. and D. Song (1994), 'Environmental quality and development: is there a Kuznets Curve for air pollution emissions?', *Journal of Environmental Economics and Management*, **27**, 147–62.

Shafik, N. (1994), 'Economic development and environmental quality: an econometric analysis', *Oxford Economic Papers*, **46**, 757–73.

Slade, M.E. (1989), 'Modelling stochastic and cyclical components of technical change: an application of the Kalman filter', *Journal of Econometrics*, **41**, 363–83.

Solow, R.M. (1974), 'Intergenerational equity and exhaustible resources', *Review of Economic Studies*, Symposium, 29–46.

Tilman, D., D. Wedin and J. Knops (1996), 'Productivity and sustainability influenced by biodiversity in grassland ecosystems', *Nature*, **379**, 718–20.

Tinch, R. (1998), 'Resilience and resource management under risk', mimeo, School of Environmental Science, University of East Anglia.

Tsur, Y. and A. Zemel (1994), 'Endangered species and natural resource exploitation: extinction versus coexistence', *Natural Resource Modeling*, **8**(4), 389–413.

Tsur, Y. and A. Zemel (1997), 'On resource management under uncertainty: the case of pollution control', Paper presented at the 8th EAERE Conference, Tilburg.

Turner, K., C. Perrings and C. Folke (1997), 'Ecological economics: paradigm or perspective?', in J. van den Bergh and J. van der Straaten (eds), *Economy and Ecosystems in Change*, Cheltenham, UK and Northampton, MA: Edward Elgar, pp. 25–49.

Turner, R.K. and D.W. Pearce (1993), 'Sustainable economic development: economic and ethical principles', in E.B. Barbier (ed.), *Economics and Ecology*, London: Chapman and Hall, pp. 177–94.

Tversky, A. and D. Kahneman (1991), 'Loss aversion and riskless choice: a reference-dependent model', *Quarterly Journal of Economics*, **106**, 1039–61.

van Tongeren, J., S. Schweinfest, E. Lutz, Luna M. Gomez and M. Guillen (1993), 'Integrated environmental and economic accounting: a case study for Mexico', in E. Lutz (ed.), *Toward Improved Accounting for the Environment*, Washington, DC: World Bank.

Vincent, J. (1997), 'Resource depletion and economic sustainability in Malaysia', *Environment and Development Economics*, **2**(1), 19–38.

Vincent, J., T. Panayotou and J.M. Hartwick (1997), 'Resource depletion and sustainability in small open economies', *Journal of Environmental Economics and Management*, **33**, 274–86.

Vitousek, P.M. and D.U. Hooper (1993), 'Biological diversity and terrestrial ecosystem biogeochemistry' in E.D. Schulze and H.A. Mooney (eds), *Biodiversity and Ecosystem Function*, Berlin: Springer, pp. 3–14.

Westman, W.E. (1985), *Ecology, Impact Assessment and Environmental Planning*, New York: John Wiley and Sons.

Westoby, M., B. Walker and I. Noy-Meir (1989), 'Opportunistic management for rangelands not at equilibrium', *Journal of Range Management*, **42**(4), 266–74.

14. Environmental technological innovation and diffusion

Carlo Carraro

1 INTRODUCTION

The difficulty of protecting the environment at a low economic cost and without harnessing economic growth, a task which is especially difficult in developing countries, has stimulated an increasing debate on the role of technical progress and on the prospective achievements of technological innovation in the field of emission abatement and low natural resource depletion.

The confidence that technical progress may provide important tools to lessen the trade-off between economic growth and environmental protection does not necessarily imply that investments in environment-friendly research and development (R&D) and innovation will be undertaken by firms, nor that this R&D and innovation can be disseminated to give all world countries the opportunity to protect their environment at a low economic cost.

This chapter addresses this issue by analysing the incentives for firms to undertake R&D and innovation, and by highlighting why market imperfections, externalities, international capital mobility and other economic factors may lead to suboptimal investments by firms in environmental R&D and innovation. This suggests that public innovation policies may become necessary to induce firms to modify their innovation strategies. Hence, the chapter analyses different types of policy mixes and discusses the role of traditional environmental policies (taxes, permits and the like) but also the effects of other policies, for example, trade or financial policies, that can affect firms' incentives to undertake environmental R&D and innovation.

The first seven sections of the paper are devoted to a synthesis of results that theoretical models have recently achieved on firms' innovation strategies, on the diffusion of innovation, on market imperfections and inefficiencies and on the trade-off between environmental protection – which calls for a wide diffusion of environmental innovation – and firms' profitability – which often induces firms to underinvest in R&D and to reduce the dissemination of environment-friendly innovation. In particular, sections 5 and 7 attempt to identify combinations of environmental, trade, industrial – including market regulation – and financial policies that can achieve a socially optimal level of environmental innovation. Section 8 focuses on empirical models and on their attempt to capture and quantify the role of innovation in reducing polluting emissions (greenhouse gas – GHG – emissions above all). These models face the difficult task of providing a consistent and behavioural modelling of innovation, coupled with the need to achieve a proper statistical identification of the model and with the goal of capturing the interaction and feedbacks between innovation and the other main economic and environmental variables. A concluding section summarizes the main achievements of the chapter, and the consequent policy recommendations, and outlines a research agenda on environmental innovation and diffusion.

2   ON THE ROLE OF ENVIRONMENTAL TECHNOLOGICAL INNOVATION (WHY DO WE NEED ENVIRONMENTAL INNOVATION?)

The development and widespread adoption of new technologies is often proposed as the main option to lessen the trade-off between economic well-being and environmental quality. With current technologies, the reduction of air, water and solid waste streams poses a difficult trade-off between increasing environmental degradation if no action is taken, and the economic costs associated with emission abatements and reductions incurred through costly investments or through a process of economic contraction. This trade-off is especially difficult with regard to GHGs where the magnitude of future environmental damage is unknown and where estimated abatement costs are likely to be significant and borne by current generations.

As said, improvements in technology can significantly alter this trade-off. There are indeed several aspects of technological innovation that affect the interactions and links between economic and environmental variables. In some cases the effect of innovation is straightforward. Innovation reduces emissions per unit of output, it lowers abatement costs and facilitates the introduction of 'greener' products. In other cases the effect of innovation may be indirect. Innovation and the resulting investment in new and improved processes of production are important for economic growth and the related use of natural resources. New products that result from innovation are crucial for improving living standards and thus the consumers' preference for environmental quality. Innovation is an important contributor to non-price competitiveness. Its effects on international competition are also relevant, as it modifies the pattern of geographical distribution of industrial activities and thus the incentive to locate plants in countries with lower environmental standards.

There is a recent body of empirical evidence which shows that a substantial reduction of important emissions, which are closely linked to economic activity, is likely to be achieved through technological innovation, rather than through the standard 'textbook' substitutabilities in response to price changes. A good example is provided by cross-country studies, carried out by Holtz-Eakin and Selden (1995), Grossman (1995) and Baldwin (1995) on World Bank data and by Galeotti and Lanza (1998) on IEA/OECD data, that show that the relation between per capita CO_2 emissions (and also other pollutants) and per capita income depicts a 'bell-shaped' curve. Data from a great number of countries show that per capita pollution increases in the first phases of development, but subsequently decreases quite sharply as development proceeds. These kinds of 'environmental Kuznets curves' are simple correlations, still in need of systematic explanation. The main determinants of the observed shape can be Engel's law, structural change of the economies and accumulation of capital; in any case, the reduction of per capita emissions seems to have little relation to prices, which are basically the same across countries. According to preliminary investigations, the diffusion of innovation related to investment seems to play a crucial role, dominating price substitutions.[1]

It is also clear from recent theoretical work by Paul Romer (1986, 1990) and Lucas (1988) that aggregate technological externalities within countries may help explain many of the observed patterns of growth across countries. The intuition is the usual one, but it is applied at the macro level. Technological ideas cannot be fully appropriated by investors (households or firms). These ideas spread, so increasing the productivity of many other households and firms. Diffusion can take place both within and across countries (in Romer's and Lucas's work, externalities are considered only within countries. Ciccone, 1996, extends their models to allow for cross-country externalities). These technological externalities are the crucial factors that lead to increased aggregate returns and endogenous growth.

If we link this latter result with those described above on the relationship between growth and pollution, the conclusion is straightforward: *technological innovation and diffusion are the engine of growth. Growth is correlated to increasing environmental efficiency. Hence, innovation and its diffusion are crucial to achieve substantial reductions of per capita emissions levels and of resource utilization.* The question is therefore how to induce firms to undertake environmental innovation. This issue will be discussed in the next sections.

3   ON THE INCENTIVES FOR ENVIRONMENTAL INNOVATION (WHY DO FIRMS INVEST IN R&D?)

As said, technical change is an important component of the mechanism that leads to timely and less costly emission control. However, it has been shown that, without adequate public policies, in many cases firms tend to underinvest and/or delay investment in environmental innovation (see Downing and White, 1986; Milliman and Prince, 1989; Echia and Mariotti, 1994; Carraro and Topa, 1995; Ulph, A., 1996; Ulph, D., 1997). Hence, public policies affecting the development and spread of new technologies may, over the long term, be one of the most important tools for environmental protection. As a first step towards designing such policies, it is therefore necessary to single out the factors driving the diffusion of new energy-saving technologies.

This is certainly an issue widely studied in the environmental literature, even if results are generally not environment specific and are usually derived from the industrial organization literature. The basic question is: why do firms invest in R&D? They do so not only to directly pursue new product and process innovation but also to develop and maintain their broader capacity to assimilate and exploit externally available innovation. Behind the 'innovative' reason for R&D are two motivating forces: profitable investment and strategic advantage. Consider the former. Allocating resources to innovative R&D will, if successful, increase a firm's profits. One can usefully conceive of this as the incentive that a firm taking a decision in isolation would face. This is why Katz and Shapiro (1987) refer to it as the 'stand-alone' incentive. The second incentive that makes firms engage in R&D is to give themselves a strategic advantage over their rivals. A better process or a better product can enhance a firm's market share. If a firm knows that its rivals are engaging in R&D then it will see its own competitive position as being under threat. This is why this force which stimulates innovation is sometimes called 'competitive threat' (or 'replacement effect').

These remarks lead to the following conclusion, that may seem trivial, but is sometimes neglected by policy makers. *Policies designed to stimulate innovation must provide an opportunity to increase firms' profits and competitiveness.* Let us consider an example. An increase in energy prices induced by an emission tax or by a system of tradable permits may lead firms to innovate to reduce energy costs. At the same time, this innovation gives these firms the opportunity to reduce the competitiveness loss with respect to firms located in countries where energy prices were not raised. However, the cost increase induced by the tax reduces the firm's profit margins, thus reducing the financial resources for investment in R&D. It is therefore crucial to identify the appropriate policy mix to achieve cost-effective R&D strategies.[2]

The economics literature has quite extensively analysed the mechanisms and incentives which lead to environmental R&D. Environmental innovation has been studied in a seminal paper by Downing and White (1986). These authors examine the effectiveness of different policies in inducing 'environmentally friendly' innovation by n identical firms. They consider a context of perfect competition and complete information for all agents: in particular, the government is assumed to know the production and abatement technology available to firms, and to be able to measure the amount of emissions discharged by each source. Moreover, in Downing and White (1986), the innovation process is modelled in a very simple manner: the authors assume that a new technology, providing firms with lower abatement cost functions, becomes exogenously and instantaneously available. Other papers on environmental innovation (for example, Magat, 1979; Malueg, 1989; Milliman and Prince, 1989) are subject to similar criticisms. Perfect competition and complete information are usually assumed; firms' innovation behaviour is modelled in a simple way; no strategic behaviour is introduced. In particular, the lack of any strategic incentives to carry out R&D is at odds with the answers to the question, 'Why do firms invest in R&D?', provided above.

More recently, environmental innovation has been analysed in the context of imperfect markets where strategic incentives and interactions among firms can be accounted for. Hence, the work by Downing and White has been extended in several directions. The timing of innovation and the role of incomplete information is analysed in Carraro and Topa (1995), the interactions between production and innovation are studied in Ulph, D. (1994). Katsoulacos and Xepapadeas (1996) analyse a case where R&D spillovers exist between firms in the process of environmental innovation, thus introducing positive externalities in addition to the negative environmental externalities. Other models are surveyed in Ulph, D. (1997) who proposes a distinction between non-tournament and tournament models in order to organize the different approaches existing in the economics literature on environmental innovation.

In a *non-tournament model* there are potentially many firms that can obtain an equivalent improvement in the production process. This could arise for one of two reasons. The first is that there may be many different research paths that firms could follow, all of them leading to the same end. Thus, while any particular firm can obtain a patent that is completely effective in protecting the output of its own successful R&D, it cannot prevent other firms from making equivalent improvements through spending equivalent amounts on R&D. Thus, in this class of models, patents can protect firms against costless imitation by rivals, but not against costly innovation by rivals. The second might be that, while the new process is of an intrinsically unpatentable nature, its acquisition involves the sinking of costs. The models of environmental innovation mentioned above belong to the non-tournament group.

In a *tournament model*, the idea is that at any moment there can only be a limited number (possibly one) of successful innovators and the issue is whether and why a successful innovator at one time is more likely to be successful subsequently. One reason why there may be just a limited number of successful innovators at any moment would be if there were just a limited number of research paths leading to a new discovery, and whoever made the discovery first got an effective patent which prevented anyone else from using the discovery, even if they arrived at it independently and shortly after the successful firm. A model of this type is described in Ulph, D. (1997).

The economics literature has also paid a lot of attention to the links between *environmental innovation* and *international trade*. There has been much debate recently about the nature of environmental policy that will be set by governments concerned about the competitive advantage their industries might obtain in a world of fierce trade competition (Barrett, 1994; Ulph, A., 1997). Some authors claim that governments will set environmental policies that are too lax (Rauscher, 1995), while others claim that policies will be excessively tough (in order to spur firms to innovate).[3] Both these claims relate to the possibility that governments may distort their environmental policies for strategic reasons, and testing them requires modelling environmental policy in a world of imperfect competition where there are strategic gains for governments which manipulate markets through their environmental policies, and for producers which manipulate markets through their R&D decisions. The next section will discuss this issue in more detail.

4 ON THE GEOGRAPHICAL DIFFUSION OF ENVIRONMENTAL INNOVATION (WHY DO WE NEED A GLOBAL PERSPECTIVE?)

There are many reasons to believe that innovation may have relevant effects on the geographical distribution of economic activities. R&D activity carried out by multinationals is often geographically dispersed (Cantwell, 1993; Kumar, 1995). R&D is often carried out by networks of firms located in different countries, including developing countries (Contractor and Lorange, 1988; Vonortas, 1991; Pietrobelli, 1996). Aggregate evidence shows that international trade generates R&D spillovers: the larger the share of imports from countries rich in R&D capital, the larger the developing countries' foreign R&D capital and the faster their rate of growth (Coe, Helpman and Hoffmaister, 1995).

The above effects need to be considered when analysing the effects of environmental policies on innovation and its diffusion. There is however another more straightforward effect that has been stressed in the recent literature on environmental innovation. This effect is due more to capital than to knowledge mobility across countries. The idea is that countries which implement tougher environmental policies than others will suffer a loss in real income as production relocates both through trade and the physical relocation of plants to countries with more lax environmental policies. This prompts concern that, in the absence of international cooperation, the freeing up of trade will lead to environmental dumping, that is, the uniform reduction by all countries in the toughness of their environmental policies. This raises two issues. The first is once more whether the potentially disruptive effects of environmental policies on resource re-allocation might be significantly mitigated through the encouragement these policies give to innovation. The second is whether environmental dumping will indeed take place when strategic innovation becomes a consideration. It has been suggested that countries might now have incentives to set excessively tough environmental policies, in order to spur the firms in their country to innovate ahead of rivals and so gain market advantage. This has become known as the 'Porter hypothesis', following the article by Michael Porter (1991) which articulated this possibility.

The issue of whether environmental policies can really have an impact on the international allocation of capital is not only a theoretical question but also an empirical one. Theoretically, firms may shift their production when they face environmental regulations (either because they add new plants in foreign sites or because they shift existing capacity abroad). However, the question is 'How significant is this phenomenon in practice?' That is: *is there considerable evidence that environmental regulations have really induced flows of capital towards pollution havens?*

Wang and Winters (1994) review most of the literature on these issues. The literature analysed by the authors specifically focuses on the empirical evidence regarding potential capital flights from industrial (OECD) countries to developing ones (non-OECD). The authors conclude that in the studies surveyed there was little evidence of capital flight from industrial countries with stringent environmental legislation to pollution havens. Other factors, such as political and macroeconomic stability, market access, market size and growth, play a much larger role in firms' location decisions. Similar conclusions have also been reached by Rauscher (1994). The author reviews some other empirical literature on the subject and again concludes that the evidence does not give much support to the hypothesis that capital tends to fly towards countries with lax environmental regulation. However, he stresses that the empirical studies may be flawed because of measurement problems. Specifically, he underlines that a major problem in the empirical assessment of the impact of environmental legislation on firms' location choices is the difficulty of measuring the strictness of environmental regulation itself (both because the proxies used may not be good enough and/or because it is extremely difficult to isolate, from aggregate data, the environmental component). These measurement problems should be kept in mind when analysing the empirical studies since they may seriously bias the results. The same doubts on the validity of some empirical studies have also been raised by Levinson (1996). The novelty of the study by Levinson (1996) is that the author examines firms' choices across most manufacturing industries, employing a wide variety of measures of environmental stringency. Contrary to the use of aggregate data, Levinson studies location choices using establishment-level data (essentially plants' births). Again, this study confirms that there seems to be only weak evidence that environmental regulations deter new plant openings.

Despite the *small amount of empirical evidence on the link between environmental policy and geographical distribution of economic activities*, the Porter hypothesis has attracted the attention of several theorists (for example, Hoel, 1995; Rauscher, 1995; Ulph, A., 1997). In Carraro and Soubeyran (1999) a firm's decision to innovate is analysed jointly with its decision to relocate its plants abroad whenever environmental policy in the foreign country is less stringent. The main conclusion of their paper is as follows. In general, three stable groups of firms emerge. Even if firms are symmetric, their equilibrium choice in response to the introduction of an environmental policy is different. Some of them relocate their plants abroad, others invest in R&D and develop new, environment-friendly technologies and others introduce the environmental innovation by buying the licences. The size of the three groups is influenced by the technological and institutional parameters prevailing in the industry. For example, the government can affect the number of firms which decide to cooperate by changing the R&D incentives and/or its trade policy.

It is therefore interesting to analyse whether innovation has significant effects when a firm is allowed to move its plants abroad in response to the introduction of an environmental policy, and if there are other policies that can increase these effects. In a recent paper, Boetti *et al.* (1998) run some simulation experiments in order to evaluate (i) the number and size of the groups of firms which are likely to emerge in the presence of an environmental tax and when R&D and innovation is accounted for; (ii) how the size of the three groups of firms is likely to change when other policy measures are adopted, for example, an industrial policy aimed at stimulating R&D and innovation, or a trade policy. They show that:

- a higher marginal tax rate does not seem to have a significant impact on firms' relocation choices (consistent with empirical findings);
- a higher R&D incentive policy increases the number of both cooperating and imitating firms, thereby reducing the number of relocating firms;

- a more stringent tariff policy that prevents imports from countries where environmental regulation is less stringent may be counterproductive.

These results clarify how important public innovation policies can be both in protecting the environment and in stimulating domestic economic growth, thus preventing relocation effects. They also suggest the importance of finding an *adequate policy mix between industrial (R&D), environmental and trade policies* in order to achieve the above policy goals. Hence, it is important to discuss carefully the issue of policy design, as is done in the next section.

5   ON POLICIES TO STIMULATE ENVIRONMENTAL INNOVATION (WHY DO WE NEED PUBLIC ENVIRONMENTAL INNOVATION STRATEGIES?)

There are three types of market failure at work when we consider the question of innovation and the environment. The first is the conventional market failure associated with externalities. If innovation results developed by one firm spill over to other firms, there is an incentive for firms to distort their innovation effort. The second is the conventional *static* market failure associated with imperfect competition – typically output is too low, prices too high and there is excessive entry. The third aspect of this market failure has only recently received serious attention. This is the *dynamic* market failure surrounding R&D and innovation. It arises fundamentally from the nature of knowledge as a public good, which is expensive to produce, but cheap to reproduce. It is particularly important for basic research, but it also holds for applied research.

This dynamic market failure gives rise to a complex set of questions which involve both innovation and its diffusion: (i) How many firms should engage in R&D? (ii) What information should they share (a) with each other; (b) with other non-innovating firms? (iii) How much R&D should each of the innovating firms carry out? (iv) What degree of protection of environmental innovation should firms be guaranteed? (v) How can public policy intervene to reduce the negative effects of market failures on innovation?

A partial solution to some of the market failures associated with R&D is the creation of a system of property rights, the most obvious one being patent protection. The problem with this is that it typically provides too much protection and so prevents socially beneficial sharing of information. In particular, it prevents a socially efficient diffusion of environmental innovation and hence reduces the environmental benefit that innovation provides. This distortion of the information-sharing aspects of R&D generates further distortions in the decisions about the amount of R&D being done. Thus we know that in non-tournament models, where many firms can achieve the same innovation, each firm typically does too little R&D, but there is excessive duplication of R&D. However, in tournament models, where there is a race to be the unique innovator, each firm undertakes too much R&D (see Ulph, D., 1997 for a survey of these models). For these reasons a lot of *the focus of technology policy is now on arrangements like research joint ventures (RJVs) which correct the distortions of the patent system by promoting more information sharing.* The difficulty now is that we have only a very limited understanding of how well these perform, mainly because, with the exception of the recent paper by Katsoulacos and Ulph (1996), the literature on RJVs treats the amount of information sharing as exogenous.

Therefore, even without the complications introduced by accounting for environmental market failures, we are far from having a complete understanding of R&D policy design. What we can conclude, however, is that *efficient innovation patterns in terms of R&D and investments cannot be achieved by a market system alone. Public policies are necessary to set guidelines, provide incentives and regulate strategic behaviour.*

Let us now include specific environmental concerns in the analysis. There are two effects of environmental policy, taxes or standards, on innovation. The *direct effect* is to alter the effectiveness of R&D in lowering costs. However, the *indirect effect* of the policy is to change the value to the firm of lowering costs. These effects go in opposite directions, though the sign depends on the nature of the policy instrument. An environmental tax or a system of tradable permits has a positive direct effect and negative indirect effect, whereas standards have a negative direct effect and positive indirect effect. These conclusions are very general and do not depend greatly on the nature of either product market competition or R&D competition (see Ulph, D., 1997). However, the balance between the two effects does depend on the nature of R&D competition. Hence, in non-tournament models it will typically be the case that higher environmental taxes will stimulate R&D, whereas in tournament models the balance between the effects depends sensitively on the competitiveness of the product market (see Jaffee and Stavins, 1995; Jung, Krutilla and Boyd, 1996).

Let us consider some specific results on optimal environmental innovation policies. Katsoulacos and Xepapadeas (1996) propose an optimal scheme of simultaneous application of taxes on emissions and subsidies on environmental R&D. The government can use receipts from taxing pollution to subsidize the firms' R&D efforts, thus implementing a recycling policy which differs from the one often proposed in the 'double-dividend theory' – where tax revenues are recycled in the labour market – and coincides with the one analysed through an econometric model in Carraro and Galeotti (1997). Furthermore, because of the R&D spillovers, the government subsidy corrects the appropriability problem that firms face when investing in R&D, while the tax corrects the pollution externality. Katsoulacos and Xepapadeas (1996) show that the optimal emission tax is less than the marginal damage, while the subsidy depends on three factors: (i) the deviation between emission taxes and marginal pollution damages; (ii) the deviation between the private and the social marginal product of R&D; (iii) firms' strategic incentives to invest in R&D.[4]

A similar framework is used in Requate (1995), where the goal is a comparison of the effects of emission taxes and tradable permits on environmental innovation in the context of an n-firms oligopoly. Requate shows that only a subset of firms would adopt the new environment-friendly technology. Moreover, both policy instruments may lead to too much or too little adoption with respect to the socially optimal rate. Taxes may cause too much adoption when little adoption is optimal and vice versa, whereas the effects of permits are the opposite of those of taxes. The incentives to environmental innovation as a tool to bypass the cost of buying permits are also analysed in Laffont and Tirole (1996). This paper shows again that firms invest excessively in new technologies as a reaction to environmental policy. This excess adoption can be mitigated by the introduction of future markets for emission permits along with the usual spot market.

The inefficiency of using a single policy instrument is stressed again in Carraro and Topa (1995), where a dynamic model of firms' environmental innovation is proposed. Here the issue is not excess adoption but rather excess timing of adoption, that is, firms tend to delay the introduction of new environment-friendly technologies. Carraro and Topa show that an environmental tax can indeed induce firms to adopt cleaner technologies, but that, without appropriate incentives, the timing of the adoption is socially suboptimal (because firms do not fully account for the environmental benefit of their innovation even when pollution is taxed). Hence, to prevent firms from delaying innovation, the government should subsidize R&D costs.

Ulph and Ulph (1996) provide a general treatment of the optimal design of environmental policy when trade effects are accounted for. They allow both governments and producers to act strategically, and producers' R&D to reduce both costs of production and emissions, but without imposing special functional forms. Their conclusions depend crucially on whether an increase in a country's environmental tax causes the costs of firms located in that country to rise or fall. In Ulph, D. (1994) it is shown that this depends on whether the increase in environmental R&D induced by the tax is more or less than the level needed to offset the direct effect of the tax increase on costs, and this in turn depends on the precise form of the relationship between emissions and R&D. Adding in process R&D does nothing to alter this.[5] If, ignoring process R&D, costs rise as a result of the tax, this will cause firms to lose market share. But this will lower the incentive to undertake process R&D and so merely exacerbate the effect of the tax on firms' costs. Conversely, if ignoring process R&D, firms' costs fall as the tax rises, this will increase their market share. In turn, this will increase the incentive for process R&D, which will simply reinforce the effects produced by the analysis in which there is only environmental R&D.

It has recently been suggested that traditional environmental policies that affect firms' costs and correct distortions through R&D subsidies may not be the most effective means of inducing environmental innovation. Recent empirical analyses emphasize the role of firms' plant size and their financial health. Kopp *et al.* (1998) find that technology adoption is positively related to the size of the plant. Past trends in energy prices and use are important control variables, but it is unclear whether 'adoption-prone' plants are more likely to have had higher energy costs in the past, encouraging them to adopt energy-saving technologies, or alternatively, whether adopters are more likely to have had lower energy costs in the past, reflecting a long-term tendency to seek greater energy efficiency. The econometric analysis performed by Kopp *et al.* (1998), which looks at the adoption of new energy-saving technologies, suggests that financial health is an important determinant of technology adoption. The effect of energy prices in this model is positive but neither statistically nor economically significant, generating only a 3 per cent swing in the likelihood of adoption (versus more than 10 per cent for both working capital and profit margin). However, looking at individual technologies instead of pooling across all technologies yields inconclusive results. The research carried out by Kopp *et al.* has therefore revealed important patterns in the adoption of new energy-efficient technologies, but also leaves unresolved some competing hypotheses. The association of financial health with technology adoption indicates that investment incentives may be an important avenue for speeding technology diffusion. It may, however, simply reflect that better-managed companies – proxied by financial health – are the ones that invest in energy-saving technologies. If that were the case, a variety of low-cost policies, for example, those which disseminate information to firms about new technologies, might also prove to be an effective means of disseminating new technologies.

The role of optimal policy mixes directed to stimulate and support environment-friendly innovation is also crucial when a dynamic perspective is accounted for. As already said, aggregate technological externalities within countries may help explain many of the observed patterns of growth across countries (Romer, 1986, 1990; Lucas, 1988). Product innovation is at least as important as process innovation in producing external effects and endogenous growth. Following the seminal work by Grossman and Helpman (1991), both Hung, Chang and Blackburn (1994) and Verdier (1995) introduce environmental variables in an endogenous growth model with product variety. Each product is characterized by a particular emission–output ratio. In the R&D stage, firms can chose the emission–output ratio of the new product introduced in the market. Designing cleaner products requires more resources to be spent in R&D. This feature naturally introduces a trade-off between the growth of product variety and the 'cleanness' of the products developed.

In this setting it is possible to show that small emission taxes need not reduce growth and may, on the contrary, boost the number of products developed in the economy. The intuitive reason is that an emission tax increases the relative price of manufactured goods, and reduces the demand for these goods and the quantity produced. This in turn releases resources to be used in the R&D sector and consequently promotes growth. Note that the issue of crowding-out emerges right away, because even in an endogenous growth model it is crucial to design a policy which stimulates environmental R&D without reducing the amount of resources devoted to other economic activities or other forms of R&D. Again a problem of optimal policy mix arises.

In Verdier (1995) there is also a comparison of the growth performance of an emission tax and a technological standard which implement the same pollution target. As expected, technological standards have a greater negative effect on economic growth than emission taxes. However, in terms of welfare the comparison is more difficult and does not lead to clear conclusions because there are potentially many market failures (outside pollution) in the economy: imperfect competition, R&D market failures, spillover effects. In a second-best world, where the regulator cannot use all the necessary instruments to correct for the various distortions, it is not clear whether emission taxes dominate technological standards. For example, for severe pollution targets, technological standards may be more efficient, in terms of welfare, than emission taxes. The reason for this result is simply that when pollution targets are severely binding, an emission tax induces industrial growth below the socially optimal rate. In other words, too many resources are devoted to environmental protection, thus crowding out resources for other economic activities.

The crowding-out issue is also raised by Goulder and Schneider (1996), whose theoretical model explicitly accounts for the possibility that increased investment in R&D by one sector (the alternative fuels sector), by demanding scarce knowledge-generating resources, might 'crowd out' investment in R&D by other sectors. To the extent that such crowding-out occurs, rapid technological change in one sector will be accompanied by less rapid change in other sectors. The model by Goulder and Schneider (1996) reveals analytically the connections between induced technical change and the costs of abatement policies and can thus explore how public policies oriented toward one industry affect R&D incentives in other industries and the economy-wide level of output and rate of technological progress. The crucial variable is the degree of inefficiency of R&D markets. If there are no such inefficiencies, the probability of R&D crowding-out is large, with consequent reduced effect on growth and pollution abatement of the proposed environmental R&D policy.

6   ON DIFFUSION PROCESSES[6]

The discussion of the previous sections mainly focused on analyses devoted to define an optimal policy mix which can provide adequate incentives to environmental, process and product, innovation. Even if diffusion processes were explicitly considered in the previous sections, particularly when analysing the role of spillovers and the impact of innovations on growth, little attention was devoted to the sluggishness and inertia of diffusion processes. These may be important problems to be faced when designing an innovation policy whose goal is to achieve environmental benefits.

There is a large body of economics research on the subject of technology diffusion. The single most important conclusion of this literature, well summarized in Jaffe and Stavins (1994), is that diffusion of new, economically superior technologies is a gradual rather than instantaneous process (Griliches, 1957; Mansfield, 1968; Davies, 1979; Oster, 1982; Levin, Levin and Meisel, 1987). Specifically, diffusion is often portrayed as a *sigmoid* curve over time. That is, the rate of adoption begins slowly, speeds up, then eventually slows down again as market saturation approaches. One justification for the sigmoid curve is based on an *epidemic* model of diffusion. Due to a lack of knowledge or confidence, the rate of adoption of a new technology increases with the growing popularity of the technology. From this intuition, it makes sense that the rate of adoption will be slow in the beginning (when there is little popularity) and in the end (when there are few non-users). In this model, the probability of adopting the technology depends entirely on the number of other firms in the industry who have already adopted it.

The pioneering work of Griliches (1957) extends this model by establishing that the diffusion of new technology can be understood in an economic framework by allowing the rate of diffusion to be partly determined by the (expected) economic return to adoption. Mansfield (1968) then demonstrates that the rate of diffusion can depend on the size of adopting firms, the perceived riskiness of the new technology, and the size of the required investment. In subsequent work, firm size has been argued to have both positive and negative effects on adoption (Davies, 1979; Oster, 1982; Boyd and Karlson, 1993). Arguments for the former are based on the resources (financial, experience, expertise) associated with large firms, while arguments for the latter hinge on potentially oligopolistic market structure which may reduce the competitive pressures to innovate. The possibility of varying diffusion rates for different technologies has been qualitatively described as the difference between different types of innovations. Minor innovations presumably diffuse quickly, innovations which are considerably more invasive diffuse more slowly (Cohen and Levin, 1989; Davies, 1979).

According to this line of thinking, economic factors (beyond firm size) influence the overall rate of diffusion based on idiosyncratic characteristics of the *technology*. Such factors do not, however, distinguish the rate of adoption by different firms. Similarly sized firms are considered to be homogeneous with respect to their rate of adoption. A natural alternative is to focus on inherent differences or heterogeneity among firms (David, 1969). This model is sometimes known as the *probit* approach, after the commonly employed statistical technique for limited dependent variables, which shares a conceptual foundation with the diffusion model (Stoneman, 1983). In this model the crucial factor for explaining the gradual diffusion process is that potential adopters are significantly different from one another in some aspects that affect the value of the innovation to them. Such aspects might include the cost of equipment, cost of learning about a new technology, cost of adapting existing processes, or future benefits of the technology. One can imagine a threshold above which it pays to adopt the new technology and below which it does not. The threshold differs across firms and, over time, the cost of the innovation may fall and/or the quality may improve, thereby lowering the threshold.

Beside idiosyncratic, firm-specific effects, the diffusion process also depends on systemic variables, that is, on the dynamics of R&D and innovation within complex social, economic and technical systems. Indeed, technological change occurs incrementally within existing technological trajectories, and only occasionally does innovation lead to the establishment of entirely new trajectories. In turn, all these trajectories are embedded within extremely complex and intricate social and technical systems in which the dynamics of change are themselves complicated, with institutional inertia and technical lock-in often inhibiting rates of change (see Rip and Kemp, 1998; Kemp, Schot and Hoogma, 1998).

Many sources of inertia govern the rate at which techno-economic systems change. These include low capital stock turnover rates in some sectors; the time needed for innovations to incubate; institutional barriers to diffusion; weak mechanisms incapable of translating political or societal imperatives into effective economic signals; and self-reinforcing loops between particular technical options and consumption patterns, which create technological 'lock-in' and discourage radical innovation.

Problems of lock-in and inertia are particularly keen in 'complex technology systems' characterized by massive investment in 'long-life' capital stock and extensive associated infrastructure, for example, transport systems and energy production and distribution systems. They are of less concern in sectors where capital stock turnover rates are comparatively low. Rates range from five years for electrical appliances, one to four decades for industrial production facilities, three to four decades for power plants, and four to ten decades for transport and urban infrastructure developments. However, even though turnover rates are low in some sectors of the economy, the inertia of overall socio-technical systems is exacerbated when the options for change within one sector or area are linked or modified by the options for change in other areas. The architecture of a building, for example, determines air conditioning requirements; and urban planning structures determine not only transportation needs but also the relative share of journeys made on foot, on a bicycle, by rail or by private car. The net result is that the inertia of an inter-related system as a whole is governed by the most inert component of the system, just as the strength of a chain depends upon its weakest link. Lock-in then stifles the opportunities for change.

Remedying structural inertia is difficult. Decision making within complex socio-technical systems takes place at many levels (households, industry, public authorities, etc.), all governed by different priorities, and diverting complete systems on to less environmentally harmful technological trajectories is a daunting task. Price signals like the ones discussed in the previous section will undoubtedly have some effect on the technological paths taken by the various actors involved in complex systems, but there are genuine fears that these prices will reflect short-term expediency rather than longer-term societal and environmental needs, and that they will be too low to overcome structural inertia as far as innovation is concerned. There is also the added complication that many parts of complex socio-technical systems are comparatively insensitive to price variations, with decisions on future behaviour driven primarily by other factors, for example, cost/speed ratios in the transportation sector, aesthetics in architecture, the price of land in urban planning.

In such situations, the important task is to make sure that future technological options are attractive to even the 'weakest-link' sectors, that is, those with high structural inertia and low price sensitivity. In fact, since 'chains' are dependent on their 'weakest links', targeting these sectors (transport, buildings, urban forms) becomes a high priority. There is, therefore, the need for socio-economic and policy research into the complementary economic and regulatory policy mechanisms which will be needed to ensure that these new technological options are adopted and diffused.

In addition, apart from research, there is also a great need for public policies supporting experimentation with new technologies, especially radical technologies for which a market is not defined. This would help suppliers to get a better idea of user requirements and the performance of technologies in real-life situations. It would also help users to develop a better understanding of new technologies and how they might benefit from them. It would also help to build a constituency for products and guide private and public actors in their policies. User experiments offer a way of breaking the gridlock of structural inertia by facilitating assessments of the claims for and against new technologies.

7   BLUEPRINTS FOR ENVIRONMENTAL INNOVATION POLICIES

It is clear from the above analysis that innovation policies need to be carefully designed according to a multi-faceted approach. On the one hand, they must promote *knowledge diffusion*, by disseminating information to firms about new technologies. They must also promote *basic learning*, by stimulating interactions between academic research and applied innovation. This is one of the most effective ways of stimulating technological spillovers, which increase growth and emission abatement at the same time (see Lucas, 1988). Finally, they should support technology diffusion, reduce inertia, and increase the amount of spillovers induced by the adoption of environment-friendly technologies.

On the other hand, policies must follow a carrot-and-stick policy. The threat of coercive regulation (see Cadot and Sinclair-Desgagné, 1996) and the higher costs introduced by a tradable permit system can act as *stimuli for energy-efficient R&D*, but must be coupled with measures to *protect firms' financial intertemporal health*, particularly for small- and medium-size firms which are more likely to suffer as a result of financial swings.

Market failures must also be offset, on the one hand, by protecting energy-efficient innovation through adequate patent rules, and on the other, by supporting *innovations obtained through research joint ventures* in order to promote knowledge sharing.

It is also necessary that policies be explicitly aimed at creating *alternative paths of development*. Some ways to do this are: support for new ideas offering long-term benefits through science and technology programmes, the creation of niches for promising technologies through government procurement policies, subsidies, regulation, experimentation, and the formulation of policy goals and targets for the medium term (Kemp, Schot and Hoogma, 1998).

Policies should also take international R&D, trade and location effects into account. Hence a high degree of *international coordination and cooperation* should characterize environmental innovation policies.

8   EMPIRICAL MODELS AND RESULTS

In many models used to assess the effects of policies designed to control polluting emissions, technical change has an exogenous representation which is quite unsatisfactory. Hence the need for a 'new generation' of environmental economic models which endogenize the linkages between economic variables (policy variables, in particular) and technical progress. Here we provide a brief description of some preliminary attempts to model induced technical change.

8.1   Innovation and R&D

Consider the GREEN model that allows for three back-stop options: a carbon-based synthetic fuel, and two carbon-free possibilities. The main hypotheses concern prices and timing of diffusion: the prices are exogenous and the back-stop technologies, once they come on stream, are available in all regions in *unlimited* quantities at constant marginal costs. The only key variable of this approach is the relative price of the technological substitution options, which is exogenously imposed at current levels; on the contrary, the technological innovation possibilities are assumed to be fixed at the present level of knowledge for the entire simulation path.

   The approaches just described do not introduce an explicit link between environmental variables and policies, technical change and economic growth. There are some recent efforts in this direction. The first one was probably proposed by Jorgenson and Wilcoxen (1990). They assume a translog unit cost function containing terms in which the input prices interact with the time trend – a proxy of technical progress. Therefore, the firms' costs depend on input prices and on the time trend. Finally, technical progress influences input demands, without interacting with any other variable. The authors show that the time trend, in addition to prices, affects the rate of total factor productivity. Thus environmental policy decisions affecting relative prices determine an endogenous change in total factor productivity. In this way, the proposal by Jorgenson and Wilcoxen partially endogenizes technical progress.

   A more satisfactory treatment of technical progress in recent AGE/CGE models relying on the concept of vintage capital can be found in Conrad and Henseler-Unger (1986) and Conrad and Ehrlich (1993). Here substitution possibilities are more feasible with the most recent capital vintages. Thus, adjusting to relative price shocks does not only depend on the elasticity of substitution but also on the capital replacement rate. This is a novelty with respect to previous CGE modelling approaches because technical change shows its effects on the firms' cost structure through a parametrization of each vintage's cost functions. Another vintage model has been proposed in Carlevaro, Garbely and Müller (1992).

Models using the idea of capital vintages have some drawbacks too, because they do not provide a precise evaluation of the mechanisms through which markets and agents can modify existing technologies toward energy-saving and environmental potentials. As an example, the model by Carlevaro, Garbely and Müller (1992) uses technical coefficients defining, say, the energy/capital ratio, which are endogenous but depend only on the future trend of energy prices. In a similar way to the technical–economic models, this approach does not explicitly take into account the economic profitability of the new technologies: the existence of a new, less polluting, technology does not imply that it will be adopted by firms.

The main difficulty faced by modellers when they try to endogenize technical change is the non-observability of this variable. This is why old-fashioned models use a deterministic trend as a proxy of technical change. And this is why this is the starting point of some *ad hoc* attempts to model technical change. For example, in Boone, Hall and Kemball-Cook (1992), Carraro and Galeotti (1996) and Dowlatabadi and Oravetz (1996), technical progress is still represented by a variable which is added to the main equations of the model. However, this variable is no longer a deterministic function of time. It is rather a stochastic function of time, in which other economic effects are also accounted for.

In Boone, Hall and Kemball-Cook (1992) (see also Hall, Mabey and Smith, 1994) the dynamics of technical change can be inferred by looking at the dynamics of factor demand (a similar approach was proposed by Gao, 1994 and Slade, 1989). In Carraro and Galeotti (1996) the basic idea is also that technical progress cannot be observed and that it must be inferred by observing the dynamics of other variables. However, the focus is on the capital stock. It is assumed that the capital stock can be broken down into two parts: the energy-saving/environment-friendly capital stock and the energy-consuming one. Each year a new vintage of the capital stock becomes operational. In this way new capital is added to the two components. The characteristics of this new capital depend on a number of economic variables which affect a firm's decision to install energy-saving capital. Among the variables which explain the dynamics of the two components, there is the amount of R&D carried out by firms. An increase in R&D expenditure can indeed increase the technological potential of the economic system and is therefore likely to produce investment in environment-friendly capital (of course, relative prices, market demand and other variables also intervene in the decision process). The amount of R&D carried out by firms depends on policy variables such as environmental taxation and innovation subsidies, and on relative prices, sales, and other endogenous economic variables. The model equations which capture the dynamics of the aggregate capital stock and its components are estimated using the Kalman filter. An indicator of environmental technical progress, which can be interpreted as an indicator of the environmental quality of the capital stock, can then be given by the ratio between the environment-friendly and the polluting capital stocks.

With this approach, the role of technical progress is completely endogenized. Let us assume, as an example, that firms are asked to pay a carbon tax. This raises the relative price of energy. This increase has two effects: it induces firms to substitute energy with other production factors (if technology is not of the Leontief type); and it raises firms' R&D expenditure, as suggested in Carraro and Topa (1994), thus accelerating technical progress, and increasing the environmental quality of the capital stock. This reduces energy demand without excessively penalizing output, but reducing energy prices. These two variables feed back into the equations determining the dynamics of technical progress.

The problem with this approach is its *ad hoc* nature. There is no explicit solution of the firms' optimization problem that determines the optimal amount of R&D and investments in the two types of capital. Therefore, links between these variables are mainly statistical, but lack a clear economic interpretation. A similar remark concerns the work by Dowlatabadi and Oravetz (1996). In this chapter, there is a direct econometric link between price variables (which depend on environmental policies) and technical change. Aside from their *ad hoc* nature, these models share another common feature. The efficacy of abatement policies is greater and the cost of curbing emissions is lower than in the case in which technical change is modelled through an exogenous trend.

The same difficulties with the observability and measurement of technical change affect the proposal by Newell, Jaffee and Stavins (1996). Here the model is more sophisticated and represents the economic structure of innovation decisions. However, the problem lies in the necessity of defining a statistical *ad hoc* model to construct the time series to be used in estimating the structural model of technological innovation. Hence, the model is still somewhat *ad hoc*, even if the problem is confined to the estimation procedure.

Of course, this problem does not exist in those models in which parameters are calibrated rather than estimated. In this case, it is possible to construct and simulate a structural model of R&D and innovation even if the price to be paid is a set of values for the model parameters that cannot easily be tested. Some preliminary but very interesting examples of this approach are contained in Goulder and Mathai (1996).

8.2   Spillovers, Diffusion, Learning-by-doing and Crowding-out

As previously said, new technologies are typically developed by the most innovative firms and not immediately available to all. Factors that influence the rate and timing of diffusion are of fundamental importance in assessing the ultimate effectiveness of the innovation. Modelling this factor is obstructed by certain characteristics of empirical environmental models. Usually, top–down models do not provide the degree of sector disaggregation that would be required for analysis at the level of the firm, while bottom–up studies do not consider strategic market behaviour that may delay the diffusion of innovation. There are however some attempts to model spillovers and diffusion.

One idea comes directly from the empirical literature on endogenous growth (see Mankiw, Romer and Weil, 1992; Ciccone, 1996). Here, the production function is specified in order to account for positive R&D externalities. These externalities, which may also depend on the volume of trade, as in the model by Grossman and Helpman (1991), are the mechanism through which endogenous growth takes place. This mechanism is empirically very relevant. For example, the Solow growth model, with physical capital only and with a share of physical capital in national income of about one-third, requires an exogenous annual growth rate of total factor productivity of 1.4 per cent to explain an annual growth rate of labour productivity of 2 per cent. The Solow model extended for human capital (see Mankiw, Romer and Weil, 1992) requires an exogenous annual growth rate of total factor productivity of 0.7 per cent to explain a 2 per cent annual growth rate of labour productivity. If we allow for externalities and technological interdependence, the exogenous annual growth rate of total factor productivity necessary to explain a 2 per cent annual growth rate of labour productivity is only 0.2 per cent (see Ciccone, 1996). It is clear therefore that the modelling of externalities plays a crucial role and greatly influences both the dynamics of the relevant variables in the 'business as usual' scenario and the effects of simulated environmental policies.

The issue of crowding-out has also received some attention in the empirical literature. Goulder and Schneider (1996) quantify the costs of carbon taxes in the presence of induced technical change and crowding-out. If there are no prior inefficiencies in R&D markets, policies that stimulate environmental R&D crowd out other forms of R&D, which implies that the gross costs (before accounting for environment-related benefits) of carbon taxes are higher than they would be if there were no induced technical change. The result may be reversed in the presence of inefficiencies in R&D markets. More importantly, the environmental benefits are likely to be larger when induced technical change is taken into account (because there is more abatement) and the benefits from the additional abatement more than compensate for the higher gross costs (whenever this is actually the case).

Another recent interesting development of the literature on induced technical change is constituted by the attempt to represent technological progress as a learning-by-doing process. The model by Grubler and Messner (1996) is based on the concept of learning curves and describes future costs and performance improvements of new technologies as a function of accumulated R&D, and learning and experience gained in diffusion of new technologies. Thus, technological learning depends on previous, accumulated investments in R&D, demonstration plants and gradually expanding niche markets.

8.3 Implementation of Already Commercially Available Technologies

This is an issue which is better captured by existing models. The bottom–up approach considers the possibility of substitution among different techniques through absolute shifts. Therefore, it risks underestimating transaction costs and being too optimistic about the potential for market penetration. At the level of the firm, elements that deserve more consideration are all those factors which impose a degree of inertia on the energy system, thereby reducing the scope for immediate adoption of available technologies. At the consumer level, market failures, such as information costs and high discount rates, can result in limited exploitation of the available options. In top–down studies, the possibility of substituting the existing technologies is no longer absolute as in the previous case, but relative to variation in the prices of the techniques, that is they are typically expressed through the concept of elasticity. Most models assign constant values to the parameters representing the elasticities. Price substitution along a given production isoquant is likely to underestimate the real impact of technology on the emission/output ratio; in particular, it does not account for changes in factor demands (that is, energy) which take place through shifts of the production isoquant. The possibility of non-price-induced energy-intensity reduction is assumed to be extremely limited in the majority of cases.

Note that most of the models described above in section 6.1 do not distinguish clearly between R&D of new technologies and the adoption/diffusion of existing best-available technologies (BATs). Being *ad hoc* reduced-form models, they tend to combine all types of technological change and, therefore, capture the dynamic effects of both R&D and the diffusion of BATs.

9   CONCLUSION AND RESEARCH AGENDA

Both theoretical analysis and empirical evidence agree on the following basic conclusion: technological innovation and diffusion are the main engine of growth. Growth is correlated with increasing environmental efficiency. Hence, innovation accomplishes a two-fold task: it stimulates growth and competitiveness and reduces pollution levels.

However, several market failures characterize existing innovation systems. Spillover effects, inefficiency in the banking sector and financial markets, risk aversion, the nature of knowledge as a public good, lack of coordination, are all elements that reduce private incentives to undertake R&D and innovation and call for public intervention.[7]

The global dimension of many environmental problems and the increasing mobility of capital and goods call for action in both developed and developing countries. It is therefore crucial to increase:

(i)   *knowledge diffusion*, by disseminating information about new environment-friendly technologies;
(ii)   *basic learning and innovation*, by stimulating interactions between academic research and applied environmental innovation;
(iii)   *technology diffusion*, by improving the quality of the role of multinationals in the global economy and by implementing technological cooperation agreements.

The long-term dimension calls for action on R&D and innovation that enhances *long-run competitiveness* in environmentally sensitive sectors, that increases *financial resources* provided by the banking sector, for example by partly involving banks in the liability process, that guarantees *protection* for energy-efficient innovation, and supports *cooperation and RJVs* designed to undertake environmental R&D.

In this framework, environmental innovation policies are structurally linked and interact with competition and industrial and trade policies. These should support R&D cooperation, increase the competitiveness of the banking system, protect innovation and introduce lender liability schemes and support trade rules that favour technology transfers.

The above conclusions are based on a large body of economics literature which is only partly environment specific. Most analyses of the role of innovation, the problems with its diffusion, the effects of different public policies, have indeed been developed independently of environmental concerns. These analyses have proved to be useful in understanding the complexity of environmental innovation, even if new elements had to be added, particularly because the main benefits provided by environmental R&D and innovation are mostly public goods. There are several research issues that deserve further attention. From a theoretical viewpoint, it would be useful to achieve a better understanding of the links between environmental, trade, industrial and financial policies. Current research is carried out in a partial equilibrium framework where each issue is analysed separately. A general equilibrium analysis of the optimal policy mix needs to be undertaken. In the previous section, we argued that environmental innovation and its diffusion are strictly intertwined. This is also an issue that needs further theoretical research (possibly using dynamic models in which inertia and lock-in effects can be explored). Similarly, there is a need for socio-economic and policy research into the complementary economic and regulatory policy mechanisms which may be necessary to ensure that new technological options are adopted and diffused.

The largest gap to fill in order to achieve reliable information for policy design concerns applied research. Existing applied analyses of environmental innovations are very preliminary and limited by lack of good data. As previously said, no empirical study is able to distinguish environmental innovation from other forms of innovation, or to distinguish between innovation and diffusion. An assessment of the incentives necessary for firms to undertake and adopt environment-friendly technologies would also be valuable in order to provide policy makers with a rough order of magnitude of the policies to be implemented. Empirical research is also necessary to evaluate innovation spillovers and their impact on aggregate growth and to quantify the constraints imposed by inertia on environmental and industrial policies. Finally, an empirical assessment of the long-term value of basic research on environmental issues (particularly on climate issues) would help in defining the optimal timing of environmental policies.[8]

ACKNOWLEDGEMENTS

The author is grateful to David Ulph, Yannis Katsoulacos and Antoine Soubeyran for useful discussions and to Henk Folmer for several helpful remarks. The author none the less bears sole responsibility for possible misrepresentations and errors.

NOTES

1. See Carraro and Siniscalco (1994). Chichilnisky (1994) stresses that differences in property rights across countries can also explain differences in the use of environmental resources.
2. Notice that recent research has highlighted the role of financial factors, rather than cost and price incentives, in stimulating environmental innovation. For example, Kopp, et al. (1998),

find that the financial health of parent firms is also strongly associated with the likelihood of technology adoption.

3. In particular, Michael Porter (1991) has argued that governments could provide a competitive advantage to their domestic producers by imposing environmental policies which are tougher than those faced by their rivals, since this will spur industries to introduce greener technologies ahead of their rivals, and enhance the long-run profitability of domestic industry. This view finds considerable support in the US administration, and is also commonly espoused in Germany and Japan. In its extreme form it suggests that environmental regulations are beneficial to both the environment and the economy.

4. A paradoxical result is that when spillovers are sufficiently small the optimal subsidy may be negative; that is, it may be optimal to tax environmental R&D. This is to avoid overinvestment in R&D, a problem also emphasized in Laffont and Tirole (1996).

5. Environmental R&D is aimed at reducing the emission/output ratio, whereas process R&D aims at lowering production costs.

6. Part of this section is based on the report 'Climate change and the challenge for research and technological development policy', prepared for the EU Commission by Carlo Carraro, Reinhard Coenen, Ken Guy, Jean-Charles Hourcade, René Kemp, Jim Skea, Walter R. Stahel, Uno Svedin and Ferenc Toth.

7. These market failures are even stronger in the case of international and global environmental problems, for example climate change. Climate change is a global, long-term, uncertain phenomenon. These features crucially reduce firms' incentives to undertake R&D and innovation.

8. On this topic, see the special issue of *Energy Economics* edited by Carlo Carraro and Jean-Charles Hourcade at the end of 1998.

REFERENCES

Baldwin, R. (1995), 'Does sustainability require growth?', in I. Goldin and A. Winters (eds), *The Economics of Sustainable Development*, Cambridge: Cambridge University Press.

Barrett, S. (1994), 'Strategic environmental policy and international trade', *Journal of Public Economics*, **54**, 325–38.

Boetti, M., M. Botteon, C. Carraro and A. Soubeyran (1998), 'On the effects of industrial, trade and environmental policies on the location choices of firms', *Revue d'Economie Industrielle*, **83**, 63–80.

Boone, L., S. Hall and D. Kemball-Cook (1992), 'Endogenous technical progress in fossil fuel demand', mimeo, Centre for Economic Forecasting, London Business School.

Cadot, O. and B. Sinclair-Desgagné (1996), 'Innovation under the threat of stricter environmental standards' in C. Carraro, Y. Katsoulacos and A. Xepapadeas (eds), *Environmental Policy and Market Structure*, Dordrecht: Kluwer, pp. 131–41.

Cantwell, John (1993) 'Multinational corporations and innovatory activities: towards a new evolutionary approach', University of Reading, Department of Economics, Discussion Papers in International Investment and Business Studies, N.172 Series B, vol. V.

Carlevaro, F., M. Garbely and T. Müller (1992), 'Vers une modélisation en équilibre général des mesures de politique énergétique en Suisse', Serie de Publications du CUEPE No. 49, Université de Genève.

Carraro, C. and M. Galeotti (1996), 'WARM: A European model for energy and environmental analysis', *Environmental Modelling and Assessment*, **2**, 171–89.

Carraro, C. and M. Galeotti (1997), 'Economic growth, international competitiveness and environmental protection: R&D and innovation strategies with the WARM Model', *Energy Economics*, **19**, 2–29.

Carraro, C. and J.C. Hourcade (eds) (1998), *Optimal Timing of Climate Change Policies*, special issue of *Energy Economics*, Amsterdam: Elsevier.

Carraro, C. and D. Siniscalco (1994), 'Environmental policy reconsidered: the role of technological innovation', *European Economic Review*, **38**, 545–55.

Carraro, C. and A. Soubeyran (1999), 'R&D cooperation, innovation spillovers and firm location in a model of environmental policy', in E. Petrakis, E. Sartzetakis and A. Xepapadeas (eds), *Environmental Regulation and Market Structure*, Cheltenham, UK and Northampton, MA: Edward Elgar.

Carraro, C. and G. Topa (1994), 'Should environmental innovation policy be internationally coordinated?', in C. Carraro (ed.), *Trade, Innovation, Environment*, Dordrecht: Kluwer Academic Publishers.

Carraro, C. and G. Topa (1995), 'Taxation and environmental innovation', in C. Carraro and J. Filar (eds), *Game-Theoretic Models of the Environment*, Boston: Birkauser.

Chichilnisky, G. (1994), 'Property rights and the dynamics of renewable resources in north–south trade', in C. Carraro (ed.), *Trade, Innovation, Environment*, Dordrecht: Kluwer Academic Publishers.

Ciccone, A. (1996), 'Externalities and interdependent growth: theory and evidence', mimeo, University of California at Berkeley.

Coe, D.T., E. Helpman and A.W. Hoffmaister (1995), 'North–South R&D spillovers', Centre for Economic Policy Research Discussion Paper Series, N.1133, London.

Cohen, Wesley and Richard Levin (1989), 'Empirical studies of innovation and market structure', *Handbook of Industrial Organization*, Volume II, Amsterdam, North Holland, chapter 18.

Conrad, K. and M. Ehrlich (1993), 'The impact of embodied and disembodied technical progress on productivity gaps – an applied general equilibrium analysis for Germany and Spain', *Journal of Productivity Analysis*, **4**, 317–35.

Conrad, K. and I. Henseler-Unger (1986), 'Applied general equilibrium modelling for long-term energy policy in Germany', *Journal of Policy Modelling*, **8**, 531–49.

Contractor, F.J. and P. Lorange (1988), *Cooperative Strategies in International Business*, New York: Lexington Books.

David, P.A. (1969), 'A contribution to the theory of distribution', Research Memorandum N.17, Research Center in Economic Growth, Stanford University.

Davies, S.W. (1979), 'Inter-firm diffusion of process innovations', *European Economic Review*, **12**, 299–317.

Dowlatabadi, H. and M. Oravetz (1996), 'Modelling US long term energy intensity: an exploration of endogenous technical change', presented at the CEC–DGXII Symposium on Prospects for Integrated Environmental Assessment, Toulouse, 24–26 October 1996.

Downing, P.B. and L.J. White (1986), 'Innovation in pollution control', *Journal of Environmental Economics and Management*, **13**, 18–29.

Echia, G. and M. Mariotti (1994), 'A survey on environmental policy: technological innovation and strategic issues', FEEM Working Paper, Milan.

Galeotti, M. and A. Lanza (1998), 'Desperately seeking environmental Kuznets', FEEM Working Paper, Milan.

Gao, X.M. (1994), 'Measuring technological change using a latent variable approach', *European Review of Agricultural Economics*, **21**, 113–29.

Goulder, L. and K. Mathai (1996), 'Optimal CO$_2$ abatement in the presence of induced technical change', mimeo, University of Stanford.

Goulder, L. and S. Schneider (1996), 'Induced technical change, crowding out and the attractiveness of CO$_2$ emission abatement', mimeo, University of Stanford.

Griliches, Z. (1957), 'Hybrid corn: an exploration in the economics of technological change', *Econometrica*, **25**, 501–22.

Grossman, G. (1995), 'Pollution and growth: what do we know?', in I. Goldin and A. Winters (eds), *The Economics of Sustainable Development*, Cambridge: Cambridge University Press.

Grossman, G. and E. Helpman (1991), 'Quality ladders in the theory of growth', *Review of Economic Studies*, **58**, 43–61.

Grubler, A. and S. Messner (1996), 'Technological change and the timing of abatement measures', mimeo, IIASA, Vienna.

Hall, S., N. Mabey and C. Smith (1994), 'Macroeconomic modelling of international carbon tax regimes', Department of Economics Discussion Paper n.94–08, University of Birmingham.

Hoel, M. (1995), 'Environmental policy as a game between governments when plant locations are endogenous', paper presented at the 21st EARIE Conference, Crete, 4-6.9, 1994.

Holtz-Eakin, D. and T.M. Selden (1995), 'Stoking the fires? CO$_2$ emissions and economic growth', *Journal of Public Economics*, **61**, 428–37.

Hung, V., P. Chang and K. Blackburn (1994), 'Endogenous growth, environment and R&D', in C. Carraro (ed.), *Trade, Innovation, Environment*, Dordrecht: Kluwer.

Jaffe, A.B. and R.N. Stavins (1994), 'The energy paradox and the diffusion of conservation technology', *Resource and Energy Economics*, **16**, 91–122.

Jaffee, A. and R.N. Stavins (1995), 'Dynamic incentives and environmental regulation: the effects of alternative policy instruments on technology diffusion', *Journal of Environmental Economics and Management*, **29**, 43–63.

Jorgenson, D.W. and P.J. Wilcoxen (1990), 'Intertemporal general equilibrium modelling of US environmental regulation', *Journal of Policy Modelling*, **12**, 715–44.

Jung, C., K. Krutilla and R. Boyd (1996), 'Incentives for advanced pollution abatement technology at the industry level: an evaluation of policy alternatives', *Journal of Environmental Economics and Management*, **30**, 95–111.

Katsoulacos, Y. and A. Xepapadeas (1996), 'Environmental innovation, spillovers and optimal policy rules', in C. Carraro, Y. Katsoulacos and A. Xepapadeas (eds), *Environmental Policy and Market Structure*, Dordrecht: Kluwer, pp. 143–50.

Katsoulacos, Y. and D. Ulph (1996), 'Endogenous information sharing and technology policy', CEPR Discussion Paper No. 1407, London.

Katz, M.L. and C. Shapiro (1987), 'R&D rivalry with licensing and imitation', *American Economic Review*, **77**, 402–20.

Kemp, R., J. Schot and R. Hoogma (1998), 'Regime shifts to sustainability through processes of niche formation: the approach of strategic niche management', *Technology Analysis and Strategic Management*, **10**(2), 175–95.

Kopp, R.J., W. Harrington, R.D. Morgenstern, W.A. Pizer and J.S. Shih (1998), 'Diffusion of new technologies: a microeconomic analysis of firm decision making at the plant level', Resources for the Future, Washington, DC.

Kumar, N. (1995), 'Intellectual property protection, foreign direct investments and location of overseas R&D activities by multinational enterprises', United Nations University, Institute for New Technologies, Maastricht.

Laffont, J.J. and J. Tirole (1996), 'A note on environmental innovation', *Journal of Public Economics*, **62**, 138–47.

Levin, S.G., S.L. Levin and J.B. Meisel (1987), 'A dynamic analysis of the adoption of a new technology: the case of optical scanners', *Review of Economics and Statistics*, **69**, 12–17.

Levinson, J. (1996), 'Environmental policy and plant location', *Journal of Public Economics*, **62**, 1–18.

Lucas, R.E. (1988), 'On the mechanics of economic development', *Journal of Monetary Economics*, **100**, 223–51.

Magat, W. (1979), 'The effects of environmental regulation on innovation', *Law and Contemporary Problems*, **43**, 4–25.

Malueg, D.A. (1989), 'Emission credit trading and the incentive to adopt new pollution abatement technology', *Journal of Environmental Economics and Management*, **18**, 297–300.

Mankiw, N.G., D. Romer and D.N. Weil (1992), 'A contribution to the empirics of economic growth', *Quarterly Journal of Economics*, 407–37.

Mansfield, E. (1968), *Industrial Research and Technological Innovation*, New York: W.W. Norton.

Milliman, S.R. and R. Prince (1989), 'Firm incentives to promote technological change in pollution control', *Journal of Environmental Economics and Management*, **17**, 247–65.

Newell, R.G., A. Jaffee and R. Stavins (1996), 'Energy-saving technological innovation: the effect of economic incentives and direct regulation', presented at the NBER Workshop on Public Policy and the Environment, Cambridge, 29–30 July 1996.

Oster, S. (1982), 'The diffusion of innovation among steel firms: the basic oxygen furnace', *The Bell Journal of Economics*, **13**, 45–56.

Pietrobelli, C. (1996), 'Emerging forms of technological cooperation: the case for technology partnership', UNCTAD, Division for Science and Technology.

Porter, M. (1991), 'America's green strategy', *Scientific American*, **264**(4), 168.

Rauscher, M. (1994), 'On ecological dumping', *Oxford Economic Papers*, **46**, 822–40.

Rauscher, M. (1995), 'Environmental regulation and the location of polluting industries', paper presented at the 50th IIPF Conference, Cambridge, MA, 22–25 August 1994.

Requate, T. (1995), 'Incentives to adopt new technologies under different pollution-control policies', *International Tax and Public Finance*, **2**, 295–317.

Rip, A. and R. Kemp (1998), 'Technological change', in S. Rayner and L. Malone (eds), *Human Choice and Climate Change*, Vol. II, Columbus, OH: Batelle Press, chapter 6.

Romer, P. (1986), 'Increasing returns and long-run growth', *Journal of Political Economy*, **98**, S71–S102.

Romer, P. (1990), 'Endogenous technological change', *Journal of Political Economy*, **94**, 1002–37.

Slade, M.E. (1989), 'Modelling stochastic and cyclical components of technical change: an application of the Kalman Filter', *Journal of Econometrics*, **41**, 363–83.

Stoneman, P. (1983), *The Economic Analysis of Technological Change*, Oxford: Oxford University Press.

Ulph, A. (1996), 'Strategic environmental policy', in C. Carraro, Y. Katsoulacos and A. Xepapadeas (eds), *Environmental Policy and Market Structure*, Dordrecht: Kluwer, pp. 99–127.

Ulph, A. (1997), 'Environmental policy and international trade – a survey of recent economic analysis', in C. Carraro and D. Siniscalco, *New Directions in the Economic Theory of the Environment*, Cambridge: Cambridge University Press.

Ulph, A. and D. Ulph (1996), 'Trade, strategic innovation and strategic environmental policy – a general analysis', in C. Carraro, Y. Katsoulacos and A. Xepapadeas (eds), *Environmental Policy and Market Structure*, Dordrecht: Kluwer, pp. 181–208.

Ulph, D. (1994), 'Strategic innovation and strategic environmental policy', in C. Carraro (ed.), *Trade, Innovation, Environment*, Dordrecht: Kluwer.

Ulph, D. (1997), 'Environmental policy and technological innovation', in C. Carraro and D. Siniscalco, *New Directions in the Economic Theory of the Environment*, Cambridge: Cambridge University Press.

Verdier, T. (1995), 'Environmental pollution and endogenous growth', in C. Carraro and J. Filar (eds), *Control and Game-Theoretic Models of the Environment*, Boston: Birkauser.

Vonortas, N.S. (1991), *Research Cooperation in R&D Intensive Industries*, Aldershot: Ashgate Publishing Group.

Wilson, D. and J. Swisher (1993), 'Exploring the gap: top–down versus bottom–up analyses of the cost of mitigating global warming', *Energy Policy*, March, 249–63.

15. On the future of environmental economics

Rüdiger Pethig

1 INTRODUCTION

Environmental economics (EE[1]) has passed its age of infancy. In terms of monographs, proceedings volumes, specialized professional journals and papers in economic journals it grew rapidly over recent decades and established itself as a discipline based on the powerful economic paradigm and reaching beyond it to capture important economy–environment interactions. As compared to its mother discipline, economics, EE is still young but this juvenile is increasingly interested in knowing where she comes from, what her present position is and, in particular, where she will or ought to go.

After a period of strong if not stormy growth, the desire for orientation and guidance increases. It materializes in new textbooks, survey articles (in specialized areas), handbooks, yearbooks[2] and conferences, which seek to identify and discuss the frontiers of research in EE. Focusing on *research frontiers* is a challenging and ambitious, if not presumptuous, enterprise, directed towards outlooks on what is perceived as the likely, promising and/or necessary agenda of *future* research.

Let me be very clear from the outset that I am neither capable nor willing to adopt the role of a prophet, a futurologist, an 'opinion leader' or a 'trend setter'. In my view, the most promising way to think about future research in EE is to let competent senior *environmental economists* (EEsts) survey their specific research topics and use their experience and overview to identify what will be, or ought to be, ahead of us. But what, then, is the possible role of a 'generalist' contribution on the future of EE? In my understanding the task assigned to me is not to outperform all the experts. I rather take it as a chance, denied to them, to focus on major broad lines and issues followed by the EE profession so far and to assess its present achievements. Thus likely future developments and desiderata are unfolded in a natural way.

One way to offer reflections on the future of EE is to centre the chapter around what I perceive to be the major likely, urgent and/or desirable substantive topics on the agenda of future research, such as global climate change, sustainable development, greening of business and energy policy (EP) issues, to name only a few. Instead, I chose the *methods* of analysis as the primary organizing principle, starting out from theoretical concepts and their ramifications, then turning to issues of interdisciplinarity and empirical relevance to finally assess the (future) impact of EE on shaping EP. Real-world environmental problems, the primary driving forces of research in EE, are also addressed, of course, but under the premise that there is not too much dispute about what the relevant substantive issues are in EE.

The subsequent analysis as well as the citation of the pertinent literature is necessarily selective, incomplete and reflects subjective appraisals and judgments that are debatable and, in some cases, certainly controversial. Even though it is inevitable that I present *my* view of the future of EE, I make some effort to draw on other EEsts' suggestions on the future research agenda without claiming, however, to offer a representative account.[3]

2   THE BACKBONE OF ENVIRONMENTAL ECONOMICS: ALLOCATION THEORY AND COASEAN ECONOMICS

The basic economic paradigm as represented by Debreu's (1959) *Theory of Value* demonstrates how decentralized coordination and allocative efficiency are achieved under idealized conditions through perfectly competitive markets. Although this neoclassical allocation theory envisages an abstract, frictionless and artificial world, it is, in my view, valuable as a framework of reference to assess the consequences of introducing imperfections. The principal deviation from the Debreu model constituting the core of EE is, of course, the presence of environmental externalities which cause the perfectly competitive markets to fail and thus define the fundamental policy-oriented task of EE as suggesting regulatory devices to overcome the associated allocative inefficiency. In the theoretical domain, Mäler (1974) is an early important contribution combining allocation theory and environmental externalities.

As is well known, the concept of externalities refers to the non-market interdependence of agents' actions which is essentially synonymous with the non-existence of (certain) markets. In the context of competitive markets it is based on the assumption that agents are both price-taking and 'externality-taking'. This view was challenged by Coase (1960) who argued convincingly that there is no reason for the absence of a market when (private and exclusive) property rights are well defined and transaction costs are zero. After the heat of the Coase debate had gone, it turned out that to a large extent EE maintained the market failure approach with the implied (Pigouvian) cause for government action, because in relevant empirical cases of environmental externalities, the qualifiers of the *Coase theorem*, zero 'transaction costs' and well-defined property rights, did not apply. Many pollution problems affect a large number of agents, rendering bargaining prohibitively costly, and/or they are related to environmental resources for which property rights are not well defined.

Nevertheless, the Coase *debate* (in contrast to the Coase *theorem*) turned out to be very stimulating for the research in EE, and it has a major impact on EE at present and in the future for the following reasons:

1. The property rights issue firmly links EE to law even though the economic notion of property rights goes far beyond the legal one. The research is not only about comparing the polar cases of private exclusive rights versus free access. It also focuses on intermediate cases, on communal rights, on non-encompassing or attenuated rights, and on the study and design of institutions through which property rights are implicitly assigned. An interesting actual case in point is the discussion of the 'take-back rule' in solid waste management. Property rights are also particularly relevant for developing countries. According to Markandya (1998, p. 464) 'neither privatization nor elaborate traditional community regulations are sufficient to guarantee that the institutional changes will be sufficient to protect the natural resource base'. He also argues that the biggest gap in our present knowledge is our limited understanding of the role of institutions which implicitly define property rights and the dynamics of institutional change.

2. The Coase theorem tells us that in a world with zero transaction costs and well-defined property rights *institutions* neither foster nor prevent allocative efficiency. Of course, the importance of this observation rests on the reverse conclusion that if transactions costs (information costs, bargaining costs, administrative costs, etc.) are significant, as in the real world, *institutions do matter*. Hence, different institutions will have different impacts on efficiency (and distribution) which, in turn, makes comparative institutional analysis indispensable. The focus on these issues is the programmatic objective of the so-called 'new institutional economics'.[4] EEsts already draw on this growing body of literature, and contribute to it, but there is a widely expressed demand and need for more systematic, in-depth analysis of institutional design, incidence and comparison. Markandya (1998) points to our limited understanding of the role of institutions in adapting to changes in the natural and human environment and concludes that a better understanding of that process 'perhaps more than any factor, is the key challenge on the research front' (p. 470).

3. If the number of agents involved in an environmental externality prob-

lem is not too large, each agent is directly affected by each other agent's action. As a consequence, with low or moderate transactions costs agents find themselves confronted with strategic uncertainty regarding the other agents' actions. This gives rise to *bargaining* or to non-cooperative reactions. Owing to the outstanding advances of game theory over the last decades, many interesting and important environmental issues have been tackled with game-theoretic methods, ranging from two-person interactions, which were the major focus of Coase (1960), to international environmental negotiations.[5]

We argued above that in its core area EE emerged as a branch of externality theory with an emphasis on the design and recommendation of policy instruments to reduce the externality-induced inefficiencies. The amazing upswing of EE in the past decades is certainly due to the increasing empirical relevance of environmental issues. When economists discussed the Pigouvian concept of externalities in the 1950s they found it hard to come up with convincing examples.[6] This situation changed dramatically, because new and large-scale environmental hazards and degradation emerged. These led to mounting dissatisfaction of the affected citizens which was then articulated and multiplied in the political arena and in the media. Even 'many economists, particularly those most visible in the media, did not realize the empirical importance of externalities until the latter started making their own headlines' (Sterner and van den Bergh, 1998, p. 252).

If EE was to play a significant role in providing relevant information for the public and for policy makers, the scientific challenges were clear: it had to come up with good advice on the effective regulation of polluting activities and it had to deliver reliable information on the order of magnitude of the allocative displacement effects caused by environmental externalities and on the net benefit of pollution control programmes.

As for the design and analysis of the impact of *EP instruments*, a huge literature has developed (Cropper and Oates, 1992) which will not be discussed here. In my view, EEsts have now a very good understanding of the regulation issue both on the conceptual and applied level, including the intricacies emerging when abstract policy proposals are to be implemented by real-world decision makers in a world with preexisting institutional arrangements (Hahn, 1989; Shogren, 1998). The professional discussion and debate on EP instruments will and will need to continue, of course.[7] But I believe that important insights have already been gained and therefore I see the major task ahead of us as improving the profession's impact on practical EP implementation (see section 7 below).

As for the *valuation* of environmental services and the benefits and costs of environmental programmes, it became evident that it was not good enough to tell policy makers that an 'uncompensated' externality, hence an inefficiency, 'was out there'. There was and still is an urgent need to be more specific about the order of magnitude of allocative inefficiencies caused by environmental externalities. To make the case for a net benefit of government intervention, environmental costs, risks and (gross) benefits need to be specified in detail and *quantified*. EE took on that challenge by developing methods and concepts of eliciting, estimating and measuring those costs and benefits. Non-market valuation became an exciting and vivid field of study which is still active and controversial (see Cropper and Oates, 1992; Smith 1997; Knetsch 2000).

The following observations are of special interest in this context: research in EE on the whole has grown rapidly during the last decades, but the number of papers dealing with 'valuation methods' and 'damage–benefit estimation' grew even more than proportionally over time both in the *Journal of Environmental Economics and Management* (Deacon *et al.*, 1998) and in the journal *Environmental and Resource Economics* (Siniscalco, 1998). This enormous expansion of the non-market valuation literature is a 'revolutionary' development which hardly anyone could have anticipated.

The availability of various methods of non-market valuation is certainly a major achievement of EE. But can the present state of the art be considered satisfactory? How well founded and reliable are these methods? In spite of significant progress that has been made, you will probably receive widely diverging results when different competent scholars are asked for independent cost–benefit appraisals. More or less scepticism seems to prevail: Deacon *et al.* (1998, p. 388) suggested that 'the "heat" has not necessarily generated "light"' (which leaves much room for interpretation) and they consider the contingent valuation method as one of the most controversial topics in non-market valuation.[8] Sterner and van den Bergh (1998, p. 249) contend that 'there are still many reasons why the numbers generated are not very reliable' and Cropper and Oates (1992, p. 729) argue that 'our ability to place dollar values on improvements of environmental quality is limited and imprecise'. Since the profession is in doubt about the reliability of its valuation methods, it is not so surprising that we have hard times convincing the public and, in particular, those policy makers who are sceptical of, or even entirely reject, the EEsts' *conceptual* approach to non-market valuation (see section 7).[9]

Much work on non-market valuation has been done in the context of rather small-scale projects. But the challenges grow exponentially when it comes to complex issues such as green accounting, dynamic economy–environment interaction, ecological tax reform or global climate change, with the urgent need reliably to assess environmental risks, damage and abatement costs in view of dynamic interdependence and likely technological innovations. The future of EE and its role in shaping EP depend heavily on further substantial improvements in operational methods of non-market valuation.

3   ENVIRONMENTAL EXTERNALITIES IN AN IMPERFECT WORLD

Imperfect Information

Imperfect and incomplete information is an important fact of life in all areas of human activities, but it is particularly serious in economy–environment interactions. The Pigouvian solution lost much of its charm when its implementation turned out to be informationally infeasible. Similarly, environmental intervention with good intentions may yield bad results due to our poor knowledge of ecosystems and dose–response relationships. Whenever new environmental hazards have arisen over the last decades, the initial situation was usually characterized by severe ignorance. Acid rain, ozone depletion and global warming are some of the more spectacular cases in point. Even though uncertainty cannot be completely removed, in general, multidisciplinary research efforts succeeded in reducing it significantly in many cases. This experience is why it is reasonable to expect the veil of uncertainty to become even thinner in the future, giving rise to the prospect that EP becomes more effective and better tuned toward supporting a sustainable development.

In the context of theoretical EE, incomplete information and uncertainty have been introduced into rigorous analysis in a systematic non-trivial way. In many cases, EE followed and applied advances in mainstream economics, most notably in risk analysis, agency theory and game theory, when strategic uncertainty is combined with incomplete and asymmetric information. EE adopted a pioneering role in the theory of decision making under the threat of irreversibility and the prospect of improved information in the future. In my view, the analytical consideration of informational aspects helped a lot to better assess and compare environmental policy options and should therefore be continued in future research.

It is worth mentioning that institutional arrangements and EP instruments, in particular, may induce or discourage agents to use or elicit environmentally relevant private information for achieving satisfactory or even efficient results. An ambitious and intellectually appealing approach was the design of demand revelation procedures (Green and Laffont, 1979) which do not seem to have reached the level of practical relevance, however.

Imperfect Competition

Imperfect competition is a particularly important real-world phenomenon. Long before environmental issues became a major concern, economists had realized that neither perfect competition (as in the referential allocation theory) nor monopoly are relevant market structures in most real markets.

Globalization tended to reduce the relative size of firms in expanding markets, but at the same time quite a few firms grew even faster and became powerful multinational agents, while smaller firms retained considerable discretion in (national) submarkets. Issues of industrial organization and (environmental) regulation arise where firms and regulators are players acting strategically and trying to take advantage of private information (see above). Major advances in game theory triggered an ever-growing literature on industrial organization which trickled down, eventually, to EP issues (Carraro and Siniscalco, 1997).

The pertinent literature is still small but growing. It applies partial equilibrium analysis almost exclusively (which is appropriate for all policy issues with small ramifications across major markets) and is (as yet) mainly theoretical. Its message is, in a nutshell, that 'no general conclusion about the effects of EP can be derived, because the presence of multiple market externalities, both positive and negative, makes the use of a single policy instrument, designed to correct for the environmental externality, largely suboptimal. As a consequence, EP needs to be designed so as to take into account the 'characteristics of the specific market and the specific environmental phenomena to be regulated' (Carraro, 1998, p. 368). I certainly agree with Carraro (p. 376) that though theoretical advances are necessary, 'an extensive empirical research program is probably even more important'.

Drawing on the experience in industrial organization (on other than environmental issues) in recent years a very large variety of models has been advanced, focusing on the same or similar issues but yielding different, partly incompatible implications. Empirical testing and analysis which was at the heart of the pre-game-theoretic industrial organization literature has hard times keeping up with the stormy theoretical development to filter out its empirically relevant aspects.

EE has yet to establish an empirical branch of industrial-organization-related analysis. That is a major task for the future, because I expect the theoretical literature will continue to grow fast, confronting us with a frustrating plurality of diverging results and recommendations, the empirical relevance of which is an open question. On the other hand, there cannot be any doubt that imperfect competition needs to be addressed more systematically than in the past for the benefit of the empirical relevance of EE and at the cost of devaluing our traditional, less complicated paradigm of perfect competition.

Preexisting Public Policy Distortions in the Competitive Economy

Whenever environmental regulation affects several major markets and their interaction as, for example, in the case of fossil fuel regulation, general equilibrium analysis is indispensable. To tackle the vast complexity of general interdependence, researchers quite often seek comfort in the world of perfectly competitive markets.[10] But even with this analytical relief, determining the impact of environmental regulation gets very complicated when the empirically obvious is accounted for, namely that (quite a large number of) distortions preexist. How messy the analysis of second best is, was first shown by Lipsey and Lancaster (1956). Public finance economists made the same discovery when they investigated the intricacies of, for example, optimal taxation and welfare-enhancing incremental tax reforms.

To the best of my knowledge EEsts did not make major efforts to embark on this kind of complex general equilibrium analysis, until a few years ago, the prospect of a double dividend from shifting the tax mix towards environmental taxes while keeping total tax revenue constant electrified the EE community. In a pioneering paper Bovenberg and de Mooij (1994) arrived at the surprising verdict that 'an environmental tax reform tends to exacerbate rather than to alleviate preexisting tax distortions' (p. 1085). This still vivid, ongoing debate on the double (or multiple) dividend is well suited to illustrate some important general theoretical as well as empirical challenges:

1. It demonstrates once again that research hot spots and hence the future directions of EE are hardly predictable. The basic idea regarding the possibility of reaping a double dividend was advanced a long time ago, for example, by Tullock (1967), but it was not put to a rigorous test by means of general equilibrium analysis until 1994.
2. We learn the lesson that if significant market interdependencies are involved, partial equilibrium analysis may be misleading. Those who 'endorsed' the double dividend using partial equilibrium analysis based their arguments on sound economic intuition which turned out, however, to be incomplete.
3. Without any intention to diminish the merits of the Bovenberg and de Mooij (1994) analysis it needs to be mentioned that its central assumptions are fairly restrictive, notably the linear technology, the absence of waste abatement and the special structure of the utility function (implying that a labour tax is second best if there is no emission tax). As a consequence we observe an ongoing discussion (to which Bovenberg and de Mooij contributed) about confirming or challenging the robustness of the general equilibrium results applying to both qualitative analysis and computable general equilibrium models.

Two important questions arise with the potential to affect on the future research in EE:

●   Will we succeed in settling the robustness issue satisfactorily or will we get lost in the stormy waters of second best in which 'anything can happen'?

● If we succeed, can we hope to get reliable *quantitative* information about both the sign of the dividends and their empirical order of magnitude?

The last point raises even deeper and more general questions: we live in economic systems with many market imperfections, partly created by government interventions, that have no direct or intentional effects on environmental issues but may well, via ubiquitous interdependence effects, affect them indirectly. For example, changes in major social policies (such as health care or social security) may have side effects on EP. Which imperfections of the third-best world matter and which can safely be neglected? What are the future standards, regarding the exclusion of interdependence effects in second-best worlds, in economics as well as in EE, for policy appraisals?

Unfortunately I have raised many questions and provided few or no answers. But I strongly subscribe to Blackorby's (1990, p. 769) statement:

> If we say that, in a second-best world, anything can happen and that that is too complex, then we will be making policy recommendations that are based on completely fraudulent thinking. Such ostrich-like behaviour risks doing more harm than good to society and certainly would relegate the study of economics to some arcane backwater of intellectual activity.

Hence there is much work ahead of us!

4   THE DIMENSIONS OF DISTRIBUTION, SPACE AND TIME

Distribution

Environmental economic analysis often appears almost synonymous to advocating allocative efficiency, where efficiency ranges from conventional cost-effectiveness of pollution control to the public provision of non-marketed environmental goods. Efficiency certainly is and remains an important issue for EE and is quite well understood because our economic paradigm with its link to welfare economics is perfectly suited to tackle it. The economic paradigm neatly separates distributional from efficiency issues via the second theorem of welfare economics. This theorem is clearly an important insight. But similar to the optimal taxation literature which emerged from acknowledging the empirical fact that non-distortionary (or lump-sum) taxes are hardly observed in real economies, EEsts need to account more seriously for the empirical fact that the implementation of any EP creates losers that are not, in general, compensated by lump-sum or other transfers. In a second-best world it is difficult, if not impossible, to separate considerations of efficiency and equity (Blackorby, 1990). Consequently, policy recommendations cannot be made without interpersonal comparisons of utility.

There are, of course, studies on distribution of income and wealth, poverty, equity, social justice and related issues both in mainstream economics and in EE. The pertinent literature in EE as addressed, for example, by Cropper and Oates (1992, p. 727 n.) and by Markandya (1998) is quite small, however, as compared to the efficiency-oriented literature. We would have no reason to worry about that if we had a good knowledge about the interface of environmental and distributional issues. But according to Markandya (1998, p. 460) the 'linkages between poverty/income distribution and EP are ... not as well understood as they need to be'. In my view, distributional issues should be given greater attention in future EE research for several other reasons:

1. Policy makers either have perceptions of social justice of their own or take account of those prevailing in their constituency, and/or they care about distributional impacts to secure their political career or survival. The polluter pays principle with its pronounced distributional implications seems to have *some* support in the political arena, but it did not turn out to be an undisputed normative guideline in political action.[11]

2. Each EP proposal whose prime goal is efficiency has distributional side effects that can and need to be accessed both in conceptual incidence analysis and empirical studies to inform policy makers. If sound research-based information is not available the political action proceeds on the basis of somewhat (ill-)perceived distributional conjectures. Quite often such assessments capture only direct and immediate effects and thus may result in flawed decisions.

3. To be more specific, consider the case of siting economic facilities with the potential of causing environmental hazards in the neighbourhood of the site (for example, hazardous waste landfills, waste incineration plants, nuclear waste deposition sites) or causing environmental degradation (for example, construction of new highways or bypasses, deforestation, deregulation of land-use restrictions). Even if the net benefit of such projects is positive, the interregional distributional effects may differ dramatically, as becomes evident in controversial political debates. In the past, EEsts offered little systematic and in-depth analysis of the *distributional* impacts of such siting decisions.

4. If EEsts restrict their analysis and advice to efficiency aspects of their EP proposals they may risk being misunderstood as taking a partisan stance

in the political (distributional) debate even if their exclusive focus on efficiency is made explicit.

5. Acknowledging that special interest groups and hence distributional considerations are relevant in the political decision-making process or, as some political economists argue (for example, Brunner, 1978), even dominate efficiency arguments, has important consequences for the future research programme of those EEsts who strive for a greater impact of EE on the implementation of EP. The distributional consequences of proposing institutions and/or instruments of EP need to be systematically considered in the *design* phase in an effort to improve their political acceptability. This issue will be discussed more broadly in section 7.

So far our focus has been on *intra-temporal* distribution. In the sustainable-development literature issues of *intertemporal*/intergenerational distribution and equity play a major role, too, or are even central to the ongoing debate. To elaborate on this topic is beyond the scope of the present chapter, but it highlights the point that the preoccupation with efficiency might have been pushed too far in the past.

Spatial Analysis

It is neither a new nor an original insight that economic activities as well as ecological systems develop in space and that in terms of quality and quantity, economic and ecological processes change and interact in space. It is obvious that space has been accounted for in EE in a variety of significant ways (see, for example, Siebert, 1985). Most notably, transboundary pollution in regional, international and global settings was and still ranks high on the agenda of EE. But even if pollutants do not cross borders, trade in productive factors and commodities renders national EPs interdependent, with the potential of strategic behaviour on the side of governments (race to the bottom?).

Quite apart from these issues with a fairly abstract connotation to space[12] there are important economy–environment interdependencies with specific and more concrete spatial dimensions that have not yet received the attention of EE research they deserve (Bockstael, 1996). Obviously most ecological systems as well as economic activities use up land, and the historical development is characterized by a process of ever-increasing land-use demands for economic purposes, quite often at the expense of ecological systems and natural habitats. Not only does this expansionary process continue, but in addition habitats are devalued by land-use fragmentation. Following Deacon *et al.* (1998, p. 394) there is a great need to know more about how 'habitat values depend on the spatial configuration of land in different uses', what are 'the determinants of changes in land-use configurations' and which are the 'appropriate policy instruments to influence these processes'. It should also be emphasized, as in Agee and Crocker (1998, p. 263), that there are mediating behavioural interactions which link economic and ecological systems (in space) and which can make significant differences in system responses. To sum up, 'the spatial dimensions of resource use may turn out to be as important as the exhaustively studied temporal dimensions in many contexts. Curiously, the profession is only now beginning to move in this direction' (Deacon *et al.*, 1998, p. 393).

Intertemporal Analysis

The first rigorous answer to the intellectual challenge of better understanding where market forces drive an economic system in the long run was the neoclassical growth model. It focused on the explanation of capital accumulation, but its reference to technical change as 'manna falling from heaven' was a major reason for the research community's fading interest. In addition, the neglect of environmental and natural resource constraints to growth made this theory unacceptable from an EE point of view. *The Limits to Growth* (Meadows *et al.*, 1972) marked an important turning point, and with advances in optimal-control techniques issues of long-term (environmental) resource use have been tackled since the 1970s. An important further impulse was the introduction of the concept of *sustainable development*, which shifted the focus of the analysis towards the dynamics and long-term development of the ecological system. Among the latest 'innovations' in intertemporal analysis is the application of *endogenous growth theory* from mainstream economics to environmental economic issues (Carraro and Siniscalco, 1997). It demonstrated that human capital formation along with increasing returns in production give rise to the possibility that 'dematerialization' of production (and consumption) *may* reconcile permanent growth and a finite resource base.

Endogenous growth theory leads us to focus our attention on what determines human capital investment and productivity. Even though this new perspective led some EEsts to be slightly more optimistic in their assessment of long-term scarcity of natural (renewable and non-renewable) resources, the proposition that technology will bail us out has not yet a sound theoretical and empirical basis (Deacon *et al.*, 1998, p. 393). Dasgupta (2000, p. 9) argues that 'the idea of unbounded consumption is science fiction. It ignores the environmental resource-base upon whose services all production and consumption ultimately depends. This base is very much finite in extent'. Changes in technology over time, in particular 'pollution-reducing' technological innovations, and their determinants, are, in my view, the single most important factor for easing the growing stress the economic system imposes on the ecological system in the long run. To better understand these issues strong research efforts are being made and need to continue along various routes. One promising line of research focuses on individual firms and their incentives to innovate, another on the impact of interacting firms on innovation (industrial organization literature); other studies investigate how technological innovation responds to natural resource scarcity and other social needs. Unless our knowledge about all these issues is substantially improved the policy guidance of EEsts on long-term sustainable development remains rather limited.

Intertemporal analysis can also relate to changes in preferences over time. Long before the appearance of EE, but also since then, there were always researchers who challenged the assumption of time-invariant preferences. The stubbornness with which most economists and EEsts upheld their credo that 'de gustibus non est disputandum' (Stigler and Becker, 1977) raised the suspicion of some advocates of changeable preferences, for example, Norton, Constanza and Bishop (1998), that EE shows traces of dogmatism. Here is not the place to discuss this issue in appropriate depth. I content myself with observing that in my view the assumption of time-invariant preferences is a convenient methodological concept suitable for many purposes of investigation. Besides, all those who find that procedure not acceptable are invited to present alternatives and convince the stubborn part of the research community about the supremacy of their approach.

So far I have focused mainly (too much, perhaps) on the dynamics of the *economic system*. Needless to say, the natural and ecological systems are also characterized by intertemporal stock–flow relationships with Lotka–Volterra models of population growth as classical prototypes and (dynamic) predator–prey models as reflections of intra-ecological interdependence (Clark, 1990). Similar concepts were applied to model stock–flow pollution issues. The important issue is, of course, the *interaction* of the dynamics of both the economic and the ecological systems. After all, the economy is sustainable if and only if the ecological system is sustainable. We find studies with hardly any interaction, with unilateral dependence, but also studies that model interdependence, even though typically on a highly aggregate and hence rudimentary level where the ecological model is usually much less structured than the economy.[13] With such models, issues of sustainability (including the threat of irreversible damage to the ecological system) can be and have been addressed, but there are good reasons to argue that a satisfactory approach requires a much more elaborate framework of analysis concerning the ecological system and its interaction with the economy.

In recent years new dynamic or evolutionary approaches have emerged that aim at accomplishing just that by radically trespassing borders and barriers of conventional environmental economic analysis. For example, Perrings (1998) draws on recent highly technical work on ecological and economic dynamics.

Preferences and technologies are no longer taken as exogenous and constant in his approach, and he models economic development and environmental change as interdependent stochastic evolutionary processes producing discontinuous path-dependent changes and repercussions in both systems. *Sustainable development* is addressed as a policy directive to 'sustain the joint systems in a desirable state or avoid it being locked-into an undesirable state' (Perrings, 1998, p. 516). The concept of *resilience* is analysed, helping to bridge the gap between the ways ecologists and economists used to think about stability issues (Levin *et al.*, 1998).

Such research programmes break new ground at the core interface of economics and ecology. In my view, they are important, ambitious and have the potential of significantly affecting the future of EE. How far this potential can be developed remains to be seen, however, because the more heavy mathematical machinery is used (for example, Markow processes in Perrings, 1998), the more limited their capacity might turn out to be in producing ecologically and economically meaningful results.

5   ENVIRONMENT–ECONOMY INTERACTIONS AND INTERDISCIPLINARITY

The work referred to in the last few paragraphs is important for future research in EE, because it places the interaction of the ecological and economic system at centre stage rather than focusing on the economic system with a small environmental appendix. This raises the more general question of how serious EEsts have been, are and should be about reaching beyond economic analysis. Again, I cannot offer here a thorough and balanced account of this issue which, in fact, would require undertaking a major research effort in its own right (an effort that would certainly be both desirable and rewarding). Instead, I content myself with the following 'stylized' appraisals:

1. As seen from base zero, EEsts achieved substantial insights, both on the conceptual and empirical level, into the links between the environment and the economic system and into EP schemes to cope with those links. But in its core domain EE tended to place more emphasis on analysing the economic system than on environment–economy interactions.
2. To study environment–economy interactions does not mean endorsing 'outdated' economics. The continuous injection of advances in both theoretical and empirical economics into EE is vital for the future of EE. The EE research community should not retreat into a niche seeking shelter against new developments in economics.

3. There is a high-priority need in EE to correct the preoccupation with economic issues by focusing more than in the past on environment–economy interactions including the impact that EP and the behaviour of economic agents have on these interactions.
4. To improve the analysis of environment–economy interactions, the empirically relevant and up-to-date knowledge of ecological and natural sciences needs to be used and integrated into EE in a more systematic way.

While point 2 above does not seem to be consensual among EEsts (Sterner and van den Bergh, 1998, p. 254), I observe acclamation for point 3 from many EEsts and from ecologists, a fortiori. Quite a few steps have already been taken in this direction, but the list of desiderata is long, as exemplified by the following sample of demands:

- 'Extractive and environmental components of resource decisions should be considered simultaneously' (Deacon *et al.*, 1998, p. 387).
- In fishery management more attention should be paid 'to ecological services, biodiversity and recreation possibilities' (Eggert, 1998, p. 399).
- In valuation, 'more complex issues related to ecosystem functions, services and characteristics need more attention' (Sterner and van den Bergh, 1998, p. 257).
- Since economic and natural systems are linked by mediating behavioural interactions, 'a systematic empirical accounting of mediating behavioral linkages can make significant differences in system responses that are estimated and in the economic valuations attached to these responses' (Agee and Crocker, 1998, p. 263).

The ambitious goal of strengthening the focus on economy–environment interaction cannot be achieved unless EEsts take a closer look at, and adopt insights, concepts and techniques developed in, the ecological and natural sciences (point 4 above). This process is under way since, as Sterner and van den Bergh (1998, p. 255) correctly observe, 'the very nature of the subject and real-life problems drive EEsts in the direction of interdisciplinary work'. But some doubts are in order about whether that 'drive' for the necessary and desirable interdisciplinary work develops sufficient momentum without devoted extra efforts. Present deficits are not hard to identify as, for example, the biological models commonly used in EE: 'Economics has largely stuck with simple paradigms that most biologists regard as useful pedagogical metaphors, but of little practical value' (Deacon *et al.*, 1998, p. 391).[14] In other words, it is desirable to shape the EE research in closer communication and contact with the state-of-the-art work in ecologically relevant disciplines.

If EEsts followed this plaidoyer for closer contact with other relevant disciplines in the field of environment–economy interactions the prospects would be favourable for narrowing the gap of communication deficits and lack of mutual understanding. Some might even already see a joint approach to the common subject matter of study at the far horizon. Even though I endorse emphatically the quest for more interdisciplinarity, I have little illusion about how hard this is to accomplish. EEsts have ample experience with both the difficulties and benefits of transdisciplinary communication. For example, referring to economics and ecology epidemiology, Agee and Crocker (1998, p. 262) observe that 'the relationships between the two disciplines can be characterized as much by tensions and recriminations about what knowledge is and how to get it as by mutual respect and reinforcement'.

Let me illustrate the tensions about how to get knowledge for the case of placing values on services rendered by nature and ecological systems. In section 2, I pointed out how central this issue is for EE and how vital and urgent further progress in methods and techniques is to getting beyond unsatisfactory statements of the type: 'We know that there is an environmental externality out there creating an inefficiency but, unfortunately, its order of magnitude is largely unknown.' The dispute *within* EE is about the best means and methods to reach the joint goal, namely measuring the (marginal) values economic agents attach to environmental goods which the market would have elicited without any research effort if it had not failed. Other researchers in the field, notably non-economists, challenge or even reject the EEsts' concept or 'philosophy' of value measurement altogether and consequently are not at all interested in debates about the appropriateness of means to reach a goal they consider inappropriate.[15]

There is nothing wrong with the existence of different views on how to get knowledge. This creates a competitive situation, and as economists we are on our home turf when talking about the benefits of competition, how it spurs efforts, creativity, etc. My suggestion is that we should try, by means of constructive further research, to demonstrate that our product is superior to the competitors' ones rather than try to let our product look better by criticizing theirs. While this competitive-market analogy has some merits, I should point to its limits, too: endorsing, and calling for, interdisciplinary work implies, of course, overcoming non-cooperative behaviour. In fact, a cooperative approach is called for!

Differences of paradigmatic approach are mainly a barrier to interdisciplinary communication and work for those researchers who feel an urge to think in narrowly defined 'schools' and 'sub-schools'. I suggest thinking of the economic paradigm (without attempting to define it) as a broad, useful and powerful 'corset' guiding our research that is very flexible and capable of absorbing new components and interdisciplinary impulses. To put it differently, the interdisciplinary dialogue need not and must not be barred by methodological differences in approaching the joint field of research. There are many indications (such as Faber and Proops, 1990; Arrow *et al.*, 1995; or Levin *et al.*, 1998) that this dialogue is happening. Even in the controversial field of non-market valuation I referred to earlier, fruitful communication and cooperation are emerging between ecologists and economists to improve linkages between ecological and economic valuation methods (Bingham *et al.*, 1995). This communication ought to be encouraged.

A few years ago the German Science Council evaluated the 'Environmental Sciences' in Germany. In its detailed and voluminous report (Wissenschaftsrat, 1994) a major finding was that university research in this field is essentially compartmentalized along department lines and hence lacks interdisciplinarity while research institutes outside universities showed a better interdisciplinary performance. The Council's clear message was that environmental sciences in academia need to shift more towards interdisciplinarity. To bring about such a shift it is certainly important to know what the obstacles are to interdisciplinary work. For one thing, it is always easier and more enjoyable to communicate among people who 'speak the same language' (that is, use the same methods) than to undergo the effort of becoming 'multilingual'. Moreover, young researchers are often reluctant to trespass into other disciplines because 'academic careers are clearly tied to proficiency within rather than between disciplines' (Sterner and van den Bergh, 1998, p. 255). (When those young scholars have become senior researchers they have become reluctant to learn 'foreign languages', unfortunately.)

6   EMPIRICAL RELEVANCE OF ENVIRONMENTAL ECONOMICS

EE owes its very existence and relevance to real-world environmental problems that concerned and still concern the broader public, the media and political decision makers. Since it is not likely that the pressure of economic activities on the ecological system will diminish, the challenge for necessary and useful research will probably even increase in the future.[16] Deacon *et al.* (1998, p. 383) are certainly right in observing that 'research on EE will be driven by policy questions, as has generally been true in the past'. In that broad sense the subject matter of EE did not and will not lack empirical relevance. On the other hand, it does not follow from the heavy emphasis of EEsts on policy questions that empirical research is dominant in EE. In fact, we have the intriguing situation that even most theoretical papers, including very abstract ones, suggest policy implications, EP instruments or institutional arrangements as a cure for some inefficiency under scrutiny, so that one might get the impression that EEsts form a community of self-declared policy advisers, not necessarily asked for their advice and often without serious intentions to promote their own recommendations in the down-to-earth real-world process of policy implementation.

This phenomenon need not be criticized if one is willing to accept the distinction between – and to admit the necessity of – *basic* and *applied* research as is widely common in the natural sciences. My experience is, however, that some EEsts devoted to empirical research do not find this position easy to accept. Having said that, I hasten to add that policy advice from the theoretical ivory tower remains useless and sterile:

(i)   if it is not accompanied by systematic research efforts to test theories and policy proposals for their empirical 'validity'; and
(ii)   if there is not an 'operative chain' of research dispersion from the ivory tower to the level of actual practical policy implementation.

As economists, we should not find it too difficult to acknowledge the necessity and advantages of the principles of division of labour and comparative advantage. But I join those who are concerned about whether the self-assignment process of researchers to the tasks I described above ensures that *all* these tasks are taken care of in an appropriate way. I do not pretend to know what the right division of labour should be, but there is some concern about theoretical knowledge piling up faster than testing the pertinent hypotheses and theory implications. It cannot be a sensible end in itself to produce an ever-increasing diversity of models and theories. We should rather strive for accumulating empirically sound theoretical knowledge. Where do we stand on this account and where are we headed?

Rather than offering a balanced answer to this important question, let me indicate my scepticism about our past achievements by referring to Sterner and van den Bergh (1998), who put together a special issue of the journal *Environmental and Resource Economics* on 'Frontiers of Environmental and Resource Economics', choosing the programmatic and ambitious subtitle 'Testing the Theories'. This special issue left me with the impression that, at present, theory testing plays a minor role only in EE. There is much work ahead of us!

The increasing specialization within the field of EE produces many important new insights and is also an appropriate response to the real-world complexities of the issues to be tackled. But it involves the risk, at the same time, that applied work does not take due notice of theoretical advances and vice versa. Both fields are important, in my view, but they must not follow disconnected autonomous paths driven by immanent forces without regard for the other. Good theory needs to 'trickle down' to application and policy implementation, and theory design should be responsive to needs and pressures at the level of application. There are only very few individual researchers whose research programme bridges the entire gap. It is therefore crucial that a sufficient number of researchers are positioned at intermediate levels of abstraction to secure the two-way communication among theorists and applied economists.

The dramatic advances in computer technology during recent years have triggered a huge productivity increase in quantitative applied work, boosting data processing, econometric work and, in particular, computable general equilibrium analysis (Conrad, 1999). This development is to be welcomed with regard to the empirical relevance of EE, and it tends to increase the attractiveness of EE for the political decision-making process, which appears to respond to 'numbers' much more than to qualitative information. As seen from the scientific perspective, the fundamental question is, of course, how reliable is the quantitative information that we are able to provide. Reliability clearly depends on the empirical soundness of the underlying theories, which brings us back to the issue of hypothesis testing. We clearly need both: producing numbers on the basis of existing theories and improving those theories to generate more reliable numbers. The finding by Deacon *et al.* (1998, p. 390) that the field of non-market valuation research 'has been dominated by application rather than testing and refining of the basic theory' suggests to me that in the future more emphasis needs to be placed on the latter.

The methods of computable general equilibrium analysis, as applied, for example, to energy taxation or transportation economics, have been significantly expanded and refined during the last few decades, and this process will certainly continue in the future. The current status of computable general equilibrium models with respect to reliability is also an important issue, of course. My impression is that this area is still characterized by competing approaches which, if applied to the same issue, may generate significantly different results. Conrad (1999) contends that computable general equilibrium analysis is useful for comparing alternative policy instruments but not for economic forecasts. He sees a large potential for future research in developing such models with features like imperfect competition, endogenous technological change, infrastructure and overlapping generations. But he also warns against too much optimism because 'the more complicated the model, the more it becomes a black box'.

The assessment of the empirical relevance of EE has yet another aspect which soon leads into the deep waters of methodology, and into which I only want to take a quick dip. I mentioned earlier that EE is firmly based on a well-developed economic paradigm, which – as most of us will agree – satisfies Sen's (1985, p. 341) desideratum: 'We want a canonical form that is

uncomplicated enough to be easily usable in theoretical and empirical analysis.' Sen then continues, 'But we also want an assumption structure that is not
fundamentally at odds with the real world, nor one that makes simplicity take
the form of naïvety.' Most of us might react to that observation as follows: we
are well aware that the economic paradigm has some limitations, perhaps
even some deficiencies or cracks, but it is still a powerful paradigm, and for
the time being there does not seem to be a better substitute on the horizon.
There have always been dissident views,[17] of course, but in recent years more
economists have begun to think twice just how much at odds with the real
world our assumptive structure is and how close some of our simplifications
come to naïvety.

To be more specific, consider our concepts of preferences, utility maximization and rational behaviour. I not only refer to the never-ceasing criticisms
from psychologists and sociologists but also, and in particular, to the mounting empirical evidence mainly from experimental economics and game theory
that people's behaviour simply does not follow our concepts of utility
maximization under constraints. Equilibrium strategies (Nash equilibria), which
game theorists consider rational behaviour in situations of strategic uncertainty about the other agents' actions, systematically fail to be adopted by
respondents in game experiments. Real-world agents' choices among lotteries, in particular when lotteries contain outcomes of low probability but high
damage like environmental catastrophes, are at odds with von Neumann–
Morgenstern expected utility theory which previously had been considered a
firm basis for explaining decisions under uncertainty.

As a response to this evidence two polar reactions are conceivable. Either
you reach the conclusion (for yourself) that some of our basic assumptions
are fundamentally at odds with the real world. You give them up as a basis of
descriptive, explicatory analysis, thus restricting their use to prescriptive,
normative purposes (to show what rational decision makers *should* do). To fill
the gap you replace 'maximizing' by concepts of *bounded rationality*, satisfying, etc. In recent years this route has been taken by quite a few economists,
among them Nobel prize winner Reinhard Selten.[18]

The alternative reaction seems to be still more widespread: it reconciles
empirical observations with the theory and thus avoids the conclusion that the
assumptions are at odds with reality by taking advantage of the enormous
flexibility of economic analysis and of the empirical voidness of the concept
of preferences. A good example is the climate change issue and the somewhat
intriguing observation that we could have a free lunch if consumers purchased all the energy-efficient utilities (for example, energy-saving light
bulbs) which are already out there. The EEsts' (and economists') prototype
reaction was, as aptly expressed by Shogren (1998, p. 565), that people 'have
or act as if they have a short time horizon' and 'preferences are preferences –

individual choices, however fuzzy, do match what society wants'. We (and here I include myself) have become used to looking at the real world in the light of our economic paradigm.[19] But isn't it somewhat disturbing that we can explain just about everything? Doesn't that mean that empirical tests of theories are quite limited in their relevance and in their role as judge to select 'good' from 'bad' theories? Haven't we a tendency to immunize our 'explanations' against empirical facts rather than – in a Popperian spirit – to accumulate empirically relevant new knowledge by making every effort to falsify our theories?

This is as far as I want to carry this argument. It is not my intention to initiate or contribute to new methodological debate which, in my view, has not accomplished much more in the past than distracting researchers from constructive substantive work. I believe, however, that the issue of preferences and rational behaviour has the potential significantly to affect the future of EE in case more and more economists cross the line.

7   THE IMPACT OF ENVIRONMENTAL ECONOMICS ON SHAPING ENVIRONMENTAL POLICY

Most EEsts who have observed and/or participated in EP formation over past decades would probably characterize the development as follows: when environmental issues entered the agenda, pollution control was the domain of administrative law, applying its traditional command and control approach. With their concepts of costs and benefits (non-market valuation) and market-based or incentive EP instruments, EEsts were not able, for a long time, effectively to promote their ideas in intricate political decision-making processes. Some progress was made over time. But it can hardly be attributed to the EEsts' impatience alone that in politics far too little use was made of the substantial value-added EE had to offer. This not only caused frustration but also led some EEsts to search for the reasons 'why the patient did not follow the doctor's orders so well' (Hahn, 1989).[20] Among the well-known central arguments are:

(i)   EEsts found it difficult to convey to the actors in the political arena the general rationale of their proposals. In the early days outright hostility towards EE was not uncommon. An important barrier to fruitful communication turned out to be that many of these actors lack basic knowledge of economics and of EE, in particular. With a background in other disciplines, such as law, political science, sociology, ecology or engineering sciences, decision makers, advisers and interest group representatives compete in policy formation, in the effort to shape the outcome according to their perceptions, interests and paradigms. After all, it was economic activities that were to blame for the environmental problems, and accepting advice based on economic concepts and methods would amount to hiring the buck as a gardener (as a German proverb has it).

(ii)   The advice EEsts offered was often based on abstract, conceptual analysis that did not pay much attention to the complexities of the political decision-making process, the importance of preexisting regulations and institutional arrangements (such as legal constraints, commands and controls) and to the costs of administration, monitoring and enforcement.

(iii) EEsts often consider their role as advocates for efficiency (Deacon *et al.*, 1998, p. 384). However, in the political decision-making process, many more criteria are taken into consideration, notably the distributional consequences of EP proposals (see above). Ignoring these criteria diminishes the prospects of political acceptability.

When these arguments are viewed against the discussion in the present chapter it is quite obvious that reducing the major deficits identified in sections 2–6 above will improve by and large the impact of EE on EP. To promote that objective in a more (pro)active way the EE research community may consider developing a constructive *research policy*. Concerning the specific areas of activism and policy instruments, I would suggest the following issues as particularly important and rewarding.

(a)   Those who share the perception that too much research effort is allocated to theoretical and conceptual work 'in the ivory tower' and too little to 'down-to-earth' empirical and applied work (which Pezzey and Park (1998, p. 552) describe as 'intellectually unglamorous but vital') might think about setting corrective incentives 'to raise the place of rigorous applied research in the academic preference order ' (Deacon *et al.*, 1998, p. 395). Editors of journals, organizers of conferences and Ph.D. supervisors have considerable means and discretion in that respect.

(b)   The observation that only few participants in policy debates 'have a grasp of fundamental economic principles' (Schultze, 1996) and hence analyse issues very differently from the economists' approach is vividly underlined by Shogren (1998) for EP in the US. We may hope that the number of students earning a degree in EE, or who at least attend advanced courses in EE and who then enter the political decision making process, rises. But EEsts might perhaps want to adopt a more active strategy: teaching programmes and workshops for administrators, political decision makers and future teachers – and thus pre-college students – could be a promising way to improve upon the present unsatisfactory situation.

(c)   Putting all the blame on the ignorance of others would be too simple. EEsts need to strive for a better understanding of the ways non-economists and politicians analyse environmental issues and for more interdisciplinarity (see above). The latter is certainly desirable independent of policy implementation, but it also enhances acceptability. There are ways to redirect incentives for interdisciplinary work along the lines mentioned in point (a).

In an attempt to foster interdisciplinary research in Germany, the Deutsche Forschungsgemeinschaft (DFG) and the Volkswagenstiftung conditioned some research grants on proposals with substantial interdisciplinary aspects. As a result, many proposals for strong commitments and 'promises' for genuinely interdisciplinary work were made, but the outcome did not always live up to these standards. Although some applicants' strategic behaviour counteracts the DFG's good intentions, such research grants appear to be quite an effective catalytic device in promoting interdisciplinarity. (Money helps to overcome barriers.)

(d)   Point (iii) above indicates the need for a good understanding of the political decision-making process as a precondition for the political acceptability of EP proposals. Therefore, greater attention to the *positive* theory of EP formation is desirable. *Public Choice* or the *New Political Economy* is now a well-established field of study, which aims at explaining the forces that drive the political process using economic methods. A clash is unavoidable if 'benevolent' EEsts 'in good faith' – or even naïvely? – offer their EP advice without taking into account the pressures and constraints self-interested political agents are exposed to when they are engaged in promoting their political career or their group's interests.

What are the implications? Should we restrict our research to the EP proposals we deem to be politically acceptable? While I agree that we should pay more attention to the issue of political acceptability when offering EP advice, I have doubts whether our anticipation of acceptability or non-acceptability should be a primary criterion guiding our choice of research programmes. For example, it is not clear to me that we should stop studying and suggesting revenue-neutral ecological tax reforms, as recommended by Pezzey and Park (1998, p. 552). These authors argue that raising large emission tax revenues would face powerful resistance from interest groups, and therefore future research should be directed towards zero-revenue market-based instruments whose acceptability is considered much greater.

The message of public choice analysis is, in my view, that EEsts interested in the implementation of research-based EP proposals should take into consideration that they become a part of the political decision-making process themselves, lobbyists for enhancing the rationality and efficiency of the process of EP formation. For lobbyists to be successful it is vital to know the rules of the game and to play the game according to those rules. The direct involvement of academic researchers in the policy implementation process is crucial, as Deacon *et al.* (1998, p. 394) point out correctly, since without such an involvement 'it seems unlikely, at least in the US, that state-of-the-art knowledge on benefits, costs and regulatory instruments will be reflected in actual policy choices'.

The preceding considerations might help to improve the impact of EE on shaping EP in the future. But, on the whole, there is no reason, in my view, to be pessimistic. In recent years the influence of EE on policy was already growing, slowly but steadily: we saw the advent of non-marginal shifts towards ecological taxation in several European countries, the successful SO_2 trading programme in the US, the application of formal procedures of appraisal for EP regulation in the European Union (Pearce, 1998) and a significant role for EEsts in the ongoing 'world-wide bargaining process' about how to cope with global climate change.

8   CONCLUDING REMARKS

As mentioned in the introduction, the preceding discussion reflects many subjective appraisals and judgments which relate both to the current state of EE and to the topics of future research agenda perceived as likely, necessary and/or desirable. While subjective components cannot be avoided in an enterprise like this, there is considerable scope for additional research, which would be desirable to generate statistical or other hard evidence on the perceived strengths or deficits of EE. For example, how much empirically sound theoretical knowledge has really been accumulated and how does empirical research and hypothesis-testing compare with other economic areas, for example, labour market economics? How much economy–environment interaction is accounted for in current EE research and what still unused potential can be drawn on from other disciplines' ecology-related knowledge? By answering these types of questions on the basis of reliable facts and figures one could certainly promote successful corrective research policies.

Embarking on reflections about the future of EE entails the immediate risk of offering a large colourful bouquet of proposals for improvements. I am not sure whether I avoided the impression that, unless we adopt the ancient Olympic motto '*citius, altius, fortius*' (faster, higher, stronger) there will be no future for EE. During a relatively short period of time EE has been established as a thriving field of study attracting bright young (environmental) economists and increasingly affecting practical EP. There is little reason to believe that this positive development will not continue. But if we direct additional efforts towards coping with the deficits identified in the discussion above, we will certainly be able to do even better.

My reflections on the future of EE were based on the premise which I share with many EEsts that economic pressures will tend to put the ecological system under increasing stress (see section 6) and will thus jeopardize the sustainable development of both the economic and the ecolcigal system, unless those with a similar perception, citizens, researchers and politicians alike, are successful in striving for effective remedy. There are different, much more optimistic assessments as expressed, for example, in an article 'Environmental Scarces: Plenty of Gloom' in *The Economist* according to which 'technology and economic freedom will make the world cleaner and will also take the pressure off endangered species'.[21] In this view future environmental problems, if there are any, will be solved without particular effort and impact of EEsts who are therefore advised to close their files. I hope I have made it clear that my perception of environmental issues, of the necessity of EE and of its future role, is quite different. In that respect I join the contributors to the Policy Forum of *Environmental and Development Economics* (1998, vol. 3, Part 4, 500–537) who responded to *The Economist* article.

NOTES

1. In the present chapter the following abbreviations are used: EE for environmental economics, EEsts for environmental economists and EP for environmental policy.
2. Among the many important contributions for orientation and guidance released in the 1990s are: Bromley (1995), Carraro and Siniscalco (1997), Constanza, Perrings and Cleveland (1997), Cropper and Oates (1992), Daly and Townsend (1993), Kneese and Sweeney (1985/1993), Markandya and Richardson (1992), Oates (1992), Sterner and van den Bergh (1998), Tietenberg and Folmer (1997, 1998, 1999, 2000), van den Bergh (1998).
3. I have paid special attention to several contributions in Sterner and van den Berg (1998) which focus on the frontiers of environmental economics.
4. See, e.g., the Symposium issue of the *Journal of Institutional and Theoretical Economics*, **149** (1993): 'The New Institutional Economics: Recent Progress; Expanding Frontiers'.
5. Negotiations about international pollution problems often involve quite a large number of players and hence may be costly. But that need not prevent successful bargaining if the stakes are sufficiently high, as in case of the global climate change issue.
6. In the early days of EE, externality theory had the dubious reputation of dealing with exceptional and largely irrelevant phenomena (Scitovsky, 1954).
7. In this future debate computable general equilibrium models will play a major role since they are very useful for ranking alternative policy measures (Conrad, 1999).
8. To indicate how difficult it is to get a clear-cut appraisal of the merits and flaws of valuation methods, consider the observation of Calthrop and Proost (1998, p. 338) that

contingent valuation techniques have been used for estimating congestion costs for perhaps 25 years and 'have been accepted in the profession long before CVM was widely
applied in environmental economics'.

9. The acceptability problem is exacerbated by ill-founded studies throwing numbers into
the public debate that do not even pass the laugh test.

10. There are ways to include market imperfections in general equilibrium analysis that will
not be discussed here. See, for example, Ginsburgh and Keyzer (1997).

11. That is particularly true in cases of transboundary pollution, but defection from that
principle can also be observed in cases of purely domestic pollution. For example, a few
years ago German farmers were subsidized to lower the groundwater pollution they
caused and this programme was defended by some EEsts (Bonus, 1986) on the grounds of
the 'Coasean principle of reciprocity'.

12. Bockstael (1996, p. 1169) quotes V. K. Smith as having noted 'that economists, when they
do deal with spatial distribution, introduce it as a constraint – as an exogenous fact, but
rarely attempt to explain it as a dimension of an economic decision'.

13. Even the static reference model is a model of rudimentary interdependence: the release of
pollutants into the environment deteriorates the state of the 'ecological system' as indicated by a variable 'pollution level' or 'index of environmental quality'. Then the ecological
system 'strikes back', causing 'environmental damage' in terms of loss of utility or
reduction in productivity which triggers reactions of economic agents, in turn. Therefore I
am willing to give a bit more credit to the achievements of the basic reference model of
EE than Agee and Crocker (1998, p. 262), who suggest that 'the standard Walrasian
paradigm ... views natural systems as vessels carrying interacting economic agents as
passengers and asks only whether allocation institutions are designed to cause the passengers to be fully accountable for the direct consequences their choices have for their fellow
voyagers. The Walrasian paradigm sets aside the state of repair of the vessel.'

14. While this is a valid criticism I am reluctant to subscribe to sweeping demands to discard
all simplifying analytical tools. A remarkable strength of economic analysis has always
been to vary the degree of abstraction in line with the purpose of investigation at hand
(and, admittedly, with an eye on tractability). For example, production technologies with
factor substitution may be reasonable to assume in aggregate analysis even though engineers may have reasons to reject that assumption at the micro level of individual firms.

15. EEsts who are still engaged in developing methods of non-market valuation are compared
by Sagoff (1994, p. 307) 'to the Japanese soldiers who were found on islands in the
Pacific years after the end of the Second World War, still fighting although the mainland
had surrendered and the cause had long since been lost'.

16. In the past decades a number of new serious environmental risks and threats have been
identified that had not been expected or anticipated – neither by the public nor by the
academic research community. I refrain from speculating on how this process will continue, but the currently known threats are severe enough to support the claim that economic
pressures will put the ecological system under increasing stress.

17. A recent sweeping attack on neoclassical (environmental) economics was launched by
Sagoff (1994), who calls for abandoning the 'dogmas' of applied welfare economics.

18. See Selten (1998) and Rubinstein (1998). It would be interesting to know how many
(environmental) economists would agree with Selten's (1991, p. 19) position that it is
better to use empirically tested *ad hoc* assumptions than unrealistic principles of high
generality and elegance.

19. Interestingly, Sterner and van den Bergh (1998, p. 254) react to Shogren's position by
noting 'that here are other views which suggest that people and firms are not striving for
individual economic efficiency and optimality'. Observe also that the debate on *X*-
inefficiency proceeded along similar lines some years ago.

20. This question has been raised ever since the rise of EE. For an early contribution and an
attempt to answer it see Haveman (1980).

21. *The Economist*, London, 20 December 1997; reprinted in *Environmental and Development Economics*, vol. 3, Part 4, October 1998, 493–9; the quote is from page 499.

REFERENCES

Agee, M.D. and T. Crocker (1998), 'Economies, human capital, and natural assets', in T. Sterner and J.C.M. van den Bergh (eds) (1998), pp. 261–71.

Arrow, K.J. *et al.* (1995), 'Economic growth, carrying capacity, and the environment', *Science*, **268**, 520–21.

Bingham, G. *et al.* (1995), 'Issues in ecosystem valuation: Improving information for decision making', *Ecological Economics*, **14**, 73–90.

Blackorby, R. (1990), 'Economic policy in a second-best environment', *Canadian Journal of Economics*, **23**, 748–71.

Bockstael, N.E. (1996), 'Modeling economics and ecology: The importance of the spatial perspective', *American Journal of Agricultural Economics*, **78**, 1168–80.

Bonus, H. (1986), 'Eine Lanze für den "Wasserpfennig" – Wider die Vulgärform des Verursacherprinzips', *Wirtschaftsdienst*, **66**, 451–5.

Bovenberg, A.L. and R.A. de Mooij (1994), 'Environmental levies and distortionary taxation', *American Economic Review*, **94**, 1085–9.

Bromley, D.W. (ed.) (1995), *Handbook of Environmental Economics*, Oxford: Blackwell.

Brunner, K. (1978), 'Reflections on the political economy of government. The persistent growth of government', *Schweizerische Zeitschrift für Volkswirtschaft und Statistik*, **114**, 549–680.

Calthrop, E. and S. Proost (1998), 'Road transportation externalities', in T. Sterner and J. C. M. van den Bergh (eds) (1998), pp. 335–48.

Carraro, C. (1998), 'New economic theories', in T. Sterner and J. C. M. van den Bergh (eds) (1998), pp. 365–81.

Carraro, C. and D. Siniscalco (eds) (1997), *New Directions in the Economic Theory of the Environment*, Cambridge: Cambridge University Press.

Clark, C.W. (1990), *Mathematical Bioeconomics*, New York: Wiley.

Coase, R. (1960), 'The problem of social cost', *The Journal of Law and Economics*, **3**, 1–44.

Constanza, R., C. Perrings and C.J. Cleveland (eds) (1997), *The Development of Ecological Economics*, Cheltenham: Edward Elgar.

Conrad, K. (1999), 'Computable general equilibrium models for environmental economics and policy analysis', in J.C.M. van den Bergh (ed.), *The Handbook of Environmental and Resource Economics*, Cheltenham: Edward Elgar.

Cropper, M.L. and W.E. Oates (1992), 'Environmental economics: a survey', *Journal of Economic Literature*, **30**, 675–740.

Daly, H.E. and K.N. Townsend (eds) (1993), *Valuing the Earth: Economics, Ecology and Ethics*, Boston: MIT Press.

Dasgupta, P. (2000), 'Discounting: Why and How?', mimeo.

Deacon, R.T. *et al.* (1998), 'Research trends and opportunities in environmental and natural resource economics', in T. Sterner and J.C.M. van den Bergh (eds) (1998), pp. 383–97.

Debreu, G. (1959), *Theory of Value: An Axiomatic Analysis of Economic Equilibrium*, New York and New Haven: Yale University Press.

Dixit, A.K. (1996), *The Making of Economic Policy: A Transactions Cost Politics Perspective*, Cambridge, MA: MIT Press.

Eggert, H. (1998), 'Bioeconomics analysis and management', in T. Sterner and J.C.M. van den Bergh (eds) (1998), pp. 399–411.

Faber, M. and J.L.R. Proops (1990), *Evolution, Time, Production and the Environment*, Heidelberg: Springer-Verlag.

Foster, B.A. (1972), 'A note on economic growth and environmental quality', *Swedish Journal of Economics*, **74**, 281–6.

Ginsburgh, V. and M. Keyzer (1997), *The Structure of Applied General Equilibrium Models*, Cambridge, MA, and London: MIT Press.

Green, J.R. and J.-J. Laffont (1979), *Incentives in Public Decision Making*, Amsterdam, New York, Oxford: North-Holland.

Hahn, R. (1989), 'Economic prescriptions for environmental problems: How the patient followed the doctor's orders', *Journal of Economic Perspectives*, **3**, 94–114.

Haveman, R.H. (1980), 'Public choice and public economics: The case of collective failure in US water quality policy', in K.W. Roskamp (ed.), *Public Choice and Public Finance*, Paris: Editions Cujas, pp. 137–54.

Kneese, A.V. and J.L. Sweeney (eds) (1985/1993), *Handbook of Natural Resource and Energy Economics*, Vols. I–III, Amsterdam: North-Holland.

Knetsch, F.L. (2000), 'Environmental valuations and standard theory: behavioural findings, context dependence and implications', in H. Folmer and T. Tretenberg (eds), 267–99.

Levin, S.A. *et al.* (1998), 'Resilience in natural and socioeconomic systems', *Environment and Development Economics*, **3**, 222–35.

Lewis, T. (1996), 'Protecting the environment when costs and benefits are privately known', *Rand Journal of Economics*, **27**, 819–47.

Lipsey, R.G. and K. Lancaster (1956), 'The general theory of the second best', *Review of Economic Studies*, **24**, 11–32.

Mäler, K.-G. (1974), *Environmental Economics: A Theoretical Inquiry*, Oxford: Blackwell.

Markandya, A. (1998), 'Poverty, income distribution and policy making', in T. Sterner and J.C.M. van den Bergh (eds), pp. 459–72.

Markandya, A. and J. Richardson (eds) (1992), *The Earthscan Reader in Environmental Economics*, London: Earthscan.

Meadows, D.H. *et al.* (1972), *The Limits to Growth*, New York: Basic Books.

Norton, B., R. Constanza and R.C. Bishop (1998), 'The evolution of preferences – Why 'sovereign' preferences may not lead to sustainable policies and what to do about it', *Ecological Economics*, **24**, 191–212.

Oates, W.E. (ed.) (1992), *The Economics of the Environment*, Cheltenham: Edward Elgar.

Pearce, D.W. (1998), 'Environmental appraisal and environmental policy in the European Union', in T. Sterner and J.C.M. van den Bergh (eds), pp. 489–501.

Perrings, C. (1998), 'Resilience in the dynamics of economy–environment systems', in T. Sterner and J.C.M. van den Bergh (eds), pp. 503–20.

Pezzey, J.C.V. and A. Park (1998), 'Reflections on the double dividend debate', in T. Sterner and J.C.M. van den Bergh (eds), pp. 539–55.

Rubinstein, A. (1998), *Modeling Bounded Rationality*, Cambridge, MA: MIT Press.

Sagoff, M. (1994), 'Four dogmas of environmental economics', *Environmental Values*, **3**, 285–310.

Scitovsky, T. (1954), 'Two concepts of external economies', *Journal of Political Economy*, **62**, 627–30.

Schultze, C.L. (1996), 'The CEA: an inside voice for mainstream economics', *Journal of Economic Perspectives*, **10**, 23–39.

Selten, R. (1991), 'Evolution, learning and economic behavior', *Games and Economic Behavior*, **3**, 3–24.

Selten, R. (1998), 'Features of experimentally observed bounded rationality', *European Economic Review*, **42**, 413–36.

Sen, A.K. (1985), 'Goals, commitment, and identity', *Journal of Law, Economics and Organization*, **1**, 341–55.

Shogren, J.F. (1998), 'A political economy in an ecological web', in T. Sterner and J.C.M. van den Bergh (eds), pp. 557–70.

Siebert, H. (1985), 'Spatial aspects of environmental economics', in A.V. Kneese and J.L. Sweeney (eds), *Handbook of Natural Resource and Environmental Economics*, Amsterdam: North-Holland, pp. 125–64.

Siniscalco, D. (1998), 'Impacts of economic theories on environmental economics: Prospects', in J.C.M. van den Bergh (ed.).

Smith, V.K. (1997), 'Pricing what is priceless: a status report on non-market valuation of environmental resources', in H.Folmer and T. Tietenberg (eds), 156–204.

Sterner, T. and J.C.M. van den Bergh (1998), 'Frontiers of Environmental and Resource Economics', in T. Sterner and J.C.M. van den Bergh (eds), pp. 243–60.

Sterner, T. and J.C.M. van den Bergh (eds) (1998), *Frontiers of Environmental and Resource Economics: Testing the Theories*; special issue of *Environmental and Resource Economics*, **11**(3–4).

Stigler, G.J. and G.S. Becker (1977), 'De gustibus non est disputandum', *American Economic Review*, **67**, 76–90.

Tietenberg, H. and H. Folmer (eds) (1997, 1998, 1999, 2000), *The International Yearbook of Environmental and Resource Economics* 1997/1998 (1998/1999, 1999/2000, 2000/2001). Cheltenham, UK and Brookfield, US: Edward Elgar.

Tullock, G. (1967), 'Excess benefit', *Water Resources Research*, **3**, 643–4.

van den Bergh, J.C.M. (ed.) (1999), *Handbook of Environmental and Resource Economics,* Cheltenham, UK and Brookfield, US: Edward Elgar.

van den Bergh, J.C.M. and P. Nijkamp (1991), 'Operationalizing sustainable development: Dynamic ecological economic models', *Ecological Economics*, **4**, 11–33.

Wissenschaftsrat (1994), *Stellungnahme zur Umweltforschung in Deutschland*, Köln.

Index

experimental economics and
environmental policy 121–2,
127–30, 136–41
information strategies for pollution
control and 90, 91, 92–3
policy implications of corporate
governance and technological
risks 287–8
policy implications of non-convex
willingness-to-pay for natural
protection 258–64
preexisting public policy distortions
in competitive economy 377–9
trade and tax policies in equilibrium
241–2
see also taxation
Govindusamy, R. 266
grandfather rights 76
Granger, C. W. J. 49
Graves, Philip E. 63, 69, 70
Gray, Wayne B. 72, 74, 76, 77
Green, J. R. 376
green electricity pricing 104
GREEN model 359
green net national product (NNP)
measure 12–30, 219
market economy 21–9
close to cooperative solution 25–9,
30
Pigouvian view 22–3
tax reforms in non-cooperative
equilibrium 23–5, 30–31
two-country economy 14–21
cooperative solution 18–21, 29–30
model 14–15
Nash non-cooperative open loop
solution 15–18, 29, 30
Greenstein, S. 155
Greenwood, Michael J. 66, 69, 70, 71
Gregory, Robin 128, 315
Griffin, R. 265
Griffiths, Charles 70–71
Griliches, Zvi 355
Grossman, Gene M. 74, 206, 320, 321,
322, 344, 354, 362
Grubb, Michael 238
Grubler, A. 363
Gulati, S. C. 201
Gunther, W. 71
Gyourko, Joseph 61–2, 65–6, 68

Hagern, C. 178
Hahn, R. W. 85, 138, 374, 391
Hall, C. A. S. 40
Hall, S. 49, 361
Hamilton, J. D. 50
Hamilton, J. T. 108–9, 135
Hammond, P. 321
Hanemann, W. 127
Hannon, C. 53
Harris, D. 219
Harrison, A. 50
Harrison, D. 204
Hartwick, J. M. 17, 219, 321
Harvey, A. C. 329
Hausman, Jerry 127, 297
Hayek, F. 157
Hayes, E. 125
hazards
warnings 105–6
see also natural disasters; risk
Heal, G. 274, 320
Heath, J. 197, 198
Heckscher-Ohlin (H-O) model 62
hedonic studies 65–6
Hege, Ulrich 279
Heidebrink, G. 320, 322
Helfand, G. 263, 265
Helioui, Khalil 219, 238
Helms, L. Jay 75
Helpman, E. 347, 354, 362
Henderson, J. Vernon 59, 72, 74, 75
Henning, John A. 59
Henseler-Unger, I. 359
Herman, Robert 221
Herriges, J. R. 266
Herzog, Henry W. 66
Hettige, H. 111
Hoehn, John P. 62, 65, 67, 68
Hoel, M. 176, 178, 179, 180, 186, 188,
321, 349
Hoffmaister, A. W. 347
Hogarth, R. M. 299
Holden, S. T. 320
Holling, C. S. 254, 323, 325, 326, 327,
328, 332
Holmström, B. 168, 169, 283, 284
Holtz-Eakin, Douglas 77, 345
Hoogma, R. 356, 358
Hooper, D. U. 328
horizontal task restructuring 169

Tinch, R. 323, 327
Tirole, J. 168, 352
Tobey, James A. 74
Tobin, James 59
Topa, G. 345, 346, 352, 361
tort law actions 96
tournament models 347, 351
Toxic Release Inventory Program 95,
    97–9, 108–10, 135
Toyota 239–40
Tracy, Joseph 61–2, 65–6, 68
trade
    international *see* international trade
    tradable discharge permits 138–40,
        167–8, 177, 179, 205
trade-offism 283–7
transaction costs, zero 374
transnational corporations 170
    environmental innovation and 347
transport 203–4
Tschirhart, J. 251, 265
Tsur, Y. 327
Tullock, G. 378
Turner, R. K. 321
Tushman, M. 155, 156
Tversky, Amos 295, 296, 320

Ulph, Alistair 177, 345, 347, 349, 352
Ulph, David 177, 345, 346, 347, 351,
    352
uncertainty 273, 313
United Kingdom
    energy efficiency in 151
    energy use and GDP in 51
    green taxes in 205
United Nations
    Centre on Transnational Corporations
        170
    Conference on the Human
        Environment (Stockholm 1972)
        97
    Development Programme (UNDP)
        207
    Environment Programme (UNEP)
        240
United States of America
    dematerialization in 229–31
    economic growth 233–4
    energy policy 48
    energy use 229, 230, 233

efficiency 151
    GDP and 51–3
environmental regulation in 131, 153
    firm location and 72, 74, 76
    green national income accounting in
        219
    information strategies for pollution
        control 90, 92–3, 94, 113
        empirical analysis 105, 106–7,
            108–10
        EPA audit policy 100–101
        green electricity pricing 104
        private enforcement actions 97,
            101–2, 106–7
        Proposition 65 99–100
        33/50 Program 99, 106, 110
        Toxic Release Inventory Program
            95, 97–9, 108–10, 135
    market-based policies 137–40, 167–8
    material flow in 227, 228
    migration within 69–70, 71
    natural disasters 300, 303–4, 306,
        308–9
    polluter-pays principle in 275
    poverty and environment in 203, 204,
        205
    quality of life indices 65–8
    service sector 214
    technological risks in 288
    tribal lands in 312–13
utility 298–9

value 10
    amenity values *see* amenity values
    ecological economics and 40–42
    ecosystems 40–42, 253–7
    valuation problem 12, 13
    valuing non-priced goods 127–30,
        374–5
van den Bergh, J. C. M. 374, 375, 385,
    387, 389
van der Linde, C. 152, 238
van Tongeren, J. 321
vector error correction model (VECM)
    51–3
Verbruggen, H. 206
Verdier, T. 354
Vietnam, poverty and environment in
    195
Vincent, J. 85, 265, 321